SUPER FAMILY VACATIONS

SUPER FAMILY VACATIONS

Resort and Adventure Guide

REVISED EDITION

Martha Shirk and Nancy Klepper

HarperPerennial
A Division of HarperCollinsPublishers

HarperCollins books may be purchased for educational, business, or sales promotional use. For information, please call or write: Special Markets Department, HarperCollins Publishers, Inc., 10 East 53rd Street, New York, NY 10022. Telephone: (212) 207-7528; Fax: (212) 207-7222.

FIRST HARPERPERENNIAL EDITION 1992

Designed by Joan Greenfield

Library of Congress Cataloging-in-Publication Data
Shirk, Martha.
    Super family vacations: resort and adventure guide/Martha Shirk and Nancy Klepper.—Revised ed.
        p. cm.
    Includes index.
    ISBN 0-06-273124-6
        1. North America—Description and travel—1981–   —Guide-books.
    2. Family recreation—North America—Guide-books.   3. Resorts—North America—Guide-books.   4. United States—Description and travel—1981–
    —Guide-books.   5. Family recreation—United States—Guide-books.
    6. Resorts—United States—Guide-books.   7. Caribbean Area—Description and travel—1981–   —Guide-books.   8. Family recreation—Caribbean Area—Guide-books.   9. Resorts—Caribbean Area—Guide-books.
    I. Klepper, Nancy. II. Title.
    E41.S48   1992
    917.304′928—dc20   91-55384

---

92 93 94 95 DT/RRD 10 9 8 7 6 5 4 3 2 1

To my favorite traveling companions—William, Tom, Bennett, and Peter Woo

M.S.

To my parents, who instilled in me a curiosity about the larger world, and to my lifelong traveling companions, Bob and Adam Klepper

N.K.

CONTENTS

ACKNOWLEDGMENTS xv

SUCCESSFUL FAMILY VACATIONS:
ARE THEY REALLY POSSIBLE? 1

How This Book Is Organized 2

    Resorts 3

    Guest Ranches 5

    Ski Areas 7

    History Places 11

    Cruises 12

    Adventure Trips 15

    Nature Places 17

About Rates 18

RESORTS

NORTHEAST 24

New Seabury Cape Cod 24	*New Seabury, Massachusetts*
The Balsams 28	*Dixville Notch, New Hampshire*
Mohonk Mountain House 31	*New Paltz, New York*
The Sagamore 36	*Bolton Landing, New York*
Four Seasons Inn on the Park 40	*Toronto, Ontario*
Skytop Lodge 43	*Skytop, Pennsylvania*
The Tyler Place 47	*Highgate Springs, Vermont*

SOUTHEAST 51

Amelia Island Plantation 51 — *Amelia Island, Florida*
The Colony Beach and Tennis Resort 55 — *Longboat Key, Florida*
Cheeca Lodge 59 — *Islamorada, Florida*
Sonesta Beach Hotel and Tennis Club 62 — *Key Biscayne, Florida*
South Seas Plantation 65 — *Captiva Island, Florida*
Callaway Gardens 69 — *Pine Mountain, Georgia*
The Cloister 74 — *Sea Island, Georgia*
The Grove Park Inn and Country Club 79 — *Asheville, North Carolina*
Kiawah Island Inn and Villas 83 — *Kiawah Island, South Carolina*
The Tides Inn 87 — *Irvington, Virginia*
Oglebay Resort 91 — *Wheeling, West Virginia*

MIDWEST 96

Eagle Ridge Inn and Resort 96 — *Galena, Illinois*
Grand View Lodge Golf and Tennis Club 99 — *Nisswa, Minnesota*
Marriott's Tan-Tar-A Resort
    and Golf Club 103 — *Osage Beach, Missouri*

WEST COAST AND HAWAII 108

The Resort at Port Ludlow 108 — *Port Ludlow, Washington*
Sunriver Lodge and Resort 112 — *Sunriver, Oregon*
Rancho Bernardo Inn 116 — *San Diego, California*
Dana Point Resort 119 — *Dana Point, California*
Hilton Hawaiian Village 122 — *Honolulu, Oahu, Hawaii*
Kahala Hilton 125 — *Honolulu, Oahu, Hawaii*
Kona Village 129 — *Ka'upulehu-Kona, The Big Island, Hawaii*
Mauna Kea Beach Hotel 133 — *Kohala Coast, The Big Island, Hawaii*

THE CARIBBEAN 138

Casa de Campo 138 — *La Romana, Dominican Republic*
Club Med Punta Cana 142 — *Punta Cana, Dominican Republic*
Boscobel Beach Resort 147 — *Ocho Rios, Jamaica*
The Hyatt Regency Cerromar Beach
    and Hyatt Dorado Beach 151 — *Dorado, Puerto Rico*

Bitter End Yacht Club   155   *Virgin Gorda, British Virgin Islands*
Hyatt Regency Grand
   Cayman   159   *George Town, Grand Cayman Island*

GUEST RANCHES

SOUTHWEST AND MOUNTAIN STATES   166
Tanque Verde Ranch   166   *Tucson, Arizona*
Wickenburg Inn Tennis
   and Guest Ranch   170   *Wickenburg, Arizona*
C Lazy U Ranch   174   *Granby, Colorado*
Peaceful Valley Lodge
   and Guest Ranch   178   *Lyons, Colorado*
Tumbling River Ranch   182   *Grant, Colorado*
Vista Verde Guest
   and Ski Touring Ranch   186   *Steamboat Springs, Colorado*
Averill's Flathead Lake Lodge
   and Dude Ranch   190   *Bigfork, Montana*
Lone Mountain Ranch   194   *Big Sky, Montana*
Mountain Sky Guest Ranch   197   *Emigrant, Montana*
Bishop's Lodge   202   *Santa Fe, New Mexico*
Flying L Guest Ranch   206   *Bandera, Texas*
Paradise Guest Ranch   210   *Buffalo, Wyoming*

WEST COAST   215
The Alisal Guest Ranch   215   *Solvang, California*

SKI AREAS

NORTHEAST   222
Mont-Tremblant and Gray Rocks   222   *Mont-Tremblant, Quebec*
Sugarloaf USA Resort   226   *Kingfield, Maine*
Killington Ski Area   230   *Killington, Vermont*

Mount Snow Resort 234   *Mount Snow, Vermont*
Stratton 238   *Stratton Mountain, Vermont*

SOUTHWEST AND MOUNTAIN STATES 243

Aspen Area Ski Resorts 243   *Aspen, Colorado*
  Aspen Mountain
  Buttermilk Mountain
  Snowmass
  Aspen Highlands
Crested Butte Ski Area 248   *Crested Butte, Colorado*
Steamboat Ski Area 251   *Steamboat Springs, Colorado*
Summit County Ski Resorts 255   *Summit County, Colorado*
  Breckenridge
  Copper Mountain Resort
  Keystone Resort
Telluride Ski Resort 260   *Telluride, Colorado*
Vail/Beaver Creek 264   *Eagle County, Colorado*
Winter Park Resort 269   *Winter Park, Colorado*
Park City Area Ski Resorts 273   *Park City, Utah*
  Deer Valley Ski Area
  Park City Ski Area
  ParkWest Ski Area

WEST COAST 279

Lake Tahoe Area Ski Resorts 279   *Lake Tahoe, California*
  Squaw Valley
  Alpine Meadows
  Northstar-at-Tahoe
  Heavenly Valley
  Kirkwood

HISTORY PLACES

NORTHEAST 288

Mystic Seaport Museum 288   *Mystic, Connecticut*
Washburn-Norlands Living History Center 292   *Livermore, Maine*

Old Sturbridge Village   296   *Sturbridge, Massachusetts*
Plimoth Plantation   300   *Plymouth, Massachusetts*

SOUTHEAST   304
Colonial Williamsburg   304   *Williamsburg, Virginia*

MIDWEST   308
Living History Farms   308   *Des Moines, Iowa*
Conner Prairie   311   *Noblesville, Indiana*
Historic New Harmony   315   *New Harmony, Indiana*
Shaker Village at Pleasant Hill   318   *Harrodsburg, Kentucky*
Mackinac State Historic Parks   322   *Mackinac Island and Mackinaw City, Michigan*

SOUTHWEST AND MOUNTAIN STATES   325
Crow Canyon Archaeological Center   325   *Cortez, Colorado*

CRUISES

THE CARIBBEAN AND THE BAHAMAS   332
Song of America   332   *Western Caribbean*
Star/Ship Oceanic   336   *The Bahamas*
M.S. *Starward*   340   *Lower Caribbean Islands*
S.S. *Jubilee*   344   *Mexican Riviera*

ALASKA   349
M.S. *Westerdam*   349   *Vancouver to Alaska*

HAWAII   354
S.S. *Constitution* and S.S. *Independence*   354   *Hawaiian Islands*

ADVENTURE TRIPS

NORTHEAST   360
Chewonki Wilderness Trips   360   *Wiscasset, Maine*
Maine Windjammer Cruise   363   *Penobscot Bay, Maine*
Hiking Inn to Inn
    Vermont's Long Trail   367   *Brandon, Vermont*

SOUTHEAST   371
Cumberland Island Camping
    Adventure   371   *Cumberland Island, Georgia*
White-Water Raft Trip on the New River   375
                       Fayette County, West Virginia
Canoeing on the Buffalo National River   379   *The Ozarks, Arkansas*

MIDWEST   384
Wagon Train Trip Through the Flint Hills   384   *El Dorado, Kansas*
Apostle Islands Sailing Adventure   388   *Madeline Island, Wisconsin*
Wisconsin Bicycle Adventure   392   *Madison, Wisconsin*
Boat-Camping in Voyageurs
    National Park   395   *International Falls, Minnesota*

SOUTHWEST AND MOUNTAIN STATES   399
Houseboating on Lake Powell   399   *Arizona and Utah*
Pontoon Boat Adventure Through
    the Grand Canyon   402   *The Grand Canyon, Arizona*
Rafting on the Colorado River   406   *Colorado and Utah*
Llama Trekking in the Big Horn Mountains   410   *Sheridan, Wyoming*

WEST COAST   414
Kayaking on the Navarro River   414   *Mendocino County, California*

NATURE PLACES

SOUTHEAST 420

Watoga State Park 420   *Marlinton, West Virginia*
Great Smoky Mountains National Park 423   *Gatlinburg, Tennessee*
Gulf State Park 426   *Gulf Shores, Alabama*

MIDWEST 431

Gunflint Lodge 431   *Gunflint Trail, Minnesota*

SOUTHWEST AND MOUNTAIN STATES 436

YMCA of the Rockies 436
   Estes Park Center   *Estes Park, Colorado*
   Snow Mountain Ranch   *Winter Park, Colorado*
The Nature Place 441   *Florissant, Colorado*
Yellowstone National Park 445   *Yellowstone National Park, Wyoming*
Pine Butte Guest Ranch 448   *Choteau, Montana*
Glacier National Park 451   *West Glacier, Montana*

WEST COAST AND ALASKA 455

Furnace Creek Inn and   *Death Valley*
   Ranch Resort 455   *National Monument, California*
National Wildlife Federation
   Conservation Summit 459   *Bellingham, Washington*
Strathcona Park Lodge and Outdoor
   Education Centre 462   *Vancouver Island, British Columbia*
Olympic National Park 466   *Port Angeles, Washington*
Camp Denali 470   *Denali National Park, Alaska*

THE CARIBBEAN 473

Virgin Islands National Park 473   *St. John, Virgin Islands*

INDEX 477

ACKNOWLEDGMENTS

We are grateful to Carol Cohen, of HarperCollins, for seeing the promise in our proposal for a family travel book and giving us the opportunity to write it, and to Helen Moore, Andrea Sargent and Deborah Brody, our editors, for their graceful editing.

Our deepest debt is to our families, whose zest for travel inspired the book and whose support enabled us to complete it. Bob and Adam Klepper and William, Tom, Bennett and Peter Woo cheerfully accompanied us on most of our trips and helped us to experience travel under the same circumstances that our readers will.

The book also would not have been possible without the competent assistance of an enthusiastic and energetic group of researchers. Gratitude for their contributions goes to Cindy Bechtel, Joan Bray, Barbara Buchholz, Abby Cohn, Patricia Corrigan, Robert Duffy, Linda Eardley, Margaret Wolf Freivogel, Terry Ganey, Jody Gaylin, Lori Kesler, Mary Ellen Noonan Koenig, Martha Kohl, Seena Kohl, Phyllis Brasch Librach, Joan Little, Michael Lloyd, Marjorie Mandel, Jo Mannies, Geoffrey O'Gara, Jan Paul, Miriam Pepper, Deborah Peterson, Alice Powers, Gail Ruwe, Kem Knapp Sawyer, Meg Selig, Dale Singer, Tom Stites, Richard Weiss, and David Wilson. Among them they have 67 children.

Various state and local tourism development officials, and publicists for many individual destinations, also provided invaluable assistance.

SUPER FAMILY VACATIONS

SUCCESSFUL FAMILY VACATIONS
Are They Really Possible?

We've all had them—family vacations that were more work than fun, outings that were a disaster from start to finish, grand trips that proved once and for all that there's such a thing as too much togetherness. When you wake up one morning in the middle of an expensive vacation and realize that you'd rather be at home, you know that something's wrong with the way you planned your family's vacation.

It doesn't have to be that way—although it is likely to be unless you take your children's vacation needs, as well as your own, into account.

We know from experience. Both of us became parents long after we had developed strong vacation preferences. Suddenly, with children on the scene, our tried-and-true vacation formulas no longer worked. No more romantic weekends at country inns bursting with antiques. No more exhilarating treks into the Himalayas. No more exciting big-city vacations. No more relaxing weeks at hideaways on Caribbean islands where disposable diapers are unheard of. The prospect of undertaking one of these trips with a child in tow was daunting. After a few hapless trips on which we tried to pretend that children hadn't changed our lives or our vacation requirements, we knew enough not to try again.

But we didn't want to stay at home. We realized that vacationing successfully with children would necessarily be different from traveling alone or as a twosome, but we were sure that it was not impossible. However, when we began looking for travel books that would guide us to appropriate places, we found none that met our needs. So we decided to write one—a book *by families* and *for families*, one that could serve as a guide for new parents, experienced parents, grandparents, and single parents.

We believe that the key to successful family vacations is planning

I

—and that means choosing a destination that's right for every member of your family. We think that the best places for families to vacation are those that offer something for everyone—for instance, tennis and golf for Mom and Dad, if they're so inclined; counselors and organized activities for the kids, with plenty of other kids around; and a selection of activities that the whole family can enjoy together. The places and vacation ideas that we feature in this book meet all these criteria. Some are strong on organized activities; some leave you alone to enjoy yourself at your own pace. Some are on the edge of big, bustling cities, with plenty of sightseeing opportunities; others are isolated. Some emphasize relaxation, others adventure. All are places where families, including our own, regularly have good times.

HOW THIS BOOK IS ORGANIZED

In this revised edition of *Super Family Vacations*, you'll find vacation ideas ranging from a few grand old resorts—the famous places that your great-grandparents may have visited—to modern beachside or mountain hideaways, guest ranches, cruise ships, and ski areas. There are "history places" that give children a glimpse into their ancestors' lives, adventure trips that provide thrills in the beautiful outdoors, and special nature-oriented places, where vacations are learning experiences. In this edition, we concentrated on finding some great new family-oriented vacation destinations that are little-known—and some unusual and little-publicized activities to take part in at places that are well known, like the greatest national parks in the United States. We offer destinations in every region of the continental United States, as well as Alaska, Hawaii, Canada, and the Caribbean. There's probably a place just two hours from your home—and many farther away.

All of the places we feature have actually been visited by one of us or one of our researchers, almost always with children along. In fact, we visited many more places than we feature here. Those that weren't appropriate for families—or that were on the margin— aren't included. We can't guarantee that your particular family will have a great time at a particular place, but we can guarantee that you'll find some destination here that appeals to you and that is within your budget range.

We've had a lot of fun researching this book. We've learned a lot about how to travel with kids—and how not to. Our children are now seasoned travelers, conversant in the advantages of one organized children's program over another, on friendly terms with Mother Nature, at ease on the ski slopes, on a sailboat, or on a horse. The experience has been broadening for them, and for us. For why travel with children unless you're going to take some time to see the world as they do? It's certainly easier to leave them at home. But if they weren't with you, you might not notice the shooting stars in the western sky, the multicolored stones at the bottom of the river you're rafting, the parrot in the hotel lobby, the buttons on the shoes of the woman who's making apple butter in the pioneer village.

For ease of use, we have divided our recommendations into seven different categories: destination resorts, guest ranches, ski areas, history places, cruise ships, adventure trips, and nature places. Within these categories, destinations are grouped by region, usually beginning on the East Coast and moving across the country. Descriptions of the appeal of each type of vacation, and some hints about how to make it work, follow.

Happy traveling!

Resorts

Resort vacations are just about the easiest family vacations imaginable. It's for good reasons that the term "destination resorts" entered the travel industry's vocabulary in the mid-1970s. This type of resort —35 of which are featured—has become a destination in itself, separate and apart from the geographical area in which it is situated. Many people choose a resort without caring about what city it's near.

At a well-run full-service resort, you are likely to find every activity imaginable, comfortable accommodations, conveniently situated facilities, a choice of eating spots, impeccable service, and an atmosphere that is conducive to having a good time.

At most of the resorts we feature, you will also find well-supervised children's programs. Why have we made that an important criterion for inclusion? Because the existence of a children's program and the ready-made playmates it provides guarantee that children will have a good time on vacation and that parents will have some time to themselves to pursue adult activities. Even if you regard your family vacation as the one time you have all year to devote to each other, you're bound to appreciate having a stimulating program in which you can place your children for just a few hours a day. For there's little point in going to a resort with a world-class golf course or round-the-clock tennis facilities if there's no one to take care of your young children so that you can play.

The nation's grand old resorts pioneered the concept of children's programs, and in recent years such programs have become a fixture at most new full-service resorts as well. The programs range from an hour or two of supervised play daily to full-fledged day camps. Some offer supervised children's dinners (followed by cartoons or games) so that parents can have a night out by themselves. Some are free to guests, and others charge a fee that can easily equal the cost of quality day care at home. Some allow drop-ins, and others require advance reservations when you book your room.

Most of the resorts also offer a variety of activities that the whole family can enjoy together, from cookouts to guided nature walks to rental bikes (in all sizes) to organized games.

Our recommendations include resorts where everything is included in the price you pay before you go, and resorts where everything is extra; resorts that are isolated, and others that are on the edge of exciting cities; resorts that are sedate and refined, and a few that are on the wild side. At one you fly on a trapeze, at others take a balloon ride, at a few others play golf on five courses.

Probably the most important thing to consider when you select a resort for a family destination is whether it will feel right for your family. If you like to show up for dinner in shorts and sandals, then one of the sedate grand old resorts is probably not for you.

How much you want to be pampered should also be a consideration. If your idea of a vacation is no cooking, then you might consider one where meals are included in the room rate. If, on the other hand, you like to make breakfast and lunch yourselves and splurge on dinner, then look for a resort whose accommodations are equipped with kitchens (the room rate may be higher, but you'll save on food).

Many of the resorts we feature are truly national in appeal. Around the pool, you'll find guests from nearly every state, and even some foreign countries. But some are strictly regional in their draw, for reasons either of remoteness or strong regional flavor.

We have also tried to include resorts in every price range; obviously, the less expensive ones won't have the range of amenities and the quality of facilities that the more expensive ones have, but all provide a quality family vacation experience. And even if your vacation budget is modest, it is possible to vacation at some of the more expensive resorts if you go in the off-season and aggressively seek information from management about cost-saving packages. The Caribbean resorts, for instance, are real bargains in the summer months, when the beaches are just as beautiful and the atmosphere just as exotic as in the higher-priced winter season.

Guest Ranches

Your wake-up call is likely to be the sound of 200 hooves pounding a hard-packed dirt trail as the horses make their way from their overnight pasture to their corral. Your days will be filled with opportunities to appreciate the joys of nature—on horseback, or on foot, or from a lounge chair by the swimming pool. Your meals will be hearty, the coffee as good as any you've ever tasted. And when you crawl wearily into a bunk bed made from lodge-pole pines, every muscle aching from the strain of your first horseback ride, you'll wonder why you never took a ranch vacation before.

If you've put off going to a guest ranch because you have no interest in horses, reconsider. Today's guest ranches offer far more than riding. All of the ranches we feature offer other activities, ranging from naturalist-guided walks to tennis, golf, fishing, swimming, panning for gold, hayrides, trap shooting, white-water rafting, back-country jeep expeditions, aerobics classes, and side trips to such nearby attractions as Yellowstone or Rocky Mountain national parks. For children, there are overnight camp-outs, nature-oriented arts and crafts, well-designed play areas, pizza-making parties (with cast-iron stoves), animal spotting, and pony rides. Besides all the planned activities, there are plenty of opportunities for serendipitous happenings—like the sighting of a moose along a trail.

And, of course, there's the riding. Even if you've never been on a horse before, all of the ranches we recommend will do their best to make an accomplished and enthusiastic rider out of you. Don't let your fears keep you from a great experience. The back of a horse offers one of the best vantage points for viewing the splendors of the West, where most guest ranches are located.

A week at a western guest ranch will give your children a glimpse into the past. They'll get a sense, maybe for the first time, of the rigors the pioneers experienced as they crossed rugged mountains and sprawling plains to reach their goal.

Don't be surprised if your children start saying "Howdy, pardner," and swaggering when they walk. A life spent caring for and riding horses must look pretty good from their perspective. And few children finish a week at a guest ranch without a new appreciation for nature, since it seems so much more accessible than at home. There must be shooting stars in the night sky in urban areas, but you're not as likely to notice them as when you're sitting around a camp fire.

Many of the families we encountered at the 13 ranches we include had been going there for years. That is typical of families who get bitten by the ranch bug: once they find one they like, they return year after year. They're treated by their hosts as family. And they, in turn, welcome new guests into the family. Many ranch guests make arrangements even before their vacation ends to return during the same week the next year to repeat their experience.

Tips to Make Your Trip More Enjoyable

- Your child's ranch experience will be enriched if you first read a few books about the West together.

- Some children may be disappointed at first by the absence of television, radios, and video games. If you explain that you're going to experience life as it was "in the olden days," most young children will be charmed. They will soon find the horses and other animals in residence at the ranch a more-than-adequate substitute.

- Before you arrive, most ranches will send you a letter advising you about what to bring. Take the advice about warm clothes seriously, since it can be quite chilly in the mountains at night. At almost every ranch, blue jeans and a few flannel shirts are all you'll need to be dressed appropriately. Some have one dress-up night a week, but all that need mean is that you put on a fresh pair of jeans. Rain gear is important.

- Riding boots are strongly recommended for vacationers who plan to ride horses. It's possible to ride a horse wearing sneakers or Topsiders, but it's much more difficult and not as safe. Buy boots early enough to break them in. And sturdy walking shoes are advised if you plan to do any serious hiking.

- If you have an infant or toddler, choose your ranch destination carefully. Unless the ranch offers child care, you'll find yourself tied down by a child who's under 6. Some ranches are better than others at arranging baby-sitting for very young children. Talk to the ranch management first about how welcome young children really are. Some will allow you to bring a baby-sitter for free.

- The weekly rates at ranches may look pretty steep to you at first glance. But before you reject a ranch vacation as too expensive, consider all that the weekly rate includes. By figuring out what your family is likely to spend at a resort on à la carte meals, a room, and sports activities, you may find that your total expenses are no more at a ranch.

- Be sure to budget money for tips to ranchhands. Rather than levy a service charge, most ranches maintain a tip pool that is divided among ranch staffers at the end of the season. Ranch managers say that most guests tip 12 to 15 percent of their total bills.

Ski Areas

No matter how great a thrill you get from schussing down an expert slope by yourself, it can't equal the joy that comes from watching your toddler make his or her first complete run down a beginner's slope, even if the skis are in a rigid wedge shape and the poles akimbo. Or the special kinship you'll feel when your 10-year-old says, "Hey, Mom, how about a run down with me?" Or that burst of pride that will overcome you as you watch your teenager conquering slopes that you wouldn't dare set ski on.

Skiing with children is one of the all-time great winter pastimes. It provides one of the few opportunities for extended outdoor activity during the winter months—amidst scenery that is inevitably majestic. And child development specialists agree that it's a terrific way for children to build self-esteem. Because it's an individual sport, there's no competition, except with one's fears and misgivings. It's a rare child who doesn't make steady progress on the slopes and take great pride in a successful run. And fortunately for once- or twice-a-year skiers, skiing is something like riding a bicycle; once you've mastered the basics, you'll never forget.

Luckily for parents, ski areas have focused their marketing incentives on families in recent years out of sheer necessity: the population on which they have traditionally counted for business, singles and childless couples between 18 and 34, is diminishing in size. Families are their best hope for future growth, and that realization, long in coming, is to your benefit. Today, families will find plenty of family-oriented restaurants, full nursery and child-care facilities, and excellent children's ski instruction programs at scores of ski areas throughout the nation.

For the non-skiers in the family, there is usually a full array of indoor activities available, from sitting by a cozy fire and watching the activity on the slopes, to taking classes in cooking or pottery, to spending the day at a spa or health club, to playing in well-equipped playrooms with one's peers. Most full-service Alpine ski areas today offer groomed cross-country trails as well.

How to choose from among the 600-odd ski areas in 39 states? Obviously, proximity is a compelling factor. If you live in western Kansas, you're not likely to head to New England to ski; Colorado is all too close, and attractive besides. Conversely, if you live in southern Pennsylvania, you're not likely to precede your skiing adventure with an expensive three-hour plane ride. Plan your family ski vacation for midweek if possible. The ski area that is packed to the tree line on weekends is likely to be gloriously deserted in midweek.

We feature 27 ski resorts that hold special attraction for families.

We've included a few in Canada that, besides providing great skiing, offer the experience of a family vacation in a foreign country.

All the successful ski areas today offer families a range of accommodations, from cozy rustic lodges, where meals are included in the rate, to budget-priced motel rooms, to modern condominiums, with all the comforts of home.

Lodges usually provide a congenial après-ski experience, with communal meals (no cooking chores for Mom or Dad), game rooms or TV lounges for the kids, and plenty of opportunities to gather around a fireplace with like-minded people and trade stories about successful runs. Motels provide attractive rates, but the benefits may be lost at the cash registers in the restaurants you'll have to frequent. Condominiums provide spaciousness—and their kitchens promise freedom from trying scenes with small children in restaurants. There are advantages and disadvantages to each option.

Distance from the slopes is a factor you'll want to consider before deciding where to stay. While ski-in–ski-out accommodations are great for expert skiers, they won't be worth the added cost if you've got an 11-month-old you've first got to deposit in the nursery or a 5-year-old who doesn't have the leg strength to manage the shuffle to the ski school. Most ski areas these days have shuttle bus service that enables you to do without a car altogether or to leave your car in the condominium parking lot.

A Note About Equipment and Clothing

Whether to buy your children's equipment or rent it is another choice you'll have to make. Most experts believe that children should have their own equipment if they are going to ski regularly. But if your family is going to ski together only once or twice a year, the cost of buying equipment is prohibitive. Most ski areas today have large stocks of children's ski equipment and can be expected to outfit your child appropriately and comfortably. Indeed, for a child who is growing, rented equipment may fit better than personally owned equipment that he or she is in the process of outgrowing.

What you wear may be the single most important decision you make during your entire ski holiday, for a cold skier is an unhappy skier. Forget style and dwell instead on comfort. Warmth and ease of movement should be the watchwords for your family's wardrobe.

Layering is the way to easily achieve both warmth and comfort, since thin layers trap warm air and can easily be shed as the day warms up. Bib pants are an excellent choice for children, complemented with a water-repellent ski jacket. A wool hat is *de rigueur*, as are good warm mittens, preferably with nylon outer covers and insulation. And a turtleneck shirt will prove more useful than a scarf in warming a child's neck (there are no loose ends to get caught in chair-lift bars or on trees).

What About Ski Schools?

Experts, without exception, recommend professional lessons for both children and adults—and not just because they're trying to keep their classes full. Remember trying to teach your 4-year-old the Australian crawl? Remember the first time you got in a car with your 16-year-old behind the wheel? Remember the frustration and awkwardness you yourself felt when you first put on skis? Eliminate an inevitably stressful situation by enrolling your child, whatever his or her age, in ski school.

Professional ski instruction is offered beginning at age 3 at most ski areas, although for the very youngest in that age group the instruction can best be characterized as snow play on skis. Many experts believe that age 5 is the best time to start children on skis. Most 5-year-olds have sufficient agility, self-confidence, and a sense of daring to enjoy the challenge. After a ski week at a well-run resort, it's a rare 5-year-old who won't be ready to ski an intermediate slope. But even most 3- and 4-year-olds love the idea of getting out on skis.

Ski Areas in the Summer?

Ski areas make marvelous summer destinations. Many operate as four-season resorts, and offer attractive price structures and a full array of recreational activities to attract summer guests. They've already got the scenery going for them. That mountain you skied down last winter looks entirely different when covered with wild-flowers in the summer. Consider visiting your favorite ski resort in the summer and take advantage of the extremely low rates. (But make sure first that it has something to offer besides cheap accommodations. There's nothing more depressing than a ski area in the summer if you're the only guests and there is nothing special to do.)

History Places

Children have a natural curiosity about the past. And creative parents constantly encourage it when they talk with their children about their own childhoods and the childhoods of their grandparents.

Whole new types of history museums have developed in recent years that re-create the history of a particular era and can be the focus of an enriching family vacation. Visitors to some simply observe the past; in others, whole families can role play and pretend they are living 100 years ago. It's history in the first person, and it's a marvelous family vacation idea.

We have included 11 wonderful history places around the country that really bring history to life for family visitors. Each does a wonderful job of explaining what life was really like in the past and of telling us about values, beliefs, attitudes, and the way people really lived. What was school like? How did parents treat their children? What did children do for entertainment before TV?

The most innovative history places take the implements and furnishings of everyday life of previous centuries out of glass display cases and put them in the hands of real people to show us what it was like to live and work in the past. It is hard to overstate how much this can improve understanding and pique your child's interest. Watching a person handle a plow behind a team of oxen—or better yet, struggling with the plow yourself—gives real meaning to the nature of farm work 100 or more years ago. Try spinning yarn to put a shopping spree at the local mall in perspective.

History places re-create or restore a real place where real people once lived; they do away with museum buildings and put visitors on a farm as it would have appeared a century or two ago, or in the streets of an authentic period town. Interpreters dress in period clothing to demonstrate crafts and describe how people lived. The emphasis is on the mechanics of producing necessities such as food, brooms, cloth, and pottery, often by hand.

The most challenging and interesting variation in historic villages are the "living history" residence programs in which you and your family stay for a number of days in a historically accurate setting and take on the roles of earlier citizens. It's like being in a time machine. You act the part of a person who actually lived 100 or more years ago. You bake the bread, hoe the garden, attend school, and play 19th-century games after supper.

Children love role playing. Adults may be a little intimidated at first, but it becomes easier with experience. And the learning is profound. Sitting on a stool in the barn and milking a cow is a long throw from peering through glass into a museum case.

Tips to Make Your Trip More Enjoyable

- Children must have a sense of history before they can relate well to history place experiences. They normally develop this capability at about 8 years of age. History places are not appropriate for younger children, who will lose interest rapidly, particularly if they are required to be observers and not participants.

- Be sure to prepare your family a little before you go. Do some reading. Talk about what life might have been like in the past and what you might expect to see and do at the museum.

Cruises

Cruises make wonderful family vacations. They offer families a complete break from routine and an escape into a fantasyland that has appeal to adults and children alike. Special children's rates—and the all-inclusive policies of most cruise lines—make taking a cruise comparable in price to staying at a 4-star resort.

In our section on cruises, we describe seven ships that have something to offer families with children of all ages. Since cruise lines typically offer similar services on all of their ships, that means that you actually have almost three dozen different ships to choose from that have proven track records with family vacationers.

Before you go, however, check to see that the cruise line's welcome mat for families hasn't been put away. Grill your travel agents well about how appropriate a particular ship is for families with children the age of yours. If they don't know, ask them to call the cruise line with your questions (cruise lines don't like dealing directly with passengers.) Find out whether you can reserve any special equipment you'll need, such as a crib, high chair, or refrigerator. And ask for a sample schedule of children's activities (that will give you an idea of how comprehensive the children's program is).

According to the Cruise Lines International Association, most of its 35 member lines now offer organized children's programs, under the supervision of trained youth counselors, to lure families. These vary from an hour of organized children's games daily to a breakfast-to-bedtime snack program that can occupy all of your child's waking hours. And the facilities used for children's activities can vary from a corner of an underutilized nightclub to a fully equipped children's playroom and nursery.

Among the attractions for children on the most family-oriented ships are special "nightclubs" for teenagers, wading pools for toddlers, libraries stocked with children's books and magazines, trained nannies, special shore excursions for children, cinemas that show cartoons and first-run family films, computer learning centers, video arcades, and collections of toys that rival those of the best-equipped day-care centers. Some lines bring along special kids' entertainers, such as magicians, puppeteers, and adults who dress as Mickey Mouse and Donald Duck. The kind of supervised events you can expect include scavenger hunts, limbo contests, aerobics and dance classes, visits to the captain's bridge, costume parties, ice-cream sundae and pizza-making parties, supervised swimming, and sports competitions. And for preschool-aged children, baby-sitting by off-duty social staff members can often—but not always—be arranged.

Then there are the inherent attractions of the cruise experience itself. What 5-year-old wouldn't be intrigued by all the nooks and crannies in a typical stateroom, small though it is? What 8-year-old wouldn't be captivated by a visit to the captain's bridge, with an opportunity to steer a massive ocean liner? What 10-year-old wouldn't revel in the freedom to explore the ship's public rooms in the company of some new chums? What teenager wouldn't swoon over the opportunity to stay up later than usual and dance to a live band with some new friends of the opposite sex?

A cruise can literally broaden your family's horizons, for the world looks entirely different from the deck of a ship than from land. Your seventh-grader might finally understand why Columbus shocked the world with his notion that the world was round, because it truly looks flat at sea. As you watch dolphins or even whales follow your ship's path across the sea, your children will get a deeper understanding of the separate world beneath the surface. And the scene in the harbor, with tugboats guiding your ship to its berth and local residents waving from the shore, is one so chock-full of excitement that only the most jaded child could remain unexcited.

About Ports of Call

One of the least attractive aspects of cruising is the vision of hundreds of ship passengers being disgorged all at once on the dock in a Caribbean harbor before they head off to the duty-free section of town, ignoring any evidence of local culture or tropical flora along the way. Small wonder that some residents of these ports treat cruise passengers as though they were merely walking opportunities to make some money. For many cruise passengers, the ports of call seem almost incidental; some don't even disembark, and many who do simply wander from one shop to another, inspecting the same duty-free merchandise that they've looked at in previous ports.

It doesn't have to be that way. With some advance planning, you can make the ports of call an adventure for your family. Make your way to the local office of the port's tourist information service (better still, write for information in advance) and find out what easily accessible attractions will appeal to children—a nice stretch of beach with gentle waves, a history museum, a local cultural center, a zoo. We offer some tips about enriching and enjoyable independent excursions with each of our entries.

But don't delude yourself that you're going to learn much about the country you're visiting. Few ships stay in a particular port longer than 12 hours, which is barely enough time for a visitor to get his or her bearings in the harbor area. This doesn't seem to bother many cruise passengers, for whom one country's straw basket is as good as another. But if you have a genuine interest in foreign cultures, you're bound to be disappointed with how little you get to experience them. Look at your port outings, instead, as an opportunity to try a small sample of the local culture—and if it appeals to you, vow to come back for more.

Tips to Make Your Trip More Enjoyable

- Although many families avoid cruises because of fear of a mishap at sea, it is virtually impossible for someone to fall off a ship's deck inadvertently. After a warning lecture about the hazards of climbing on the deck's fence, or interfering with safety equipment, or going into forbidden areas, you can give your mature 8-year-old the run of any ship without too much worry. Just make sure he or she knows where to find you—and that you always have an agreed-upon time and place to meet.

- Most ships have two seatings for meals. The earlier one is almost always the best bet for families because at the later one the crowd tends to be older, and dressier clothes are expected. You'll find the servers on the ships we describe friendly to children and eager to accommodate your special needs. Ask to be seated alone or at a table with another family whose children are similar in age.

- A short cruise, three or four days in length, is the best bet for families with preschool-aged children, and a good way for any family to sample cruise life and find out whether it's appealing.

- Don't hesitate to ask your cabin steward to do whatever he can to make life easier for you. He'll be happy to provide endless supplies of ice for cooling children's juices, fresh fruit for toddlers, extra pillows and blankets, and anything else you need.

- Take seriously the cruise line's tipping suggestions. On most lines, cabin stewards, waiters, and busboys are paid abysmally poor wages, and really do rely on tips to earn a living wage. Don't try to save money on your vacation by shortchanging them.

Adventure Trips

Family adventure trips can provide some of the most satisfying vacation experiences—closely shared family activities in settings of beauty and grandeur, the joy of living close to nature, the self-satisfaction that comes with learning a new skill. But it is important to understand what makes family adventure vacations work.

Nature is equally fascinating for adults and children, but the participation goes on at different levels. Parents see majestic mountains; young children see colorful rocks and interesting insects. Young children just don't see what we see. And we are often blind to their perceptions until we stop, observe, understand, and share them. Outdoor adventures are great family trips when family members can participate at their own levels and, at the same time, share the experience. The only mistake you can make in choosing an outdoor trip is to fail to adequately consider the needs and interests of every family member.

This book offers a selection of 13 outdoor adventure trips that will please many families—canoeing, hiking, rafting, cycling, camping, sailing, riding a covered wagon across the prairie—but you have the obligation to your family to choose carefully. If the stops on a gravel bar are frequent and long, your young child will not enjoy the raft trip, no matter how beautiful the scenery. Your indifferent teenager may not lift an eye to the canyon walls, but come alive only when the raft drops into a hole in the rapid and snowmelt water floods the boat.

Go with an Outfitter, or Go It Alone?

Going on an outdoor adventure with a first-rate outfitter is an excellent way to experience the out-of-doors. Good outfitters understand that individual needs vary, and they know a family won't be pleased with a trip unless every individual in the family is happy. They help in offering a variety of trips, in setting age limits on some of the trips they offer, and in varying the activities on each trip. Abide by their guidelines. Read their literature carefully, and if your questions aren't answered, contact them for more information. The good ones are happy to oblige.

Even to a veteran of adventure vacations, an outfitter offers some of the same advantages as to the neophyte: uncommon luxury in the out-of-doors, freedom from everyday chores, an introduction to a new area, a gain in the confidence that you can do it yourself the next time. The outfitter is likely to know the best places to stop for the night on a particular river and the most likely place to see wildlife. A good outfitter will also know the rudiments of first aid, which is a definite plus when you're traveling with children.

On the other hand, there are limits to what an outfitter can do for you. The outfitter can't reduce the volume of water in the river and make the rapids a little less scary. The outfitter can't make the sun shine when a three-day rain settles in on the lakes. The outfitter can't arrange a command performance by wildlife. If you and your family members are not physically and temperamentally suited for the trip, you will be miserable, no matter how good the outfitter.

Outdoor adventures are a lot more enjoyable when other families and children are in the group. Ask the outfitter if other families are joining the trip you are considering.

Nature Places

If your family wants an outdoors-oriented vacation, several considerations might steer you toward a nature place rather than an adventure trip. One is comfort. A family that wants to enjoy nature but still enjoy creature comforts will choose a nature place over an adventure trip for an outdoor family vacation. A family that wants to enjoy nature and camp will favor adventure trips. Nature places allow families to be out in nature by day and "home" in their snug rooms by night.

The lower physical demands and greater creature comforts of nature places make them a better choice for families with young children. For the same reasons, nature places might be ideal for an intergenerational family get-together where grandparents, parents, and children unite for some time together in a wonderful natural setting.

The organized learning component is a second compelling reason for choosing a nature place. Most of the 16 nature places described in this book have professional naturalists and ecologists on staff. Their program offerings usually vary in intensity, allowing you to choose casual introductions to nature or more serious experiences. Several offer the opportunity to earn college credit in special study programs during your stay.

Tips to Make Your Trip More Enjoyable

- If a bit of hiking is involved and your young children have never been on a hike, take them to the local park and try it out. Discover how fast they move when left to set their own pace. How do they react to being pushed along a bit? What interests them? Consider the skills that would enhance the experience for family members.

● If your child will have the opportunity to snorkel on a tropical reef for the first time, get a mask and snorkel and experiment in the bathtub and in the local swimming pool before leaving home.

● Go to your library or a bookstore and find some books that relate to the upcoming adventure trip. Read to your younger children about the cultural and natural history of the area you will visit. Read about the skills you will use to paddle the canoe or guide a horse.

● Preparation is important, not only for your children but also for you. Anticipating how other family members will react helps you react (or refrain from reacting) when the moment of truth—the first rapid, or the first 45-degree hillside, or the first swarm of yellowjackets—arrives.

● Nothing contributes more to comfort in the out-of-doors than appropriate clothing and equipment. Heed recommendations from the outfitter or nature place staff, and don't cut corners. If the outfitter says bring a warm sleeping bag, you run a significant chance of suffering through long, cold nights if you bring that light summer bag that you already have stashed in the attic.

ABOUT RATES

Rates at vacation spots change as frequently as hemlines—and the trend is usually upward. They do go down sometimes, if, for instance, there's a glut of hotel rooms in a particular area, or political unrest has scared off potential visitors, or a destination has suddenly and inexplicably become unfashionable. But the reality at most destination resorts and ranches is a five- to ten-percent increase each year in both off-season and high-season rates.

Rather than list specific rates for each destination we discuss and risk being almost immediately out of date, we have instead created categories and assigned each place we discuss to a category, and to more than one if there's a wide range of rates. The category list will give you a rough idea of the cost for two adults for a room without meals; each entry tells you whether or not children stay for free (if they're younger than 12, they usually do) or receive discounts.

Here are the categories to which we have assigned the vacation destinations, based upon their per-night, room-only rate for two adults:

$ Inexpensive: Under $80 a day
$$ Moderate: $80 to $110 a day
$$$ Expensive: $110 to $160 a day
$$$$ Very expensive: Over $160 a day

Published rates are not always directly comparable, because some of the places we discuss are all-inclusive—i.e., one rate covers all meals and all activities, along with a room—and others are either American Plan (three meals), Modified American Plan (breakfast and dinner), or European Plan (no meals). For purposes of comparability, at ranches and American Plan resorts we have subtracted $35 a day per adult from published daily rates to arrive at a basic room rate, even if a room-only rate is not available to guests. In instances in which two meals a day are included in a Modified American Plan rate, we have subtracted $25 per adult to arrive at a basic room rate.

For resorts, ranches, and cruise ships where many otherwise expensive recreational activities are covered by the basic rate (such as horseback riding, scuba diving, or greens fees), we have subtracted an "activities allowance" of $25 a day per adult to arrive at a basic room rate.

We know that the formula is complicated, but we hope it will permit you to compare the basic costs of destinations more easily. The cost of a cruise, for instance, might not seem so high in comparison to a week-long stay at a beachfront hotel if you factor in the meals and activities that are included in the cruise rate and that cost extra at the hotel.

At some places, where there is a range of charges for accommodations, you will find a destination assigned to two categories, such as Moderate and Expensive. You can count on reduced rates during the low season at almost all destinations, but you might not find such amenities as organized children's activities then. When you inquire about current rates, be sure to ask about package plans and weekend rates that might provide more advantageous rates than the published nightly rate.

Obviously, many families would not consider a $75-a-night room inexpensive, nor would it be if all you were getting was a roadside motel. Each of the destinations we describe, however, provides much more than a bed in which to sleep. Before you decide that a particular place is too expensive for your budget, research carefully all the amenities, services, and recreational opportunities that the basic rate includes.

1. Children can pretend to be boat captains at South Seas Plantation's waterfront playground. *(Photo: Martha Shirk)* **2.** The children's petting area, part of the 65-acre Good Children's Zoo at the Oglebay Resort in Wheeling, West Virginia, is just one facet of the resort that families can enjoy. *(Photo: Oglebay Resort)* **3.** Sailing is a popular pastime at Boscobel Beach Resort. *(Photo: Bruce Byers)* **4.** Children pause during a "bike hike" at Amelia Island Plantation. *(Photo: Amelia Island Plantation)*

5. A staff member helps fit a young visitor with a hula skirt at the children's program of Kona Village on the Big Island in Hawaii. **6.** Children anxiously line up for the start of a big race at The Tyler Place in Highgate Springs, Vermont. *(Photo: Wayne S. Tarr)* **7.** At New Seabury Cape Cod in Massachusetts, children take part in organized activities for part of the day as well as fishing and bicycling.

RESORTS

4

5

6

7

NORTHEAST

New Seabury Cape Cod
New Seabury, Massachusetts

No matter what you want from a vacation—a cozy villa where you can hear the ocean through your open window, challenging and top-rated golf or tennis facilities, fine dining, quaint and historic surroundings less than an hour away, or a comprehensive children's program so the whole family is taken care of in grand style—you can find it at New Seabury Cape Cod.

On the south shore of the Cape, between Falmouth and Hyannis, the sprawling 2,000-acre resort allows you to do as much, or as little, as you want.

The steady stream of traffic toward Cape Cod on summer weekends proves vacationers are attracted to the area like bargain hunters to Filene's Basement in Boston. The mixture of quaint New England charm and the seashore is irresistible.

As one admittedly biased employee of the resort put it, "Once you're here, there's no reason to leave if you don't want to." But if you do, all the attractions of the Cape Cod peninsula beckon.

ACCOMMODATIONS: **$$$** The New Seabury complex, which celebrated its 25th anniversary in 1987, is made up of 165 villas in villages. Guests live in the comfort and convenience of homey surroundings with separate sleeping and living rooms, but they still receive the convenience of housekeeping services.

Maushop Village offers units that typify what the rest of the world thinks of as Cape Cod living. Right on Popponesset Beach, they were designed to recall 19th-century Nantucket cottages, with white picket fences and narrow, winding lanes. Contemporary California-style patio homes are available at another village, known as The

Mews, where some units even have their own private swimming pools. Tidewatch Village, another waterfront area, is located between the greens of the complex's golf courses and the water of Nantucket Sound. All villas have balconies or decks designed to take full advantage of the views.

New Seabury is open year-round. Rates are highest in summer, with bargains available in early June. Maushop Village units are not air-conditioned, depending instead on ocean breezes for natural cooling. All villas offer fully-equipped kitchens, including utensils and table settings for 6. Many units include washers and dryers.

DINING: Only The Seabury restaurant is open year-round. In the summer, breakfast and lunch are available under the outdoor gazebo at the Marketplace Café (either eat-in or take-out). There are also beachfront cafés serving soups and sandwiches so you never have to leave the waterfront area.

On summer evenings, families searching for a casual meal can eat at the Marketplace Café or in the lounge at Popponesset Inn. More elegant dining is available in the summer either at the Country Club or at the dining room at Popponesset Inn, featuring New England seafood, of course. Men are asked to wear jackets in the evening at the more formal restaurants.

The general store in the Popponesset Marketplace has basic supplies so that you can make your own light breakfast in your villa.

ACTIVITIES

 Sixteen courts; pro shop, instruction.

 Two challenging 18-hole golf courses. The Blue Championship course, surrounded by water in a spectacular setting, has been ranked as one of the top 100 in the nation by *Golf Digest*. The Green Challenger course is less demanding.

 In the Atlantic Ocean from three miles of pristine beach or in several attractive pools.

Sailboat rentals, instruction.

Rental bicycles (summer only) in a shop in the Popponesset Marketplace.

 Hundreds of acres have been preserved in their natural state for wildlife refuges and hiking.

 Room with Nautilus equipment, aerobics and aquatic exercise classes; jogging, walking along the many tree-lined winding roads and parallel paths.

 New Seabury serves as the home for Summer Concerts by the Sea, a series of several concerts featuring conservatory bands, guitar duos, wind quartets, and soloists.

FOR CHILDREN: During the summer, 4- and 5-year olds can take part in "Summersalts" activities, including swimming instruction, exercises, and a variety of arts and crafts. Half and full-day programs are offered.

"Adventurers" is offered to children ages 6 through 13, from 9 A.M. to 3 P.M. Monday through Friday. The activities are organized around theme weeks. Typical themes include "A Whale of a Time," when studies of whales end with a whale-watch boat trip; "Working on the Railroad," climaxed by a trip on the Cape Cod Railroad; and "Kid Video," where participants create and star in their own music videos. Children who sign up for one week or more of the supervised activities receive a T-shirt.

"Teen Challenge" is for children in grades 8 through 10; lessons in sailing, karate, golf, tennis, and advanced lifesaving are offered.

Children taking part in the organized activities must bring their own golf and tennis equipment, if they are involved in those sports, plus lunch and a cold drink. Fees for the full-day programs are comparable to the cost of a quality day-care program at home. Half-day programs cost little more than you'd pay a baby-sitter. Early registration is advised.

Baby-sitting for younger children is also available.

NICETIES: Some units have a guest book to sign, and reading the comments of others who have stayed there before you gives a nice sense of community that other, less personal resorts cannot match.

A "video tour" of New Seabury is offered daily in the executive offices to acquaint guests with all the resort has to offer.

OF INTEREST NEARBY: Cruises to Nantucket and Martha's Vineyard leave from both Falmouth and Hyannis, each about 10 to 15 miles away, and automobile ferry service is available from Woods Hole. Since the boat rides are about four hours round-trip, set aside a full day for each of the excursions. Advance reservations are advised.

The island of Martha's Vineyard is known as a paradise for artists and photographers. There are tiny fishing villages to discover, old colonial homes in Edgartown, gingerbread cottages in Oak Bluffs, and breathtaking views, such as the colored clay cliffs of Gay Head. Wildlife refuges offer a pristine look at the island, including the state lobster hatchery at Oak Bluffs. Many special events take place on the island in the summer. Sightseeing is best done either by tour bus or by bicycles available for hire at the pier.

Nantucket Island is a former whaling port, complete with cobblestone streets and historic landmarks. Art galleries, restaurants, and shops are located in many of the old mansions on the island. You can tour Nantucket by bus, by bicycle, or on foot. Fishing, public beaches, and two public golf courses round out the activities.

Back on the Cape, less than an hour away by car, is Sandwich, on the northern coast. Children will enjoy the Yesteryears Doll and Miniature Museum, filled with historic dolls and dollhouses. The Sandwich Glass Museum displays exquisite examples of the area's glass artistry, and the Heritage Plantation is a 76-acre site featuring various crafts, a military museum, and restored automobiles, as well as gardens, nature trails, and a working mill. The plantation is open from 10 A.M. to 5 P.M. daily from mid-May to mid-October.

Whale-watching trips can be taken from Provincetown.

FOR MORE INFORMATION: Write New Seabury Cape Cod, Box B, New Seabury, MA 02649, or call (508) 477-9111. From Massachusetts, call (800) 752-9700; elsewhere in New England and in New York and Philadelphia, call (800) 222-2044.

The Balsams

Dixville Notch, New Hampshire

Once every four years, tiny Dixville Notch makes the news. Its 30 permanent residents are usually the first in the nation to vote in the presidential election. For the rest of the time, Dixville Notch is content to be known simply as home to one of New England's most prestigious and successful resorts.

The Balsams has been a summer resort since 1866. It began with a clapboard inn and grew dramatically with a 1916 stucco addition. It is the addition, with its red tile roof, that gives the inn its European flavor. Add Lake Gloriette in the foreground and the towering White Mountains in the background, plus 15,000 acres of virtually undeveloped land, and it is obvious why The Balsams has the well-deserved nickname "The Switzerland of America."

Like most grand resort hotels, The Balsams had its heyday in the early part of this century, when guests came for the entire summer. Warren G. Harding, Franklin Roosevelt, and Will Rogers enjoyed the healthful New Hampshire air, golf, and leisurely formal dinners. But the Depression and World War II sent The Balsams into a downward spiral.

The engineer of The Balsams' modern-day resurgence was a former caddy at the hotel, Steve Barba. Five years after Barba and his partners—general manager Warren Pearson, chef Phil Learned, and maintenance foreman Raoul Jolin—took it over, the Balsams turned a profit. Today the hotel operates from late May through mid-October and mid-December through March at near capacity. Its historic buildings are being slowly and splendidly renovated and restored to their turn-of-the-century grandeur.

But it is more than excellent facilities that constitutes the secret of The Balsams' success. Barba and his staff make an extra effort for each of their 400 guests. Their personal touch is obvious from the bottle of New Hampshire maple syrup that welcomes each guest to the beautifully manicured garden with 30,000 flowers. As Barba notes, "We do not sell land, space, or time. . . . The Balsams is one of the last hotels of this scale being run as a hotel catering solely to overnight guests."

ACCOMMODATIONS: **$$** to **$$$** The 232 rooms and suites at the Balsams are comfortable, clean, and cozy. They are New England simple with painted Ethan Allen furniture, wall-to-wall carpeting, and beautiful views of either the lake or the mountains. Generous walk-in closets are a vestige of the time when most guests came for "the season" of two months or more. Many of the rooms have fireplaces.

The Balsams has four categories of rooms, ranging from standard to deluxe. Children are charged $6 times their age per night, with a minimum charge of $24. Rates include all meals and activities. Guests are responsible for gratuities and their bar bill.

Very few guests come for just one night; 40 percent come for 10 days or more.

DINING: The Balsams provides its guests with three meals daily. Every meal is an event. Cuisine is largely continental, with many New England specialities.

Breakfast may be ordered from the menu or selected from a sumptuous buffet. The Balsams' luncheon buffet is renowned. Guests may choose from 10 hot dishes, 20 cold dishes, salads, cold cuts, fruits, breads, and 20 desserts arrayed on tables that stretch 100 feet across the dining room.

Dinner is the most formal meal of the day; jackets are required for men and dresses for women. Dinner offers a choice of eight entrées. Two or three special children's entrees are always offered.

For dinner, some parents order room service for their children (there's a nominal service charge), and enjoy a leisurely dinner alone.

ACTIVITIES

Six courts, three clay and three all-weather. A tennis professional offers private and group lessons and complimentary clinics. Guest tournaments are regularly scheduled. No court fees.

On a spectacular 18-hole mountaintop golf course designed by Donald Ross in 1912 (6,804 yards). A separate nine-hole executive course is designed for beginners. No greens fees.

In Lake Gloriette or a heated outdoor pool next to the lake.

 Pedal boats, canoes, and rowboats are available at no charge for use on Lake Gloriette. An old-fashioned paddlewheel cruise boat takes guests on tours of the lake.

In the lake. The hotel's kitchen will clean and cook your catch.

 Hiking is a challenge in the White Mountains surrounding The Balsams; a naturalist guides walks. Guests have reported seeing moose, bear, and fox just a short distance from the hotel.

Shuffleboard and horseshoes; a game room with video games and a Ping-Pong table. The Balsams offers a lecture series to guests with topics ranging from "A Naked Eye Supernova in Our Lifetime" to "Yankee Humor."

At night there are first-run movies and cabaret shows, dancing in the Switzerland of America Ballroom, a late-night piano bar in the Patio Garden Lounge, and a lively combo in the Wilderness Lounge.

Ice skating, snowshoeing. The Balsams Wilderness Ski Area, with 12 trails, bustles during the Balsams' four-month ski season; rentals available. (Dixville Notch gets an average of 250 inches of snow a year.) For Nordic skiers, The Balsams has 70 kilometers of groomed trails; rental equipment available.

FOR CHILDREN: From July 4 through Labor Day, The Balsams operates a free comprehensive children's program called "Camp Wind Whistle." The program is staffed by three counselors, and usually serves 15 to 25 children, ages 5 to 12.

The counselors meet the children at 9:30 at the children's play-room, 7 days a week, and organize a busy day of hiking, games, arts and crafts, swimming, and boating. The afternoon program ends at 4 P.M., but resumes at dinnertime, with activities available until about 9 P.M. Parents who want sitters can make arrangements through the front desk.

Every recreation area at The Balsams is extremely well supervised. Parents can feel confident letting their older children swim at the pool or the lake, under the watchful eye of lifeguards, or play on the playground.

For teenagers The Balsams offers "The Minor's Cave," off the main lobby. It is operated on Wednesday and Saturday nights by the recreation staff, and features rock videos, movies, and music. Refreshments are non-alcoholic and half-price to guests under 21.

During ski season The Balsams has a nursery at the base lodge for children through age 6. Hours are 9 A.M. to noon and 1 P.M. to 4 P.M. Parents must care for their children during the noon hour. Older children can participate in the Wind Whistle Ski School free of charge.

NICETIES: The Balsams has a small library stocked with 1940s best-sellers. There's always a jigsaw puzzle in progress.

There are several shops located on the first floor of Hampshire House. The Balsams Gift Shop also carries magazines, books, and film. Several boutiques sell clothing and supplies for golf, tennis, and swimming. Every summer Peter Lear returns as the resident silversmith. Lear sells his own creations and will also custom-make and repair jewelry.

There are no television sets in The Balsams' rooms. For diehard watchers, a large-screen television set is located off the main lobby.

FOR MORE INFORMATION: Write The Balsams, Dixville Notch, NH 03576, or call (800) 255-0800 from New Hampshire or (800) 255-0600 from elsewhere in the U.S. and Canada. A video brochure is available for a $35 refundable deposit.

Mohonk Mountain House
New Paltz, New York

No travel literature can adequately prepare you for your first glimpse of Mohonk Mountain House. About two miles past a simple gate-house on a country road in New York's Shawangunk Mountains, it looms ahead: a magnificent red-roofed Victorian castle, a relic from another century. Because of its splendor and rich history, the Mountain House and its surrounding land were declared a National Historic Landmark in 1986, rewarding the owners for more than a century of extraordinary stewardship. Mohonk is owned by the Smiley family, descendants of twin brothers Albert and Alfred Smiley, who purchased the spectacular site in 1870 after Alfred discovered it on a hike.

The hotel sits at one end of a half-mile-long, 60-foot-deep natural mountain lake about two hours northwest of New York City. Rugged glacial outcroppings rise dramatically from the water. Surrounding the Mohonk property is a 22,000-acre unspoiled natural area comprising state parks and private preserves. It is as much the so-called Mohonk experience as the beautiful setting that draws guests back generation after generation.

That "experience" reflects Mohonk's heritage. The Smiley twins were schoolteachers and devout Quakers, who built their grand hotel on the site of a rowdy tavern where overly-rambunctious guests were chained to trees. The Smileys banned liquor, cardplaying, and dancing in favor of nature walks and daily prayer services. Even today, there is no bar or cocktail lounge, although you can get a drink with lunch and dinner or order a bottle to drink discreetly in your room. There is no smoking in the dining room or parlor, jackets are required at dinner, and a prayer service is offered every morning during the busy summer season.

The carriage roads (yes, there is a horse-drawn carriage ride) are so well-groomed you can actually push a baby stroller on them, and the views of the lake and the Mountain House as well as the surrounding valleys are truly spectacular. Walk or jog a mile away from the lodge and you're as likely to see a family of deer as a family of fellow guests. Or stroll up to the Sky Top, a stone tower that marks the highest point on the property, and look out at six states.

Mohonk is also renowned for its 40 special weekends, with themes like Cooking, Mystery, Tennis, Star-gazing, Fitness, or Tower of Babble (foreign-language instruction).

ACCOMMODATIONS: $$$ Mohonk Mountain House has 276 rooms, about half with working fireplaces and two-thirds with balconies. Most have good views of the lake (even-numbered rooms) or the mountains to the west (odd-numbered rooms). There are some adjoining rooms that share a bathroom—perfect for a family with small children. All rates, except for these adjoining rooms, are per room, per night, for two persons, and include three meals per person and afternoon tea.

The peak season is May through October. Weekly rates are available. For families, the double occupancy rate applies to the first two occupants of double-bedded rooms, with a children's rate available for children sharing the room. In adjoining rooms, the first three occupants are charged the full rate regardless of age, and each additional occupant age 2 to 12 is charged a children's rate. Children under 4 stay free.

DINING: All meals are taken in either the Main Dining Room or a smaller dining room. Food at Mohonk is abundant. Early-morning coffee is available from 7 to 8 A.M. Breakfast, served from 8 to 9:30 A.M., is a bountiful buffet. Continental breakfast is served from 9:30 to 11 A.M.

A luncheon buffet is served from 12:30 to 2 P.M. During the summer, a barbecue lunch is also offered outdoors. The evening meal is served from 6:30 to 8 P.M. and offers selections from a menu.

Guests have the same waiter—and the same table—for all their meals. Make your reservations early to ensure a seat in the Main Dining Room, which has an incredible view.

ACTIVITIES

Four red clay and two Har-Tru courts, two lighted platform tennis courts; pro shop, lessons, rental equipment, tournaments, partner matchup.

Nine-hole, Scottish design, par 35 course, open from April through October; 18-hole putting green.

In Mohonk Lake; inner tubes and beach chairs provided.

Mohonk Lake. Rental boats available.

Mohonk Lake. Rental equipment available.

 The 5,000-acre Mohonk Preserve protects the area's natural beauty and encourages visitors to appreciate it. Educational and interpretive nature programs are offered year-round. Maps of trails through the preserve are available.

Guided English or Western-style trail rides four times a day from April through October.

Indoor Fitness Center with a Universal weight machine, exercise bicycles, ballet barre, saunas, and showers. Classes are offered regularly. Massages are available.

The energetic activities staff organizes guest tournaments in putting, croquet, lawn bowling, Ping-Pong, shuffleboard, softball, volleyball, and platform tennis, as well as hayrides, skating parties, snow-tubing outings, guided jogs and rock scrambles, prayer services, and afternoon tea. Lots of special activities are offered for families, including cookouts, barn museum tours, forging demonstrations, softball and volleyball games, and outdoor movies.

 Ice-skating, ice fishing, cross-country skiing on groomed and double-tracked trails; equipment rentals.

FOR CHILDREN: There's a well-organized children's program, whose underlying philosophy is "Let kids be kids." It emphasizes outdoor activities and nature appreciation. The program is available daily except Monday during the summer and on weekends and holidays after Labor Day.

"Mohonk Tykes," for 2- to 4-year-olds, meets from 9:30 A.M. to 12:30 P.M. in a facility equipped with a wide selection of toys, including a play tunnel, rocking horses, blocks, puzzles, and lots of art materials and books. Parents are welcome to stay or drop in whenever they like. The Tykes play mostly indoors, but are also taken out for walks, games, and pony rides.

Three separate programs for older children meet from 9:30 A.M. to 12:30 P.M., recess for lunch with parents, and resume from 2 to 5 P.M.

Children aged 5 and 6 are called "Explorers" and engage in such activities as peanut hunts, croquet, swimming, field games, ice cream making, and frog hunts.

Children aged 7 and 8 are called "Scramblers." They go on hikes, swim, take pony rides, run an obstacle course, make arts and crafts projects, and go on scavenger hunts.

The "Adventurers" are the 9- to 12-year-olds, who go rock scrambling, swim, play putt-putt golf, hike, fish, play field games, and make kites.

Each evening there are either activities for children only (5- to 12-year-olds) or entertainment for the whole family.

There are no special activities for teenagers or for children under 2. Baby-sitting can be arranged.

NICETIES: Late arrivals on Friday nights may order a late supper between 8 and 10 P.M.

The Mountain House is accessible to wheelchairs, and Guest Services can provide a special chair with pneumatic tires for outdoor use.

There's a laundry in the basement of the Mountain House.

If you run out of diapers or other essentials during your stay, the staff will purchase them for you in a nearby town for a small service charge.

OF INTEREST NEARBY: If you're driving from New York City, budget some time to explore the small towns along the way, which are dotted with antiques shops and interesting restaurants.

Newburgh, about 15 miles from New Paltz, was George Washington's headquarters for more than a year during the Revolutionary War, and later was a center of the whaling industry. Washington's headquarters, at Liberty and Washington streets, is now a state historic site. Local sightseeing maps and brochures are available at the Chamber of Commerce, 72 Broadway.

At Rhinebeck is the Old Rhinebeck Aerodrome, a collection of antique airplanes built between 1908 and 1937. Barnstorming rides may be available in an open cockpit biplane. Call (914) 758-8610 for hours.

Hyde Park, about 45 minutes from Mohonk across the Hudson River, is the home of the Franklin D. Roosevelt Library and Museum, and Roosevelt's home. The museum is excellent, and the home, through which tours are available, provides you with an intimate glimpse into the Roosevelts' family life. Call (914) 229-8114 for hours. Nearby is the Eleanor Roosevelt National Historic Site, her private retreat. Call (914) 229-9115 for hours.

FOR MORE INFORMATION: Write Mohonk Mountain House, New Paltz, NY 12561, or call (914) 255-1000 or (212) 233-2244 (within New York City).

The Sagamore
Bolton Landing, New York

For most of a century, the Sagamore has been a luxurious resort with an exclusive clientele. Built in 1883 on Green Island near "Millionaire Row," the Sagamore quickly became the center of Lake George's glittering social life. America's wealthiest families spent leisurely summers boating on the lake and enjoying sumptuous meals in the Sagamore's dining room.

After World War II, the hotel went into gentle decline and closed in 1981. It was completely rehabilitated and reopened in 1984 under the aegis of developer Norman Wolgin, a Philadelphian who traditionally summered at Lake George, and under the management of the Omni chain. In its newest incarnation, the Sagamore is "An Omni Classic Resort and Conference Center."

Wolgin has managed to maintain the Sagamore's charm while adding the Omni's sleek management style. Guests can still enjoy morning coffee or cocktails in the Sagamore's magnificent portico with its stunning view of the lake and the Adirondack Mountains, just as their predecessors did a hundred years ago.

ACCOMMODATIONS: $$$ to $$$$ The Sagamore has a total of 350 rooms and suites divided between the Victorian Landmark-style main building, new lodges adjacent to the original hotel, and the

Hermitage, an executive retreat. All of the rooms in the main building were renovated in the early 1980s.

Summer rates in the main building are offered under the Modified American Plan (MAP). Children 3 to 18 pay reduced rates; children under 3 stay and eat free.

Better suited to families than the original hotel are the new lodges. Each lodge suite has its own kitchen, small patio, dining area, living area (with sleep sofas), private baths, and one or two bedrooms. Color television sets are in the living rooms and bedrooms. MAP rates are also offered here, and are somewhat lower than in the old building. Ask about the Family Fling package, which includes some special amenities.

DINING: Breakfast, served in the Sagamore dining room, is an experience not to be missed. In addition to a buffet of hot and cold entrées, a trio of chefs makes omelets to order.

The Sagamore has many options for dinner. The most elegant is the Trillium Room (there's a surcharge for MAP guests). Three other dining options are included in the MAP. The Sagamore Dining Room serves American regional cuisine. The Club Grill, 2 miles from the hotel on the golf course, has a 1920s style and is a treat for adults and older children. Least intimidating to children for lunch and dinner is Mr. Brown's, serving informal meals in a casual, clublike atmosphere. Low-calorie specialties are available at all meals.

In the summer, the hotel organizes special event meals at the Pool Terrace. This casual dining is a natural for young families. One of the most popular events is a clambake with unlimited portions of clams, lobster, and seafood salad.

All of the restaurants at the Sagamore have children's menus.

ACTIVITIES

 Two indoor and four outdoor courts.

 Eighteen-hole Scottish-style course designed by Donald Ross. Located two miles from the main hotel, it can be reached by a regular shuttle bus. Golf professional Tom Smack is available for clinics and tournaments.

Indoor pool and whirlpool at the hotel. In Lake George from a sandy beach (even in the middle of the summer the water is frigid). Parents should bring life jackets or "floaties" for young children, since there is no children's pool or shallow pool area.

From May 1 through October 15, sailboat and powerboat rentals are available at the docks adjacent to the beach for pleasure outings, water skiing, or fishing. Three outings a day are offered on the *Morgan*, a 72-foot replica of a turn-of-the-century touring vessel.

Lake George abounds with lake and rainbow trout, salmon, perch, pike, and bass. Charters and equipment available.

The Sagamore Spa is a luxurious European-style health spa with exercise equipment, a loofah room, saunas, steam and massage rooms, whirlpools, and hot and cold plunge pools. Facials and complete massages are available by appointment.

In the evenings during the summer, the Sagamore offers movies or its dinner theater revue.

Cross-country skiing on groomed trails across the golf course; ice-skating on the flooded tennis courts. Downhill skiing is available at the West Mountain Ski Center, in nearby Glens Falls, with six chair lifts and 19 trails (some lighted for night skiing). Half an hour from the Sagamore is Gore Mountain, with 41 trails; complimentary shuttle.

Hardy guests may want to participate in the Lake George Winter Carnival in January and February. Events include polar bear swimming, ice fishing, and outhouse racing.

One of the first impressions you get of the Sagamore is of multicolored parachutes high above Lake George. The sport is parasailing, and instead of dropping from planes, the participants are pulled by motor boats. Children as young as 4 have parasailed there. Also offered are sunrise hot-air balloon flights. Both activities are expensive.

FOR CHILDREN: The Sagamore's free children's program operates daily in the summer season and on holidays and selected weekends in the winter, for children 3 to 13. Activities are offered from
9 A.M. through 9 P.M. Supervised children's lunches and dinners
are available (there's a charge for meals).

The program is supervised by adult counselors. The toddler
group, ages 3 to young 5s, listens to stories, swims, does art projects,
and plays games at the resort's inventive playground. Older children
(mature 5- to 13-year-olds) swim, participate in golf and tennis clinics, go on scavenger hunts, play kickball and volleyball, and attend
movies. Theme parties are held daily for both groups.

Baby-sitters are also available.

NICETIES: In mid-afternoon guests may enjoy a complimentary
tea or lemonade with chamber music at the Lakeside Pavilion, or
they may opt for high tea in the Veranda, with its 180-degree view
of the lake.

Parked on the Sagamore's gracious circular driveway during the
summer is a surrey with a horse and driver for complimentary tours
of the grounds. In the winter, horse-drawn sleigh rides are given
over the snow-covered golf course.

OF INTEREST NEARBY: Lake George is a paradise for history
buffs. Half an hour north of Bolton Landing is Fort Ticonderoga, a
pre–Revolutionary War fort, which has a military museum. In Lake
George Village, 10 miles south, Fort William Henry was the site of
the last battle of the French and Indian War.

Children find Lake George Village a wonderland of amusement
and theme parks, including The Great Escape, with its Desperado
Plunge flume ride, and Gaslight Village.

Saratoga Springs, about half an hour from Lake George, is well
known for both its racetrack and its performing arts center. The
track is the oldest in America, and races are held in August. The
Performing Arts Center, an open-air theater, draws the Philadelphia
Orchestra, the New York City Ballet, and many top theater and
show business performers.

FOR MORE INFORMATION: Write The Sagamore, P.O. Box 450, Bolton Landing, NY 12814, or call (800) 358-3585.

Four Seasons Inn on the Park
Toronto, Ontario, Canada

Only 20 minutes from the hustle and bustle of cosmopolitan downtown Toronto, the Four Seasons Inn on the Park has the ambience of a country resort. Families can spend a busy morning soaking up culture and adventure in one of North America's most interesting and family-friendly cities and then repair to the hotel pool for an afternoon of relaxation.

Located next to the beautiful 600-acre Wilket Creek Park, the Four Seasons Inn on the Park provides recreational opportunities unthinkable at most urban hotels—tobogganing and cross-country skiing in the winter and swimming, tennis, bicycle riding, horseback-riding and hiking in the summer. Because of the excellent children's program, parents who need to be in Toronto on business often bring their children along, contributing to a festive atmosphere amid the elegance of the hotel.

This AAA five-diamond hotel manages to serve both business travelers and family vacationers well. Set amidst lovely gardens in a courtyard are a playhouse and excellent playground equipment. And the concierge staff is as willing to help visiting parents find a babysitter as to fax business documents for a conference attendee. The Four Seasons group has built its fine reputation on attention to detail —from complimentary overnight shoeshining right down to the colorful bumper pads in the cribs!

ACCOMMODATIONS: **$$** to **$$$** The 568 guestrooms, including 26 suites, are located either in the main building or in the Tower Suites. The rooms are spacious and beautifully furnished, with sitting areas. Each room has a mini-bar and remote-control color television, and some have balconies. Parents of small children can request a first-floor room that opens onto the courtyard and its play-grounds. Children under 16 stay free of charge.

DINING: There are two restaurants, a poolside snack bar, and two cocktail lounges. Seasons is the hotel's premier restaurant; it features continental and nouvelle American cuisine in an elegant atmosphere. The Harvest Room is a cheerful and friendly family-style restaurant; children will enjoy coloring their special menu. Lunch and afternoon snacks are served at the outdoor Cabana Café. Room service is available around the clock.

ACTIVITIES

Three tennis courts (bubbled for winter play), five squash courts, and five racquetball courts at the Parkview Racquet & Fitness Club on the premises; court fees.

Guests have privileges at the nine-hole Flemingdon Golf Course, five minutes away, and the beautiful and exclusive 18-hole Parkview Golf & Country Club, 30 minutes away.

A heated indoor pool with adjacent whirlpool, 25-meter out-door pool, and separate diving pool. During the summer, a portable splash pool is provided for toddlers.

Complimentary bicycles are available for riding on miles of trails in adjacent 600-acre Wilket Creek Park, which is also a jogger's paradise.

There are shuffleboard and badminton courts in the courtyard and a gymnasium and indoor track at the Racquet Club; massages.

Late-night dancing and entertainment in the Copper and Ter-race lounges. Special social activities are offered during holiday periods for families.

Complimentary cross-country skiing equipment available for use on 16 miles of groomed trails through Wilket Creek Park. Complimentary toboggans for use in the park.

FOR CHILDREN: Daily during the summer and on every weekend during the rest of the year, the Inn offers "InnKids" a free supervised children's program for children between 5 and 12; children under 5 may participate if accompanied by a parent or baby-sitter. The program is supervised by a full-time staff member with a background in childhood development; a ratio of one adult to eight children is maintained. The program attracts about 20 children a day.

The children gather at 9:30 A.M. in the V.I.K. (Very Important Kid) Room next to the indoor pool. The day typically begins with swimming and games in the indoor pool, followed by lunch. In the afternoon, children enjoy arts and crafts, outdoor games, storytelling (in the "hideaway hut"), and more swimming. The program ends at 4 P.M.

The courtyard contains terrific playground equipment and plenty of run-around room for young children, as well as a pond filled with fish and frequented by ducks. A game room next to the V.I.K. Room has the usual assortment of video games.

NICETIES: The pool attendant will lend your child water toys, water wings, or a lifejacket.

The housekeeping department keeps on hand a full stock of baby supplies, such as strollers, high chairs, diapers, wipes, thermometers, pain relievers, bottles, and pacifiers.

Among the offerings from room service: milk and cookies at bedtime and popcorn and pizza for snacks.

OF INTEREST NEARBY: On weekends, pack a picnic lunch and join the locals on their family outings by ferry to the Toronto Islands, especially Centre Island, which has an excellent amusement park called Centreville, miles of biking trails, formal gardens, fishing ponds, playgrounds, beaches, and a free tram.

The Ontario Science Centre, less than a mile from the hotel (ask for directions to the path through the park), is one of the best of its kind, with hundreds of hands-on exhibits in a striking building.

The Metro Toronto Zoo has more than 4,000 animals displayed in naturalistic settings scattered across its 710 acres. Locals like to ski around the zoo in the winter!

The Royal Ontario Museum has mummies, dinosaurs, and suits

of armor, as well as a Ming tomb, an Islamic home, and a Buddhist temple. Adjacent McLaughlin Planetarium has an excellent theater with laser light shows and special shows for children. The Art Gallery of Ontario, a few blocks away, has the world's largest collection of sculptures by Henry Moore, as well as his seashell and bone collection.

Families can ride a glass-walled elevator to the top of the CN Tower, the world's tallest free-standing structure, for a panoramic view of Toronto and Lake Ontario.

Ontario Place is a futuristic lakefront theme park featuring a terrific Children's Village amusement area, a Waterplay Area with a 370-foot waterslide, restaurants and shops, a three-dimensional movie theater, boat rides, and the Canadian Baseball Hall of Fame and Museum.

Black Creek Pioneer Village, on the outskirts of town, is an excellent living-history museum that evokes the feel of life in Canada in the 19th century.

FOR MORE INFORMATION: Write the Inn at 1100 Eglinton Avenue East, Toronto, Ontario, Canada M3C 1H8, or call (416) 444-2561.

Skytop Lodge
Skytop, Pennsylvania

"Secluded in the Poconos," the mood-setting advertising slogan used by Skytop Lodge in Pennsylvania's glorious Pocono Mountains, is an understatement. Amidst the garish billboards for the Poconos' other famous resorts, we did not see a single directional sign for Skytop.

Seclusion is what attracts visitors to Skytop—that and a wide array of seasonal outdoor activities, a genteel, old-fashioned atmosphere, impeccable personal service, and endless opportunities to just relax. Staying at Skytop, one has the feeling of belonging to a private club, and for good reason—it *was* a private club until the late 1970s.

Founded in 1928 by rich New Yorkers as a golf retreat, Skytop remained a haven for members only until the increasing age of its members and the skyrocketing costs of running a full-service resort forced it to open its doors to "those who will be congenial at the Club."

Today, the resort is overrun with families, many from Philadelphia and New York City, each within a two and a half hour drive. On a typical weekend, toddlers waddle the length of the long, old-fashioned Pine Room, which functions as the resort's living room. On the lower level, teenagers play exuberant games of Ping-Pong or billiards, gorge themselves on old-fashioned ice-cream sundaes, watch a wide-screen television set, or waste a month's allowance on video games. And at any hour of the day, the heated indoor pool is likely to be the venue for a game of water tag or splash Daddy.

Skytop still reflects the manner and customs of a bygone era. Constructed of granite and topped with a slate roof, the main building sits in an imposing setting on a plateau ringed by gentle hills, looking much like the administration building of a 200-year-old college. The Pine Room, with its overstuffed chairs, flowered draperies, and grandfather's clock, is your great-grandmother's parlor writ large. To its rear, the library provides a quiet, smoke-free environment for letter writing and reading. Game rooms recall the era in which families gathered to play table games rather than watch TV. A glassed-in sun porch furnished with Adirondack lawn chairs overlooks gardens and manicured lawns in the foreground, with the Delaware Water Gap, one of the East's outstanding natural attractions, in the background 20 miles away.

ACCOMMODATIONS: $$ to $$$ Skytop has 183 rooms, most in the main lodge. They are various sizes; all have full bathrooms and have been redecorated since 1989. Under the family plan, children 17 and under stay and eat free if they share their parents' room. There are nine cottages with four bedrooms each.

Three full meals a day are included in the room rates. A service charge is added to the bill, and tipping is discouraged.

DINING: Mealtime is an event at Skytop, and guests are encouraged to dress for dinner, though sportswear is appropriate for breakfast and lunch. Breakfast, served from 7:30 to 9 A.M., includes such regional favorites as Philadelphia scrapple and steamed finnan haddie. Lunch, served from noon to 1 P.M., includes a choice of four appetizers, relishes and crudités, two soups, and entrées ranging from Maryland crab cakes to braised Swiss steak. Vegetables, served family style, and a choice of three salads and six desserts round out the meal.

Dinner, served from 7 to 8 P.M., allows the chef to show off. There's usually a choice of five entrées.

Cocktails, wine, and beer may be purchased in the dining room or enjoyed before dinner in the Tap Room, a cocktail lounge on the lower level. If hunger pangs strike anytime during the day, a lower-level tea room serves light snacks and ice-cream sundaes.

ACTIVITIES

 Five Har-Tru tennis courts and two all-weather courts; instruction, pro shop.

Eighteen-hole golf course, rated among the finest in the country, with only an 84-foot variation in grade over the entire course; three putting greens and a practice hole, pro shop, instruction.

 Heated indoor pool, large outdoor pool (new in 1989), kiddie pool; swimming in small lower lake.

Rental rowboats and canoes at the Boat House on the 74-acre Upper Lake (small privately owned sailboats also are welcomed). Daylong or half-day-long canoe trips can be arranged on the Delaware River, about 20 miles away, through Kittatinny Canoes, Inc.

Fishing for bass, catfish, pickerel, perch, and sunfish in the lake on the grounds at no charge. Or, for a charge, you can fish in one and a half miles of private stream stocked with brook and brown trout; mounted trout on the walls of the lobby attest to past successes. The chef will prepare your catch.

 Rentals available; miles of marked trails.

Nine miles of marked trails crisscrossing the resort's 5,500 acres. Topographical map supplied to each guest, interpretive walks led by the staff naturalist in July and August.

Off premises at Carson's Riding Academy near Mt. Pocono.

Fitness center with whirpool and sauna; lawn games such as lawn bowling, horseshoes, croquet, archery, badminton, miniature golf, and shuffleboard.

Barbecue at the base of the ski slope at 12:30 P.M. on Saturdays in the summer; movie showings scheduled throughout the week; hayrides in summer and fall. Piano concerts most Friday evenings in the Pine Room; Saturday night dances; periodic night walks and stargazings.

Skiing at nearby Jack Frost Mountain, Big Boulder Ski Area, and Camelback, short slope on premises; cross-country skiing on groomed trails; ice-skating on 6,000-square-foot-rink; sledding on resort's hills and tobogganing on 350-foot slide onto Skytop Lake (equipment provided).

FOR CHILDREN: Skytop's free children's program, called the "Camp in the Clouds," operates five and a half hours a day, daily except Sunday, in July and August. The program is geared toward children from 3 to 12, but children as young as 2 (even in diapers) can be included. The day's schedule of activities is adjusted to take into account the ages and abilities of the children present.

A converted boat house on the shore of Lake Skytop serves as the playroom and activity center. From 9:30 A.M. to noon, children participate in activities ranging from arts and crafts to storytelling, or take group instruction in swimming, golf, tennis, archery, badminton, croquet, boating, and fishing. One morning a week, the group goes by van to the Pocono Playhouse in nearby Mountain-home, Pa., for a children's play. On another morning, the staff naturalist leads a nature walk. After a break for lunch with their families, camp resumes at 2 P.M., with swimming the primary afternoon activity. The camp director, who has teacher training, is assisted by two college students.

In the off-season, there are many scheduled activities that are suitable for older children. Board games are available in the game rooms on the main level.

NICETIES: Continental breakfast is served in the Pine Room for early risers. A selection of local and national newspapers is available.

The library is stocked with several thousand volumes, including children's books, which can be checked out.

Flowers can be ordered to grace your table during your visit.

FOR MORE INFORMATION: Write the Skytop Lodge, Skytop, PA 18357, or telephone (717) 595-7401 or (800) 345-7759 from Connecticut, New York, New Jersey, Delaware, and Maryland; in Pennsylvania, (800) 422-7759. The Pocono Mountain Vacation Bureau is at 1004 Main St., Stroudsburg, PA 18360, phone (717) 421-5791.

The Tyler Place
Highgate Springs, Vermont

It is not the food or the accommodations that make The Tyler Place so appealing. While both are more than adequate—cottages and suites are comfortable and nicely decorated, but not deluxe, and meals are home-cooked and healthy, but not haute cuisine—it is the resort's overwhelming friendliness that is its main attraction. Guests make fast friends and come back year after year, often during the same week so they can see the same people (they're also happy to meet new guests).

The resort occupies 165 acres on Lake Champlain's shore, only a few miles from the Canadian border. From its opening in 1945, The Tyler Place has been managed by the Tyler family. Frances Tyler and her late husband decided to open a resort that offered a place for young families to relax with their children. The Tyler Place's philosophy has evolved into "separate, but equal" facilities for adults and children. The six separate children's programs are well-supervised, highly structured, and very successful.

The Inn is the social hub of The Tyler Place. It houses the dining facilities, a cocktail lounge, recreation rooms, and the only public telephone at the resort.

ACCOMMODATIONS: $$ The 27 cottages at The Tyler Place, decorated with Waverly fabrics, have a quaint charm, and are comfortable enough to earn a three-star rating from the Mobil travel guide. Every cottage has a fireplace and from one to four bedrooms, including an air-conditioned master bedroom. The cottages are priced according to their proximity to the lake or the Inn. Although all meals are served at the Inn, each cottage has a small kitchen. Well-behaved pets are permitted in the cottages.

In addition to the cottages, there are suites in the Inn, more modern than the cottages but not as charming. The suites are air-conditioned and designed with the parents' privacy in mind. There are no telephones or television sets in the rooms or cottages.

The Tyler Place operates on the American Plan. For most of the summer, registration and departure are on Saturdays; guests must stay for a week. During spring, early summer, and early fall, a two-night minimum stay is required. Special rates at the beginning of the summer and early fall are available at a 20 to 35 percent savings, with the same services and meals.

The Tyler Place does not permit tipping, but adds a 10 percent service charge to each bill.

DINING: In general, children and adults dine separately, but may eat breakfast together in a special room.

Older children and adults choose from similar menus; the food is filling and wholesome, and Vermont dairy products are often served. Young children have their own special menu. All meals are served semi-buffet style, and guests usually choose among three entrées. Picnic baskets can be arranged for family outings.

Dinner is at 6:30 P.M. and is preceded by a 5:30 P.M. cocktail hour with a cash bar. Most couples socialize during a leisurely candlelit dinner before picking up their children at 8:30 P.M.

Dress at all meals is informal except for Saturday's Get Acquainted Party and some special evening events, when jackets are suggested for men.

ACTIVITIES

Privileges at nearby indoor facility. Six outdoor courts. Round-robin doubles, singles tournaments.

Privileges at three country clubs, 15 to 45 minutes away.

In the heated pool or in Lake Champlain. Children's wading pool.

Sailing, sailboarding, kayaking, canoeing, powerboating, and water-skiing on Lake Champlain. Canoe trips on Rock River.

Fish are plentiful in the lake (a license is required for adults, available in nearby Swanton). Motorboats can be rented.

Twelve mountain bikes and 42 one-speed bikes for guests' use on country roads.

Basketball, softball, tennis, champagne cruises on a pontoon boat, soccer, badminton, and archery. Frequent competitions in all sports.

On some evenings, there's a DJ, square-dance caller, or Vermont storyteller. On Parlor Game Night there are spirited games of charades and Pictionary. On Monte Carlo Night there are bingo and roulette. By the end of the week even the most inhibited guest joins the lip-sync contest with a prize for the best contestant.

FOR CHILDREN: "The jewels in our crown are our children's programs," says Frances Tyler, proprietor of The Tyler Place. The programs operate from 8:30 A.M. to 1:30 P.M. and from 5:30 P.M. until at least 8:30 P.M. Children as young as 2 can participate. There are separate programs for six age groups: "Junior Midgets" (2- and 3-year-olds), "Senior Midgets" (4- and 5-year-olds); "Juniors" (6- and 7-year-olds); "Pre-Teens" (8- to 10-year-olds); "Junior Teens" (11- to 13-year-olds); and "Senior Teens" (14- to 17-year-olds).

Each group participates in sports, lake activities, swimming, talent shows, hayrides, and other activities, all geared to their age level.

All groups are well-supervised by college students who are enthusiastic and creative.

Afternoons are reserved for family activities.

The Tyler Place is one of the few resorts that will make arrangements for child care for children as young as one month. Local high school girls, most known personally by the Tyler management, are available as parent helpers, either on a live-in or live-out basis or for occasional baby-sitting. In the spring and summer, infant care is available at the Infant Center.

NICETIES: The Tyler Place publishes a list of its guests each week, the names of their children, and their home addresses. Not surprisingly, many children who have become summer friends become winter pen pals.

At the end of the week each camper gets a picture of his or her group. A professional photographer is available for family photos.

Guests post notices seeking partners for bridge, tennis, or other sports.

OF INTEREST NEARBY: Highgate Springs is equidistant from three interesting tourist areas: Montreal, Stowe, and the Shelburne Museum.

The Tyler Place posts events of interest in Montreal. Most guests who have made a trip there feel that it is a city better appreciated by adults than by children.

However, the Shelburne Museum is a perfect family jaunt. Shelburne has been called "a collection of collections." Most of its buildings have been brought from other places and reconstructed at Shelburne. Children love the *Ticonderoga*, a luxury side-wheeler that used to cruise Lake Champlain. Not to be missed are the antique doll collection and the hand-carved miniature circus parade, so long that it is displayed in its own semicircular building.

Stowe is well known as the home of the von Trapp family, of *Sound of Music* fame. It is also a tourist area in the summer, with many quaint craft shops.

FOR MORE INFORMATION: Write The Tyler Place, Highgate Springs, VT 05460, or call (802) 868-3301.

SOUTHEAST

Amelia Island Plantation
Amelia Island, Florida

In the midst of the environmental devastation that developers have wrought through much of Florida, a few resorts stand out as models of what thoughtful, ecology-minded development can be. Amelia Island Plantation, a 1,250-acre complex on Florida's northernmost barrier island, 29 miles northeast of downtown Jacksonville, is a jewel of a resort that has been cited in numerous competitions for its environmentally-sound master plan. The resort opened in 1974 and has been expanded substantially since then. The developers have successfully integrated a full-service, four-star resort into a beautiful piece of property that once seemed fated for strip-mining.

Where else can you wander on a marked trail around the perimeter of a 900-year-old Indian burial mound in between playing a round of golf and swimming in the Atlantic Ocean? Where else can your child climb a ladder into a treetop hideaway and pretend he's Robinson Crusoe? At how many other resorts can you go out for a morning walk and encounter members of Greenpeace trying frantically to save a beached loggerhead turtle just below the main swimming pool?

Amelia Island's villa-type accommodations are scattered throughout a spacious property covered with moss-draped live oak, palmetto, magnolia, and palm trees and bordered by a wide, four-mile-long beach; 230 species of birds have been sighted there.

ACCOMMODATIONS: $$ to $$$ Amelia Island has daily, weekly, monthly, and long-term rentals available in both hotel rooms and 600 one- to four-bedroom villas with complete kitchen facilities. The villa units are all individually owned and decorated to the owner's taste. Prices rise with newness and proximity to the ocean. Each cluster of villas has a slightly different character. High season runs from mid-March to the end of April. Rates are much lower in the winter and during some parts of the summer.

DINING: The kitchens in the villas are fully equipped; groceries can be purchased at the large supermarkets in Fernandina Beach. A convenience store on the property sells a limited selection of canned, frozen, and fresh foods, liquor, and baby supplies.

Amelia Island's six restaurants vary greatly in atmosphere, price, and type of food. The Dune Side Club, just off the hotel lobby, has a spectacular ocean view and serves continental cuisine. The Verandah, located at Racquet Park, serves fresh, locally caught seafood for dinner and makes families feel welcome. The Beach Club, near the main swimming pool, serves casual lunches and dinners, with live entertainment and dancing nightly in the summer.

The Coop, in the cluster of shops near the main entrance, is perfect for children, serving cooked-to-order fast-food at breakfast and lunch.

There also are snack bars at the Beach Club swimming pool and some other pools.

ACTIVITIES

Two Deco-Turf II, 19 Fast-Dry and four Omni-Turf courts, three lighted; professional instruction; pro shop.

Twenty-seven holes designed by Pete Dye and 18 holes designed by Tom Fazio. The golf courses are among the most picturesque anywhere, with sweeping views of the Atlantic Ocean on the Oceanside Nine. The Oakmarsh and Oysterbay nines feature 6,372 yards of twisting fairways, marsh views, and greenery.

Twenty-four pools and the Atlantic Ocean (the best pool for families is at the Beach Club, which has a wading pool for toddlers, and an adjoining wooden playground).

Asphalt and wooden bike trails; rentals available, including childseat-equipped adult bikes and junior-size bikes.

Wooden trails wind through miles of "sunken forest," the valley between the primary and secondary dune lines. Descriptive signs identify flora. Boardwalks on the edge of the marshlands at Drummond Park provide a perfect vantage point for bird watching or taking in the sunset.

 At nearby Seahorse Stables.

At the health and fitness center at Racquet Park (sauna, whirlpool, Nautilus, Universal equipment, racquetball courts, indoor/outdoor lap pool, organized classes). The Baker International Wellness Clinic has a sports medicine program.

Freshwater and saltwater, charters available through Amelia Angler at the Beach Club.

The recreation staff publishes a monthly calendar of events designed to provide something to please everyone every day. On a typical Saturday in June, for instance, the schedule includes high-energy exercise, beginners' racquetball, a golf clinic, beach volleyball, poolside bingo, ocean seining, and a mixed doubles tennis round robin.

In the evening adults may enjoy dancing at the Beach Club; live music and cocktails in the Admiral's Lounge, and family movies two or three times a week. Dances and barbecues are sometimes scheduled at Walker's Landing, a lovely spot on the marsh.

FOR CHILDREN: Amelia Island has a delight for children around virtually every corner. It has the best collection of playgrounds of any resort we've seen, from the climbing structures right outside the reception center (perfect for stretching travel-weary legs), to the elaborate wooden structures overlooking the ocean next to the Beach Club pool, to the replica of a tall-masted schooner on Aury Island, to the Robinson Crusoe–type treetop structure at Drummond Park.

Aury Island has a special fishing pier just for kids; the recreation staff can provide tackle and bait. Kids also will enjoy fishing from the walkway behind the Coop.

The organized children's program is called "The Most Fun Under the Sun," and an energetic staff of counselors works hard to make it attractive to children. The program runs during Thanksgiving week, the five or six weeks surrounding the Easter holidays, and from Memorial Day to just after Labor Day.

Preschoolers between 3 and 5 can join the program from 8:30 A.M. to 1 P.M. Monday through Saturday for a fee. Lunch, usually with known child-pleasers like peanut butter and jelly or hot dogs, costs extra. Activities include safety tips, exercises, fishing, shell collecting and crafts, feeding goldfish, and pool games.

Children from 6 to 8 can take part in half-day or full-day programs (they're cheaper if paid for by the week). A typical day includes beach soccer, a swim in the ocean, fishing at the Coop, beach games, a walk through the dunes and discussion of the dune's ecosystem, a kickball game, arts and crafts, relay races in the pool, and a scavenger hunt. Lunch is optional.

Children between 9 and 12 have their own half- and full-day programs (again, there's a modest fee). They take field trips to nearby factories, the Jacksonville Zoo, the Jacksonville Airport, a Waterslide, nearby state parks, and local restaurants. Nature education is emphasized.

The program is run by the plantation's full-time youth program director and is staffed by between 12 and 14 senior college students working toward degrees in recreation. A lengthy list of local babysitters also is available at the front desk; it gives their ages and what hours they are usually available.

NICETIES: Ten complimentary trams ply the roads within the complex so that you can forget about driving while you're there.

A 900-year-old 60-foot-high burial mound for the Timucuan Indians has been excavated and carefully restored at Walker's Landing. It is one of Florida's finest and largest Indian burial mounds. Descriptive markers explain the life-style of the Timucuans.

OF INTEREST NEARBY: Fernandina Beach, a 15-minute drive from the resort, is a charming town. A 30-block downtown area dotted with Victorian homes has been listed in the National Register of Historic Places. It is perfect for long, leisurely walks followed by lunch in one of numerous good restaurants. It's fun for the kids to watch the shrimp boats come in with their catch in the early morning. Fernandina Beach was once the busiest shrimping port in the nation.

The Fort Clinch State Park at the northern tip of Amelia Island has a pre–Civil War fort that kids love to explore. Costumed interpreters help bring the past alive.

FOR MORE INFORMATION: Write Amelia Island Plantation, Highway A1A South, Amelia Island, FL 32034, or call (800) 874-6878.

The Colony Beach and Tennis Resort
Longboat Key, Florida

After a fast game of tennis, what could be better than watching the sun set over the Gulf of Mexico, taking a relaxing walk along a white, sandy beach, or unwinding with a massage and whirlpool? Those are among the options at The Colony on Longboat Key, a resort on a small island off the western coast of Florida. Longboat Key has the feel of an out-of-the-way place, offering privacy, charm, and lush greenness. But it's only a 10-minute drive to Sarasota and its shopping, attractions, and nightlife.

Several luxury resorts have been developed on Longboat Key since World War II, with The Colony being the first, but the key's environment has been treated with respect. Strict state laws protect the flora and fauna, and local ordinances control growth and development. There are no billboards and little commercialism. Even the key's shopping center is almost hidden among the trees. The Colony's low-rise buildings blend unobtrusively into the 18 acres of sand and carefully manicured grounds. There are ponds, fountains, palm trees, and flowers everywhere.

Originally a small, beach-bungalow type of place, The Colony was bought in 1969 by Dr. M. J. "Murf" Klauber, an orthodontist from Buffalo, N.Y., who had become hooked on Longboat Key during a visit and decided he wanted to make it his home. In 1973, all but 12 of the original 114 bungalows were razed and replaced with 18 two-story frame buildings. In 1974, a six-story clubhouse was added. Since 1983, more than $5 million has been spent to upgrade and redecorate facilities. "We took the resort from shack-elegant to beach luxury," said the owner.

ACCOMMODATIONS: $$$$ The Colony offers 235 spacious one- and two-bedroom suites, all with kitchen facilities and balconies. All suites have a large master bedroom with a king or two double beds, a marble bath with a separate dressing area, a family-sized living room with color television and comfortable rattan furniture covered in bright tropical prints, a dining area, and a modern kitchenette. A closet in the living room has twin Murphy beds.

The two-bedroom suites have a second-floor loft bedroom with twin beds and a second bath. All of the suites are only a short walk from the beach and the tennis courts.

DINING: The resort offers a variety of restaurants, ranging from simple to sophisticated. The award-winning Colony Restaurant is the most elegant. It offers breakfast, lunch, and dinner in an airy room with a spectacular view of the pool and beach. The restaurant has a delightful children's menu with poems describing the entrées, beverages, and desserts.

Bamboo's, on a patio overlooking the beach, offers lunch in a casual setting. Windows is a casual restaurant that serves dinner only.

Kids will love Jimmy Murfy's, a thatched-roof beachside snack shop offering such lunchtime favorites as hamburgers, hot dogs, French fries, and milk shakes.

For a quick snack or the ingredients for whipping up a light meal in your suite, there's Tastebuds, a mini-grocery and gourmet deli.

ACTIVITIES

Twenty-one courts, (two lighted for night play); no court fees. Teaching pros promise to find a tennis partner custom-matched to your game, whether you're an adult or a child. If an appropriate partner is not available, a pro will play with you at no charge (that's almost like getting a private lesson free). Clinics and private lessons are also offered, as well as tennis camps from May through December.

 Privileges at nearby Meadows Country Club and Prestancia.

 Large pool smack in the middle of the beach, which provides a lovely setting.

 Laser class racing sailboats are available for the use of guests, as well as windsurfers. There are also a few scaled-down windsurfers for young children, and a simulator on shore for practice.

 Deep-sea fishing charters can be arranged.

 Men's and women's health clubs offer steam rooms, saunas, whirlpools, and five kinds of massages by appointment. In addition, an aerobics and fitness center offers aerobics classes and the use of exercise equipment.

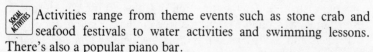 Rentals available.

Activities range from theme events such as stone crab and seafood festivals to water activities and swimming lessons. There's also a popular piano bar.

FOR CHILDREN: Children aged 4 to 12 can participate in the Colony's year-round complimentary children's program, "Kidding Around." Recreational activities are offered daily from 9 A.M. to noon and again from 1 P.M. to 4 P.M. (children must be picked up for lunch). They include swimming, building sand castles, treasure hunts, nature hikes, shell collecting, shell crafts, fishing, movies, and games. Activities are centered in the thatched-roof "tiki hut" near the pool, with playground equipment nearby. In bad weather, activities shift to the Kidding Around Room, which has a big-screen television set, games, puzzles, and arts and crafts supplies.

The children's program is directed by full-time employees with degrees in recreation and related fields assisted by college interns.

Children aged 7 to 14 who are budding tennis players can enroll in tennis clinics.

During holiday periods and in the summer, complimentary movies for children and teens are shown several evenings a week. And a conference room is turned into a video game room that is open from 7 to 11 P.M. nightly. The Colony will gladly make arrangements for baby-sitters, usually employees of the resort.

NICETIES: Suites feature a "mini-spa" bath with steam shower and whirlpool. The suites' many amenities include reading lights above the beds, lighted magnifying mirrors, and wall-mounted hair dryers in the dressing area.

OF INTEREST NEARBY: The Ringling complex in Sarasota, about a 15-minute drive from Longboat Key, is the rich legacy of John Ringling, founder of the Ringling Brothers Circus. The complex includes the John and Mable Ringling Museum of Art and the bayfront Ringling residence, which was built in 1925 at a cost of $1.5 million. The Florida State Theater, The Asolo, is right next door.

Children will love seeing a training session of the Lipizzan stallions of Austria, under the direction of Colonel Ottomar Hermann. From January through March, the free outdoor sessions are offered on Fridays and Saturdays at the Lipizzans' winter home in Myakka City, about a 30-mile drive from Longboat Key.

Sarasota is the spring-training home of the Chicago White Sox; games are played nearly every other day in March in Payne Park. Also training within easy driving distance of Sarasota are the Philadelphia Phillies, in Clearwater; the St. Louis Cardinals, in St. Petersburg; the Toronto Blue Jays, in Dunedin; the Cincinnati Reds, in Tampa; the Pittsburgh Pirates, in Bradenton; and the Texas Rangers, in Port Charlotte.

The Marie Selby Botanical Gardens are on a lush 16-acre peninsula along Sarasota Bay, just minutes from the resort.

FOR MORE INFORMATION: Write The Colony Beach and Tennis Resort, 1620 Gulf of Mexico Drive, Longboat Key, FL 34228, or call (813) 383-6464 or (800) 237-9443.

Cheeca Lodge
Islamorada, Florida

You don't have to go all the way to the Caribbean to find azure seas, live coral reefs, lush tropical flora, rare birds, freshly caught seafood, and balmy breezes. The Florida Keys can provide all that, as well as a family-oriented resort that rivals any in the United States for attention to detail.

Cheeca Lodge, on a spit of land between the Atlantic Ocean and the Gulf of Mexico, is a compact, self-contained vacation destination that offers boundless opportunities for activity in an atmosphere that is also irresistably conducive to relaxation.

Although it has facilities that are unparalleled in the Keys, Cheeca Lodge's strongest card is its commitment to preserving the area's rare beauty and special charms. In 1990, the resort won the Gold Key Environmental Achievement Award from the American Hotel & Motel Association for its unique environmental education programs for guests.

ACCOMMODATIONS: $$** to **$$$$ Cheeca Lodge's 203 accommodations include beautifully furnished ocean-view and gulf-view rooms in the main lodge and 64 one- and two-bedroom villas, each equipped with a living room and kitchen, in about two dozen low-rise buildings scattered around the property. All units are air-conditioned, with ceiling fans, and most include private screened-in balconies and mini-bars. Special packages are available. There's no charge for children under 17 who share their parents' rooms (limit two children per room.)

DINING: Breakfast, lunch and dinner are served in the Ocean Terrace Grill, a casual open-air dining room and terrace next to the main pool. The Raw Bar overlooking the Atlantic Ocean serves a variety of fresh Keys seafood for lunch, along with hot dogs and hamburgers. Dinner is special at the Atlantic's Edge Dining Room, a lovely semi-circular room with sweeping views of the ocean. The chef specializes in freshly caught local seafood and the Sunday brunch is the culinary highlight of the week. Children's menus are available, although children who wish to order off the regular menu receive a 50 percent discount.

There are also many restaurants located within a few miles of the lodge.

ACTIVITIES:

 Six lighted, Laykold courts; instruction available. Court fees.

 On a par-three, nine-hole executive course.

 Three pools; two freshwater and one saltwater. Swimming in the Gulf of Mexico from the lodge's 1,100-foot stretch of beach.

 Rental windsurfers, Hobie cats, glass-bottom paddle boats, and rafts. Arrangements can be made for parasailing.

 Half-day and full-day excursions for tarpon, grouper, wahoo, mackerel, barracuda, and sailfish as well as guided expeditions on the shallow flats of Florida Bay for bonefish, snapper, and redfish. Rental equipment available at the Beach Hut for fishing from the 525-foot lighted pier.

 Cheeca Divers offers day and night skin- and scuba-diving trips; instruction and equipment rental available.

 Five hot tubs, resident masseur.

 Nightly entertainment in the Light Tackle Lounge.

FOR CHILDREN: "Camp Cheeca" is Cheeca Lodge's award-winning program for children from ages 6 to 12. The program's goal is for children to have fun while learning about the fragile ecology of the Florida Keys.

Camp Cheeca operates every Friday, Saturday, and Sunday through the year and nearly every day between Memorial Day and Labor Day. Full-day and half-day rates are available. The morning session runs from 9 A.M. to noon and the afternoon session from 1 P.M. to 4 P.M., with a supervised lunch at the Tree House for an extra charge.

On a typical day, participants play getting acquainted games, followed by hands-on instruction in marine life identification. Then they'll take a walk along the resort's own nature trail or along the beach, trying out their newfound powers of plant and animal identification, before heading to the lap pool for some water games.

After lunch, there's likely to be more learning about sea creatures during a "Fashion a Fish" session in which the children create their own fish and discuss its attributes. That's often followed by the resort's most popular activity for children: catch-and-release fishing from the pier with a hand line. Snorkeling along the pier's underwater nature trail in the shallow water just off the beach is also popular. Kids will see a 16th-century cannon, an underwater archaeological mapping station, and a prime example of a turtle grass ecosystem.

Periodic field trips are scheduled to John Pennekamp Coral Reef State Park, the Dolphin Research Center, and the Theater of the Sea. The tennis pro offers individual and group lessons for children.

NICETIES: There's always a pile of sand toys available under one of the thatched-roof huts on the beach.

Each unit also includes a VCR (be sure to bring your kids' favorite tapes!) and a hair dryer.

OF INTEREST NEARBY: Theater of the Sea, on Windley Key, just north of Islamorada, offers glass-bottom boat rides and a performing dolphin show.

John Pennekamp Coral Reef State Park, the only underwater state park in the continental United States, is just 20 minutes away. Snorkeling, diving, and sightseeing trips are offered to the reef.

The state of Florida offers boat rides and guided walking tours to Lignum Vitae and Indian Keys. Lignum Vitae, on Islamorada's gulf side, is home to many rare trees that are over 10,000 years old, as well as other rich plant life. Indian Key, on the Atlantic side, was Dade County's first county seat and is a state historic site.

Key West, a colorful community of artists, writers, shopkeepers, treasure-hunters, and great chefs, is just 82 miles south.

FOR MORE INFORMATION: Write Cheeca Lodge, P.O. Box 527, Islamorada, FL 33036 or call (800) 327-2888.

Sonesta Beach Hotel and Tennis Club
Key Biscayne, Florida

It is just after dawn as you take a cup of coffee out to your balcony overlooking the Atlantic Ocean. A luxury cruise ship is silhouetted against the sun, a red orb inching up over the Atlantic. In a few minutes, pool attendants begin rearranging the deck chairs, and a tractor is driven out to rake the sand. A lone father and son make their way to the beachside playground, while an early-morning sailor pushes a catamaran out to the turquoise sea. In the foreground, palm trees sway gracefully in the breeze, and sea gulls and pelicans begin their day-long search for sustenance.

A new day has begun at the Sonesta Beach Hotel and Tennis Club.

This luxury hotel stands like a Mayan temple on a beautiful 500-foot stretch of beach on Key Biscayne, a palm-fringed island with a semi-tropical air just a short ride from downtown Miami. The island is just close enough to Miami to put all of its vices and virtues within easy reach, and just far enough away so that none of the hubbub intrudes. The hotel, opened in 1969, was the third constructed on the island, which is mainly residential, with large pockets of land reserved for public use.

The Sonesta Beach has an international air about it because it is a popular vacation destination for Europeans and South Americans. It also has the feel of a small hotel, despite its nearly 300 rooms and extensive group meeting facilities.

ACCOMMODATIONS: $** to **$$$$ The 293 guest rooms in the hotel are tastefully furnished and decorated in light, airy colors. Half have balconies overlooking the ocean (the ocean view is worth the extra cost); the other half have balconies overlooking the island and, off in the distance, the bay. The rooms come with either a king-size bed or two double beds and stocked mini-bars.

The 13 nearby Sonesta Villas, with two to five bedrooms, have private swimming pools, living and dining rooms, and full kitchens. All hotel services are available to villa guests except room service. The villas are rented for a minimum of five nights.

Package plans at a lower cost than the published rates are frequently available. Rates plummet in the summer.

DINING: The Two Dragons Restaurant features Chinese (Cantonese, Mandarin, or Szechuan) and Japanese food at dinner only. The Rib Room is famous for its expansive brunch; it also serves breakfast, lunch, and dinner. The Greenhouse Café serves inexpensive breakfasts, lunches, and dinners, and will pack its items for eating on the beach or in your room.

The Snackerrie, built to blend in with the sea grape trees on the beach, serves interesting snacks. Since the playground is a stone's throw away, you can enjoy a quick snack while your children cavort in the sand. Drinks are served at the Seabreeze pool bar, Seagrape Beach bar, Desires, and the Bar of the Two Dragons.

There are numerous restaurants elsewhere on Key Biscayne. Dick Clarke's American Bandstand Grill is a fun place in Miami's Bayside complex.

ACTIVITIES

 Ten Laykold tennis courts; pro shop, rental equipment, lessons.

 Privileges at the 18-hole Key Biscayne Golf Course, three minutes away.

 Atlantic Ocean and beachfront swimming pool. Snorkeling and scuba-diving trips can be arranged.

 Catamarans, kayaks, aquabikes, and wind-surfer rentals at the beach.

Deep-sea fishing charters at nearby Key Biscayne Marina or the Miami Marina.

 Rentals available, including bikes with child seats, children's bicycles, and quadricycles.

 Fitness center on the hotel's lower level, with whirlpool, sauna, steam room, exercise room, and massage room. Exercise classes are held daily.

 Jewelry-making workshops, limbo contests, card and board games, volleyball, tug-of-war on the beach, and organized excursions to nearby shopping centers, museums, and attractions.

FOR CHILDREN: The complimentary "Just Us Kids" children's program runs year-round. The program entertains children between 5 and 13 from 10 A.M. until 10 P.M., with a break between 5 and 6 P.M. Children can participate for any amount of time you choose. Each morning, the program features sightseeing expeditions to such popular attractions as Metrozoo, the Seaquarium, and the Museum of Science. The children return to the hotel for lunch together, usually at the Snackerrie on the beach, and then begin an afternoon of beach and pool activities and games. Many of the afternoon activities take place at the wooden playground on the beach; you can easily see what's going on from your chaise longue at the pool.

At 6:30 P.M., the children are taken to dinner at one of the hotel's restaurants, where they can choose from special children's menus. The evenings feature movies, outings to the Treasure Island Amusement Park, ice-skating, crafts classes, or games in the game room.

The headquarters for the program is the video game room children on the hotel's lower level. The counselors keep a closet full of kids' games and crafts materials to pull out on rainy days.

The children's program's counselors are college students, and in the periods when the program is most utilized, there may be 15 on the staff. Many are bilingual. Baby-sitting for younger children can be arranged through the hotel's housekeeping service.

NICETIES: Participants in the Just Us Kids program receive T-shirts and hats.

Newspapers are delivered to your door every morning.
The hotel's literature is printed in both English and Spanish.

OF INTEREST NEARBY: The Bill Baggs Cape Florida State Recreation Area occupies over 900 acres on the southern tip of Key Biscayne, an easy bike ride from the hotel. It has a historic lighthouse and museum and a reconstructed keeper's home and office, as well as lovely picnic facilities and beaches.

Key Biscayne is only 10 miles southeast of Miami, so all of the city attractions are just a short drive away.

Miami Seaquarium, on the causeway linking Key Biscayne to the mainland, is a 60-acre park with marine life displayed in four show areas (including Flipper, America's most beloved dolphin, and an orca whale.) It also has aquarium exhibits and a refuge for shore birds.

Parrot Jungle and Gardens is a marvelous private park with hundreds of beautiful birds on display. You can feed them and converse with them and watch several shows.

The Venetian Pool in nearby Coral Gables is a wonderful free-form swimming pool fed by underground artesian wells. There are small grottoes to swim into and waterfalls to swim under.

Biscayne National Park, about an hour's drive from Key Biscayne, provides unparalleled snorkeling and diving opportunities on a pristine reef. Call (305) 247-2400 for information about glass-bottom boat trips, canoe rentals, and snorkeling expeditions.

FOR MORE INFORMATION: Write the Sonesta Beach Hotel and Tennis Club, 350 Ocean Drive, Key Biscayne, FL 33149, or call (305) 361-2021 or the Sonesta Hotel's central reservation service at (800) 343-7170.

South Seas Plantation
Captiva Island, Florida

Legend has it that the island of Captiva was used in the 1800s to sequester the female captives of pillaging pirates. Today, it is the site of one of the most comfortable, yet unimposing, seaside resorts in North America, South Seas Plantation.

Sprawling across the entire northern half of a barrier reef island off the western coast of Florida near Fort Myers, South Seas Plantation has two and a half miles of the best shelling beach in North America, a wildlife refuge that harbors thousands of migratory birds, and some of the most beautiful flora this side of Tahiti. Interspersed among the mangrove swamps and coconut palm groves are all the recreational facilities and amenities you'd expect at a full-service resort.

The atmosphere at South Seas is quiet and low key. You can spend all your time lying on a virtually deserted beach or take part in one of the most ambitious social programs in southern Florida. You can grab a bite to eat at Cap'n Al's Pub or dress up for the resort's elegant continental restaurant, the King's Crown.

Captiva and its sister island Sanibel are among the most attractive resort areas in Florida. Development has been guided by a concern for the ecology of the area and its natural beauty.

ACCOMMODATIONS: $$ to $$$$ South Seas offers a wide range of accommodations, from hotel rooms to four-bedroom beach houses. Most of the 600 guest quarters have full kitchens. The accommodations are all tastefully furnished; cable television (with HBO) are provided. All have screened-in porches or balconies with lovely views.

The accommodations are clustered in small villages, each with its own character and ambience. Like to watch the comings and goings of 100-foot yachts? Then stay at the Marina Villas, overlooking the resort's small but busy yacht harbor. Is tennis your top priority? Then the Tennis Villas, right next to the courts, may be for you. Do you like hearing the roar of the surf all night long? Then rent a beach house or cottage.

DINING: The resort offers a range of eating options, from casual to elegant, as well as two small grocery stores that stock everything you'll need to cook in your own kitchen.

The most informal restaurant—and the most fun for kids—is

Cap'n Al's at the marina. It serves traditional breakfasts (you can sit outside and watch the early-rising yacht crews swab their decks) and reasonably-priced lunches. At night, Cap'n Al's features all-you-can-eat barbecues and buffets.

Chadwick's, near the resort's entrance gates, specializes in local seafood and serves breakfast, lunch, and dinner.

The lovely King's Crown Restaurant, in a converted key lime warehouse on the island's northern tip, is the resort's formal restaurant. Children are best left with a sitter.

If you venture off premises for a meal, have it at the Bubble Room, just a short drive down Sanibel-Captiva Road. This special restaurant will appeal to the child in every adult, and every child will adore it. It is decorated with antique toys and 1940s memorabilia; an electric train whizzes along a track mounted over the bar and meanders on through one of the dining rooms.

Another fun place to eat is the Mucky Duck on the Captiva Beach, which features pub food. Parents can dine at picnic tables while their children play in the sand.

ACTIVITIES

 Twenty-two Laykold courts, many lighted; pro shop, rental equipment, instruction, game-arranging service.

 Nine holes bordered on three sides by the Gulf of Mexico, 2,946 yards, par 36; pro shop, rental equipment, instruction.

 Gulf of Mexico and 18 freshwater swimming pools; half a dozen hot tubs.

 Rental sailboats and powerboats available on site. Steve and Doris Colgate's Offshore Sailing School is based here, offering instruction for both beginners and accomplished sailors. *Sports Illustrated* has called it the best sailing instruction program in existence.

 Pier fishing; charters available at the marina for tarpon, grouper, snook, and redfish fishing.

 Rentals available, including bikes with child seats. Bike path runs the length of Captiva and Sanibel.

Guided nature hikes and seining expeditions for the whole family.

 Volleyball, shuffleboard, croquet, Ping-Pong equipment and a full-service fitness center are available.

Well-rounded social program. Many of the scheduled activities are suitable for the whole family (water volleyball, beach walks, ice-cream socials, shell craft instruction, canoe outings).

The bar in Chadwick's features live entertainment and dancing on weekends.

FOR CHILDREN: South Seas' children's programs will keep your children happy with a variety of activities for a fee. "Pelican Pals" welcomes children aged 3 to 5 from 9:30 A.M. to noon on weekdays. "Captiva Kids," for children aged 6 to 8, operates from 9:30 A.M. to 2:00 P.M. The "Castaway Club" is for children 9 to 12. "Tropical Adventure," a separate program for teenagers, provides activities mainly in the late afternoon and evening. All run in the summer and during specially designated winter months; during other periods, there are occasional activities for all ages.

The children's programs are staffed by full-time employees, all with college degrees in recreation. They are supplemented by interns, each in his or her last semester of college. Staff members will gladly baby-sit during their free time.

Pelican Pals stresses age-appropriate activities such as puppet making, ball games, shell collecting, lunch preparation, and playground activities. Children in the Captiva Kids program take part in ball relays, lawn games, sand sculpting, seining, and Frisbee play, with a lot of time in the pool and on the beach. The Castaway Club goes canoeing and swimming and makes crafts. Tropical Adventure features Ping-Pong tournaments, poolside pizza parties, movies, pretend casino, snorkeling lessons, and non-alcoholic happy hours. The recreation staff also schedules special events for moms and tots and families.

Pirate's Cove, a video game room, is open from 9 A.M. to 4 P.M. Children can borrow games, books, and sports equipment from the activities office. An attractive playground outside Pirate's Cove also provides hours of fun.

NICETIES: Propane-powered trolleys travel the resort's roads continuously, discharging and picking up guests along the way.

OF INTEREST NEARBY: One of the main reasons to spend your vacation on Captiva is the proximity of the J. N. "Ding" Darling National Wildlife Refuge. Hundreds of species of birds winter here. Serious bird-watchers set up their tripods along the dirt road through the refuge, hoping for a glimpse of the nesting osprey or the elusive roseate spoonbills. Your children will delight in the almost sure sighting of one of the resident alligators. A small museum at the entrance to the refuge explains the significant role the refuge plays in the island's ecology.

One of the most pleasant outings on the island is a canoe ride along the Commodore Creek Canoe Trail through the refuge. Canoes can be rented for a modest charge at the Tarpon Bay Marina. The water is shallow, so children 4 and over could accompany you safely. But for a truly tranquil morning, leave the children behind. It may be the high point of your entire vacation.

Excursion boat rides to Cabbage or Useppa cays make nice outings. The biggest thrill comes from seeing dolphins play in the boat's wake.

FOR MORE INFORMATION: Write South Seas Plantation, P.O. Box 194, Captiva Island, FL 33924, or call (800) 237-3102; in Florida, (800) 282-3402.

Callaway Gardens
Pine Mountain, Georgia

The gambit around the swimming pool here is not "Where are you from?" but, rather, "How many years have you been coming here?" It is a rare guest who is here for the first time, and a rare first-timer who ends a week's stay not intending to come back.

What contributes to guests' intense loyalty is a gorgeous physical property, an exhausting schedule of planned activities, an indefatigably friendly and helpful staff, an atmosphere of southern hospitality, and one of the best children's programs anywhere. Callaway Gardens pioneered the concept of a children's program in the 1950s and has been fine-tuning it ever since.

Callaway Gardens is located on an idyllic site in the foothills of the Appalachians about 70 miles south of Atlanta. It is among the very few American resorts operated by a not-for-profit foundation, in this case the Ida Cason Callaway Foundation, whose stated purpose is "to provide a garden of natural beauty where people may find relaxation, inspiration and a better understanding of the living world." The foundation's intent was to preserve in its natural setting the native plant life of the southeastern region and to restore the land to its previous beauty and diversity.

The resort's facilities (rated four-star by Mobil) are dispersed throughout a 2,500-acre botanical garden that draws tens of thousands of day-trippers from around the country each year. The gardens include miles of azalea trails featuring over 700 varieties; holly trails with over 450 varieties; a model vegetable garden that serves as the backdrop for a nationally televised garden advice show, and numerous other trails through hills and vales. A state-of-the-art greenhouse and garden complex, the John A. Sibley Horticultural Center, features spectacular flower displays and functions as an educational center as well. A restored pioneer log cabin set in a woods is interesting to visit, as is the Ida Cason Callaway Memorial Chapel, a charming stone retreat used for meditation, weddings, and regular organ concerts.

Many recreational activities center on Robin Lake, which is said to have the longest inland man-made beach in the country. Waterskiers crisscross each others' wakes off in the distance, while children frolic in the guarded, roped-off areas close to shore. The *Robin E. Lee Riverboat* toots as it passes by with another load of sightseers. A miniature golf course and volleyball, badminton, tennis, and shuffleboard courts provide more diversion, while a playground provides an outlet for toddlers' climbing instincts. And for those who just want to relax, there are comfortable cane-backed rockers to sit in and observe the passing sideshow.

Just a stone's throw from all this is the Big Top, where the Flying High Circus from Florida State University performs all summer long. Once or twice a day, the 50-member circus puts on a performance of near-professional quality, complete with high-wire acts, trapeze artists, jugglers, and clowns (but no animals). In between shows, the performers serve as counselors in the children's program.

ACCOMMODATIONS: $$ to $$$ Callaway Gardens has a range of accommodations, from 350 rooms at the Callaway Gardens Inn to 49 Mountain Creek Villas, to 155 two-bedroom cottages. From June through August, cottages are rented for one or two-week periods only to families with children as part of the Summer Recreation Program.

The cedar cottages, scattered throughout a fragrant pine forest, have all been built since 1985. Each has a fully equipped kitchen with dishwasher, beautifully furnished dining and living room with fireplace, two bedrooms with two double beds each, two baths, screened porch with barbecue grill, and a deck.

DINING: Families in the summer recreation program eat most of their meals in their cottages; groceries are available in the nearby town of Pine Mountain. A snack bar called the Flower Mill is located in the cottage area and offers breakfast, lunch, and dinner at moderate prices; teenagers like to gather here at night. Hearty meals with a country flavor are available at the Country Store, a restaurant and specialty shop about two miles from the cottages.

In the inn, the Plantation Room offers extravagant breakfast, luncheon, and dinner buffets, and the fancier Georgia Room offers continental cuisine. To our minds, the loveliest restaurant on the property is the Veranda, a continental-style restaurant that overlooks the serene Mountain Creek Lake. On the floor above the Veranda is The Gardens, a less formal restaurant with two nightly sittings and entertainment. Children are happily accommodated at all the restaurants.

ACTIVITIES

 Nineteen lighted tennis courts (eight Har-Tru and 11 Plexi-Pave); two racquetball courts; instruction available. Pro shop.

Three 18-hole courses and a nine-hole executive course; instruction, two pro shops.

A beautiful pool and hot-tub complex, with a limited snack bar, located in the cottage area; smaller pool at the Inn; guarded swimming area in Robin Lake.

 Rental paddle boats, fishing boats, and sailboats on 175-acre Mountain Creek Lake. Water-skiing instruction on Robin Lake (free ski time is available almost daily, as are sailboat rentals, for participants in the Family Recreation Program). Canoe trips can be arranged on the Flint River, 35 miles east of Callaway Gardens, with an accompanying naturalist; children must be 12 years or older.

 Bass and bream fishing in Mountain Creek Lake (fee, license required).

Adult bicycles (with child seats) and children's bicycles can be rented by the hour, day, or week.

Narrated walks through the vegetable garden; early-morning bird-watching expeditions; strolls through the herb garden; hikes on mountain trails and through the nearby Cason J. Callaway Memorial Forest.

 At nearby stables.

Year-round skeet and trap shooting; dove, deer, and quail hunting can be arranged in season (license required, available in town).

The range of group activities here will leave you breathless. Many are free to persons staying in the family cottages; for others there are small fees. A typical day offers the option of participating in a bus tour of the gardens, attending an organ concert in the chapel, touring the Sibley Center, watching the circus, watching the once-or-twice-daily water-ski performance, or going to a movie. That's not all. You can run in an early-morning 5,000-meter fun run, take part in an arts-and-crafts session, go on a guided walk through Mr. Cason's vegetable garden, attend golf or tennis clinics, learn to juggle or to walk a tightrope, or go roller-skating.

In the evening guests can enjoy entertainment in the Vineyard Green Lounge, twice-weekly family cookouts, performances by the LaGrange College Summer Theater four nights a week, and family movies three nights a week.

FOR CHILDREN: Callaway Gardens is proud of its summer children's program (entirely free to cottage guests), and with good reason. For 1- and 2-year-olds, care by mature staff members is available from 9 A.M. to 3 P.M. Mondays through Fridays: the Toddler Center maintains a ratio of 4 children to 1 adult. Organized activities are available from 9 A.M. to 3 P.M. for children between 3 and 6 at the Early Childhood Center near Robin Lake. Children are separated by age for a morning of art, free play, storytelling, and circus activities. Lunch is served (there's a small charge), and afterwards the children are taken to swim in a shallow, roped-off area of the lake. The counselors are generally elementary school teachers or college seniors.

Children between 7 and 12 can attend a day camp under the Big Top. They are divided into three age groups, and activities include games, swimming, arts and crafts, sports, water-skiing, tennis, bike hikes, and acting workshops. Their program also runs from 9 A.M. to 3 P.M. and includes lunch (extra charge).

Teenagers between 13 and 16 have a program that begins at 9 A.M. and ends at 4 P.M. and includes lunch (extra charge). They take part in some of the nature programs, as well as water-skiing, beach activities, golf instruction, arts and crafts, tennis, and sailing (only for teenagers 15 and over).

Teenagers 16 and over (the hardest group to please) have the use of a game room near the Flower Mill. The room is equipped with electronic games, Ping-Pong, and board games. A disc jockey provides the music for a dance once a week.

Children's movies are shown Tuesday and Thursday evenings at 7 P.M. at Laurel Hall.

A special children's fishing program is available from 6:30 to 8 A.M. Monday through Friday. Poles, bait, and transportation to a fishing lake are provided for a small charge.

Baby-sitters are available. The resort will send you a list of available sitters before you arrive, or provide it when you get there. Since many are employees, you can meet them before you hire them.

NICETIES: Each week, the president of Callaway Gardens meets guests for continental breakfast (the resort's treat) at Robin Lake Beach. He takes all questions and complaints; not infrequently, the exchange results in changes in the program or fees the following year.

Shuttle bus service is provided among the inn, villas, cottages, Robin Lake Beach, golf courses, and tennis courts from 8:30 A.M. to 11 P.M. daily.

A coin laundry across from the pool makes it possible to do your laundry in between dips in the pool.

OF INTEREST NEARBY: Georgia operates Franklin Delano Roosevelt's old retreat at nearby Warm Springs as a state park. The home has been left much as it was when he died; another home nearby has been converted into a museum, with presidential memorabilia. The nearby springs where Roosevelt underwent rehabilitation for polio have fallen into disrepair, but are interesting.

FOR MORE INFORMATION: In Georgia, call the reservations office at (800) 282-8181; elsewhere, call (404) 663-2281. Write Callaway Gardens, Pine Mountain, GA 31822-9800.

The Cloister
Sea Island, Georgia

There are a few resorts in the nation to which a visit is like a voyage back in time. The legendary Cloister, on Sea Island, just off Georgia's southern coast, is one of them. Visiting Sea Island is like stepping back into another era, into bygone days when ladies and gentlemen—and even their offspring—dressed for dinner and tea was an event, not just a drink. Television was introduced here only in the mid-1980s—and only after prolonged debate. The compromise between opposing factions of management was to hide each television set in a lovely armoire so that its presence wouldn't intrude into guests' lives unless they invited it.

But The Cloister is more than just a historic relic. It's a place where you can sample southern cuisine (peanut soup on ice is standard fare), ride on a jeep train to a "plantation supper," play a spirited game of bingo, dance to either reggae or waltz music, or go for a horseback breakfast ride. Above all, it's a place for families to enjoy each other.

Many of The Cloister's guests are members of families that have been coming here for generations. And there are many multi-generational families here at any one time.

The main hotel has intense romantic appeal, with its terra-cotta roof, vaulted windows, and grand piano in the Spanish Lounge. The Spanish moss for which Georgia is famous, the palm trees, the abundance of spring-blooming azaleas, and five miles of impeccably groomed beach are all part of The Cloister's lush surroundings. What makes a vacation here so inviting is the special combination of great natural beauty (10,000 acres of unspoiled forest and marshes) and attractive structures (there are no high rises or strip shopping centers to be seen). It's probably no accident that it was on Sea Island that Eugene O'Neill, perhaps America's greatest playwright, wrote his only happy play, *Ah, Wilderness!*

ACCOMMODATIONS: $$ to $$$ You may choose from small rooms with a double bed, larger rooms with a sitting alcove and wet bar, large beachfront rooms, or guest house suites. You will find them more than comfortable; many of the 264 rooms are quite elegant with lovely views. Many of the 450 privately owned luxury homes in the Sea Island cottage colony also can be rented through Sea Island Properties.

Rates include three full meals. Special spa, tennis and golf packages are available. Children who share a room with their parents are charged only for meals on a scale that rises with age (there's no charge for children 2 and under). The high season is spring.

During the Family Festival, from early July through early September, there is no charge for children's meals (that's true also during the Christmas and New Year's holidays).

DINING: Eating is an experience at Sea Island, with extravagant meals offered three times daily in the Cloister Dining Room or, as an alternative, at the Sea Island Beach Club, a short walk away; the Sea Island Golf Club; or the St. Simons Island Club (the latter two are a short drive). Fresh flowers decorate tables set with crisp linen tablecloths at every meal. Breakfasts are sumptuous, and the buffet lunches are formidable (the Beach Club is a nice venue for this meal). Dinners are elegant and delectable seven-course affairs.

Men must wear jackets for dinner in the Cloister Dining Room, and jackets or long-sleeved sweaters for breakfast and lunch (dress at the Beach Club is more casual). Women are expected to dress up too, and most little girls have ribbons in their hair; boys too young for jackets seem to favor suspenders. On Wednesday and Saturday nights, it is customary for guests to wear gowns or dinner jackets with black ties, but many of the younger guests forgo that tradition.

The majority of children accompany their parents to meals. However, children ages 3 through 11 may eat dinner together in the children's dining room during the summer and at Christmas and Easter. Supervision is provided from 6 to 9 P.M.

ACTIVITIES

Eighteen fast-dry clay composition tennis courts, with professional instruction available. Clinics and guest round robins scheduled each week. Golf and tennis magazines consistently rate The Cloister's facilities among the top in the nation. No court or greens fees for players under 19.

Five golf courses with a total of 54 holes, many of which have beautiful views of the Atlantic Ocean; state-of-the-art Golf Learning Center. The greens are interrupted by lovely groupings of azaleas and huge live oaks. Four nine-hole courses designed by Coit and Alison: Seaside, 3,371 yards, par 39; Plantation, 3,343 yards, par 36; Retreat, 3,506 yards, par 36; Marshside, 3,258 yards, par 37. Eighteen-hole course at St. Simons Club, 6,308 yards, par 72, designed by Joseph Lee. Driving ranges, putting greens, instruction, pro shop.

Two large pools and a wading pool that overlook the ocean and The Cloister's five-mile-long strip of beach. Pool chairs and towels available without charge.

Rentals of inland boats and oceangoing sailboats available; one and a half hour sightseeing cruises.

Nearby waters abound with trout, bass, drum, flounder, whiting, croaker, and sheepshead.

Rental fleet numbers 550—including tandems, bikes with children's seats, and children's bikes.

Regularly scheduled nature walks.

The Long family has managed the stables since 1948, and it's a favorite hangout for little girls, who are allowed to help groom and pamper their mounts. The Longs care for more than 40 horses and offer lessons in the ring or on a trail. Ride through the marsh and picnic on the beach. On morning rides, you may even spot a porpoise.

Three skeet courses; instruction, rental equipment.

Full service spa. Services include facials, massage, Swiss shower, hydrotherapy, and other aesthetic treatments. Exercise/cardiovascular equipment, classes, and personal assessments.

Movies, lectures on the history of the area and the resort's founding, bridge tournaments, and guided walks; croquet, badminton, and other lawn games.

Bingo is one of Sea Island's big evening attractions for families; the games on Tuesdays and Thursdays frequently attract more than 100 guests. Plan to join in the line dancing when the game is over. If you've never done the bunny hop or the alley cat, you'll learn quickly. Another Sea Island highlight is the Friday evening Plantation Supper, outdoors at the torch-lit Ocean Grove by the beach.

Nightly dancing (except Sunday) is popular with adults; you'll hear everything from beach music to reggae to waltzes.

FOR CHILDREN: The Cloister offers a supervised children's program from June through Labor Day and during the Thanksgiving, Christmas, and Easter school breaks. The best time for families to visit is from early July through Labor Day, during the Family Festival. Not only are children under 19 not charged for accommodations, but there is also no charge for meals and children's activities.

Junior staffers (college students) will keep 3- to 11-year-olds occupied from 9 A.M. until 3 P.M. daily except Sunday. The list of activities reads like a summer camp brochure—shuffleboard, lawn games, scavenger hunts, pony rides, sand-sculpture contests, nature walks, kite flying, croquet, jeep rides, and morning and afternoon swims. The junior staffers are all warm, friendly, and energetic.

Children under 3 may participate in these activities if accompanied by a parent or sitter. Advance registration is required.

Older children will enjoy the many sports and social activities, from bicycling to bingo. Children over 11 seem happy to spend time on their own at the Beach Club, where they swim and play shuffleboard or Ping-Pong.

On rainy days, the resort schedules movie parties, magic shows, and arts and crafts classes. Sometimes there are cooking classes and classes on "modern manners."

The holidays offer excuses for other activities—a dance for teenagers on New Year's Eve, an Easter sunrise service and egg hunt, fireworks and dancing on the Fourth of July, and a Thanksgiving harvest celebration.

Baby-sitters are easy to come by.

NICETIES: If you ask for a crib in the room, you'll also get a baby basket complete with baby lotion, washcloths, and wipes.

During the cooler months, afternoon tea is served in the Spanish Lounge. In late evening, you'll find a tray set out with milk and cookies (graham crackers or ginger snaps).

For early risers, continental breakfast is available.

OF INTEREST NEARBY: Sea Island is one of Georgia's Golden Isles. St. Simons, adjacent to Sea Island, has many older homes as well as one of the nation's oldest continuously working lighthouses, and other points of historical interest.

Jekyll Island, to the south, was once a vacation destination for the Rockefellers, Morgans, and Vanderbilts, and is now a state park. You can tour the historic district (called Millionaires' Village) or enjoy the wildlife refuge, beaches, and picnic sites. Like Sea Island, Jekyll Island and St. Simons are accessible by car.

Cumberland Island, farther south, is now a national seashore on which cars are not permitted. The island may be reached by boat from the mainland. It offers wonderful opportunities for nature study and solitude.

FOR MORE INFORMATION: Write The Cloister, Sea Island, GA 31561, or call (800) 732-4752.

The Grove Park Inn and Country Club
Asheville, North Carolina

Built into the western slope of Sunset Mountain and overlooking the city of Asheville, the Grove Park Inn and Country Club has a spectacular setting. The hotel was built in 1913 from enormous boulders brought from local quarries. "Built not for the present alone, but for ages to come, and the admiration of generations yet unborn"—that was the motto of its founder, Edwin Wiley Grove, a pharmaceutical firm owner from St. Louis.

In its 75-plus-year history, the hotel has hosted such illustrious guests as inventor Thomas Edison, President Franklin D. Roosevelt, and industrialists Harvey Firestone and Henry Ford. F. Scott Fitzgerald did much of his writing in the 1930s from his own special room here. Like many of the nation's grand hotels, it was taken over by the State Department during World War II and used first as an internment center for Axis diplomats and later as a rest center for Navy personnel. Returned to recreational use in 1945, it underwent a number of management changes and expansions. In 1984, it was updated with a new heating system and additional facilities and became a year-round resort. It is listed in the National Register of Historic Places.

With a country club, a large sports facility, playground, and children's program, the Inn offers plenty of activities to keep you on the grounds. But with the Smoky and Blue Ridge mountains within easy reach for hiking and sightseeing, there's also plenty to do beyond.

ACCOMMODATIONS: $$$ The Main Inn offers rooms decorated with antique light fixtures and authentic mission oak furnishings; the rooms open in toward one of the country's first hotel atriums and have views looking either over the gardens and hillside or toward the distant mountains. The Sammons Wing and the Vanderbilt Wing (opened in 1988) are modern additions, designed to complement the Inn's naturalistic architecture. In all, there are 510 rooms.

Low season is from January through March. Various package plans are available that include meals, golf or tennis fees, or admission to sights such as the Biltmore House. Children under 17 are free.

DINING: The Grove Park Inn features several fine restaurants, each with its unique atmosphere and cuisine. The Sunset Terrace offers a spectacular setting along with a traditional American–continental menu; open only in warm weather, the terrace looks toward the Blue Ridge Mountains and is a lovely place to linger over lunch.

The Blue Ridge Dining Room and Terrace serves breakfast, lunch, and dinner in a lovely setting in the Inn's new Vanderbilt wing. The Horizons Restaurant, specializing in innovative versions of classical dishes, is open for dinner only. As in all the Inn's restaurants, reservations and jackets for men are necessary.

At the Country Club is the Pool Cabana, which serves hamburgers and hot dogs for lunch. Most suited to family dining with younger children is the Carolina Café, which serves three meals a day.

Pisgah View Ranch, 30 minutes from Asheville on Route 1, serves family-style meals in a large, homey dining room. Reservations are required for all meal sittings, so call in advance (667-9100); during the summer and fall, entertainment such as square dancing or bluegrass music is provided after dinner.

ACTIVITIES

 Six Laykold courts outdoors, three Plexi-Pave courts indoors; squash and racquetball courts also available.

 Eighteen-hole, 6,301-yard course, designed by Donald Ross, winds in front of the Inn. The course features rolling hills, tree-lined fairways, and winding streams, with strategically placed traps.

 Indoor pool on the eighth floor of the hotel's Sammons wing, outdoor pool at the Country Club.

Workout rooms, Nautilus equipment, whirlpools, saunas at the Sports Center.

Game room, an antique car museum, horse-drawn carriage rides. The Christmas season brings visits from Santa, sing-alongs with the staff chorus, and festive decorations.

FOR CHILDREN: Next to the Sports Center there's a playground for children, equipped with a climbing center, corkscrew slide, swing, and horizontal ladder. The Inn runs two supervised activity programs for children, ages 3 to 5 and 6 to 11, from 9:30 A.M. to 4:30 P.M. every day except Sunday from late May through Labor Day, and on winter weekends. Evening sessions are held from 6 to 10:30 P.M. on Fridays and Saturdays. The activities include nature hikes, crafts, swimming, and low-key instruction in tennis, racquetball, and badminton. The fee includes meals.

A "parents' night out" program is offered from 6 to 10:30 P.M. on Friday and Saturday nights throughout the year at the activity room at the indoor pool. The charge includes movies, pizza, and soft drinks.

Baby-sitting can be arranged through the Housekeeping Department with a 24-hour advance notice.

NICETIES: Rows of rocking chairs stand near the landscaped front entrance.

A shuttle bus runs frequently between the Inn and the Country Club.

OF INTEREST NEARBY: Asheville's major tourist attraction is the Biltmore House. You'll probably want to allow at least a half day to tour this immense mansion and the beautiful gardens and winery. While children under 11 are admitted free, this might be better enjoyed when the kids are in the children's program.

The Western North Carolina Nature Center is a small zoo and mini-farm with both indoor and outdoor exhibits. The nocturnal hall, with its collection of owls and opossums, will delight your children, as will the small petting area. A picnic area on the Nature Center grounds borders the Swannanoa River and makes a good spot for a lunchtime romp.

Fifty miles south of Asheville, the Cherokee Indian Reservation has attractions to interest all ages. The Museum of the Cherokee Indian is a good place to start, with audio-visual exhibits that tell the story of the Cherokee people and their eventual journey on the Trail of Tears. Across the street is the Qualla Arts and Crafts Mutual, Inc., which offers authentic Indian work. The Oconaluftee Indian Village gives visitors an overview of 18th-century Cherokee life and is run by the nonprofit Cherokee Historical Association.

The town of Cherokee is on the border of Great Smoky Mountains National Park, where your family will find plenty of wonderful spots to hike or picnic. An outdoor amphitheater is the scene for the summer production of *Unto These Hills*, a dramatization of Cherokee history from 1540 to the Trail of Tears in 1838.

FOR MORE INFORMATION: Write to The Grove Park Inn and Country Club, 290 Macon Avenue, Asheville, NC 28804. Or call (704) 252-2711 or (800) 438-5800 for reservations.

Kiawah Island Inn and Villas
Kiawah Island, South Carolina

As if to confirm to the visitor Kiawah Island's dedication to preservation, he or she is likely to be greeted by white-tailed deer leaping across the road, an alligator peering out from a lagoon, or an egret pausing in its fishing activities. This resort has won dozens of awards for planning, architecture, and environmental sensitivity.

Built in 1976 on an undeveloped beach 21 miles south of Charleston, the resort encompasses about half of a 10,000-acre barrier island. Several miles of beachfront remain undeveloped, reputedly the longest stretch of privately owned and undeveloped beach on the East Coast. Even in the developed area, you still feel as though you're in the midst of a maritime forest, for each grouping of villas has been designed to blend into the surrounding forest of palmetto, live oak, loblolly pine, and magnolia.

Kiawah is a sprawling resort. After you check in, you follow the bellhop's van to your accommodations in your own vehicle. Unless you stay at the Kiawah Inn, your villa is likely to be at the end of a long and winding road. Except in the vicinity of the Inn, Kiawah is almost eerily quiet. No overhead lights shine on the roads at night, and even the Inn lighting is dim, because nesting loggerhead turtles are disturbed by light. The island is home to over 140 species of birds, 18 species of mammals, as well as 30 species of reptiles and amphibians.

The resort is divided into two parts—West Beach, which includes the Inn, and East Beach, which includes the 21-acre Night Heron Park and the Conference Center. Two new beachfront hotels are being developed in East Beach. Each section has its own amenities.

Like most South Carolina resorts, Kiawah is essentially a year-round resort, though business drops off considerably in winter, when temperatures dip into the 50s and can be as low as the 30s. The climate permits year-round golfing, tennis, and other land sports, however.

ACCOMMODATIONS: $$$ to $$$$ If you want to minimize driving, consider accommodations closest to the activity you are most likely to pursue. Ocean lovers would do well to take a room at Kiawah Island Inn or a beachside villa. Inn rooms have mini-bars, but no kitchen facilities; however, the one- to four-bedroom villas have fully equipped kitchens as well as washers and dryers.

Non-beachside accommodations are clustered near the tennis centers, the golf courses, the park, or the pools, almost all overlooking one of the beautiful lagoons interlacing the island. Families with pool-happy small children would be well-advised to choose one of the three locations near a pool—either the Inn, Turtle Point, or Night Heron Park. Prices for non-beachside accommodations are lower. All beachside villas have balconies, and all landside villas have screened-in porches.

Kiawah Island Inn and Villas offers golf, tennis, and family packages at lower-than-daily rates. There are 150 inn rooms and 300 villas available on the rental program. Rates are considerably lower during the winter months.

DINING: Families with villa accommodations may find it easiest to do their own cooking. Groceries are available at the General Store, a convenience food shop on site, or at a supermarket about four miles toward Charleston along a scenic two-lane road.

Kiawah's flagship restaurant, the Jasmine Porch, located at the Inn, is the only restaurant that serves breakfast, lunch, and dinner. The fare is delicious and the atmosphere pleasant.

In East Beach, the Indigo House serves lunch and dinner daily. One of the lunch offerings is an attractive seafood and salad buffet. Jonah's, in the Straw Market shopping area in West Beach, is open from 11 A.M. to 10 P.M. for lunch, snacks, drinks, dinner, and dessert. Scoopers, an ice-cream shop in the Straw Market, serves from 11 A.M. to 9 P.M.

Snacks and drinks are also available at various activity centers around the resort, including the Inn pool area, which has a lounge and a cabana, and the golf and tennis areas.

About half a mile from the entrance to the resort, Bohicket Marina offers a fine seafood restaurant, the Privateer. There is also a pizza parlor that delivers.

ACTIVITIES

Twenty-three Har-Tru courts and five hard courts, two lighted. Pro shop, daily clinics for adults and children. Kiawah Island Inn and Villas has been named one of the 50 best tennis resorts in the country by *Tennis* magazine. Court fees.

The 6,223-yard, par 71 Marsh Point course, designed by Gary Player, challenges golfers with 13 water-hazard holes and undulating greens. For those who prefer more challenge, the Jack Nicklaus–designed course at Turtle Point, with 6,889 yards, par 72, offers long, narrow fairways and three scenic oceanside holes. Tom Fazio is the architect of a third course, Osprey Point (6,840 yards, par 72). Pete Dye built the Ocean Course, with every offering dramatic views of the Atlantic. The Ocean Course hosted the 1991 Ryder Cup matches. All courses have clubhouses, pro shops, driving ranges, and putting greens.

In the Atlantic Ocean from a south-facing beach; low rolling surf, water temperature in the 80s in the summer. The three pool complexes—at Night Heron Park, Turtle Point, and the Inn—are popular gathering places. The Inn has an upper-level pool for adults only and a lower-level pool for families. All have baby pools.

 Sailboat and windsurfer rentals are available through Kiawah Island Inn.

 Charter fishing excursions from nearby Bohicket Marina.

 Kiawah Kollege offers weekly canoe trips, bike tours of the marshlands, and seining, crabbing, and bird-watching expeditions.

 Rentals with child seats and helmets available; 14 miles of paved trails also used by walkers and joggers.

Jazzercize or water aerobics classes.

Typically, Sunday evenings in the summer feature an ice-cream social followed by a family movie. Monday is bingo night; Tuesday, beach cookout night, and so on.

FOR CHILDREN: Kiawah Island Inn and Villas offers supervised activities for children during the summer, from 9 A.M. to 4:30 P.M. The program is offered for 3- to 12-year-olds, Monday through Friday, for a modest fee.

For young children, Night Heron Park has a small playground with a variety of equipment on a sand base. For the 4- to 6-year-old group, a "tiny tot" tennis program is offered from 8:30 to 9 A.M., Monday through Friday in the summer, for a nominal charge.

Activities for teenagers are scheduled daily, including volleyball, pizza parties, and pool parties.

Kiawah Island Inn and Villas provides guests with a list of baby-sitters who set their own rates.

NICETIES: The tennis pro will match you with partners of equal ability in case you're not traveling with one.

Glossy magazines, *Kiawah, Legends,* and *Oak Tree Hotel,* are placed in every guest accommodation. They tell you everything you could possibly want to know about the resort.

OF INTEREST NEARBY: Tours to Charleston can easily be arranged through the Inn's guest services coordinator, or you can go off by yourself to tour the historic district at the tip of the peninsula. Charleston's historic homes, gardens, museums, forts, wharves, and shops make this a worthwhile trip. A cruise of the harbor or to Fort Sumter, where the Civil War began, are fun and educational diversions for children and adults.

FOR MORE INFORMATION: Call (800) 654-2924 for reservations and rates or (803) 768-2121 for more information, or write Kiawah Island Inn and Villas, P.O. Box 12357, Charleston, SC 29422-2357.

The Tides Inn
Irvington, Virginia

The setting of the Tides Inn could not be more exquisite. This small, special resort is located on a dot of land surrounded by water on three sides, creating a quiet haven. You'll enjoy the natural beauty of Carter's Creek and find it provides a sheltered spot for sailing and canoeing.

Water is definitely the controlling element here. The Inn is located eight miles up the Rappahannock River from the western shore of the Chesapeake Bay, enabling guests to arrive by yacht.

The Tides Inn is both comfortable and unpretentious. It is family run, and every effort is made to make guests feel at home. This was the tradition started by E. A. Stephens and his wife, Ann Lee Stephens, who opened the Tides Inn in 1947. When the Stephenses first bought the point, they found it overgrown with honeysuckle, briers, and vines. They cleared the land and built the inn using native wood. The cypress you see today in the View Room and the Dining Room came from a swamp 20 miles from the Inn.

The Stephenses traveled to Europe to look for many of the Inn's fine furnishings. They found the carpets in Brussels, the Sheffield silver and Chippendale furniture in England, and some of the prints in Paris. The silver honeymoon cups (from which couples still drink on Monday nights) were brought from the Netherlands.

The Stephenses' son, Bob Lee, and his wife, Suzy, took over when Bob Lee's father retired in 1963. Bob Lee started working here in 1947 as an elevator boy. He and his wife share the same commitment to understated luxury and "quiet quality." And now their oldest and youngest sons, Lee and Randy, have begun to take over. Family is, indeed, fundamental at the Tides Inn!

ACCOMMODATIONS: $$$ When the Tides Inn first opened in 1947, there were 47 rooms. Now there are 110 in the Main Building, the East Wing, the Garden House, the Lancaster House, and the Windsor House. Many rooms have balconies or patios. Family suites are also available.

All of the rooms are light and airy. E. A. Stephens had planned for every guest to enjoy the view. "So few places I stay are built the way I like them," he said. "I'm building this one my own way." So most of the rooms have windows 13 feet wide and almost five feet tall, set so low you can lie in bed and look out at the view.

Rates include three meals daily. There is no charge for children ages 1 to 10, and children's rates apply up to age 16.

DINING: The Tides Inn is well known for its excellent southern cooking. You'll find an abundance of Chesapeake Bay specialties as well. The dining-room employees all wear name tags showing how many years they've been on staff.

Soft-shell crabs are a delicacy you'll find on the menu every evening. Other entrées will vary, but you'll find a wonderful selection —everything from roast goose with fennel to baked ocean grouper with crabmeat. The Sunday night Seafood Buffet is also a real treat.

Guests will delight in breakfast (Mr. Stephens's favorite meal). The main breakfast is served from 8 to 9:30 A.M. A continental breakfast is also available, from 7:30 to 8 A.M. and from 9:30 to 11 A.M.

If you take an early-afternoon cruise on *Miss Ann,* you'll have lunch aboard. You may also choose to eat in the Dining Room or on weekends at the Captain's Quarters, an informal dining room. Or walk down to the Summer House next to the saltwater pool and enjoy a casual buffet luncheon, served between 12:30 and 2:30 P.M. Snacks and drinks are available at other times.

For a change of scenery, dine at Cap'n B's, located at the Golden Eagle Gallery Club House, two miles away. (There's a courtesy van service.) Cap'n B's offers an interesting history, with a building modeled after a house in New Orleans, and Cajun food.

Or you may wish to explore the Tides Lodge for lunch. This facility is located just across Carter's Creek and is operated by Mr. Stephens's brother.

ACTIVITIES

 Four outdoor courts, two clay, two all-weather. No court fees.

Three courses in beautiful settings. There are the 18-hole Golden Eagle course (6,943 yards, par 72), the 18-hole Tartan course at the Lodge (6,500 yards, par 72), and the nine-hole Executive course (par three). Pro shop, instruction. Complimentary greens fees in March and December.

 Saltwater pool next to a beach looking out on the creek, shallow end for children.

 Miss Ann, The High Tide, and *Star Tide* depart once or twice daily on cruises—a cove cruise on Carter's Creek, a bay shore picnic, or a luncheon cruise. Sailboats, canoes, and paddleboats are also available without charge.

Ponds on the golf course are well stocked for freshwater fishermen. The dock master can also arrange saltwater fishing. Local captains will take guests fishing for spot, croaker, or bluefish.

Complimentary, including tandems and bikes with child seats.

Play pavilion with pool, Ping Pong, croquet, and shuffleboard. If you're planning a trip in the fall or spring, ask about the weekend specials, such as watermen's weekends, country weekends, and historical promotion week.

Dancing several nights a week, movies, slide shows, shipboard-style horse racing, bingo, or a golf clinic.

FOR CHILDREN: A free supervised program for children ages 4 to 12 is available from Memorial Day through Labor Day, Monday through Saturday. Two college-age counselors supervise the program from 10 A.M. to 5 P.M. At least one night a week they supervise a children's dinner.

Children meet in the playroom for games and crafts. They usually have lunch at the Summer House by the pool. Afternoon activities include swimming, paddleboating, beach trips, or a movie.

The children's favorite activity is crabbing in Carter's Creek. They use chicken wings tied to strings for bait and nets to catch the crabs. The children may also visit a local crab house, where they'll get an insider's view of the seafood industry.

Children are free to participate in the program as much or as little as they please. Most parents leave gratuities for the counselors.

Teenagers do not participate in the supervised program, but find plenty to do—canoeing, sailing, tennis. The pool is a particular magnet; it's open 24 hours a day.

Baby-sitters are available at reasonable rates.

NICETIES: You'll find a retractable clothesline in the bathroom, as well as a coffee and tea maker in the room.

Chambermaids will bring an iron or hair dryer on request.

Small pets (under 50 pounds) are welcome to stay with guests in the soundproof Garden House wing.

OF INTEREST NEARBY: Christ Church is only a mile or two away in Lancaster County and is a beautiful example of colonial church architecture. It is cruciform in design and has a rare three-decker pulpit. The church was built between 1730 and 1734 at the expense of Robert Carter, former Acting Governor of the Colony of Virginia. (Older children will be interested in discovering that Robert Carter's descendants include three signers of the Declaration of Independence, two presidents of the United States, and eight governors of Virginia.)

Stratford Hall, the plantation home and birthplace of Robert E. Lee, is one of Virginia's most beautiful historic homes and only an hour's drive from the Tides Inn. The views of the Potomac are spectacular. Stratford Hall is located off SR 214.

About half an hour's drive from the Tides Inn you'll find the Yorktown Battlefield. The film *The Siege of Yorktown*, which is shown at the Visitor Center, is well worth seeing. While you're at the Visitor Center, don't miss the military tents used by George Washington during the Yorktown campaign. Also ask for the map outlining two self-guiding auto tours through the battlefield. The Yorktown Victory Center also shows a movie, called *The Road to Yorktown*.

Take the Colonial Parkway and you'll arrive in Williamsburg in about an hour.

FOR MORE INFORMATION: Write The Tides Inn, Irvington, VA 22480, or call (800) TIDES INN.

Oglebay Resort

Wheeling, West Virginia

Surrounded by the breathtaking splendor of the West Virginia hills, Oglebay Resort is a resort for all seasons. Set among 1,500 acres in the highlands of northern West Virginia, this former summer estate of industrialist Colonel Earl Oglebay was willed to the people of Wheeling, West Virginia, for "recreational and educational purposes." Today, Oglebay serves as a nationwide model for municipal parks.

This exceptional resort offers choices for every age. Families can be as active as they choose. Depending upon the season, the recreational options range from tennis, downhill and cross-country skiing, golfing, and classes at the arboretum to feeding and petting the animals at the children's zoo, boating, and picnicking.

Oglebay offers numerous seasonal and weekend packages that are great for family visits, including Getaway Winter weekends, Spring Flings, Easter Golf Package, and Christmas and New Year packages. The best-known Oglebay events of the year are the renowned Oglebayfest, in October, featuring ethnic food, parades, and fireworks, and the Festival of Lights from early November through February weekends.

ACCOMMODATIONS: $ Wilson Lodge has 204 attractively decorated and reasonably priced rooms, most with balconies or patios. Chalets and suites with spacious living rooms and one or more connecting bedrooms are perfect for families.

Oglebay also offers 35 cabins in natural woodland settings. The family deluxe cabins are rustic but have all the conveniences for year-round comfort: open stone fireplaces, central heating, completely equipped kitchens, and direct-dial telephones. All have living rooms, four bedrooms, and one or two baths; they sleep up to 14 people.

For serious golfing families who want to be located as close to the course as possible, there are golf cabins on the fairways of the Speidel course. These are deluxe, fully equipped accommodations with spacious living rooms and kitchens, four bedrooms, two baths, air-conditioning, and color television. These cabins can sleep five couples or up to 15 family members.

Rates for Wilson Lodge rooms are lowest in winter. In the summer, family deluxe and golf cabins are rented on a weekly basis only. Linens are not included in the cabin rates but can be rented.

DINING: The friendly atmosphere and a fine array of traditional and special meals make dining at Oglebay a treat. The Ihlenfeld Restaurant in Wilson Lodge offers daily family specials and a varied children's menu for those under 14. The Sunday brunch is lavish.

There are many other places to eat at the resort: Hamm Clubhouse Grill at the Speidel golf course, offering breakfast and lunch through the golfing season; Par 3 Clubhouse, Schenk Lake Boat House, and the Good Zoo.

ACTIVITIES

Nine Har-Tru and two Gras-Tex lighted courts, and two lighted paddle tennis courts at the Crispin Center. Within Wheeling Park there are six additional Har-Tru courts and four rubberized courts in an air dome that extends the tennis season through the winter months.

Three 18-hole courses. The Speidel course, designed by Robert Trent Jones, features multiple tee placements and has been the home of the West Virginia Ladies' Professional Golf Association Classic. Clubhouse with grill room, locker room facilities, pro shop; instruction available. The Crispin Center course is a beautifully landscaped year-round facility that traverses the West Virginia hills. Practice (par three) course adjacent to 30-tee driving range. Both of these facilities are lighted for night use. There's also a miniature golf course near Schenk Lake.

A large outdoor pool complex with a separate toddlers' pool is located at Crispin Center. Youth and adult lessons are available. Wilson Lodge has an indoor aquatic complex with a Polyne-

sian-motif pool, a Jacuzzi, and a whirlpool set among natural vegetation and waterfalls.

 Pedal boat and canoe rentals at Schenk Lake.

 Bass and catfish fishing at Schenk Lake. Fee for fishing; no
license required.

 Miles of wooded trails and meadows invite family hikes, and
formal gardens and an arboretum provide less strenuous walking opportunities. Gardening activities take place in the Garden Center. The Oglebay greenhouse features seasonal floral displays, which
visitors are encouraged to tour. Formal terrace gardens adjoin the
greenhouse and Wigginton Arboretum.

 Lessons in a ring at Oglebay's riding academy. Horse shows
held throughout the summer.

Skiing is the primary winter activity at Oglebay. Runs are from
900 to 1,600 feet in length with a 330-foot vertical drop. Three
Poma lifts serve the ski area, day and night. A snow-making system supplements natural snowfall, which averages only 40 inches
annually. Professional instruction, rental equipment (including
children's gear). Cross-country skiing, sledding, and tobboggan-
ing on the rolling hills of the resort; ice-skating in a covered rink
at nearby Wheeling Park. There are winter workshops on ice
fishing and cross-country skiing nature trips. The Oglebay Ski
Lodge is located on the slopes, with a fireplace, lounge, and snack
bar.

Cocktail lounge with entertainment at night year-round.

FOR CHILDREN: Specialized camps for youngsters are held at the
Children's Center, which encompasses the Brooks Nature Center,
the Miniature Golf Park, a playground, picnic sites, Schenk Lake,
and the Good Zoo.

The Brooks Nature Center holds special exhibits and programs
throughout the year. Storytelling, Appalachian music, nature walks,

self-guided nature trails, and astronomy lectures are all conducted here. On summer evenings there are campfires with songs, games, and storytelling. The astronomy program includes slide presentations and star-gazing through a refractor telescope in the Nature Center Observatory. The center has a book shop with a wide selection of children's and outdoor books.

The Good Children's Zoo is a 65-acre haven for animals and families. Oglebay is the only resort with a zoo that is fully accredited by the American Association of Zoological Parks and Aquariums. The zoo's collection includes bison, elk, deer, bear, and otter. Children can feed and pet deer and goats.

The curvy slide in the walk-through Red Barn is an enticing play area. A train, the 1863 vintage *C. P. Huntington,* takes visitors on a one and a half mile circuit through the bison range and over a waterfall.

Within the zoo, visitors can glimpse into the past by visiting a reproduction of a late-19th-century West Virginia farming, logging, and mining community, complete with model-train exhibit. The zoo also houses the Benedum Natural Science Theater, with wildlife shows on a 180-degree screen.

During the summer months, zoo camp programs for children ages 4 through 12 provide a marvelous adventure with lots of animal handling, games, arts and crafts, and movies (advance reservations are advised). The Farm Festival, Zoo Olympics, and science "playshops" are other summer activities for families.

OF INTEREST NEARBY: Oglebay guests have privileges at nearby Wheeling Park, where a 350-foot water slide is part of the pool facility.

Oglebay Institute's Stifel Arts Center is the headquarters of arts and crafts for the valley. Exhibitions, festivals, and arts programs are offered throughout the year.

The Mansion Museum is in a structure that dates from 1832 and was once Colonel Oglebay's home. The museum depicts life in the Ohio valley in the 19th century. It houses period rooms and a major collection of glass.

Exhibits and a craft shop are part of historic West Virginia Independence Hall, at Sixteenth and Market streets in Wheeling.

Jamboree U.S.A. Capitol Music Hall is the site of a famous country music show.

FOR MORE INFORMATION: Write Wilson Lodge, Oglebay, Wheeling, WV 26003, or call (800) 624-6988; in West Virginia, call (304) 242-3000.

MIDWEST

Eagle Ridge Inn and Resort
Galena, Illinois

Eagle Ridge Inn and Resort is located in the rolling hill country of northwestern Illinois, six miles from the quaint town of Galena. Although reminiscent of New England, Eagle Ridge is solidly Midwestern in its informality and its relaxed way of life. The resort offers an outstanding array of year-round recreational activities on its spacious 6,800 acres, which include the lovely 220-acre Lake Galena. The resort is a favorite vacation escape for Chicagoans; the Loop is just 153 miles away.

Galena was once the largest Mississippi River port north of St. Louis. Its economy was built on streamboating, lead mining, and the Blackhawk Indian War. Today, it has one of the highest concentrations of preserved mid-19th century buildings in the Midwest. Ninety percent of Galena's buildings are listed in the National Register of Historic Places, including one of the homes of Ulysses S. Grant. Many preservationists believe that Galena has the finest collection of period architecture in the Midwest.

ACCOMMODATIONS: **$$** to **$$$$** The 66-room Inn overlooking Lake Galena offers four types of rooms, including some with fireplaces and four-poster beds. Children under 18 stay free in their parents' room.

An alternative to the Inn are the 200 resort homes overlooking the lake or nestled deep in the woods or along the fairways. These are condominiums, cottages, and townhouses with one to four bedrooms. All are fully furnished, with well-equipped kitchens, fireplaces, washers and dryers, and daily maid service.

Twelve special packages are offered throughout the year, including golf, family, western adventure, and riverboat gambling packages (the latter includes a gambling expedition on the Mississippi River).

DINING: The Dining Room is the resort's formal restaurant, with great views of rolling hills and the lake. Jasper Maltby's Restaurant and Ice Cream Parlour offers families an informal dining atmosphere. Children will delight in the old-fashioned ice-cream palor offerings. Food and beverages are available poolside and in the pro shops. The General Store has groceries, gourmet items, beverages, and all the essentials to prepare your own meals.

ACTIVITIES

 Four outdoor latex courts, court fees. Instruction.

On two 18-hole championship courses—the 7,012-yard North Course and the 6,762 South Course, both par 72—designed by Roger Packard. There's also a 2,700 yard, 9-hole East Course (par 34). *Golf* magazine ranks Eagle Ridge among the "Best Golf Resorts in America." Driving range, putting green, two pro shops, club and cart rentals.

 Large heated indoor pool at the inn, swimming beach on Lake Galena.

 Rental Sunfish, canoes, pedalboats, aquafish, catamarans, and pontoon boats from the boat dock.

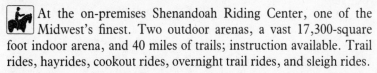 At the on-premises Shenandoah Riding Center, one of the Midwest's finest. Two outdoor arenas, a vast 17,300-square foot indoor arena, and 40 miles of trails; instruction available. Trail rides, hayrides, cookout rides, overnight trail rides, and sleigh rides.

On 40 miles of trails. Several trails near the inn are designated nature trails with interpretive signs.

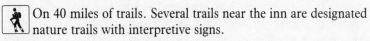 Indoor fitness center with exercise equipment and daily classes, including aerobics, swimnastics, and lap swims. Outdoor fitness trail with 21 exercise stations.

Mississippi River cruises, tours of historic Galena, poolside bingo, squirt-gun tag, pontoon tours of the lake, adult crafts, family movies, canoe races, and seasonal holiday events.

Cross-country skiing on 36 miles of groomed trails. Ice-skating rink and toboggan run; instruction, rental equipment.

Nearby Chestnut Mountain Resort offers downhill skiing on 16 runs served by two triple lifts, one quad-chair lift, and six rope tows. Slopes lighted for night skiing. Rental shop, Ski Wee program for 4- to 10-year-olds.

FOR CHILDREN: The "I Am an Eagle Ridge Kid" youth program runs every day but Sunday between Memorial Day and Labor Day and welcomes 3- to 12-year-olds. Trained counselors lead children in games, swimming, arts and crafts, boating, and special field trips. Children can join the program for half days or full days for a modest fee (lunch included). The program also operates over the Christmas holidays, Thanksgiving, and Presidents' weekend.

Organized teen activities include volleyball, alpine slide outings, casino nights, and pizza parties.

Kid's Night Out programs are held each Saturday from 7 to 10 P.M. and are centered around themes like carnival, beach party, and pirate's night.

Baby-sitting is available, with a three-hour minimum.

NICETIES: The grocery delivery service will stock a resort home with the foods of our choice before your arrival or at any time during your stay.

Each resort home has a VCR, and the resort has an ample supply of rental tapes.

OF INTEREST NEARBY: The main street of historic Galena has an abundance of shops, and restaurants, and historic homes. The Galena/Jo Daviess County History Museum presents a 15-minute film on Galena's history and has permanent exhibits on the town's past. The Old General Store Museum is an excellent reproduction of a 19th century general store.

The Ulysses S. Grant Home State Historic Site preserves a home given to Grant, a native son, by grateful citizens after the Civil War.

Galena's Kandy Kitchen is owned and operated by the third generation of a candy-making family whose patriarch was the creator of "Chuckles." Tours include tastings.

Riverboat cruises are offered regularly on the Mississippi River near Galena.

FOR MORE INFORMATION: Write Eagle Ridge Inn and Resort, U.S. Route 20, Box 777, Galena, IL 61036 or call (800) 892-2269 or (815) 777-2444.

For general tourist information, write Galena/Jo Daviess County Convention and Visitors Bureau, 101 Bouthillier St., Galena, IL 61036.

Grand View Lodge Golf and Tennis Club
Nisswa, Minnesota

This resort has all the essentials of an authentic north-woods retreat —a rough-hewn log lodge, towering pines, thousands of flowers lining wood-chip paths, a gorgeous lake setting, and every kind of family activity, including golf and tennis.

A cedar log lodge built in 1919, now on the National Register of Historic Places, is the center of activity at the 900-acre complex, which is three hours north of Minneapolis. It houses the main dining room, a comfortable varnished pine lobby complete with big-game trophies and a small library, and 12 upstairs rooms. Hidden away in the woods is a two-story annex that can easily accommodate a crowd.

The resort offers a variety of water sports on the big Gull Lake, and the other activities available during a typical summer week require a four-page newsletter to list. While a large number of guests are from Minnesota, the resort draws from as far away as California and regularly has some foreign visitors. Families often make it an annual reunion spot.

The resort is ideal for families for whom a vacation means freedom from cooking. Most guests sign up for a two-meal-a-day plan that is plentiful enough so that they don't mind missing a midday meal. If they're hungry, they can buy a snack on the beach.

Less than a half mile away is Roy Lodge on Roy Lake, and two and a half miles away is Gull Haven on Gull Lake. Both are rustic log cabin complexes owned by Grand View Lodge. The cabins are rented almost exclusively by the week, and the settings are more intimate and quiet. Families who stay here may participate in most activities at the Lodge, sometimes paying small extra fees; the disadvantage is that participation involves a drive.

ACCOMMODATIONS: $$ to $$$ Grand View Lodge has 12 lodge rooms and 65 cabins of varying sizes (plus 11 at Roy Lodge and 10 at Gull Haven). Except at Roy Lodge and Gull Haven, rates include breakfast and dinner. Lakefront cabins and more modern cabins are more expensive than basic cabins. Children 6 to 12 years old pay two-thirds of the adult rate, and children 3 to 5 years old pay one-half the adult rate. Children under 3 pay a modest daily "crib" rate. In addition there is a 15 percent service charge (in lieu of tipping). There is a two-night minimum stay.

The MAP rate includes tennis and golf and use of many boats. Extra fees are charged for rentals of golf carts, motors for boats, or water bikes.

The cabins are in various stages of upgrading—from brand-new furnishings to 1970s era decor. Some feature two bedrooms, fireplaces, two bathrooms, kitchenettes, and decks. Telephones were added to the cabins in 1987. Television is confined to a single large-screen unit in the main lodge lobby.

Roy Lodge and Gull Haven housekeeping units are more economical. Guests at Roy Lodge and Gull Haven are provided bed linens, but are expected to bring their own towels and clean their own cabins during the week. Many families cook in and use the main dining room at Grand View Lodge on a pay-as-you-go basis.

The resort season runs from late April to mid-October, with the most popular family months in July and August.

DINING: Breakfast is either ordered from the menu or chosen from a buffet, depending on the size of the crowd. Hours are 8 to 9:30 A.M. Continental breakfast is available until 10 A.M. Lunch is served from noon to 1:30 P.M. Sundays are brunch days.

A typical dinner features Minnesota's famous walleyed pike, a choice of Caesar salad or garden salad, a wonderful wild-rice soup or seafood cocktail, and a choice of desserts. Dress is casual, with no shorts allowed during dinner hours.

Guests eat either in the Pine Dining Room or the main dining room, which features shiny green tables with forest paintings on the tops. In addition, a beach snack bar is open during the day.

ACTIVITIES

Eleven Laykold tennis courts surrounded by gorgeous flowers and woods; pro, private, or group lessons; partner match-up. (Small charge for Roy Lodge and Gull Haven guests.)

The Pines, an 18-hole course, is one of the top-rated courses in Minnesota. The 9-hole Garden Course is lined with birch trees.

In roped-off areas of Gull Lake or Roy Lake (no lifeguards) or in an indoor-outdoor swimming pool. Nearby whirlpool.

Boats available for water-skiing and fishing; also "playaks" (small plastic kayaks), pontoons, and canoes (no charge).

Rental bikes available; weekly organized rides. Extensive trail system nearby.

The weekly events run the gamut from morning aerobics, horseback riding, skiing, trips to Nisswa for shopping, beach parties, and bingo, to a talent show.

A beach bar and a main lodge bar called the Totem Pole are open for nighttime drinking and music.

FOR CHILDREN: The children's counselors—all college students —run a free, camp-like activities program six days a week. The 3- to 13-year-olds meet daily from 9:30 A.M. to noon. Six- to 13-year-olds are entertained again from 1:30 to 3:30 P.M., and all children may attend supervised dinner hours that include beach dinners and movies from 5:30 to 8 P.M.

A crew of four counselors easily handles an average crowd of 25 children; however, more staff is drafted for the busiest summer family weeks. The making of yarn dolls, jewelry, and nature plates and lots of playground activities keep the youngest set busy. The older kids are treated to earth ball games, trips to water slides, and sports events. Free golf and tennis lessons are offered.

Children who have participated in the program for an entire week often take part in a weekend talent show featuring staff and guests.

No supervised activities are available Sundays.

Baby-sitting can be easily arranged with the front desk. College-student employees, many of whom live in the older cabins on the property, are often willing to sit, and the resort also has names of in-town sitters who will drive to the resort.

Teenagers are offered specials on tennis and water-skiing and seem to particularly enjoy the main lodge's downstairs game room with video games and pool tables.

NICETIES: The flower planting program was designed by a horti-culturalist, and a guided walk is offered each week. Some 24,000 flowers cover the grounds, creating a vibrant contrast with the deep-shaded woods.

For those who can't wait for 8 A.M. breakfast, the lodge offers coffee and a newspaper delivered to your cabin door for a small fee.

OF INTEREST NEARBY: Within a 15-minute drive are Paul Bunyan Center, Indian mounds, and Brainerd International Raceway. Farther away, but worth the drive, is Itasca State Park, home of the headwaters of the Mississippi River.

In nearby Brainerd, kids love the Paul Bunyan amusement park featuring the famous talking giant. (Paul calls out a personal greeting to each child as they climb up his giant shoes.) The park is manage-able in size; a visit of just a few hours is adequate.

The small town of Nisswa is even closer to the resort and features several nice shops for browsing on rainy summer days. Also close by are more tennis courts, water slides, go-carts, and Deer Forest, featuring storybook characters to wow the little travelers.

FOR MORE INFORMATION: Call the reservations office at (800) 432-3788 (summer only in Minnesota) or (800) 345-9625 (elsewhere year-round) or write Grand View Lodge, South 134 Nokomis, Nisswa, MN 56468.

Marriott's Tan-Tar-A Resort and Golf Club
Osage Beach, Missouri

Hidden away in the forests of Missouri, along green hillsides and moss-covered cliffs and miles of curving lake shoreline, is a giant of a resort. It is Marriott's Tan-Tar-A Resort and Golf Club, one of the largest resorts in the Midwest.

Tan-Tar-A sprawls across more than 400 acres of hushed woods and winding trails that overlook the beautiful Lake of the Ozarks. The lake, created by Bagnell Dam, is said to be the largest privately owned man-made lake in the United States and one of the largest in the world. Its 1,375-mile shoreline snakes in and out of the countryside, creating innumerable coves in which to fish and explore. Tan-Tar-A is on the eastern side of the 129-mile-long lake.

Tan-Tar-A is located in the middle of Missouri, about midway between St. Louis and Kansas City, and is a popular weekend getaway destination through the year. Tan-Tar-A, which means "one who moves swiftly," opened in 1960. The resort received both the Mobil 4-star and the AAA four-diamond ratings in 1991.

ACCOMMODATIONS: $ to $$$ Nearly 1,000 guest rooms, suites, cabins, and villas are scattered throughout the grounds, from moderately priced but comfortable hotel rooms to condominium-type suites with all the amenities. The main lodge has 365 rooms in four interconnected buildings; in addition, there are some "islanders," which are separate one- and two-bedroom suites.

There are also about 600 "estates"—mostly low-rise condominiums that are individually owned, designed, and decorated and rented by Marriott to Tan-Tar-A guests. Many are right on the lakeshore. The styles of the estates range from Cape Cod to sleek and modern to rough-sawn rustic. The most remote estates are two miles away from the main lodge and the recreation area. A shuttle operates 24 hours a day.

A typical estate has a living room, dining area, full kitchen, one to five bedrooms, and one or more baths. Many have stone fireplaces in the living room and decks off both the living room and bedroom, from which you can enjoy a lovely view of the lake, framed by tall oak trees, or the Hidden Lakes Golf Course.

Rates are highest in the summer; winter rates are exceptionally low. Several package rates are available that include room and meals or recreation passes.

DINING: Tan-Tar-A has four moderate to upscale restaurants, plus a sandwich shop and poolside snack bar. Three of the restaurants—Happy House, Cliff Room, and Windrose—are in the main lodge area. Of the three, Happy House is the most casual. You can eat breakfast, lunch, or dinner inside or outside on an appealing multilevel terrace. The children's menu comes on a balloon.

The Cliff Room also is nice for family dining at lunch or dinner, but is more formal. Its Sunday brunch is very popular.

The Windrose specializes in seafood and romance (it's better to go without the children). Diners may sit inside or outside on a patio overlooking the marina and enjoy continental cuisine. The Windrose is open only for dinner, and closes in the off-season.

Breakfast and lunch are served at the Oaks, located at the Oaks Golf Course, in spring, summer, and fall.

Families on the run may choose from a variety of sandwiches and pizza at the Grille, which opens early and closes late. Sandwiches, snacks, and drinks also are available at the Jetty poolside bar by the Arrowhead Pool, and at Mr. D's Deli & Lounge.

ACTIVITIES

Six outdoor (four lighted) and two indoor courts; pro shop, court fees. Four indoor and two outdoor racquetball courts.

The rolling hills of the resort are dotted with 27 holes of PGA-rated championship golf (an 18-hole, 6,805-yard, par 71 course and a nine-hole, 3,015-yard, par 36 course, both designed by Robert von Hagge and Bruce Devlin); pro shop, instruction, driving range, putting green, rental equipment. John Jacob's Golf School operates in the summer.

 Five swimming pools (one indoors) or from a sandy beach on the lake; water-skiing.

 Rental canoes, pedalboats, sailboats, fishing boats, ski boats, excursion boat rides.

 Lake of the Ozarks is one of the finest fishing lakes in the country; rental equipment, guides.

 Rentals available.

 Stable, trail rides through the woods, hayrides.

Spa with exercise equipment, aerobics classes, massages. Marked jogging tails.

Bowling, billiards, and lawn games. Tan-Tar-A prides itself on making holiday weekends spectacular. On Labor Day weekends, for instance, guests might enjoy an Ozark barbecue, a dance on the lakefront featuring 1960s music, an ice-cream social, carnival games for the kids, and the resort's own version of "Wheel of Fortune." Several cocktail lounges, nightclub entertainment.

Enclosed ice-skating rink, rental skates; cross-country skiing on golf course (no rentals).

FOR CHILDREN: "Camp Tan-Tar-A" operates from 9:30 A.M. to 3:30 P.M. Monday through Friday during the summer for children between the ages of 5 and 12. Youngsters swim, create their own artwork, feed the fish, play games, go on a treasure hunt, and make ice cream. The staff includes schoolteachers and others with recreation expertise. The daily fee includes lunch.

Activities are centered at the Playhouse, a two-room cabin equipped with books, blocks, trucks, a kid-size kitchen, dress-up clothes, and television. Large picture windows brighten the room, showing off the carpet splashed with a hopscotch-and-checkers pattern.

Teenagers up to 17 years old have a special program just for them, which includes beach volleyball, paddleboat races, and video game contests. Prices vary, depending on the activity.

Baby-sitting is provided in guests' rooms for a fee by employees and members of the community who have been screened by the resort.

Families seeking togetherness can play at the Garden of Games. This area, across from the main lodge, has a hillside miniature golf course, bocci, a kiddie play park, a moon walk, and a turtle track. Motorbikes and touring carts can also be rented here.

A supervised children's dinner is held at the Grille Monday through Saturday during the summer and on weekends during the rest of the year.

NICETIES: There's no need to want for anything, since the resort has more shops than some suburban malls. You can buy clothing, shoes, jewelry, brass, crystal, crafts, floral arrangements, groceries, and live fishing bait. You can get your hair done in the salon and have your portrait taken in turn-of-the-century attire.

If you'd like to see some of the sights outside the resort, Hertz car rental is available at the main lodge.

OF INTEREST NEARBY: A few miles east of Tan-Tar-A is the Lake of the Ozarks State Park, the largest state park in Missouri, with camping, boating, fishing, hiking, horseback riding, playground equipment, and the Grand Glaize Beach. Also nearby is the Ha Ha Tonka State Park, which has some of the most beautiful scenery on the lake, as well as picturesque ruins of an old castle.

Within a 25-minute drive of Tan-Tar-A are three caves that offer tours—Bridal Cave, Fantasy World Caverns, and Ozark Caverns.

Visitors can also tour Bagnell Dam. And nearby Osage Beach has shopping centers, factory outlet stores, and small shops with country crafts and antiques—and countless video arcades.

FOR MORE INFORMATION: Call (800) 826-8272 or write Tan-Tar-A at State Road KK, P.O. Box 188, Osage Beach, MO 65065-0188.

WEST COAST AND HAWAII

The Resort at Port Ludlow
Port Ludlow, Washington

Getting to The Resort at Port Ludlow can be an adventure in itself. Visitors can get there via seaplane, roads, or ferries, but the truly adventuresome will want to charter a boat in the Seattle harbor and fish during the two- to three-hour trip across Puget Sound.

No matter how the journey is made, a vacation at The Resort at Port Ludlow rewards the traveler. This is a wonderful vacation place, with magnificent views of the Olympic Mountains to the southeast and the islands and waters of Puget Sound at the doorstep. The accommodations are first rate, with a wide choice of luxurious condominium units. The food is memorable. And the possibilities for recreation are boundless, with a good marina and one of the nation's most scenic golf courses heading the list.

All this and family activities too. Families are more than welcome at The Resort at Port Ludlow. Good facilities and services for children are built into the recreation program.

ACCOMMODATIONS: **$$** to **$$$** A lumber mill once stood at the site of The Resort at Port Ludlow. It folded in the Great Depression, but its owners, the Pope and Talbot Company, retained the land and eventually developed the present-day resort. A few traces of the old mill can still be seen in the concrete foundation for a huge furnace, now a picnic area, at the tip of Burner Point and a small lagoon, now enjoyed by swimmers and boaters, which once impounded logs awaiting processing at the mill.

Beautiful native wood siding, wood-shingled roofs, and exposed interior beams link the buildings, with 180 units, including 50 suites, to their forested surroundings. Guests can choose from indi-

vidual guest bedrooms or full condominium units with a loft bedroom, living-room–dining-room area, completely equipped kitchen,
a private balcony or deck, and a fireplace.

The peak season is May through October; spring and fall rates
are lower. There is no charge for children under 12.

DINING: The Harbormaster Restaurant is a short walk from the
accommodations at Port Ludlow and serves three meals a day. The
food is delicious, with the salmon, halibut, crab, and oysters of
the Pacific Northwest heading the menu. A children's menu is also
available. Niblicks serves lunch at the pro shop.

Other seafood restaurants of note are an easy drive from Port
Ludlow. You might guess that the 3 Crabs Restaurant in Dungeness,
40 minutes away, serves crab, and it does, along with wonderful
other seafood. Port Townsend, with its main street of beautifully
restored Victorian buildings, also has several good seafood restaurants.

Guests who want to prepare some of their own meals can buy
provisions in the resort's general store. More substantial shopping is
available in Hadlock, 20 minutes north of the Resort.

ACTIVITIES

Seven Plexi-Pave courts, no fees. Equipment rentals.

Championship 6,800-yard golf course designed by Robert
Muir Graves: the American Society of Golf Course Architects
rates it among the top one percent of the best-designed courses in
the nation. Pro shop, snack bar, putting green, driving range, instruction.

Heated pool shielded from the wind by glass walls; also, lagoon
swimming.

The Marina at Port Ludlow, with 300 slips, is one of the largest
on Puget Sound. Several charter companies will equip you
with dinghies, 21-foot Victory day sailers, 27-foot Ericson sailers, or
even larger boats. On sailing trips of one or more days you can
explore Mats Bay, Port Townsend, the city of Victoria in Canada,

or the San Juan Islands. Skippered sightseeing cruises and moonlight champagne cruises can be arranged. Complete instruction.

 Charters from the Marina. Puget Sound waters are famous for their fishing; record-setting salmon and halibut are taken here. The Marina also has crabbing equipment for rent. Good clamming is available near the Hood Canal Bridge, a short drive away.

 Rentals, including children's bicycles, available. The resort provides maps with cycling, jogging, and walking routes.

The Beach Club complex houses a squash court, exercise equipment, and saunas; rental equipment.

The peninsula leading out to Burner Point has a volleyball court, a basketball backboard, a nine-hole pitch-and-putt golf course, and picnic facilities. Pool and Ping Pong tables and video game room at the Beach Club. During the peak summer season, the resort offers tours to various attractions on the Olympic Peninsula.

Friday and Saturday night bonfires at Burner Point, complete with marshmallows and hot dogs, are family affairs.

FOR CHILDREN: Most of the adult activities at Port Ludlow will appeal to children as well. In addition, the Recreation Office lends equipment for volleyball, badminton, croquet, lawn bowling, softball, Frisbee, football, tetherball, basketball, fishing, lawn darts, snorkeling, horseshoes, and t-ball.

Organized children's activities are scheduled during the summer months for children 5 and older. Many of these fall on weekends, when the children of Port Ludlow homeowners join in. Activities include games, a t-ball competition, nature hikes, a treasure hunt, an aqua scout race, or beachcombing. At spring vacation time and on summer holiday weekends, the schedule steps up to three or four organized children's activities a day.

NICETIES: Rental cars are available at Port Ludlow.

Most of the employees of the Resort come from the surrounding rural area of the Olympic Peninsula. Their warmth and friendliness add to the pleasure of your stay.

OF INTEREST NEARBY: The Olympic Peninsula is a marvelous family playground. Olympic National Park and Olympic National Forest offer snow-capped mountains, rain forests, hot springs, and unparalleled views. U.S. 101 rings the Olympics with access roads radiating from 101 into the mountains. The drive to Hurricane Ridge is particularly rewarding, with its views of the Olympic Mountains, the Strait of Juan de Fuca and the San Juan Islands.

Canada is only a 90-minute ferry ride from the United States out of Port Angeles. The ferry docks in the city of Victoria on Vancouver Island. In summer months, the car traffic backs up at the ferry landing and long waits develop. But there is always room on the ferry for foot passengers. On a day visit, leave your car in Port Angeles and take public transportation in Victoria.

In Port Angeles, visit the Arthur D. Feiro Marine Laboratory just east of the Ferry Terminal. Its tanks contain a fine collection of Puget Sound marine specimens. Watch the crabs and starfish feed, and handle the marine life in the touch tank.

The Dungeness Spit is the nation's longest sand spit and the center of a network of bays and estuaries that teem with birds, marine life, and seals. Take a picnic lunch and enjoy a walk along this seven-mile stretch of sand.

A trainer of animals for Hollywood movies established the Olympic Game Farm near Sequim, not far from Port Ludlow. A wide variety of North American and some African animals are displayed here. Self-guided driving tours are available.

Pope and Talbot, the developers of The Resort at Port Ludlow, began their Northwest logging operations at Port Gamble, across the Hood Canal Bridge, a short drive from the Resort. The sawmill at Port Gamble has been in operation since 1853, and the original New England–style buildings of this company town have been beautifully restored. There's a museum in the basement of the general store.

FOR MORE INFORMATION: Write The Resort at Port Ludlow, 9483 Oak Bay Road, Port Ludlow, WA 98365, or phone (800) 732-1239 (in Washington) or (206) 437-2222 from out of state.

Sunriver Lodge and Resort
Sunriver, Oregon

Sunriver Lodge and Resort is a place for family rest and recreation in all seasons of the year. Located in the Oregon high-desert country in the shadow of the Cascade Mountains, Sunriver boasts a wonderful summer climate and easy access to Cascade Mountain skiing in the winter. From March through October, opportunities for warm-weather outdoor activities abound. Lovers of golf, tennis, cycling, canoeing, white-river rafting, swimming, and fishing are in their element here. From November through late spring, Sunriver is a short distance from excellent downhill and cross-country skiing.

Sunriver is a resort built to harmonize with its surroundings. An investor from Portland who came to the Bend, Oregon, area in the 1960s with the intention of building a simple fishing cabin recognized the potential of the site. Determined to preserve the natural beauty of the location, he carefully developed this 3,300-acre tract of ponderosa pine forest and meadows bordering the Deschutes River. And now, despite the fact that the Sunriver development has 1,500 homes, over 650 condominiums, and 1,400 year-round residents, the natural beauty has been preserved.

ACCOMMODATIONS: **$$** to **$$$** The lodge building houses the front desk, concierge, recreation management offices, shops, and restaurants. Accommodations are in nearby condominium-style units or in lodge bedroom units. Lodge suites have fully equipped kitchenettes and a loft bedroom. All units have magnificent stone fireplaces and decks, with tasteful furnishings. Lodge suites comfortably accommodate an additional child or two on a sofa bed.

It is also possible to rent one of more than 100 vacation homes or condominiums in the Sunriver development through the Sunriver Lodge rental program.

Rates are highest in the peak summer months and in the Christmas holiday period. Spring and fall golf and recreation packages are available, as are three- to seven-day winter ski packages.

DINING: Two restaurants are located in the main lodge building. Both overlook the Deschutes River with the high Cascades as a backdrop.

The Provision Company, open for breakfast, lunch, and dinner, is a very comfortable place for families.

The Meadows Restaurant is the resort's gourmet eatery for dinner. On Friday nights, The Meadows serves up a fabulous seafood buffet on a long table burdened with fresh Pacific Ocean fish, oysters, crab, and clams. And on Sundays it's the scene of a champagne brunch. Men must wear jackets here.

A few hundred yards from the lodge is Sunriver Country Mall, with restaurants and a supermarket. You'll find Chinese, Mexican, and Italian food and any number of establishments that serve sandwiches or deli fare. The supermarket is large and contains everything you need for meals in your own kitchenette.

ACTIVITIES

Twenty-eight outdoor Plexi-Pave courts; three indoor courts and five racquetball courts at the Sunriver Racquet Club. Pro shop, instruction, tournaments, rental equipment, summer tennis camps.

Two 18-hole courses. The North Course (5,911 yards, par 72) was designed by Robert Trent Jones, Jr., and is considered to be one of his best. The South Course (6,560 yards, par 72) was designed by Fred Federspiel. Both play through beautiful mountain scenery. Pro shops, instruction, clinics.

Two heated swimming pools. The Olympic-size South Pool is closest to the lodge. It has a separate wading pool with a maximum depth of one and a half feet, two spas, saunas, and changing rooms. Lessons in swimming, scuba diving, water polo, water basketball, water volleyball, and water aerobics.

Canoes can be rented at the marina for use on placid stretches of the Deschutes. Vans leave the marina daily for half-day and full-day white-water raft trips.

In the Deschutes River at Sunriver's front door. A guide service can provide half-day and full-day fishing trips on other nearby rivers.

More than 25 miles of paved bike paths snake through the Sunriver development. The Lodge Bike Shop rents more than 175 bikes ranging from a monster five-seater to tandem bikes and 10-speed, three-speed, and single-speed cruisers, some with child seats. Children's bicycles, some with training wheels, are also available.

From its large and attractive building near the marina, the Nature Center's professional staff mounts excellent exhibits on the natural history of the Cascades and high desert, including many hands-on activities for children. Snakes, lizards, birds of prey, and scorpions are on display. The Center offers an impressive schedule of classes and guided hikes.

Sunriver Stables has guided horseback rides throughout the summer and on winter weekends. Trails wander over the Deschutes River meadows and into the pine forests. Longer rides afford wonderful views of the Cascade Mountains. Day trips, wagon ride cookouts, and riding lessons are available.

An indoor lap pool, a spa, saunas, and an exercise room with a full range of equipment at the Sunriver Racquet Club; daily aerobics classes.

In August, the Music Festival brings professional musicians to Sunriver for a series of classical music concerts. Bus tours to the nearby High Desert Museum and to Mt. Bachelor for a chair-lift ride leave the lodge five days a week.

Sunriver is only 18 miles from the Mt. Bachelor ski area. The ski season extends from mid-November until mid-spring. The lodge operates a shuttle to the slopes. The Sunriver ice-skating rink operates during the winter, and sleigh rides are offered over snow-covered lanes. Ten miles of groomed cross-country trails on the golf course; equipment rentals and lessons.

FOR CHILDREN: Between 9 A.M. and noon on summer and holiday season mornings, the "Kid's Klub" is in session for children 6 through 12. Kid's Klub activities include field trips to places like Benham Falls or a fish hatchery, canoeing and swimming, arts and crafts, and games. Lunch is included in the fee.

Organized activities for teenagers include inner-tube floats, trivia contests, Frisbee, golf, bicycle rodeos, video game competitions, and dances.

Sunriver also has a fully licensed day-care center, "The Playroom," for children 3 months through 10 years of age.

Near the lodge is a fine children's playground with great equipment, including a wonderful log stockade and fort.

NICETIES: The Sunriver Country Mall has a wide variety of shops where you will find the clothing you forgot to bring or the perfect gift for that person back home. You can even drop in on the stockbrokers to check on your stocks.

OF INTEREST NEARBY: The Oregon High Desert Museum, 8 miles from Sunriver, has excellent exhibits on the natural and social history of the region. Lectures on birds of prey and feedings of the Museum's two otters, Bert and Ernie, are scheduled daily.

Lava River Cave is three miles from Sunriver. Bring flashlights, or rent a lantern at the cave, or better yet, do both and conduct your own tour of a mile-long lava tube formed thousands of years ago.

The Lava Cast Forest, nine miles up a good dirt road off Highway 97, provides an opportunity to walk over a lava flow on good paths and view the largest collection of lava cast trees in the world. Picnic tables and potable water are available at the parking lot.

Drive to the top of a volcanic cinder cone at Lava Butte, which is skirted by Highway 97 between Sunriver and Bend, Oregon. The Lava Lands Visitors Center is at the foot of the cinder cone.

FOR MORE INFORMATION: Write Sunriver Lodge and Resort, Sunriver, OR 97707, or call (800) 547-3922; in Oregon call (800) 452-6874 or (503) 593-1221.

Rancho Bernardo Inn
San Diego, California

Tucked away in the San Pasqual Mountains 30 miles northeast of downtown San Diego on the road to Escondido is an oasis called the Rancho Bernardo Inn. The inn is perfectly situated to take advantage of San Diego's world-renowned weather, with an average year-round temperature of 70 degrees, cool nights, and more hours of sunshine than any other major resort area of the country.

Within a 45-minute drive are Sea World, the San Diego Zoo, Wild Animal Park, Old Town, La Jolla, Del Mar, Mexico, sailing, fishing, and Pacific Ocean beaches—prime ingredients for a first-class family vacation.

But even without all the attractions nearby, the Inn would be a destination in its own right. The decor is a mix of Indian, Mexican, and early California motifs that impart an atmosphere of genuine warmth like that found in an intimate inn. Families feel comfortable here.

The Inn's grounds are abloom with tropical plants. Eight "haciendas"—two- and three-story buildings—house 287 guest rooms. Many of the courtyards between these buildings have fountains that delight both ear and eye. The Inn has an assortment of guest amenities, including reading and game rooms and car rental. Separate shops serve the golfer, the tennis player, and the person looking for a tasteful gift.

Many families return year after year for the atmosphere, the setting, and the facilities. Another attraction is the Inn's outstanding children's program, which operates during major holidays and the summer.

ACCOMMODATIONS: **$$$** Rooms are tastefully furnished; most have patios or balconies that overlook the golf courses or swimming pools. The one- and two-bedroom suites are particularly attractive for families, and children under 13 are free. Special golf and tennis packages are available.

DINING: El Bizcocho is the gourmet dining room, serving French cuisine for dinner and an elegant champagne brunch on Sundays. The Veranda Room, a charming restaurant with some patio dining, offers breakfast, lunch, and dinner at moderate prices. Both restaurants have sweeping views of the golf courses and mountains beyond.

ACTIVITIES

 Twelve hard-surface courts, four lighted and two designed for major tournaments. Five-day and two-day tennis colleges.

 Four golf courses. The par-72 West Course was the site of the 1963 San Diego Open. In addition, there are three nine-hole executive courses that offer a variety of conditions. Five golf pros, clinics, and group and private lessons.

Two outbound pools.

Aerobics and fitness classes held several times a day.

 Volleyball, badminton, Ping-Pong, and shuffleboard. Over holidays, there are movie screenings for adults and children, theme cocktail parties, fun runs, and special buffets.

FOR CHILDREN: Over the Christmas and Easter holidays and in August, the Inn operates a free children's holiday camp for children from 4 to 17, and a full-blown camp it is. The program is run by Jeff Crosswhite, an outdoor educator and recreation leader who hires an experienced staff, including outdoor educators, a crafts specialist, and college recreation majors. Crosswhite and his crew have all the parent-reassuring bona fides—education degrees, first-aid certificates, resuscitation training, water safety training, and so on.

The camp runs from 9 A.M. to 9 P.M. daily. About 18 children take part each day, for a kid-to-counselor ratio of nearly four-to-one. A guest suite has been converted into a well-equipped playroom for the program's use.

The staff divides its charges into three groups, ages 4 to 7, 8 to

11, and 12 to 17. The groups each have some separate activities, but one of the really effective aspects of this program is the frequent combining of the three age groups.

A typical day starts at 9 A.M. with table games, followed by arts and crafts, swimming, and a scavenger hunt for everyone.

Some parents return from their morning's activities and pick up their children for lunch. Other parents deposit children and head off for a quiet lunch together while the children eat with their counselors on the patio at The Veranda Room (there's a charge for meals).

Lunch is followed by ball games and other activities for all age groups. At 2 P.M., the children dress and assemble for supervised water games. After plenty of swim time, the afternoon starts to wind down, and the older children go off to have a game of soccer while the younger children settle down for story time.

In late afternoon, the older children may play hide-and-seek or miniature golf, while the younger children are busy with arts and crafts. Before dinner the older children stage a basketball game, and the younger children act out their fantasies in a drama class.

A group dinner is served at 6 P.M. in The Veranda Room, although many children eat with their parents. In the evening, children stage a carnival with games, costumes, prizes, and treats. At 9 P.M., exhausted counselors give up their charges to their parents.

NICETIES: Rancho Bernardo Inn's service is outstanding. The staff goes out of its way to be accommodating, as one guest discovered when she offhandedly mentioned that she had hoped there would be more scheduled aerobics classes. The next day her wish was fulfilled.

An unusually nice touch is the high tea served daily from 4 to 5 P.M. in the Inn's Music Room. On Sundays, complimentary Bloody Marys and screwdrivers are served there.

OF INTEREST NEARBY: San Diego's Sea World, a 100-acre marine park, is sure to delight all family members. The shows are fun, and there is even a marvelous children's playground, Cap'n Kids World, to enchant the younger children.

Balboa Park is San Diego's cultural center, with galleries, gardens, and museums. Mission Bay Park is San Diego's recreational "heart" and has miles of beach.

San Diego Zoo is renowned for its natural habitats. The Zoo's separate Wild Animal Park is located within five miles of the Inn. It features bird and animal shows, a hiking trail, and a 50-minute monorail ride that gets you close to the hundreds of animals that roam freely within the park.

Pacific beaches come in every size and shape. One of the largest and least crowded is Torrey Pines State Beach, beneath the cliffs of the well-known Torrey Pines State Park. Stop at Torrey Pines Glider Port to watch the hang gliders.

The nearby community of La Jolla has attractions for the whole family—beaches, coves, snorkeling, scuba diving, surfboarding, shopping, restaurants, galleries, a contemporary art museum, and even a children's museum.

Scripps Institute of Oceanography, in northern La Jolla, has a small aquarium and an outdoor tidal pool.

FOR MORE INFORMATION: Write Rancho Bernardo Inn, 17550 Bernardo Oaks Drive, San Diego, CA 92128, or call (800) 854-1065; in California call (800) 542-6096.

Dana Point Resort
Dana Point, California

On a bluff overlooking the Pacific Ocean, midway between Los Angeles and San Diego, is a luxury resort that manages to evoke both the charm of Cape Cod and the casual ambience of southern California. Surrounded by 42 acres of brilliant, emerald green public park, the Dana Point Resort promises guests that "the view follows you everywhere," and it never disappoints.

Dana Point Harbor was discovered in 1835 and has long provided shelter to yachtsmen, but it only became a destination for tourists traveling overland when the hotel opened in 1987. The area below the hotel now draws day-trippers from all over southern California who are attracted by a 2,500-slip harbor with two separate marinas, a fine public beach and park, an interpretive center, and three-themed shopping area: The Pavilion, Mariner's Village, and Dana Wharf.

The Dana Point Resort is perfectly situated to provide easy access to the tourist attractions of both Los Angeles and San Diego. But at the same time it provides a soothing refuge from the congestion and fast pace of southern California; you need never leave the premises to have a good time.

ACCOMMODATIONS: $ to $$$ Dana Point's 350 rooms and suites are beautifully decorated in colors that evoke the seaside setting—blues, grays, and sands. Most rooms have private terraces; all have remote-control TVs, clock radios, two phones, lounging robes, and twice-daily maid service.

The concierge level accommodations offers such added amenities as complimentary continental breakfast, cocktails, and desserts. For budget-minded travelers, the Cape Cod rooms on the top floor are the least expensive. Special promotions during slow periods (just before and after Christmas, for instance) can make a stay here inexpensive.

DINING: Breakfast, brunch, and dinner are served in Watercolors Restaurant, which has gorgeous harbor views. The chef specializes in California cuisine, with an emphasis on inventively prepared fresh vegetables and seafood. The Sunday Champagne Brunch draws diners from as far away as Los Angeles. An elegant afternoon tea is served Wednesdays through Sundays in Lantern Bay Lounge.

The children's menus are printed on Frisbees, which they may take home. Room service is available from 6 A.M. until 2 A.M. Poolside service is available at lunch.

There are numerous other restaurants in Dana Point and nearby Laguna Beach.

ACTIVITIES

 Three lighted cement courts, slow to medium; rental equipment, court fees.

 Privileges at five nearby courses, ranging from classic Scottish links to short executive courses.

Two pools with ocean views, adjacent hot tubs. Swimming in the Pacific Ocean from the beach at Doheny State Beach.

Charters, rental sailboats available at Dana Point Harbor, just below the hotel. Parasailing, wind-surfing equipment available.

Deep–sea fishing expeditions available from Dana Wharf Sportfishing; half-day, twilight, and three-quarter-day excursions.

Rental bicycles available for use on nearby streets and paved biking trails.

Miles of walking trails leave from the park in front of the hotel. Dana Point offers an excellent vantage point for watching the migration of California gray whales from January to mid-March. A naturalist and whale expert offers lectures Saturday nights during the whale season.

Health club with sauna, steam rooms, Jacuzzi, workout equipment, massage therapists. Outdoor basketball court, Ping-Pong tables, horseshoe pits. Fitness parcourse in neighboring park.

Piano music most nights in Lantern Bay Lounge; live music and dancing on weekends in Burton's. Poolside orchestral concerts are held monthly between April and September.

FOR CHILDREN: "Camp Cowabunga," the resort's children's program for 5- to 12-year-olds, operates from 10 A.M. to 4 P.M. and 6:30 P.M. to 9:30 P.M. every day during the summer and on all weekends through the rest of the year. There's a fee.

A typical day starts with a special coded message with the day's activities slipped under your door. Participants gather in the camp's playroom (Room 1055) or at the tennis courts for such activities as kite-making and flying. T-shirt art, walks, group tennis lessons, pool games, and arts and crafts. Field trips go to the nearby Orange County Marine Institute, Doheny Beach State Park Interpretive Center, and the *Pilgrim,* a replica of Henry Dana's tall ship.

In the evenings, children can eat dinner together, make origami or jewelry, play video games, watch movies, and go on a moonlit hike to the state park's amphitheater, where counselors will regale them with stories, point out constellations, and toast marshmallows. Baby-sitting can be arranged for younger children.

There's a terrific playground and basketball court just down the hill from the resort in a public park.

NICETIES: Complimentary coffee and muffins are served each morning in the lobby.

The concierge keeps a selection of board games, basketballs, volleyballs, kites, and croquet sets for use by guests.

OF INTEREST NEARBY: Doheny State Beach, Lantern Bay Park, and the Dana Point Marina, all adjacent to the resort grounds, offer plenty of activities for families. The Orange County Marine Institute has aquariums featuring local specimens and offers opportunities for hands-on learning experiences. Excursions are offered on the *Pilgrim*, which is moored at the Institute. You can also spend hours exploring the tidepools nearby or just watching the windsurfers.

The Mission at San Juan Capistrano is just a few minutes away.

Laguna Beach, just north of Dana Point, has scores of unique shops along its scenic streets.

Disneyland and Knotts Berry Farm are each about an hour from the resort.

FOR MORE INFORMATION: Write Dana Point Resort, 25135 Park Lantern, Dana Point, CA 92629 or call (800) 243-1166 (800-533-9748 in California); FAX: (714) 661-3688.

Hilton Hawaiian Village
Honolulu, Oahu, Hawaii

Just a few generations ago, Waikiki was an untidy collection of taro patches. Today, its beach has become an icon of international tourism and is one of the most visited vacation destinations in the whole Pacific region.

If you want to be where the action is on Waikiki, there is no better place than the Hilton Hawaiian Village, a "has-it-all" resort with something for everyone. Recent renovations have given the Hilton a decidedly Hawaiian ambiance with acres of lush tropical gardens, displays of live native wildlife, and a 10,000-square foot, two-tier swimming pool complete with lava waterfalls, and beds of tropical plants.

Among the big lures for families: a free, fun-packed children's program. And Hilton Hawaiian Village is also a shopper's paradise, with scores of shops and boutiques on the premises. The many shops in the Waikiki neighborhood are only a short walk away.

ACCOMMODATIONS: $$$ to $$$$ The hotel has more than 2,500 rooms in four towers—Rainbow, Tapa, Diamond Head, and Ali'i—and is the largest resort on Oahu. A whole floor of each tower is given over to non-smoking rooms. The rooms are spacious and beautifully decorated. Many have a view of Waikiki Beach.

The Ali'i Tower provides the most deluxe accommodations, with many special services included—preferential seating in hotel restaurants and nightclubs, full concierge services, and its own health club, sauna, and swimming pool.

There is no charge for children when they occupy their parents' room. (State law limits room occupancy to four).

DINING: The Hilton Hawaiian Village has 10 restaurants. Bali by the Sea is the headline restaurant, with elegant continental cuisine and many awards to its credit. The Golden Dragon serves up magnificent Chinese cuisine, including Imperial Beggar's Chicken and Peking Duck.

Other restaurants offer more casual dining. The Rainbow Lanai Restaurant features nouvelle Hawaiian and Pacific cuisine and has many menu items that are low in sodium, cholesterol, and calories. The Village Steak and Seafood Restaurant offers a daunting seafood buffet every Friday and Sunday.

Children's menus are available in all restaurants.

ACTIVITIES

A free shuttle transports guests to the Turtle Bay Hilton and Country Club on the north shore of Oahu for tennis, golf and horseback riding.

The huge Super Pool is a magnet for hotel guests, and Waikiki Beach is only a few steps away. The small, quiet Hilton lagoon is a perfect place for small children.

Surfboard and sailboat rentals at the beach. The Hilton *Rainbow I* catamaran sails on champagne breakfast cruises, a sunset sail that includes dinner and dancing, and tours of Pearl Harbor. Excursions are also available in Atlantis submarines.

Guided walking tours of Waikiki and the crater of Diamond Head.

Lei making, hula lessons, and instruction in such ancient Hawaiian games as stone rolling and spear sliding. Some evenings, Don Ho and his Polynesian review hold forth in the Dome Showroom, and on others there's a Polynesian magic show. The Tropics Surf Club features top-flight Hollywood entertainers. And every Tuesday afternoon the Polynesian Cultural Center brings Polynesian dancers, musicians, and artisans to the Hilton's Village Green for a demonstration of one of the rich Polynesian cultures.

Every Friday evening a musical and dance tribute to King David Kalalaua, the "Merrie Monarch," is held on the Super Pool terrace, climaxed by a fireworks show over Waikiki Beach. On other evenings, terrace entertainment includes the Chinese Lion Dance or hula dancing by Hawaiian children.

FOR CHILDREN: A free children's program is available year-round Monday through Saturday for children 3 to 12 years of age. A cruise on the hotel catamaran, tropical bird shows, Hawaiian storytelling and games, treasure hunts, and a children's "olympics" are among the hotel-based activities.

The program also includes excursions to the Honolulu Zoo, Waikiki Aquarium, Dole Pineapple Cannery, and the Children's Museum. Parents are welcome on off-site excursions if there is room on the van. Lunch and snacks are included.

NICETIES: The Disney channel and three other cable channels are free in rooms.

The staff of the Hilton makes genuine efforts to impart some of Hawaii's rich culture to guests.

OF INTEREST NEARBY: Pearl Harbor, site of the Arizona Memorial, is the most visited tourist site in Honolulu.

Other excursions popular with families include the Honolulu Zoo and Aquarium, the Sea Life Park at Makapuu Point, the Dole Pineapple plant, the Polynesian Cultural Center, and the Bishop Museum, with its world-famous collection of Hawaiian and Polynesian art and artifacts.

FOR MORE INFORMATION: Write Hilton Hawaiian Village, 2005 Kalia Road, Honolulu, HI 96815-1999 or call (800) HILTONS.

Kahala Hilton
Honolulu, Oahu, Hawaii

On the opposite side of Diamond Head and 15 minutes from the hubbub of Waikiki is the Kahala Hilton. Exit the brash commercialism of Honolulu and enter the quiet elegance of one of Honolulu's best hotels.

Built in the 1960s by Conrad Hilton and maintained as one of the flagships of the Hilton fleet, the Kahala Hilton has been the Honolulu hotel of choice for a generation of political leaders, big-name entertainers, and captains of industry. When two-thirds of the guests are repeat customers, you know there's something special.

The Kahala district of Honolulu is an area of expensive homes and the Waialae Country Club, site of the annual Hawaiian Open. It is also the historic site of the 1795 invasion of the Island of Oahu by King Kamehameha the Great in his successful quest to unite the Hawaiian Islands.

The six and a half acres of hotel grounds sit between the Country Club and the ocean. Waters from the springs that gave the Waialae-Kahala area its name flow through the gardens of the hotel and cascade down a rock wall into a one and a half acre saltwater lagoon. The grounds are beautifully landscaped with dense tropical foliage. The lagoon is populated by reef fish, jackass penguins, sea turtles, and two dolphins.

Beyond the lagoon is the hotel's oval swimming pool, and beyond that are 800 feet of perfectly kept beach with a view of Diamond Head from one end and Koko Head from the other.

The dolphins provide for rare excitement. By day, they dart playfully about the lagoon and surface occasionally to greet a guest. By night, they move swiftly and silently through the water; the ambient light catches the occasional flank or tail. Watching them is a magical experience. The pool and lagoon are only a few feet apart, and the deck between them is just above water level. So it is possible to slip into the pool with the water up to your chin and peer across the deck toward the lagoon and find a dolphin staring back at you. The penguins have a small pool of their own, and the sea turtles move slowly around a pool that is close to the Hala Terrace Restaurant.

ACCOMMODATIONS: $$$$ In an age of expensive hotel land and pint-size hotel rooms, the Kahala Hilton's 369 rooms are unusually spacious. Each has a sitting area with comfortable chairs and a desk in addition to two double beds or a king-size bed. Furthermore, each room has a large dressing area separated into his and her domains. Rooms look out on the lush hotel grounds, the ocean, the hotel lagoon, or mountains. Some of the Kahala Hilton's rooms open onto the beach and are particularly suited for active families.

Rooms without balconies and with views of the mountains or hotel grounds are the least expensive. A wide variety of luxury suites is available. There is no charge for children sharing a room with parents (limit of four persons to a room).

DINING: The hotel has three restaurants and a poolside snack bar.

The Maile Restaurant is world renowned and the consistent winner of dining awards from travel magazines. In its plush setting, kimono-clad waitresses provide the best of service, and guests order from a continental menu with dashes of Hawaiian and Oriental cuisine. The Maile is open for dinner, and men are requested to wear jackets, although ties are optional. The chefs of the Maile prepare a special Sunday Buffet Brunch served beside the dolphin lagoon.

The more casual Hala Terrace looks out on the beach. It features a variety of American favorites and is open for all meals. On Sunday evenings the Terrace serves up a sumptuous buffet.

The casual Plumeria Café overlooks the grand drive in front of the hotel. It serves lighter lunches and dinners. The Plumeria's pastries are fantastic—pineapple–macadamia nut loaf, macadamia nut cream pie, fresh fruit tarts, and chocolate mousse cake.

The Gazebo at the poolside serves drinks and snacks. Its milk shakes, sandwiches, and fruit salads are popular with children.

Children's menus are available in all restaurants and from room service.

ACTIVITIES

 Privileges at six lighted courts at the exclusive Maunalua Bay Club, seven minutes away by complimentary hotel shuttle van. The Club occupies a two-acre beachfront property.

 Public courses nearby.

 The hotel is located on Maunalua Bay, which is well protected from the prevailing winds. The ocean here is usually an ideal place for younger children to swim. The hotel pool is marvelous, and its proximity to the dolphin lagoon allows children to keep track of the dolphins' antics and do dolphin imitations of their own. The dolphins perform three shows daily.

At the beach, guests will find rafts and equipment for snorkeling, kayaking, and pedalboating.

Spa, sauna, exercise equipment, and snack bar at the Maunalua Bay Club.

Music for dancing is performed nightly except Sunday at the Maile Restaurant. Six nights a week, the Terrace is the scene of one of the longest-running floor shows in Honolulu, the Danny Kaleikini Hawaiian Revue.

FOR CHILDREN: "Kamp Kahala" is the Kahala Hilton's children's program for 6- to 12-year-olds. The day camp–style program operates during the summer and in the Christmas and Easter vacation periods. The program is free; the only charges are for transportation for outings and admission fees.

The program starts at 9 A.M., when a hostess meets parents and children at the penguin pool. The program breaks for lunch at 11:30 (children eat with their parents) and resumes at 12:30, ending at 3 P.M.

Activities include arts and crafts, beach activities, and excursions. Children learn traditional Hawaiian games, make masks, and do origami or mosaic work. They build sand castles and paint with sand at the beach. Excursions may be to one of several excellent beach parks, Sea Life Park, or the Honolulu Zoo.

In-room baby-sitting is easily arranged.

NICETIES: A delicious pineapple, chilled and sliced for immediate enjoyment, is delivered to your room on arrival.

Dressing robes and slippers are provided in each room.

A delightful afternoon tea is served daily in the Plumeria Cafe.

The hotel staff members are exceptionally friendly and go far out of their way to be helpful. Guests who have returned to the Kahala Hilton repeatedly can all recall special services that have been performed for them, like the batch of favorite cookies served up by a chef or the orchid brought from an employee's home garden.

OF INTEREST NEARBY: The hotel's shuttle bus takes guests to downtown Waikiki. Among the attractions of interest to families are the Honolulu Zoo and Aquarium, the Sea Life Park at Makapuu Point, Pearl Harbor and the *Arizona* Memorial, The Polynesian Cultural Center, and the Bishop Museum, with its world-famous collection of Hawaiian and Polynesian artifacts.

FOR MORE INFORMATION: Write the Kahala Hilton Hotel, 5000 Kahala Ave., Honolulu, Oahu, HI 96816, or phone (800) 367-2525 or (808) 734-2211.

Kona Village
Ka'upulehu-Kona, The Big Island, Hawaii

The drive from the Kona Airport to Kona Village, on Hawaii's Big Island, crosses ancient lava fields; no people inhabit this lunar landscape. But tucked away in a pocket of land the lava flows missed lies Kona Village. It is a true hideaway, with no other resorts and no human settlements in the vicinity.

Kona Village is on the ocean at the site of the ancient Hawaiian village of Manuahi. Today, the historic remains of this site are integrated into the resort, making this a place of archaeological significance as well as one of natural beauty. The ancient village people thrived by fishing and trading; the modern resort is built around pools of water that were the fish ponds of Hawaiian kings. Petroglyphs are found over more than 15 acres of Kona Village; guided walks help visitors explore these historic sites.

Families have the option of being busy every moment of the day or of relaxing in the hammock outside their *hale* (guest house) and enjoying the tropical beauty of this world-class resort. Fifty percent of the guests each year are return visitors. Few would think of challenging the resort's claim that it's "the most dreamed about place on earth."

ACCOMMODATIONS: $$$ to $$$$ Kona Village is built around the ancient stone platforms of the historic Hawaiian village. Guests stay in one of 125 *hales* scattered throughout the 82-acre village site. Some perch on the side of ponds, others face the beach, and still others are in lush tropical vegetation or in lava gardens.

Hale architecture was inspired by traditional Micronesian and Melanesian housing; the influence is reflected in the shape of each unit, in the thatched roofs, and in details like rope lashing on moldings and door frames. Some *hales* have the shape and roof line of Fijian or Samoan traditional houses; others mimic Tahitian, New Hebridian, or Maori housing styles.

Hale interiors are smashing. Bedspreads and pillowcases are silk-screened or hand painted by local artists. Much of the furniture and accessories are the works of Hawaiian and Pacific island craftsmen. *Hales* vary from two-person units to two-bedroom suites for up to five people. Many *hales* have lanais, or screened-in porches. Ceiling fans and trade winds do the cooling; there are no air-conditioners. All *hales* are equipped with small refrigerators and coffee makers. In keeping with Kona Village's get-away-from-it-all philosophy, there are no phones, television sets, or locks on the doors (safe-deposit boxes are available for valuables).

The resort operates on the full American Plan. Children's rates are available and rise with age. There is a minimum stay requirement in the Christmas season.

DINING: Meals are usually taken in the Hale Maona, a dining room inspired by New Hebrides longhouse architecture. Rare 19th-century murals depicting Hawaiian life hang in the dining room. Breakfast is served from 7:15 to 9:45 A.M. Lunch is served buffet style on a patio adjacent to the dining room. Buffet tables are laden with fresh seafood and salads. Box lunches can be arranged if you're going on an outing.

Dinner menus feature local fresh seafood, veal, roast beef, and steaks. Successful fishermen can have their catch prepared for their own evening meal. A *keiki*'s, or children's, menu is available, with fish, chicken, and the ubiquitous hamburger.

Guests book for one of three seatings at dinner. The 6 P.M. seating is recommended for families with children.

Some evening meals feature themes, such as Luau Night, with pig the centerpiece of a traditional South Pacific feast, and the Western Paniolo Steak Fry. At least once during your stay you'll want to eat dinner at the Hale Samoa, which features exquisite cuisine in a grownups-only setting (there's a $10 surcharge).

If you desire a dinner that will provide memories for years to come, consider the dinner cruise aboard the 54-foot luxury sailing yacht *Makani Kai* (there's an extra charge).

The Kona Village dress code absolutely forbids jackets, ties, or fancy dress at any meal.

ACTIVITIES

Three lighted Laykold courts, no court fees. Rental equipment, group and private lessons. The Activities Shack displays a matchup sheet for persons looking for tennis partners of equal ability.

Privileges at several outstanding golf courses at other resorts on the Kona Coast.

Two freshwater pools, including one used mainly by families. The sandy beach adjacent to the Activities Shack is the best place for ocean swimming. There are six additional beaches, each with its own character. Snorkeling gear is available in children's as well as adult sizes. The Shipwreck Bar at the main pool is the converted hull of the *New Moon*, a 42-foot schooner owned by Johnno Jackson, the founder of Kona Village.

Small sailboats and outrigger canoes are available at no extra charge. There are daily cruises on a glass-bottom boat, *Hooloko*, and a daily sail and snorkeling cruise goes out on a 38-foot catamaran; the half-day trip visits a secluded beach and the world-class coral reefs off the Kona Coast. Quality snorkeling gear, snorkeling instruction, a marine life lecture, and refreshments are included in the cruise fee. An extra-charge sailing school is available to teenagers and adults who are beginners or novice sailors; the fleet ranges from small Sunfish and Lasers to a 38-foot catamaran and a 54-foot sloop.

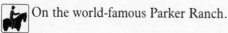

On the world-famous Parker Ranch.

Programs on Hawaiian weaving, Hawaiian toys, origami, sand art, feather crafts, seed and shell work, and Hawaiian quilting; pictograph tours; hula or ukulele lessons; guided walks; imu ceremony; poi pounding; Hawaiian games; fishing contests. Ping-Pong, volleyball, and shuffleboard equipment available at the Activities Shack.

In the evening cocktails are served at a bar in the Hale Samoa, which is also the scene of nightly music for entertainment and dancing.

Kona Coast waters are superb for scuba diving. Daily charters are available, and night dives are made once each week. A range of scuba instruction is offered, from a single introductory dive to full NAUI open-water II certification (seven-day minimum). Special family instruction rates are available.

FOR CHILDREN: Some families, or *'ohana*, have been coming to Kona Village for three generations, attracted here by the truly authentic Hawaiian experience. It's more than simple arts and crafts; it is Hawaiian people sharing their history and culture through activities that are entertaining and enjoyable. Staff members like Auntie Eleanor have been showing children how to play Hawaiian games and string leis for years.

Activities offered year-round include such novel pursuits as paddling outrigger canoes and exploring petroglyphs. For children under 5, accompanied by an adult or baby-sitter, the activities are numerous and range from hula lessons to fishing contests to coconut husking. Those 6 to 12 engage in tidal pool exploration, ukulele lessons, star-gazing, kite flying, and a host of other activities. For teenagers, there's snorkeling, volleyball, sailing, scuba diving, tennis, and swimming—and much more.

Baby-sitting arrangements can be made on 24 hours' notice. A supervised children's dinner is offered at 5:30 P.M. daily, followed by social activities until 9 P.M.

NICETIES: You are welcomed in Hawaiian style with a lei and tropical drink. Registration includes an orientation to the resort. Throughout your stay, you are pampered in many small ways, such as fresh Kona coffee beans and coffee-making equipment in your room and turn-down service at night.

Families will appreciate the washing machine and dryer on the premises.

The Island Copra Trading Company is the resort's general store. It stocks film, swim and resort wear, beverages, sundries, and gifts.

OF INTEREST NEARBY: Deep-sea fishing, circle island tours, and volcano tours can be arranged through the concierge. Rental cars can be arranged at the resort for day trips around the Big Island.

FOR MORE INFORMATION: Write Kona Village, P.O. Box 1299, Ka'upulehu-Kona, HI 96745, or phone (808) 325-5555 or (800) 367-5290.

Mauna Kea Beach Hotel
Kohala Coast, The Big Island, Hawaii

There are only a few dozen truly world-class resorts, and Mauna Kea Beach Hotel is indisputably among them. Built by Laurance S. Rockefeller in the early 1960s, this luxury resort features a spectacular setting, fine surroundings, and the attention to service one expects of establishments in its league.

Rockefeller obtained a 99-year lease from the famous Parker Ranch for this superbly situated bayside land with a perfect crescent beach on the Kohala Coast of the island of Hawaii. The island itself is one of vast contrasts dominated by two gigantic mountains, both over 13,000 feet at the summit. One is snow covered, the other an active volcano, and between them stretches a vast prairie.

Renowned architects and decorators created the hotel, golf course, and tennis courts out of scrub grazing-land and lava flow. The hotel has an atrium-style design, with fish pools, waterfalls, and palm trees and tropical vegetation at the base. A half-million plants were brought in as part of the landscaping effort. Robert Trent Jones Sr. designed an award-winning golf course, which he considered to be one of his best.

Rockefeller obtained more than 1,600 art objects from Hawaii, the Pacific rim, and the Orient to place in the public areas of the hotel. A seventh-century pink granite Buddha from India is probably the resort's most valuable possession. (A matching sculpture from the same temple site is in the collection of the Art Institute of

Chicago.) A guide to the hotel's art can be found in each room, and twice-weekly tours by an art historian are available.

Mauna Kea Beach Hotel boasts one of the highest staff-to-guest ratios in the world, with 310 rooms and 800 employees.

ACCOMMODATIONS: $$$$ Simplicity and elegance are a hard combination to achieve, but the accommodations in the low- and medium-rise buildings at the Mauna Kea meet this goal. In the walk from the elevator to your room you pass art objects from New Guinea, Fiji, or Thailand. The room furnishings are made from teak and willow. Floral serigraphs or originals by a contemporary Hawaiian artist, John Young, grace the walls. Each room has floor-to-ceiling wooden-louvered panels and sliding glass doors that open to a private lanai with views of the ocean or mountain.

The Mauna Kea offers the Modified American Plan, which includes breakfast and dinner, and the European Plan (no meals included). There is no meal charge for children under 5; children 5 to 12 pay reduced rates.

DINING: The Mauna Kea has four restaurants that have won many awards over the years, as well as snack bars at the beach and the golf course.

The Terrace features Japanese-style *teppan yaki* cooking in the evening and a renowned lunchtime buffet with as many as 150 items.

The Pavilion is open for breakfast and dinner. The Pavilion's flagstone terrace faces the sea and is an exceedingly pleasant place to take breakfast. Evenings feature contemporary cuisine and music for dancing.

The Garden's menu is based on Hawaiian regional cuisine and varies daily with the availability of fresh ingredients. The Batik's menu features the cuisines of southern France and northern Italy.

The weekly luau feast is held on Tuesday evenings at a special site above the sea a short walk from the hotel. The menu includes the traditional pig with short ribs; steak, fish, and chicken are thrown in for good measure.

If you prefer a quiet dinner alone, you can order from the room service menu and let the resort's attentive staff serve a feast at the table on your lanai.

Through the years the Mauna Kea has cultivated and encouraged local Hawaiian sources to supply the ingredients for its kitchens. Local herb and spice growers, a fish smokehouse, fruit growers, abalone fishermen, and cane-syrup producers have been given their start or helped along by the resort's chefs as a way of guaranteeing the finest fresh ingredients for the hotel's tables.

Some of the restaurants require jackets for men and dresses for women in the evening; The Terrace and The Pavilion do not. A children's menu is available at all restaurants.

ACTIVITIES

Eleven Plexi-Pave courts in the resort's 13-acre oceanside tennis park, two in the beachfront wing. These facilities are highly praised by *Tennis* and *World Tennis* magazines. Lessons, clinics, round-robin tournaments, and partners arranged through a nationally recognized tennis rating system are available. Tennis packages are offered from May through October.

The 18-hole golf course has been selected as Hawaii's finest and as one of America's 100 greatest by *Golf Digest*. The famous third hole with its tee shot over the crashing Pacific surf is one of "America's 100 greatest holes," according to *Golf* magazine. Four tees at each hole make this a challenging course for golfers of every ability. Golf packages are available from April through mid-December.

In the pool and at the beach, which has a gentle surf. Scuba-diving and snorkeling lessons daily in the pool. Coral reefs stretch for 20 miles along the coast, and underwater visibility is sometimes 200 feet.

The Beach Activities Desk has the equipment necessary to enjoy snorkeling, sailing in 12-foot Lasers, wind surfing, and boogie boarding. Wind-surfing and sailing lessons.

Charters available for deep-sea fishing.

After dinner, walk along the torch-lit trail toward North Pointe and stop at a coastal area lighted by floodlights to watch the manta rays "fly" back and forth under the water as they feed on microscopic organisms.

The Mauna Kea has its own stables on the nearby Parker Ranch, the largest privately owned ranch in America. Guided trail rides are available five days a week. Picnic and sunset rides.

Fitness center with Lifecycles, Nautilus equipment; aerobic exercises every day, and water exercise classes three days a week. An 18-station exercise trail and a hilly two-mile jogging trail skirt the golf course. Sauna and massage facilities.

Craft activities or outings daily. Hawaiian lei making, flower arranging, *lauhala* weaving, and quilting instruction are frequently offered. Shuffleboard, croquet, and volleyball equipment available; card games scheduled. An art historian leads two tours a week and introduces guests to the resort's impressive art collection.

Nightly dancing in the Pavilion and under the stars on the Batik terrace. Movies are shown three nights a week, and buttered popcorn is served. Stargazing is offered once a week.

The resort can arrange helicopter sightseeing, full- or half-day deep-sea fishing charters, and hunting expeditions for wild boar, bighorn sheep, or game birds on the slopes of Mauna Kea.

FOR CHILDREN: The complimentary children's program is designed for children ages 6 to 11. It operates from mid-June through Labor Day and in the Christmas and Easter holiday periods. The program starts at 8:30 A.M., includes lunch, and ends at 4:30 P.M. Evening programs are also available, from 6:15 to 9 P.M., and include a children's dinner in one of the restaurants.

Morning activities generally start with games or a scavenger hunt and move on to hikes, beach activities, or fishing. Lunches are taken at The Terrace or at picnic spots. The after-lunch pace allows for quieter activities like crafts or movies and picks up again in mid-afternoon with swimming at the resort's pool.

The evening children's program starts with dinner and ends with movies.

Baby-sitting can be arranged for younger children. The resort requires an advance notice of 24 hours.

NICETIES: Everyone receives a fresh flower lei on arrival.

All rooms have cool cotton *yukatas*, or Japanese hand-screened summer kimonos, for lounging.

Turn-down service and an orchid on the pillow are special evening touches.

You may not be aware of some things that make your stay more pleasant—like the custom room-service carts that move silently or the resort's computerized guest history program that keeps records on each guest's preferences and needs.

OF INTEREST NEARBY: There are many historic sites in the area. Ancient Hawaiian temples are located just a mile from the hotel. In the other direction are additional sites of archaeological significance, including petroglyph fields and ancient fish ponds.

Sleepy coastal villages and the Lapakahi State Historical Park, with its restored Hawaiian fishing village, evoke Hawaii's pre–jet age past. The great Hawaiian king Kamehameha, who united the Hawaiian Islands, was born not far from the present-day resort. At his birthplace, Mo'okini, you can see one of the largest and oldest of the ancient Hawaiian temple platforms.

An hour away is Pu'uhonua O Honaunau, the City of Refuge, one of the best restored of Hawaii's ancient sites and a National Historic Park. A little farther are Volcanoes National Park and the observatory on top of Mauna Kea, which has scientists in residence who help you explore the skies on summer Saturday nights.

FOR MORE INFORMATION: Write the Mauna Kea Beach Hotel, One Mauna Kea Beach Drive, Kohala Coast, HI 96743-9706, or call (800) 882-6060; in Hawaii, (808) 882-7222

THE CARIBBEAN

Casa de Campo
La Romana, Dominican Republic

This sprawling 7,000-acre resort on the southeastern coast of the Dominican Republic calls itself "the most complete resort in the Caribbean," and for once it's not hype—this resort has it all. Casa de Campo, which in Spanish means "a house in the country," was built by Gulf & Western in 1974 on the site of an old sugar plantation. It is still surrounded by 240,000 acres of sugar cane that make up what is believed to be the largest privately held sugar plantation in the world. The resort was bought from Gulf & Western in 1984 by the Fanjul family of West Palm Beach, Florida, along with the surrounding sugar cane acreage, and is operated as part of the Premier Resorts & Hotels group.

In 1988 the Dominican Republic was the third most visited destination in the Caribbean, after Puerto Rico and Jamaica. It offers easy connections to major cities in the United States, a balmy tropical climate, lush greenery, a rich history, and friendly people who make visitors feel welcome. Although the Spanish language is spoken here, many Dominicans speak English, which makes it an easy country in which to get around, and a rewarding one to explore.

Casa de Campo, with a capacity of about 1,500 guests, attracts an interesting mixture of North Americans, South Americans, and Europeans. In the summer and during the Christmas holidays, it attracts a great number of families.

ACCOMMODATIONS: **$$$** to **$$$$** Casa de Campo has 367 hotel rooms, which it calls *casitas*, most of them in low-rise groupings near the main hotel complex. The *casitas* are roomy enough for a family of two adults and two young children, and feature two double beds, a balcony or terrace, walk-in closet and dressing area, and cable television. The decor was designed by Oscar de la Renta.

Another option for families is a rental villa. The 250 rental villas range from one to six bedrooms in size and come with a full-time maid (for a modest extra charge, you can also have a butler or nanny). The exquisitely decorated villas offer the ultimate in luxury; many have private swimming pools. The maid will cook breakfast (provisions come from a central commissary). The cost of a small villa is comparable to a *casita*.

Rates are considerably lower in the summer than in the winter. Numerous package plans are offered.

DINING: There are nine restaurants on the property. In the main hotel is Tropicana, a dinner-only restaurant that frequently features a massive seafood buffet and at other times specializes in Oriental food, and Café el Patio, which serves casual breakfasts, lunches, and dinners (it's the best bet for families). Many guests take lunch at the snack bar by the main pool. Guests at the beach can grab lunch or a light snack at Las Minitas, the beachside restaurant. The Lago Grill is a casual place for breakfast and lunch.

Many of the resort's restaurants are tucked away in the scenic splendor of Altos de Chavon, the replica of a colonial village that is just a short shuttle bus ride from most accommodations. Café del Sol is a quiet spot that features oversized pizzas, sandwiches, salads, and native specialties for lunch and dinner. For casual dining at night, there's El Sombrero, which serves Mexican food. Fine gourmet cuisine is offered at night at Casa del Río, high on a cliff overhanging the Río Chavon. La Piazzetta is a lively trattoria featuring Italian cuisine and strolling musicians.

A 10 percent service charge is added to all restaurant bills.

ACTIVITIES

Nineteen courts, many lighted for night play, arranged around a country club complete with pool, pro shop, and outdoor dining facilities.

Two distinctive golf courses designed by Pete Dye. The oceanfront Teeth of the Dog course has been called the best golf course at any resort in the world by *Golf* magazine; it's the only course in the Caribbean to be rated among the world's top 100 courses. The Links, Dye's inland course, has one of the longest and broadest driving ranges anywhere. Golf country club, pro shop, restaurant, and elevated observation lounge.

 Fourteen pools. The main swimming pool complex, with its tables shielded by thatched roofs, is always a center of activity; there's a separate shallow pool for children, as well as a separate lap pool. Minitas Beach, the resort's man-made beach on the Caribbean, is an active spot during the day, with hundreds of sunbathers (and seabathers), wind surfers, and small-boat sailors.

 From the marina, rental sailboats and sailing and snorkeling trips to Catalina Island.

Deep-sea or snook fishing in the scenic Río Chavon, whose banks are dotted with palm trees and roamed by wild pigs.

 A stable of horses is available for one-, two-, and three-hour trail rides. During the polo season, from October 1 to May 31, there are three polo games weekly at the Equestrian Center. Polo instruction is also available. In between games, it's fun to visit the stables and watch the horses being lovingly cared for.

A fitness center with fully equipped gym, including exercise bicycles, roller massage, rowing machine, Universal weight-lifting center, sauna, whirlpools. Racquetball and squash courts.

Golf clinics, aerobics classes, Spanish and merengue lessons, introduction to wind surfing, and fashion shows held weekly.
    Live entertainment is offered at night in numerous lounges.

FOR CHILDREN: Casa de Campo operates one of the few full-fledged children's programs in the Caribbean. Aimed at 6- to 13-year-olds, it operates from July 1 through mid-August and over the Christmas holidays. Part-day and full-day fees are offered. Occasional activities are scheduled for teenagers.
    Many Americans who reside year-round in the area use the program as a day camp for their children. There are four bilingual

counselors and a program director, most drawn from the staff of the nearby English language school.

The program runs from 9:15 A.M. to 5 P.M., Tuesday through Sunday, with lunch provided either at Minitas Beach or Lago Grill. Children are separated into two or three age groups. Among the activities featured daily are swimming lessons, beach games, rides on a horse-drawn cart, pony and horse rides, a sailboat excursion, golf and tennis lessons, and arts and crafts. Weaving and pottery instruction is given by the artisans at Altos de Chavon.

For younger children, there's a staff of 50 nannies who can be engaged on an hourly, daily, or weekly basis.

Playgrounds are located near the golf club and at the beach.

NICETIES: There are always plenty of plush beach towels available at the main pool and at the beach.

A shuttle system links all of the resort's facilities and eliminates the need for a rental car. But four-passenger rental golf carts are very popular with families; they enable you to zoom around the property to your heart's content.

Volleyball, dominoes, checkers, chess, Scrabble, bingo, and backgammon equipment is available from the concierge.

Bottled water is provided in all the rooms.

OF INTEREST NEARBY: Altos de Chavon, the resort's $30 million replica of a 16th-century colonial village, is a site to behold. Built in a spectacular setting on the top of a cliff overlooking a gorge created by the Río Chavon, the village looks like a movie set. It draws tourists from all corners of the country with its boutiques, art galleries, restaurants, Taino Indian museum, and small stone church. International stars such as Frank Sinatra, Sergio Mendes, and Julio Iglesias are regularly featured in its 5,000-seat Grecian-style amphitheater. Professional artists are in residence for months at a time, as well as 200 boarding students at the junior college operated there by the Parsons School of Design, the Caribbean's only college-level training school in the arts.

Excursions to Santo Domingo can be arranged through a tour operator at the hotel or taken on your own. Old Santo Domingo is a treasure trove for history buffs. Many of the original 16th-century buildings have been restored and others lovingly re-created. There are also numerous museums that document the Caribbean's early Indian and European history.

FOR MORE INFORMATION: Call the Miami sales office at (800) 877-3643—in Miami, call 856-5405—or write Premier World Marketing, 2600 S.W. Third Avenue, Miami, FL 33129. The hotel's direct phone number is (809) 682-2111.

Club Med Punta Cana
Punta Cana, Dominican Republic

If the name Club Med conjures up visions of nubile 22-year-olds in string bikinis and muscle-bound Lotharios, consider these recent visitors to Club Med Punta Cana: 70 children (27 of them under the age of 4) and their parents, six obviously pregnant women, and at least five sets of grandparents.

Oh, the nubile 22-year-olds and the Lotharios were there, but the atmosphere was distinctly wholesome and the appeal to families strong. The Club Med organization operates six family-oriented villages among its 16 villages in North America; in any given year, thousands of children vacation at them.

A strong contender for the title of Most Beautiful of all Club Med villages is the village at Punta Cana on the remote southeastern tip of the Dominican Republic. Here, the beach is breathtakingly lovely, banked on one side by a grove of coconut palms and on the other by the azure waters of the Caribbean Sea. A coral reef several hundred yards from shore serves as a brake on the action of the waves, so swimming is safe and relaxing. The sand is the perfect texture for castle building, and chaise longues beckon adults.

An integral part of the Club Med concept is quality control. Little differs from one village to another. The buffets can always be counted on to be lavish and well prepared, with a few locally inspired dishes thrown in for atmosphere. Sports are varied and active, and participation encouraged. The GOs (short for *gentils organisateurs*, the French term for "congenial hosts") are all attractive and fit. Even the music which ends the nightly shows is the same at each village (you can buy a tape of it to take home).

Club Med's repeat rate among GMs (*gentils membres*, its term for guests) is high. Families for whom the idea of a Caribbean vacation in a sheltered setting is appealing know they can count on Club Med to provide the same kind of vacation year after year, at whatever village they choose.

ACCOMMODATIONS: $$ The rooms are small, but adequate, with two or three single platform beds and a small, built-in vanity. A short corridor leading to the doorway contains two closets with built-in shelves, a bathroom with a shower stall and sink, and a separate toilet area. Although the window will open, it is unscreened. Walls are whitewashed concrete block, and the floors red tile. Doors can be locked only from the inside, but room safes are provided.

All meals and most activities are included in the rate. During certain periods of the year, children 2 through 5 are free at Punta Cana and the other family-oriented Club Med villages. There are a few adjoining rooms.

DINING: Food is prepared by both French and Dominican chefs, and the influence of both cuisines is obvious. All meals are served buffet style in a large open-air dining room with a circuslike atmosphere; one guest described it as comparable to his college's cafeteria. Guests are seated as they arrive at tables for eight, so unless you arrive at the same time as newly made friends, you're likely to be seated with someone else.

A breakfast buffet is served from 7:30 to 9 A.M. Late-risers can eat in the cocktail lounge until 11:30 A.M.

Lunch, served from 12:30 to 2 P.M., features eight to 10 buffet tables. Dinner is served from 7:30 to 9 P.M. On perhaps five of the seven nights of the week, there's a particular theme, such as Asian Night, Italian Night, or Seafood Night. There's always a selection of wonderful appetizers (carpaccio one night, raw tuna in garlic sauce another) and several seafood, meat, chicken, and pasta entrées. Complimentary Dominican wine and beer are served.

Children can either take their meals with their parents or eat together as a group in a special area equipped with child-size furniture. Parents must accompany children under 4 to this area at dinnertime (the children's dinner is at 6:30 P.M.).

For a special treat, guests can reserve a table at the beachside annex restaurant, La Hispaniola. There, you'll be served by waiters and enjoy French specialties in a more relaxed atmosphere. Reservations are taken at 12:30 P.M. daily, and filled within five minutes. A second specialty restaurant, La Cana, serves late lunches and Italian specialties for dinner.

ACTIVITIES

 Ten tennis courts, five lighted for night play. Instruction, weekly tournaments.

 Large pool; separate pool for children at children's center; ocean swimming.

 Instruction offered daily in water-skiing, wind surfing, kayaking, snorkeling, and sailing, plus free time to enjoy these sports.

 Available at extra charge from off-premise concessioner.

Before-breakfast stretch exercises, before-lunch water exercises, and aerobics classes. Many guests also take advantage of the instruction available in such circus activities as juggling and high-trapeze artistry. Volleyball, basketball, and archery equipment.

Periodically through the week, special activities such as a wind-surfing regatta (with free sangria and barbecue) or a free happy hour are offered.

There's nightly entertainment in the theater, staged by the GOs. A highlight of the week is the circus performance in which both adults and children show off their newly learned skills. The bars and disco stay open until the last guest leaves.

FOR CHILDREN: Throughout the year, the Club offers three separate programs for children: the "Petit Club," for children 2 through 4; the "Mini-Club," for children 5 through 7; and the "Kids' Club," for children 8 through 11. In addition, when there are large numbers of teenagers present, special activities are offered for them.

Three recently built low-rise buildings near the perimeter of the property house all the children's activities. In addition, there's a special shallow pool for kids, which is guarded during swimming times. Scuba diving lessons are offered for 4-to-12-year-olds.

The children's program is staffed by special children's GOs, all of whom have college degrees and experience in child care. Each serves a six-month stint at the village before moving on to another village. When we visited, most were outgoing, energetic, and enthusiastic. Most speak both French and English.

The Petit Club features such activities as sand-castle building, jumping on a trampoline, splashing about the pool, free play, and arts and crafts. Children may be left in the program from 9 A.M. to 5 P.M., and returned to it again from 7:30 P.M. to 9 P.M., but few children of this age do well for such a long period of time. Because of the high child-adult ratio that can result during busy periods, it's best to leave a young child in the program for only a two- or three-hour stretch. There are designated hours during the day when children can be brought to the program, but they be taken away at any time. Counselors will feed children lunch in their special section of the dining room, and put them on mats for an afternoon nap.

The Mini-Club is a more active program, featuring circus activities, pool games, swimming instruction, beach activities, arts and crafts, and performances in one or two evening shows.

The best of the children's programs is the Kids' Club. There, your 8- to 12-year-old children can learn archery, water-skiing, snorkeling, sailing, tennis, and circus skills.

Private baby-sitting is all but impossible to arrange. Some families do so by approaching the local staff of housekeepers and waitresses, but few of them speak English.

NICETIES: There's a Dominican physician in residence each week, as well as two nurses. There's no charge for children's visits, and only a nominal charge for adults. Commonly needed drugs are kept on hand.

The hostess, stationed most of the day in the cocktail lounge, has a supply of old paperback books and games such as checkers, backgammon, and Scrabble that you can check out.

There's a classical music concert daily featuring taped music. Chairs are set up in the coconut grove.

OF INTEREST NEARBY: Punta Cana is quite remote, without even a local market to visit. The only way you'll get to see anything of the Dominican Republic is to take one of the two excursions offered twice weekly—one to Altos de Chavon, a replica of the 16th-century colonial village at the Casa de Campo resort about 90 minutes from the Club, the other to Santo Domingo. There's an extra charge for the excursions.

Although it sounds hokey, Altos de Chavon is actually a spectacular tourist destination. Created at a cost of $30 million on a cliff overlooking the Río Chavon, the stone buildings are filled with restaurants, boutiques, art galleries, and artisans' workshops; in addition, there's a quaint church and a museum about pre-Columbian Indian life. The view of the Río Chavon gorge is stunning.

Santo Domingo is the oldest city in the Western Hemisphere and has a lovingly restored historic district. Club Med's excursion allows about six hours there (following either a 45-minute flight in a small plane or a three-hour ride by mini-bus) during which guests are taken to lunch and on a tour of historic sites and the local market. It's an excursion best taken without children.

FOR MORE INFORMATION: Call (800) CLUB-MED, or write Club Med Sales, Inc., 40 West Fifty-seventh Street, New York, NY 10019.

Boscobel Beach Resort
Ocho Rios, Jamaica

Until the mid-1980s, Jamaica was a tourist destination catering mostly to couples and singles. With resorts with names such as Hedonism II and Couples, what family would even consider Jamaica as a destination for a family vacation? Then, in 1987, came Boscobel Beach Resort, on the site of the refurbished Playboy Club on a lovely cove about 15 minutes from downtown Ocho Rios. Children now have the run of the place where Playboy bunnies once entertained.

This glistening beachside resort on Jamaica's north coast resembles nothing so much as a permanently moored cruise ship. There's an activity every hour of the day, including the wee hours of the morning, and plenty of deck chairs and chaise longues in which to relax between activities. There are lavish buffets and elegantly prepared dinners—and free drinks and even cigarettes. There is a host of social directors—and a select group of Super Nannies to care for your children. And then there's the Caribbean Sea—a mosaic of turquoise, royal blue, and aquamarine that beckons constantly.

Although the main buildings have been in place for more than two decades, the resort has an all-new feel since it was extensively refurbished after Hurricane Gilbert in 1988. Most of the guest rooms are grouped in two three-story buildings that look out over tropical gardens, the pool, and the sea beyond.

ACCOMMODATIONS: **$$** to **$$$** Boscobel Beach has 228 guest rooms, most with ocean views. Most are "junior suites"—exceptionally spacious rooms with separate sleeping and sitting areas; 14 have two bedrooms. The rooms are beautifully decorated and equipped with ceiling fans, air-conditioners, refrigerators, telephones, radios, and cable TV. The tubs are tiled and sunken, and the balconies are large, with plenty of seats. Roll-away beds and cribs are available.

Rates are lowest in the late spring, summer, and fall. Up to two children under 14 are free in each room, and children over 14 who are sharing their parents' room get a 25 percent discount from the adult rate. The rate covers all meals, including drinks; all activities; transfers to and from the airport at Montego Bay; and three off-premises excursions. A single parent traveling with two children pays no supplement. No tipping is permitted.

DINING: The chef here tries to use as many local vegetables and fruits in the cuisine as possible, and provides a wonderful opportunity to taste such exotic offerings as ackee (a scrambled-egg-like vegetable), cho-cho (similar to squash), and curried goat. In addition, there is no better coffee in the world than Jamaican Blue Mountain, and you'll get to drink bottomless cups of it at every meal (served, in the British style, with evaporated milk).

A breakfast buffet is served daily from 7:30 to 10 A.M. on the Jippi Jappa Terrace overlooking the swimming pool and the sea beyond. Alternatively, you can ask for a continental breakfast to be served in your room, and enjoy it on your balcony.

Lunch is also served buffet style on the Terrace and generally features five entrées, including one sure child-pleaser, and an extensive array of salads. The dessert table is irresistible. A separate snack bar at the beach will cook to order hamburgers, hot dogs, and french fries for those who don't want to leave their beach chairs.

A children's dinner is served from 6 to 7 P.M. on the Terrace. The regular dinner is served from 7 to 10 P.M. in the open-air dining rooms upstairs and in an Italian restaurant in the luxury wing (new in 1990). Many families choose to eat together at least some evenings during their stay.

ACTIVITIES

 Four Laykold courts.

 Privileges at Superclubs' golf courses in Runaway Bay; no greens fees. Professional instruction available.

 Two large pools, daily scuba-diving and snorkeling lessons and thrice-daily excursions to the reef (free use of all equipment).

A half dozen sailboats and windsurfers and a powerboat for water-skiing are available to guests. The staff will even provide sailing, water-skiing, and wind-surfing lessons, or take you out for a spin (child-size life preservers are available). A glass-bottom boat makes several trips daily to the reef for coral and fish viewing.

 Aerobics and dance exercise classes on the Terrace; beachfront gym with weights, exercise equipment, Ping-Pong, Jacuzzis.

 Instruction in hat-making, Jamaican culture, bicycle tours, arts and crafts, sand-sculpting, basket-weaving, a reggae dance class, and tennis and table tennis tournaments.

At night, the Jippi Jappa Terrace comes alive with the sounds of a steel band or a reggae group. One night each week, a local cultural group performs. The disco opens at 11 P.M. The piano bar offers a romantic site for a drink.

FOR CHILDREN: Boscobel operates one of the most ambitious children's activity programs in the Caribbean. The kids' center is a circular, mostly glass-walled building just outside the lobby. It is open daily from 9 A.M. to 10 P.M. and accepts children between 6 weeks of age and about 12 years, although most children over 9 seem to find other things to do.

The center is staffed by seven local women whom the resort calls "Super Nannies." Separate activities are offered for 3- to 5-year-olds, and 6- to 11-year-olds. Among the activities are "Mousercise," swimming lessons, pool games, shell hunts, arts and crafts, nature walks, donkey rides, reggae dance classes, glass-bottom boat rides, computer play, treasure hunts, movies, and patois classes.

The facility is equipped with about a half dozen Atari computers, which seem to be a real hit with the over-6 set. Cribs are made up for napping babies, and cushions and quilts are spread on the floor in front of a giant-screen TV for toddlers who don't want to miss some of their favorite cartoons. Snacks are served, and the staff will arrange to feed your child lunch if you wish.

Old McDonald's Farm, just behind one of the hotel wings, features several dozen exotic birds and small farm animals and is very popular with children. Its cock will ensure that you are awake early. There also are several swing sets and an expansive grassy play area.

Sitters can be hired for the late evening. Children under 6 must be accompanied by a sitter if they are in the kids' center after 6 P.M.

NICETIES: There's a lot to be said for staying at an all-inclusive resort, where you never need to dig into your pockets to pay for a thing. Children can easily get accustomed to walking up to a bartender and asking for "a strawberry daiquiri—without the rum, please."

The resort is largely accessible to wheelchairs (there's an elevator to the beach). Several families were accompanied by children in wheelchairs when we visited and had no trouble getting around.

Fresh beach towels are delivered to your room each evening so that you'll be well prepared if you go for an early-morning swim. In addition, there are large supplies at the beach and pool.

The staff at the children's center keeps a birthday book and sends their former charges cards on the appropriate day.

OF INTEREST NEARBY: Dunn's River Falls is one of Jamaica's premier tourist attractions, and the resort makes the Falls easy to experience by scheduling a daily outing. The Falls cascade 600 feet down a series of steplike rock outcroppings into the sea. No visitor is either too young or too old to enjoy playing in the many ice-cold pools along the way. But to really experience it, you have to climb the Falls, which is done with the help of a local guide.

The resort also offers daily tours to nearby Prospect Plantation, which offers a tram ride past fields of bananas, pineapples, sugar cane, coffee, limes, and pimento—and samples along the way. The plantation also is the site of the scenic White River Gorge.

Ocho Rios is a 20-minute drive from the hotel, and most guests make at least one foray into the town by tourist van to shop the many straw and souvenir markets.

FOR MORE INFORMATION: Write Boscobel Beach at P.O. Box 63, Ocho Rios, Jamaica, or call (800) 858-8009 or (809) 974-3291; in New York, call (516) 868-6924. For general tourist information, write the Jamaica Tourist Board, 866 Second Avenue, New York, NY 10017, or call (212) 688-7650.

The Hyatt Regency Cerromar Beach
Hyatt Dorado Beach
Dorado, Puerto Rico

It is possible to take a vacation to an exotic island paradise where you don't need a passport, don't have to change your money, and don't need to brush up on your French or Spanish because most of the natives speak English. The place is Puerto Rico, where a rich broth of culture has been simmering for eons, as Indian natives mingled with settlers from Spain, England, France and the Netherlands and slaves from West Africa. The island is a protectorate of the United States.

The Hyatt resorts in Dorado, a beautiful area on the north shore about 22 miles west of the San Juan airport, are truly world-class. Originally, the ground on which the two Hyatt resorts now stand was a coconut and grapefruit plantation. It later became a private playground for Laurance Rockefeller, who opened the Dorado Beach resort to the public in December 1958. Cerromar Beach, the sister resort, opened in 1971, two miles down the road.

In 1985, the Hyatt Hotel chain bought both resorts for $40 million and lavished time and attention—and another $75 million—on renovation. It has been money well spent; the hotels are beautiful. And with a mean year-round temperature of 76 degrees, outdoor sports are possible anytime.

The hotels' grounds are heaven on earth for the serious horticulturalist—and the weekend gardener. The 1,000-acre properties are verdant with nearly 600 species of tropical plants. Beehives produce honey for the kitchens, and the resort's own coconut palms are the source of meat and milk for tropical drinks.

ACCOMMODATIONS: **$$$** to **$$$$** The Dorado Beach is made up of low-rise buildings with four suites in each and a total of 300 rooms. The suites have terra-cotta tile floors and bamboo frames around king-size beds and are awash with the tropical colors associated with Caribbean island hideaways. Deluxe rooms and beach-side units called casitas, in small clusters but with private patios, cost more than standard hotel rooms. Rates include breakfast and dinner.

The Cerromar Beach has 504 rooms, including 19 suites, in a seven-story building; most rooms have a view of the sea, and many have private balconies. The rooms are spacious, with marble baths, tile floors, and tropical furnishings.

Rates at both hotels drop considerably—as much as 60 percent—after the high season, which generally lasts from mid-December to late April. A Modified American Plan package can be purchased for an additional charge at the Cerromar Beach. At both hotels, children 15 and under are free when they stay in their parents' room (limit two children per room.)

DINING: Most dining at the resorts is done in spacious, windowed rooms with spectacular views of the ocean.

The favorite of the hotels' Austrian-born chef, Wilhelm Pirngruber, and of many guests is the Su Casa Restaurant. The restaurant is in a colonial mansion that was the home of the plantation's original owner and features Pirngruber's gourmet Caribbean and Spanish specialties, which rely largely on fresh seafood and unusual spicing.

At the Cerromar, Medici's, the main restaurant, features Northern Italian and Caribbean cuisines and fresh seafood. The Costa de Oro features oversize cuts of grilled meat and delicious desserts.

The outdoor Swan Café at the Cerromar, open for breakfast and lunch, is a triple-level restaurant next to the river pool. The Sunday brunch here is hard to beat, with its extensive array of fresh seafood, Caribbean specialties, and made-to-order omelets.

The main restaurant at the Dorado Beach is the open-air Ocean Terrace, which is open from morning through dinner and is a delightful spot to sip coffee, eat from the breakfast buffet, and watch the ocean. It has nightly theme parties. This is also a good place to stop with the kids. The Surf Room is more formal.

All the restaurants offer children's menus with entrees under $3; children can also choose from the regular menu at a 50-percent discount.

ACTIVITIES

 Twenty-one Decoralt-surface courts, some lighted. Private and group lessons, pro shop; court fees. Special "Caribbean Sports

Academy" package features two hours of instruction and two hours of supervised play (golf, tennis, or windsurfing.)

Four 18-hole courses designed by Robert Trent Jones. The two courses at the Dorado are regarded as among the great seaside links of the world; they wind through tropical forests and citrus groves, out along the Atlantic Ocean, and past a chain of lakes and a man-made lagoon. Chi Chi Rodriguez is the resort's executive director of golf.

The Cerromar claims the longest swimming pool in the world, 1,776 feet long, or 526 feet longer than the Empire State Building is high. It takes 15 minutes to float from one end to the other. The pool, which cost more than $3 million to build, is actually five free-form pools connected with 14 waterfalls and four slides. The pool features a 187-foot spiral water slide, a swim-up bar, and a lounge with underwater seats, a subterranean Jacuzzi, water volleyball and aerobics courts, and a kiddie area. The pool is beautifully landscaped with more than 30,000 plantings.

The Dorado Beach has three swimming pools. And of course, there's the Caribbean.

 Deep-sea fishing and scuba diving trips can be arranged.

 Rentals available, including adult-sized tricycles.

Spa Caribe, new in 1988, offers computerized body composition analyses and exercise and diet recommendations, Powercise exercise machines, Dynacourt warm-up equipment, aerobics classes, massages, and skin and body care programs. Miles of jogging trails.

Spanish lessons, gourmet cooking classes, sightseeing tips, art expositions, carriage rides, scuba shows, ice-carving exhibitions, movies, snorkeling tours, and garden walks.

At the Cerromar Beach, a large open-air bar and cocktail lounge called the Flamingo Bar offers live entertainment nightly. El Coqui is a new sports bar there. Both hotels have casinos, which means they're quite lively at night.

FOR CHILDREN: "Camp Coqui," a professionally supervised children's activities program for youngsters from 3 through 15 operates from June 1 through Labor Day, and during the Christmas and Easter holiday periods at Cerromar Beach, but welcomes children staying at the Dorado Beach. The hours are from 9 A.M. to 4 P.M. daily and again from 6 to 10 P.M. A fee is charged.

A typical day in the children's program starts with registration between 9 and 9:30, followed by outdoor games, such as jump rope, hopscotch, soccer, castle building, or kite flying. Then come pool games, such as swimming relays, raft relays, pool volleyball, and treasure hunts. At 11:30, lunch preparation begins, after which there are indoor activities such as bingo, coloring, arts and crafts, Spanish lessons, board games, movies, and cartoons, followed by outdoor games and more pool games.

The evening schedule starts with a get-acquainted session between 6 and 6:30, followed by dinner in the main dining room, movies, cartoons, quiet games, or clown and mime shows.

Facilities for children include a good playground at Cerromar Beach, which is equipped with climbers, tunnels, and swings. Bilingual babysitters can be obtained for in-room child care.

NICETIES: Luxuriously thick terry robes, an umbrella hanging in each closet, and a driver with a golf cart willing to tote you around are a few indications of how these resorts pamper their guests.

A San Francisco–style cable car (on wheels) shuttles guests betweeen the resorts.

Recipes of some of the resort's most popular Caribbean-style dishes are gladly proffered to guests.

OF INTEREST NEARBY: Don't miss Old San Juan. It is a maze of little streets with street vendors, fancy department stores, galleries and charming cafés that offer heady concoctions of coffee and who-knows-what-else, as well as tropical drinks. Old San Juan is an interesting architectural study, with many well-maintained colonial-era buildings that are painted in pastel colors.

Also of interest is the old walled city of San Juan, which displays miles of cement walls, parapets, lookout towers, and cannons. It offers spectacular views of the ocean and city.

The Caribbean National Forest, commonly called El Yunque, has 28,000 acres of rain-forest vegetation and is the only tropical forest in the U.S. National Forest System. The forest offers great hiking trails and provides a home for the very endangered Puerto Rican parrot. El Yunque is about 50 miles southeast of San Juan.

FOR MORE INFORMATION: Write the Hyatt Regency Cerromar Beach or the Hyatt Dorado Beach, Dorado, Puerto Rico 00646, or call Hyatt Resorts Puerto Rico at (809) 796-1234.

For reservations call (800) 233-1234; in Nebraska, call (800) 228-9001; in Alaska and Hawaii, call (800) 228-9005.

Bitter End Yacht Club
Virgin Gorda, British Virgin Islands

The British and American Virgins are located in one of the best sailing areas of the world. They promise sailors warm air and water temperatures year-round, steady trade winds, sheltered anchorages, and unspoiled beauty.

The easternmost of these mountainous islands form a rough ellipse that defines a great cruising basin. The popularity of sailing in this region is apparent even as you fly into Virgin Gorda—the water below is dotted with sails. Boats anchored off the white sand beaches cast shadows on the sandy bottom below. Coral reefs are everywhere.

Sparsely populated Virgin Gorda itself has an up-and-down profile of green mountains. Leaving the airport, the taxi climbs to the top of Mount Gorda and descends the other side to Gun Creek on North Sound. There, a launch waits to ferry you to the Bitter End Yacht Club.

Bitter End is one of the great sailing resorts of the Caribbean. It welcomes families and offers a wide variety of sailing and water-based recreational activities. At Bitter End, steep hillsides covered with flowering bougainvillea and hibiscus fall to white sand beaches that ring a secluded sound. "Paradise" is a cliché, but paradise it is.

ACCOMMODATIONS: **$$$$** Rates vary with the season, with stays around Christmas and Easter the most expensive. Rates are lowest in the summer.

Bitter End has 81 accommodations in several categories. Chalets, the most luxurious accommodations, perch high on the hillside with great views of North Sound and the yacht harbor. They have over 600 square feet of space, air-conditioning and ceiling fans, balconies, two queen-size beds, marble baths, and garden-view showers. Hillside Villas are open and spacious with private decks overlooking the sea, twin beds, ceiling fans, two-sink bathrooms, and enormous showers with private views of a garden or the sea. Beachfront Villas are slightly older and smaller. Villas are arranged in groups of two (larger families could rent both and have two bedrooms and two baths).

Another option is to sleep on a Cal 27 sailboat moored at the Bitter End dock. The Cals sleep four and have hookups for electric lights and running water. Daily maid service is included.

Rates include all meals, and for stays of seven nights or more, unlimited day sailing, daily snorkeling trips; entry into Sunday regattas; and a manager's cocktail party.

A variety of packages is available. The summer family package is a great enticement to a summer vacation here. From the beginning of May to the beginning of November, Bitter End charges two adult family members the lower summer rate, throws in a second room and bath for two or more children, and charges only a flat daily rate for each child.

DINING: You are a captive diner at Bitter End, since there are no other restaurants for miles around. But oh, to be at the mercy of these chefs more often! The food in both restaurants is marvelous.

The English Carvery is located in a striking open-air pavilion surrounded by tropical gardens. The menu features roast meats and poultry served in an elegant, candlelit atmostphere. The Carvery's location is quiet and secluded.

The Clubhouse Steak and Seafood Grille is at the harbor and docks. Fresh fish and Caribbean lobster head the menu.

Breakfasts and lunches at The Grille are healthy, ample buffets. The poolside bar offers sandwiches.

Families can obtain packed lunches of sandwiches or cold roast chicken to take on boating excursions.

ACTIVITIES

 There's a freshwater swimming pool with a four-foot depth throughout. Each day, the *Ponce de Leon* pontoon boat takes snorkelers out to Eustatia Reef, a short distance from Bitter End. Life belts and flippers in all sizes are available. Bring your own mask and snorkel or purchase these in the resort's shop.

Guests have unlimited use of most of the resort's sailboats, which include windsurfers, Sunfish, Lasers, Rhode 19s, and J-24s; sailing and wind-surfing lessons available for an extra charge. Boston Whalers are always available for exploring within North Sound. *Paranda*, the Bitter End's 48-foot catamaran, takes guests on sunset cocktail sails and makes at least one trip each week to Dog Island for swimming and snorkeling.

A number of trails crisscross Virgin Gorda and can be used for family hikes.

Bitter End has rowing shells, an excellent way to get some exercise. The roadway along the Bitter End waterfront is suitable for jogging.

Scuba diving on Virgin Island reefs with the Kilbride family is one of the adventures of a lifetime. Bert Kilbride was made "Keeper of the Wrecks" that litter Anegada and other Virgin Island reefs by Queen Elizabeth. No one knows these waters better. The Kilbrides offer daily scuba trips and beginning instruction. They furnish tanks, weights, and backpacks. You can bring your own regulator, fins, mask, and snorkel or rent them.

FOR CHILDREN: During the summer, Bitter End offers a complimentary half-day sailing instruction program daily to children between 6 and 16 whose families are staying there on the family plan.

Bitter End Yacht Club does not encourage stays of families with children younger than 5 or 6, but the staff has great patience with older children and welcomes them in all the activities. This is a good place for your older child to learn to snorkel, sail, or wind-surf.

Children return again and again to the large fish tank at the harbor dock, which is lighted at night. It holds a fascinating collection of sea turtles, tarpon, sharks, blowfish, remora, and other tropical species. Lobster boats call occasionally and replenish the restaurant's supply, which is stored in the adjacent lobster tanks.

The Sand Palace Theater plays several movies a day on its large video screen. Those scheduled early in the evening are generally suitable for children.

The Flipper, one of only two dozen "aquascopes" made in France some years ago, takes children and their parents on a one-hour tour of Eustatia reef. Passengers ride in a submerged compartment of Plexiglas with unobstructed views of the coral and marine life on the reef on both sides. The tour includes views of the cannon and anchors from a Spanish galleon.

NICETIES: When you arrive at your room, you'll find fresh flowers and a complimentary bottle of Virgin Islands rum. The flowers are replaced every day.

The breakfast juice bar includes a bottle of chilled champagne, and rum punch is one of the luncheon drink options.

Each room has a coffee maker and small stocked refrigerator. Maid service is twice daily.

Dinner in The Grille is by early and late sittings. Each day, the staff will seat you at a different table. In the process, you'll meet a widening circle of other guests at adjacent tables.

Bitter End Yacht Club stretches for nearly a mile along the shore of North Sound. You can reach any point in a few minutes at a leisurely pace, but a pontoon boat provides a free taxi service along the waterfront.

OF INTEREST NEARBY: The 50-foot excursion boat *Prince of Wales* makes day-trips several times a week. Visit the Baths, where huge boulders on the beach form grottoes and pools, or Anegada, the only coral atoll in the Virgin Islands, and the site of over 300 shipwrecks. Pirates used to light false beacons on Anegada to lure ships onto the rocks. A sightseeing and shopping trip to Road Town on the nearby island of Tortola is another option.

FOR MORE INFORMATION: Write the reservation office, Bitter End Yacht Club, 875 N. Michigan Ave., #3707, Chicago, IL 60611, or call (800) 872-2392 or (312) 944-5855.

Hyatt Regency Grand Cayman
George Town, Grand Cayman Island

Ask any serious scuba diver or snorkeler for a list of the world's great diving spots, and the Cayman Islands are certain to be on it. The coral reef just off North Sound on Grand Cayman offers some of the most accessible snorkeling and diving in the Caribbean in water so clear that visibility is often 150 feet. The awesome sponges, magnificent corals, and colorful fish that you'll see here will make diving experiences elsewhere pale in comparison.

This British colony occupies three tiny islands in the Caribbean, equidistant from Cuba and Jamaica. Grand Cayman, the largest of the three, is the main tourist destination. Visitors are drawn to its unique combination of British politeness and Caribbean mellowness. People also come for the climate (the lowest recorded temperature ever was 68 degrees), the breathtaking aquamarine water, and the low-key ambience.

The Hyatt Regency Grand Cayman, which opened in 1986, is the most complete family resort in the Caymans.

ACCOMMODATIONS: $$$$ Most guests stay in the 236 luxury hotel rooms in seven low-rise buildings. Connecting rooms and a few suites are available. All rooms have ceiling fans and air conditioning, mini-bars, and room safes (there's a charge.) The rooms are decorated in soothing pastels, with bleached ash, rattan, wicker, and teak furnishings. Either a king-size bed or two doubles should be specified when reservations are made.

About two dozen individually owned villas bordering the golf course can also be rented. These have full kitchens, washers and dryers, a patio or balcony, and one to three bedrooms.

DINING: Guests eat breakfast in the Garden Loggia, an airy room opening on to a garden, which offers a buffet with cooked-to-order eggs and piano music in the background. The restaurant, which has both indoor and outdoor seating, is also open for lunch and dinner, and serves snacks outdoors until midnight. On Friday evenings, there is a prime rib carvery and lavish seafood buffet. Children can choose from an assortment of inexpensive items on the children's menu or eat for half-price from the regular menu.

Hemingway's, at Hyatt's Brittania Beach Club, serves lovely lunches and dinners both inside and outside, with gorgeous views of the Caribbean. The menu features some Caribbean specialties, as well as classic continental offerings. Also at the Beach Club, the Pool Grille serves sandwiches throughout the day. The Brittania Grille at the golf course serves sandwiches, salads, and light meals.

For villa guests, Foster's Food Fare, two blocks away, offers all the necessary groceries.

ACTIVITIES:

Two Plexi-paved lighted courts, no fees; rental equipment available. Adults' and children's clinics, private lessons.

Brittania, the island's only golf course, is here. Designed by Jack Nicklaus, the 3,202-yard course can be played three different ways: as a nine-hole regulation course, an 18-hole executive course, or an 18-hole "Cayman ball" course. The Cayman ball has pimples instead of dimples and is half the weight of a regular ball.

The main free-form, freshwater pool covers more than a third of an acre and is lushly landscaped. There's a swim-up bar and whirlpool. Two smaller pools are located at the Britannia Beach Club and near the Brittania villas. The island's famed Seven-Mile Beach (it's actually just five!) is a short walk along a landscaped path.

Instruction and rental pedal-boats, aqua trikes, windsurfers, sailboats, and jet skis at the Beach Club. For a novel experience, rent the inflated Banana Boat, which is towed by a powerboat. Sunset, dinner, and star-gazing cruises on The Spirit of Ppalu, an excursion catamaran.

 Marlin, tuna, dolphin, and wahoo expeditions on charter boats that depart from the hotel's small marina.

 Rental bikes and mopeds at the Beach Club.

Few guests leave without exploring the offshore coral reefs. Snorkeling or scuba-diving instructions and expeditions are offered daily on *The Spirit of Ppalu*, and on two Red Sail Sports dive boats. The excursion to Sting Ray City is a must.

Water aerobics classes daily in the main pool; land-based stretching sessions.

Croquet on a formal English lawn, organized water volleyball games. The manager holds a cocktail reception every Tuesday night.

FOR CHILDREN: "Camp Cayman" welcomes children between 3 and 15 for daily activities during the summer and over school holidays and on weekends the rest of the year.

The program, for which an hourly fee is charged, features snorkeling or sailing expeditions, T-shirt painting, visits to the Cayman Island's treasury and history museum, movies, beach activities, tennis lessons, and pier fishing. It usually operates from 10 A.M. to 4 P.M., and 6 to 8 P.M. Participants receive a Camp Hyatt cap and magic slate.

NICETIES: An impressive collection of both modern and ancient sculpture is scattered around the property.

Frick and Frack, two parakeets who live in a cage in the Loggia Lounge, will delight your children throughout their stay.

Dave Miller, a Caymaner whose family has lived on the island since 1655, leads excellent personalized tours around the island. He knows the best snorkeling places and can even satisfy a personal interest in Cayman beekeeping techniques. Call 70643 or 71047 to make arrangements.

OF INTEREST NEARBY: Grand Cayman is short on conventional tourist attractions. The Turtle Farm is the island's main tourist draw. It's the only facility in the world for raising green sea turtles for commercial use. Several thousand green sea turtles and Kemp Ridleys, an endangered species, are released into the sea each year to replenish the natural population.

Hell, a patch of eerie dead coral formations, is of primary interest to visitors who want an unusual postmark on their postcards.

The Cayman Islands National Museum, which opened in 1991 in an old courts building on the waterfront at Hog Sty Bay, has exhibits on the islands' natural and cultural history.

FOR MORE INFORMATION: Call (809) 949-1234; FAX (809) 949-8528. For reservations, call (800) 229-9001 from Nebraska, (800) 233-1234 from elsewhere in the continental U.S. and Canada, and (800) 228-9005 from Alaska or Hawaii.

1. Families can enjoy two daily trail rides at the Lone Mountain Ranch in Big Sky, Montana. *(Photo: Don Breneman)* **2.** Even very young children can take a turn on one of the gentle horses at Mountain Sky Guest Ranch. *(Photo: Martha Shirk)* **3.** Children can take part in trail rides as part of a free children's program at the Flying L Ranch in Bandera, Texas. **4.** Trail rides at the C Lazy U Ranch in Granby, Colorado, are only one of many activities parents can enjoy with their children. **5.** Lunch is served outside at Mountain Sky Guest Ranch to take full advantage of the spectacular scenery. *(Photo: Martha Shirk)* **6.** Children delight in cart rides pulled by Luigi, the beloved donkey at the C Lazy U Ranch in Granby, Colorado. **7.** After a day of horse riding, hiking, swimming, or fishing, guests at the Tanque Verde Ranch in Tucson, Arizona, have plenty of room and facilities to rest and relax. *(Photo: Manley Commercial Photography)*

GUEST
RANCHES

5

6

7

SOUTHWEST AND MOUNTAIN STATES

Tanque Verde Ranch
Tucson, Arizona

The Tanque Verde Ranch has been a working cattle or horse ranch since the 1860s. Founded on a land grant from the Spaniards, it was the site of frequent Apache ambushes and a crossroads for Don Esteban Ochoa's mule trains before it was transformed into a guest ranch in the 1930s. Since 1957 it has been owned by the Cote family, which has gradually turned it into one of the premier guest ranches in the Southwest.

Set in the foothills of the Rincon Mountains on the eastern edge of Tucson, the ranch commands a sweeping view of Tucson and the mountain ranges that ring it. The vegetation is typical of the upper Sonoran Desert, with the desert's signature cactus, the impressive saguaro, visible at every turn. The ranch owns 640 acres, and its eastern border is the rugged 1.3-million-acre Coronado National Memorial Forest, and its southern border the 63,000-acre Saguaro National Monument, so there is plenty of space to ride and roam. And it's the riding that brings guests back here time and time again —that, and the comfortable accommodations, bountiful meals, and relaxed ambience.

ACCOMMODATIONS: $$$ Up to 150 guests stay in four small "ramada" rooms or 56 larger adobe-look casitas, all attractively furnished with a mixture of antiques and southwestern-style furniture. The larger casitas have fireplaces, with a more-than-adequate supply of mesquite wood just outside the door. Each accommodation has an outdoor patio or sitting area so that you can take in the majestic views, day or night. The rooms have no television sets, although a few are available to rent if you absolutely cannot do without; in addition, there's a large-screen set in the living room in the main ranch building. Many units have refrigerators for storing snacks and drinks. A coin-operated laundry facility is available.

DINING: Memorable meals are served in a large, western-motif dining room with a wall of glass overlooking the outdoor pool and surrounding mountains. Meals are included in the room rate; the menu is posted daily on a bulletin board outside the main building. Most breakfast items are on a buffet, but eggs, hotcakes, French toast, and breakfast meats are cooked to order. Lunch also is usually a buffet.

Dinner offers a choice of entrées, with something to please every palate, including the calorie conscious. The hostess attempts to seat guests at different tables for each meal so that by the end of your stay you will have met nearly everyone there. This is helpful to new guests, since repeat guests can offer a wealth of helpful hints.

Beer and wine are served with meals for an additional charge. Dietary restrictions can be accommodated.

The ranch encourages children over 4 to take their meals together in the special children's dining room, but children are welcome to join you in the main dining room if you prefer. The dining-room staff will gladly fill a baby bottle or provide you with children's snacks to take back to your room.

ACTIVITIES

Five Laykold courts, several of them lighted, supervised by a tennis pro between November and April.

Privileges at six courses in Tucson.

Heated indoor pool; the outdoor pool serves as a popular gathering place for families after the afternoon ride. A waterfall—with cascading hot water—is both scenic and therapeutic if you place your shoulders directly in the water's path.

The Rincon Mountains foothills have numerous trails for hikers; a map is provided in each guest room. One of the unique features of the ranch is a bird-banding program, held every Thursday morning at the crack of dawn. Master bird banders licensed by the U.S. Fish and Wildlife Service capture and band wild birds in the only year-round banding operation in the state. More than 60,000 birds of 155 species have been banded. Guided nature walks are offered six times each week by a naturalist.

With 115 horses, Tanque Verde has the largest stable of riding horses in Arizona and a skilled wrangling staff that can size up your level of ability—and psychological preparedness—in a glance. Two or three scheduled rides are offered daily, as well as two riding lessons (all included in the room rate). Each lesson ride is divided into two groups, beginners and lopers. Rides range from one-hour jaunts on ranch property to all-day rides across the Saguaro National Monument. Breakfast rides, which feature pancakes cooked over an open fire, are especially popular.

El Sonora Spa is a health facility equipped with a heated indoor pool, saunas, whirlpool, and exercise equipment. Equipment for lawn games and basketball at the front desk.

Catch-and-release fishing for largemouth bass in the ranch's spring-fed Lake Gambusi; tackle provided.

Programs are offered each evening for the entire family, including bingo, square dancing, snake demonstrations, lectures on desert ecology, and demonstrations of Indian crafts. Once or twice a week, an evening cookout is held in the Cottonwood Grove, with dancing under the stars and cowboy singing and music. Adults gather before dinner in the Dog House, a converted bunkhouse that serves as a cocktail lounge. Lockers are available to store each guest's liquor, which must be bought by the bottle at the ranch office.

FOR CHILDREN: This is the only ranch in southern Arizona with an organized children's program. It operates daily from mid-November to May 1 and serves children between 4 and 11. Baby-sitting is available for younger children, and special, less regimented activities are provided for those over 11.

The complimentary daily program begins with breakfast at 8 A.M. in the children's dining room, just behind the main dining room. From there, children usually go on an hour-long ride. Parents are welcome to ride with the children, but children under 12 may not go on the adult rides.

The morning program ends at 10:15 A.M., about the same time the adults' trail ride concludes, and resumes with lunch at noon. After lunch, a second ride is usually offered. For those who don't want to ride, swimming, nature walks, games and arts and crafts are offered. The afternoon program ends at 3:30, and the children meet again at 6 for dinner. Between the conclusion of dinner and 8:15 P.M., they usually go to the Tack Room for games or storytelling.

All-day rides, punctuated by a cookout lunch on the mountain, are offered occasionally for children 7 and up. And each week there is usually at least one trail ride to Cottonwood Grove, followed by a picnic lunch and a sing-along with the ranch hands.

The program is run by two counselors, but when there are large numbers of children in the program, extra staff members are added.

If there are many teenagers staying at the ranch, a teen table is set up in the dining room, and other activities are arranged.

NICETIES: Fresh fruit, coffee, and herbal tea are available nearly around the clock in the dining room. Early risers can snack on Danish rolls and coffee beginning at 6 A.M.

Major plant specimens are labeled so that you can quickly become familiar with desert plants.

The front desk maintains a stock of fruit juice in large cans, as well as soda, six-packs of beer, and bottles of liquor. A coin-operated beer and wine machine is located in the Dog House.

The staff makes a supply run into town once a week and will gladly pick up necessities for you for a small charge. Guests are welcome to ride along.

OF INTEREST NEARBY: The Arizona Sonoran Desert Museum is world famous for its living exhibits featuring 200 species of animals and 300 species of plants native to the Sonoran Desert. It's a drive of an hour or more from the ranch.

Sabino Canyon provides a look at another type of environment. A motorized tram takes visitors on a nine-mile ride up the canyon; you can get off at numerous points and picnic or hike. The cascading river creates many deep pools that are popular swimming holes.

Old Tucson is a former movie and TV show location, with shoot-'em-up gun fights re-enacted daily. There are rides and shops and buildings designed to suggest the flavor of Tucson in the 1860s.

Saguaro National Monument East is just outside the entrance to the ranch. A visitors center offers a slide show and lectures on the desert environment.

FOR MORE INFORMATION: Write Bob Cote, Tanque Verde Ranch, 14301 E. Speedway, Tucson, AZ 85748, or call (602) 296-6275.

You can get general tourist information from the Metropolitan Tucson Convention and Visitors Bureau at 450 West Paseo Redondo, Tucson, AZ 85705, or telephone (602) 624-1817.

Wickenburg Inn Tennis and Guest Ranch
Wickenburg, Arizona

At this remote Arizona guest ranch, a family can recapture the spirit and adventure of the Old West, become intimately involved with the history and ecology of the Sonoran Desert, and experience the comfort of a luxury resort.

The Wickenburg area of Arizona, 70 miles from Phoenix, has been a destination for outsiders ever since the Prussian emigrant Henry Wickenburg hurled a rock at his stubborn burro and discovered, on closer inspection, that the rocks he was tossing about contained gold—the richest find in Arizona and the start of the Vulture Mine. Eventually the gold ran out, the miners and gamblers moved on, and the cowboys and cattle moved in.

The Wickenburg Inn Tennis and Guest Ranch is an activity-oriented resort where tennis, horseback riding, nature study, and arts and crafts are pursued in a spectacular western ranch setting. The inn sits astride two arroyos in the center of its own 4,700-acre desert wildlife preserve. At Wickenburg, the wild Sonoran Desert surrounds you. The vegetation is mesquite, burro bush, and 50-year-old saguaro cactus. Deer, jackrabbits, and birds are abundant, and roadrunners are frequently seen sprinting through the grounds. Bird feeders attract finches, Gamble's quail, white wing doves, and mourning doves.

The inn's lodging units, called casitas, are placed along winding paths. Park your car on arrival and forget it. All the getting around for the rest of your stay can be accomplished on foot or horseback.

ACCOMMODATIONS: $$ The inn is on the full American Plan. The accommodation charge includes all meals and most activities. Children between 2 and 12 are charged a modest daily rate to cover their meals, and children under 2 are free. Rates vary by season, with summer rates the lowest; over Thanksgiving, Christmas, and the spring vacation periods, a surcharge is added.

The ranch lodge has six guest rooms, but most families choose one of the 41 rustic-looking but luxuriously appointed casitas. Each has 18-inch thick walls of traditional adobe brick and high, beamed ceilings. The two-story deluxe casita suites have their own private sun decks. Each casita has a wood-burning fireplace and a small kitchen with refrigerator, sink, and a two-burner stove.

DINING: The dining room is decorated with an eclectic assortment of antiques. Most tables look out on desert vistas. The inn's American Plan meals feature a delicious assortment of American and southwestern specialties. The food is plentiful and fresh and features home-style soups, breads, and pastries.

A Saturday night steak fry under the desert sky is the culinary highlight of the week. Families travel to the cookout by horseback or hay wagon. Steaks and chicken are prepared over a mesquite fire; beer biscuits, cowboy beans, fried spuds, and Dutch oven cobbler round out the meal. After dinner, families and staff gather around a crackling camp fire for stories and join in guitar-accompanied songs. Later, when the fire dies down, guests ride back to the inn under a spectacular desert sky.

ACTIVITIES

 Eleven hard-surface courts, special rebound walls, ball machines, stroke developers, and daily and weekly clinics under the tutelage of tennis pros. Tennis clinics in three-day and five-day formats are offered year-round.

At the nearby Wickenburg Country Club or at Rancho de los Caballeros.

An attractive heated outdoor swimming pool and sun deck; huge hilltop hot tub (a perfect place to enjoy a bottle of wine at sunset or under a starlit desert sky).

The inn's naturalist-in-residence leads day walks and star walks; children delight in identifying the constellations and learning their legends and lore. The inn's Desert Nature Center houses displays and a natural history library; a self-guided nature trail starts here. The inn maintains a checklist of the wildlife that has been sighted within the Preserve, and guests are encouraged to add to the list. (So far visitors have recorded 173 species of birds, 30 mammals, 29 reptiles, and five amphibians!) An all-day van trip (extra fee) takes guests to Oak Creek Canyon, with its colorful cliffs and unusual rock formations, and to the historic ghost town of Jerome and the incomparable Grand Canyon.

Western pleasure rides are available for all guests; the slow pace is perfect for families, photographers, and nature lovers. The intermediate ride and advanced ride are for more experienced riders; they mix walking, trotting, and cantering. All-day rides to a box canyon, rides with the inn naturalist, sunrise and sunset rides, and deluxe overnight pack trips can also be arranged during the winter season. Regardless of your equestrian skills, join the Dudeo held on some Friday afternoons. Expert and beginning riders and children 6 years of age and up compete in fun-filled and often hilarious contests on horseback.

Join your children and let your creative energies flow at the inn's well-supplied crafts center. Materials are available for bead handiwork, weaving, sketching, pottery, sand painting, and leatherwork, with instruction available.

On some evenings there are programs for the entire family—a disco with everyone dancing or perhaps a camp fire with songs and the telling of tall tales.

FOR CHILDREN: During the Thanksgiving, Christmas, and spring school vacation holiday periods the Wickenburg Inn offers an action-oriented children's program for youngsters 4 through 12 years. Qualified counselors supervise activities for children in two age groups: 4 through 6 and 7 through 12. A fee is charged.

The day program of the 4–6 group runs from 8:45 A.M. to 4 P.M. Parents join their children for lunch at the corral bunkhouse. Arts and crafts, walk and lead rides at the stables, visits with the naturalist at the Nature Center, nature walks, swimming, tennis lessons, supervised games, and other special events fill the day.

The preteen program for 7- through 12-year-olds includes trail rides, Dudeos, tennis clinics, arts and crafts, square dances, nature hikes, swimming, and special trips. The program runs the same hours as the younger children's programs: from 8:45 A.M. to 4 P.M., with a break for lunch with parents. At 5:34 P.M., children may eat with counselors or, if they wish, join their parents for dinner later. Evening events might include a cookout, hayrides, a Nature Center program, camp-fire storytelling at Squirrel Banks, star walks, movies, or square dances.

There is no daily program specifically for teenagers, but your teenager is sure to make friends with peers. All of the inn's scheduled adult activities are suitable for teenagers, and the inn plans some teen activities each week, such as a teen tennis tournament, a Dudeo, and a dance. At mealtime your teen can join other teens at a special dining-room table.

Children under 6 years are not allowed to ride on the trails, but wranglers are happy to walk children around the corral on a horse.

Evening baby-sitting can be arranged, with advance notice.

NICETIES: On arrival, guests find complimentary baskets of fruit and half-bottles of wine in their casitas.

The small casita kitchens are well stocked with a variety of fruit juices, soft drinks, liquor miniatures, and mixes. Guests keep a tally of their consumption, and the total is added to their bill.

A bookshelf full of paperbacks from yesteryear can be found in each casita, and there are flashlights to take on nighttime desert walks.

Fresh fruit is available in the lodge lounge throughout the day.

OF INTEREST NEARBY: Small, historic Wickenburg village and its western museum are nearby. Frontier Street in Wickenburg is restored to resemble the Wickenburg of 80 years ago. Other relics of historic Wickenburg are the Little Red School House of pioneer days and Santa Fe Railroad steam locomotive Number 761 that once hauled passengers and freight on the route between Chicago and the Southwest.

The ghost towns of Weaver, Stanton, and Octive are in the Wickenburg area and make an interesting day trip.

Further afield are Joshua Forest with a large concentration of prehistoric Joshua trees (less than an hour away) and Oak Creek Canyon and Sedona (a two and a half hour drive).

FOR MORE INFORMATION: Write Wickenburg Inn Tennis and Guest Ranch, P.O. Box P, Wickenburg, AZ 85358, or phone (800) 528-4227; in Arizona, (602) 684-7811.

C Lazy U Ranch
Granby, Colorado

When C Lazy U became the first dude ranch to put in a swimming pool and tennis courts, other ranchers scoffed at what they termed a country club atmosphere. But now that swimming pools are a common feature of guest ranches, and a few others have gone so far as to lay tennis courts, C Lazy U has taken on a more flattering nickname, the Cadillac of Dude Ranches. It is, after all, the only ranch in the United States to merit a five-star rating from the Mobil guide and a five-diamond rating from AAA.

C Lazy U is posh, by ranch standards, and attracts an upscale crowd. The cottages have all been extensively renovated, with interiors that are indistinguishable from a first-rate hotel room or suite. The dusty lane that cuts through the ranch is flanked by manicured lawns, and the amenities include an indoor racquetball court, sauna and whirlpool, recreation room, and lounge.

But that's not to say it's not a ranch. Riding is taken seriously here. Scores of guests saddle up each morning and afternoon.

Opened to guests in 1934, the 2,500-acre ranch is spread over a valley (altitude 8,300 feet) in north-central Colorado about three hours from Denver. Ringing the valley is a ridge of foothills leading to Rocky Mountain National Park and the Arapaho National Forest. From atop the ridges, riders look out over the mirrorlike surfaces of Grand Lake, Granby Lake, and the headwaters of the Colorado River.

ACCOMMODATIONS: $$$$ The ranch has 41 units and can accommodate as many as 120 guests, up to half of whom are likely to be children during July and August. Two- to four-unit cottages feature breezy front porches, spacious rooms with cathedral ceilings and stone fireplaces, walk-in closets, and fully modern bathrooms.

There are no television sets or telephones, and room keys are not issued, although you may lock yourself in at night. Each unit has a safe.

The peak season is between the last week of June and the first week of September. There are no children's rates for children 6 and over; children under 6 years old receive a discount and may not ride on trails. The rates include room and meals, trail rides and other activities, and a supervised program for children. Alcoholic beverages, ice cream, and skeet shooting are extra. Daily rates are available in early June and September.

DINING: Breakfast may be ordered from the grill or chosen from an expansive buffet. Lunch is a lavish buffet, dished out poolside. It may include soup, a full salad bar, chicken salad or other sandwiches, fresh pineapple and other fruit—and home-baked cookies.

Dinner is a gourmet affair served in the dining room on the second floor of the main lodge. Waitresses bring drinks and your meals to long tables of eight to 10 persons. Cookout buffets are served around the pool each Wednesday and Saturday night.

Drinks are served poolside from 11 A.M. to 5:30 P.M. daily and in the lodge before and after dinner. And for the sweet tooth, ice-cream concoctions are dished up at the Patio House Ice Cream Parlour before and after dinner.

Breakfast is the only meal a family eats together. Children eat lunch and dinner with their camp counselors.

ACTIVITIES

 Two Laykold courts, racquetball court.

 At Pole Creek Golf Course, 14 miles away. Green fees, instruction.

 Heated outdoor pool.

 White-water rafting on the Colorado River is available through a local outfitter each Friday.

 A fishing guide is available to lead serious fishers to the best spots. Casual fishing in a stocked lake or in Willow Creek.

 Guided early-morning hikes.

 Each guest is assigned his or her own horse from a string of 140 gentle horses. Trails cover a 40-square-mile area, some of it open range, and other parts rugged, mountainous terrain that passes through aspen and pine forests. Except for Friday morning's family ride, adults ride separately from children, who are grouped with their counselors; all-day picnic ride on Thursday. Individualized lessons available. The week culminates in the "Shodeo"—a staff and guest rodeo—on Saturday afternoon.

 Indoor racquetball court, whirlpool.

Skeet and trap shooting available for a fee.

Nordic skiing on 20 miles of groomed trails; ski equipment provided. Alpine skiers are shuttled 25 miles to Winter Park, where there are 93 trails and 18 lifts. The smaller Silver Creek ski area is only 10 miles away. Guests also enjoy ice-skating on the lake, sleigh rides, sledding and tubing.

Square dancing, camp-fire sing-alongs, musical entertainment.

 The ranch has a few head of cattle that would-be wranglers can help drive to pasture in the afternoon.

FOR CHILDREN: The ranch has operated a full children's program since 1949 for children 3 and older.

A staff of at least six well-trained counselors is on hand to make sure the children are kept happy and safe. Children can be in their care from just after breakfast until 8:30 P.M., with hour breaks after the kids' lunch and before dinner.

The youngest age group, 3- to 5-year-olds, spends some time on horseback, but the counselors take the reins. The children ride Big Bertha, a mare of 30 or 40 years, and the Shetland pony Toby Tyler, or ride in a donkey cart pulled by Luigi. When they're not "horsing around," the little kids feed the colts, pick flowers, finger paint, and play Duck, Duck, Goose.

The older kids get their first introduction to horseback riding in the ring on Monday morning. They're divided by ability and sent out on morning and afternoon rides. Thursday is an all-day ride to the top of Old Baldy, where they sometimes meet their parents for lunch. The same day, the younger kids hike up a smaller hill called Three-to-Five Baldy for games and lunch. On Friday families ride together, affording Mom and Dad a chance to admire the progress their child has made in controlling a horse.

Between trail rides, the children go swimming, play on the playground, fish, or play other games. All ages usually come together for evening activities. A ranch favorite, Capture the Flag, is played in the lane outside the main lodge a couple nights a week.

NICETIES: When you check in, you'll get a roster of that week's guests and their hometowns to help you get acquainted.

In your room, you'll find a small basket of fruit and snacks, along with an extensive toiletries tray.

All rooms are equipped with humidifiers, coffee/tea makers and blow dryers.

Logs are laid in the fireplace each morning, and an extra supply of firewood is stacked outside your door.

Coffee is served on the veranda outside the main lodge at 7 each morning, followed by an optional hike.

OF INTEREST NEARBY: Grand Lake, which, at an altitude of 8,100 feet, lays claims to the country's highest yacht club and golf course, is just 20 miles away. The glacial lake, 12 miles long and a mile wide, attracts boaters, swimmers, and trout fishermen.

Estes Park, about 60 miles away across the breathtaking Trail Ridge Road, is filled with shops, restaurants, and recreation opportunities. For those seeking solace in the mountains, Rocky Mountain National Park offers almost unlimited hiking trails.

FOR MORE INFORMATION: Write to the ranch at P.O. Box 379, Granby, CO 80446, or call (303) 887-3344.

Peaceful Valley Lodge and Ranch Resort

Lyons, Colorado

Peaceful Valley Lodge and Ranch Resort is a handsome, carefully conceived all-season ranch resort whose goal is a happy and shared family experience. Owned and operated by Karl and Mabel Boehm and their family, it is large enough to include activities for all tastes and small enough to be flexible and intimate. A plaque on the wall in the dining room proclaims "He who enters is a stranger but once!" and symbolizes the emphasis on informality, hospitality, and personal attention to each guest.

Located in the South St. Vrain Canyon near Rocky Mountain National Park just 60 miles from Denver, the Swiss chalet–style lodge and Alpine-type cabins seem a bit out of place until the ranch's history is explained. The founder of the current ranch, Karl Boehm, was an Austrian refugee from the Nazis who trained in the Rockies when he was a member of the U.S. ski corps, the Tenth Mountain Division. On the night that Boehm and his Kentucky-born wife, Mabel, purchased the ranch in the mid-1950s, the ranch buildings burned, and the Boehms built from scratch using architectural features Karl remembered from the Austrian Alps. The overall effect is charming.

A unique feature of the ranch is its Alpine-style chapel overlooking the valley and the jagged mountains that form the Continental Divide. Worship services are held Sunday mornings and Wednesday evenings in the summer. The lodge is open all year.

ACCOMMODATIONS: $$ to $$$ There's a wide variety of accommodations in separate buildings: the Main Lodge (21 rooms), the Edelweiss Chalet (12 rooms), and 11 freestanding cabins. Some of the rooms include sitting rooms; others have separate vanity and dressing areas. All the rooms are tastefully decorated with attention to detail and comfort. The capacity is about 120 guests.

The cabins each have one to three bedrooms and a living room with a fireplace; some have hot tubs or Jacuzzis. Some have porches overlooking the St. Vrain River, which runs through the property. Other cabins are located in the woods.

The larger cabins have a minimal occupancy requirement and are very well suited for larger families. The largest separate cabin, Seven Gables, has 10 rooms grouped around a common living room. Isolated from the Main Lodge, it is perfect for large family reunions.

There are three rate categories—best, superior, and moderate—according to different appointments and room size. Week-long stays are required in the summer. Children's rates are available. Children 2 and under are free.

DINING: Meals are served family style in a bright pine-paneled dining room, each table set with fresh flowers. The breakfast bell rings at 8 A.M., but guests have until 10 A.M. to amble in. Lunch is served to all at 1 P.M., and dinner at 6:30 P.M. Wine and beer are available before dinner at the Edelweiss Room and can be served with dinner.

The food is traditional American cooking with a few European dishes thrown in (Wiener schnitzel is one of the chef's specialties). The variety of vegetables and salads at meals enables one to keep to a diet, although willpower will be required to resist the delicious pastries, desserts, and freshly baked rolls. The staff is responsive to special diet needs.

A variety of table sizes permits different seating arrangements; you can meet new people or remain within your own family group. During the summer, there are separate children's tables.

Throughout the week there are special dining highlights, such as a poolside barbecue, chuck-wagon breakfast on the mountain, and other cookouts.

The coffee shop is open during the day for soft drinks, coffee, pie, cakes, and ice cream.

ACTIVITIES

 One outdoor hard-surface court.

 Public course in nearby Estes Park.

 In a large indoor solar-heated pool; adjacent sauna, whirlpool.

 Half- or full-day rafting trips can be arranged through an out-fitter in Fort Collins.

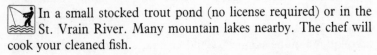 In a small stocked trout pond (no license required) or in the St. Vrain River. Many mountain lakes nearby. The chef will cook your cleaned fish.

Scheduled all-day trips to the back country via four-wheel-drive vans or bus. A number of hiking trails begin at the lodge and lead into the Roosevelt National Forest lands surrounding the lodge.

Large string of gentle horses. Trail rides are scheduled each day along a variety of routes that accommodate varying abilities; instruction offered. There are all-day rides, breakfast rides, lunch rides, and supper rides. Once a week there is a gymkhana (a combination horse show and rodeo) at which guests are both participants and spectators. The ranch has large indoor and outdoor arenas. An overnight pack trip is offered into the high country of the Indian Peaks region from Wednesday morning through Thursday noon for an additional fee.

Horseshoes, volleyball, shuffleboard, and organized excursions to ghost towns.

Square dancing, talent shows, melodramas, sing-alongs, kaffee klatsches, slide shows, movies, and naturalist talks are held in the evenings.

 Cross-country skiing, snowshoeing (equipment can be rented), and sleigh rides.

FOR CHILDREN: Special full-day programs for young children over 3 and teenagers include riding, swimming, crafts, fishing, games, nature lore, and hiking. Parents may take their children in and out of the program as they please.

Children under 6 do no trail riding but ride in a pony cart or in the ring. Older youngsters may ride twice a day (one trail ride, one horsemanship lesson).

There are well-trained counselors assigned to each group. Special arrangements can be made for child care for younger children for an hourly fee. A counselor helps the teen group plan its own schedule of activities, including special camp-fire programs, hikes, and trail rides.

The playground, with its wooden fort and gigantic sandbox, is the center of daily activities for the younger set; they also enjoy the petting farm, with kid goats, lambs, calves, and foals. Older children gravitate to the game room next to the dance hall, where they can play foosball, pool, air hockey, Ping-Pong, or Pac Man.

Family Day, an outing into the mountains, is scheduled weekly for the enjoyment of parents and children. You can climb a mountain ridge for a view of a big glacier basin or hike to a waterfall.

NICETIES: Riding or hiking boot rental is available at the Sport Shop, as well as tennis racquets, tennis shoes, and fishing equipment.

A clock-radio in each cabin and a coin-operated set of washers and dryers are useful amenities.

OF INTEREST NEARBY: Central City is a renovated gold mining town filled with a variety of shops. There is a museum and a 20-minute gold mine tour. The renovated Opera House holds performances Tuesday through Sunday in the summer.

Estes Park is the entrance to the Rocky Mountain National Park. From mid-May to mid-September you can ride the aerial tramway to the summit of 8,700-foot Prospect Mountain. The Estes Park Area Historical Museum has exhibits on local Indians, early settlers, and a homestead cabin.

FOR MORE INFORMATION: Write Karl E. Boehm, Peaceful Valley Lodge and Ranch Resort, Box 2811, Lyons, CO 80540, or call (303) 747-2881.

Tumbling River Ranch
Grant, Colorado

The first thing you notice when you pull into Tumbling River is the friendliness that blankets the air. It's not just the staff that lays out the welcome mat, but the other guests as well. They take their cue from Jim and Mary Dale Gordon, transplanted Texans who bought the ranch in the early 1970s.

Tumbling River was established as a guest ranch in the 1940s. It had been homesteaded in the 1890s on a tight 200 acres of wilderness wedged between mountains in Pike National Forest on the front range of the Rocky Mountains. Five miles of Geneva Creek—the so-called tumbling river—cut through the ranch.

At the upper end of the ranch is the five-level main lodge, built by a 1920s-era mayor of Denver. It houses five guest rooms, each with a fireplace and bath, two lounges, and a dining room that affords a picture-postcard view of bighorn sheep on the rocky cliffs that the Gordons have dubbed Flag Mountain. A half dozen cabins, the Gordons' house, the Trading Post, a swimming pool, whirlpool, rec room, and corral are also clustered on the upper ranch.

Down the road is the lower ranch, or Pueblo. Louise Porter, Adolph Coors's daughter, brought Taos Indians from New Mexico in the late 1920s to build the lodge of stucco, stone, and hand-carved wooden beams. On the first floor are spacious living and dining areas built around large stone fireplaces; upstairs are seven airy guest rooms.

ACCOMMODATIONS: $$ to $$$ Cabins and individual rooms at the upper ranch are furnished in charming antiques. Bookshelves are lined with mysteries and novels. All cabins and individual rooms have porches and fireplaces, which always have firewood laid and kerosene-soaked sawdust ready to ignite.

Guest rooms at the Pueblo are larger, more comfortable, more modern, and furnished in a southwest decor.

Children's rates are available. Discounted rates for adults and children apply in early June and again in September. The rates cover lodging, meals, horses, the children's program, and all activities except overnight pack trips and raft trips. The ranch's capacity is about 60.

DINING: A bell is rung each morning, noon, and evening to signal that chow time is 15 minutes away. Guests and some staff members sit together at tables for six or eight; Pueblo guests eat in the dining room there. Food is served family style, all you can eat, and the recipes have all been developed and tested on the staff by Mary Dale. Breads and desserts are all homemade and baked daily.

A typical dinner is barbecued steak, fettucini, fresh asparagus, warmed spiced apples, and banana fudge pie. Candlelight-and-wine dinners are served for adults only two nights a week. On other nights, families eat meals together.

Simple hors d'oeuvres are served in the lounge in the main ranch house before dinner each evening. Setups and cocktail mixes are on hand, but you must bring your own liquor or buy it in a nearby town.

ACTIVITIES

 Heated outdoor pool, adjacent whirlpool. Hot tub and cabana at the Pueblo.

 White-water raft trip through the Brown's Canyon section of the Arkansas River. Children should be at least 8 years old.

In a pond stocked with rainbow trout. No fishing license is needed. Anglers almost surely will want to sign up for the overnight pack trip. You'll ride above the timberline to Shelf Lake next to the Continental Divide for an afternoon of fishing. A short ride farther is the overnight camp, complete with mattresses. You'll have a steak cookout that evening and a hearty breakfast the next morning before riding back to the ranch.

Mary Dale leads an early-morning walk to gather wildflowers on Saturday. You can also take a jeep trip into remote, unspoiled areas along the routes once taken by old stagecoaches and trains. You'll find evidence of the Ute Indians along with trappers' dilapidated cabins. Rock collectors can spend an afternoon at the old mines with a pick and shovel.

Rides of varying lengths are offered each day. There's a breakfast ride on Tuesday, a brunch ride on Tuesday, and a trail ride that winds up at a lunch cookout at Duck Creek Thursday. Wednesday's all-day ride takes guests to a point near the Continental Divide. On Thursday, people who are game can ride up to the snowy mountain peaks on the overnight pack trip. On Saturday, everyone gathers at the arena at 2 o'clock for a rodeo. It's a chance for kids and adults to show their new-found skill in controlling their horses. There's barrel racing, pole bending, the keyhole turn, an egg toss, and a boot scramble. Everyone gets ribbons.

Rec hall with Ping-Pong and pool tables. There are lots of off-ranch excursions each week. Vans take guests each Tuesday over Guanella Pass to the quaint mining town of Georgetown for an afternoon of shopping and a ride on a narrow-gauge train. On Fridays, there's a van trip to South Park City Museum, a restored western town in Fairplay. Each Monday, a hay-packed pickup truck takes guests to Jack's Mine, an old mining town above the timberline.

Square dancing, hootenanny, and a guest talent show are held in the evenings.

FOR CHILDREN: A children's program, geared to three separate age brackets, operates from 9 A.M. to 6:30 P.M. Tuesday through

Friday and up till the rodeo on Saturday. Children ride separately from their parents, but sometimes meet up with them on the trail for lunch. But the program is very flexible: anytime you want to spend an afternoon fishing or swimming with your child, just let the counselor know.

A counselor leads the 3- to 5-year-olds on ponies. When they're not riding, they're likely to keep busy playing games, swimming, jeeping, or making pressed-flower pictures or painted horseshoes to take home.

Almost every morning, children aged 6 to 11 take their horses out on trails with a counselor and wrangler at the head and tail. The rest of the day offers a full menu of activities: a train ride in Georgetown, climbing on antique locomotives at South Park City Museum in Fairplay, Ping-Pong and pool, swimming, and fishing (they love to see the cooks serve that day's catch).

Teens often join the adults on the all-day rides and jeep trips or take a raft on the Arkansas River. Tuesday is a special teen day, when the energetic youths master the climb up Flag Mountain and plant flags in its rocky soil in the morning and take a special trail ride in the afternoon.

During Tuesday's candlelight dinner for the grown-ups, kids are treated to their own weenie roast and play the all-time favorite game, Capture the Flag. And Thursday evening is a spaghetti dinner followed by bingo and other games.

And the kids never tire of tagging after the ranch pets. There are Daisy and Molly, golden retrievers, Catman, a tabby cat, ducks, geese, and calves.

NICETIES: On arrival, each guest is given a *concho*, or leather neckpiece, with his or her name on it and the ranch's brand. Wearing the *conchos* helps the guests get to know each other's names quickly. The horses have them, too. You'll also get a roster of staff members and the week's guest roster, listing the guests' names, hometowns, and children's names and ages.

In your room, you'll find a small basket of fruit with a hand-printed welcome note.

If you want, coffee will be brought to your cabin door at 7 A.M., giving you time to wake up before the breakfast bell sounds.

There's a guest laundry with commercial-size washers and dryers and free soap.

OF INTEREST NEARBY: Georgetown, known as the Silver Queen of the Rockies, is an hour's drive over a narrow dirt road that winds through Guanella Pass. Said to have been the greatest producer of silver in the world in the 1880s, the old mining town now is a motherlode of antiques and crafts shops, restaurants, old hotels, and historic buildings. It's also the home of the narrow gauge railroad, the Georgetown Loop, on which you can take an hour's ride.

Also nearby is the historic mining town of Fairplay, with its locomotives and western town of restored buildings assembled from all parts of Colorado.

FOR MORE INFORMATION: Write Tumbling River Ranch, Grant, CO 80448, or call (800) 654-8770.

Vista Verde Guest and Ski Touring Ranch
Steamboat Springs, Colorado

Vista Verde, aptly named, is located in a small green jewel of a valley in the Rocky Mountains of northwestern Colorado. There are exquisite views in all directions, and wildlife is abundant, with frequent sightings of deer, elk, beavers, eagles, marmots, and even an occasional bear. In the summer, wildflowers are everywhere, despite the elevation of 7,800 feet.

The 1,600-acre ranch is a working cattle and horse operation surrounded by the 1.1-million-acre Routt National Forest, with over 100 lakes and 900 miles of mountain streams, and the Mount Zirkel Wilderness Area, a 140,000-acre area restricted to foot and horseback travel. The snow-capped peaks of the Continental Divide can be seen on clear days.

Vista Verde is intimate and family-oriented. The number of guests typically ranges between 25 and 32. The owners' goal is to provide a wilderness experience with the comforts of home. The staff is well trained and includes many employees who are outdoor enthusiasts with an interest in the natural sciences. Guests are invited to experience some of the ranch work activities, including riding herd on 200 head of cattle, checking fences, and helping with haying operations.

ACCOMMODATIONS: $$$ The nine cabins are inviting and provided with all amenities. They embody the philosophy of the ranch: simple comfort, attention to detail, and charm. Along with modern bathrooms, there are small touches that recall the past: calico curtains, quilts, old photographs, and dried-flower arrangements.

The family-size cabins sleep six; two bedrooms are upstairs and one downstairs. They are made from hand-hewn logs of native pine and spruce; each has a small kitchenette and comfortable living room with a wood-burning stove or fireplace. All have small front decks that overlook a small stream.

Rates cover accommodations, all meals, and all activities and excursions. The minimum stay is one week in July and August; guests arrive on a Sunday. Children's rates are available. The ranch closes in May and November.

DINING: The food is traditional American cooking with a gourmet flair, served family style in the main lodge or on picnic tables near the outdoor barbecue. Portions are large, and seconds are always available. The chef is a Culinary Institute of America graduate, and his training shows in the taste, variety, and attention to presentation.

Special diets can be accommodated with advance notice. Bread and pastries are home-baked, the eggs collected each day from the chicken house, and the beef raised on the ranch. Wine may be purchased at dinner. Families eat together.

Throughout each week there are scheduled breakfast cookouts, and lunch and evening barbecues. Trail lunches are provided as needed for the all-day trips.

ACTIVITIES

 Privileges at courts five miles from the ranch.

In a lake. Hot tub and sauna.

All-day rafting trip on the upper Colorado River included in the rate. Guests who want more river floating should ask about the Ranch Float Trip package, which consists of five days at the ranch and a two-day float.

Trout fishing in nearby mountain streams and lakes. One of Colorado's finest fly fishermen holds a weekly clinic.

There's an attractive log spa overlooking the valley. It has a large whirlpool, sauna, cold tub, showers, and exercise room. A masseuse comes out to the ranch once a week.

All-day hike to Mica Basin or Gilpin Lake, sometimes on the old Wyoming Trail once used by cattle rustlers and outlaws.

Guests are matched with one of 55 horses, which becomes theirs for the entire week. Rides are usually two and a half hours long on trails that wind throughout the forest and wilderness area; they are limited to five or six guests and a wrangler. An all-day ride along the South Fork of the Elk River, with lunch on the trail, is scheduled during the week. On Saturdays, the staff and guests participate in an exhibition of horseback riding, games, and skills called a gymkhana. Overnight pack trips can be arranged for an extra charge.

Guided gold-panning expeditions, organized games, hayrides. Evening programs include sing-alongs, slide shows, square dancing and, of course, pleasant conversation in the antiques-furnished living room of the main lodge. Television and games are also available there. On Friday evenings guests attend the rodeo in Steamboat Springs.

A rock-climbing clinic is conducted one afternoon a week. Mountain bike tours of the Routt Forest are offered. Hot-air balloon rides can be arranged.

Cross-country skiing on 12 miles of marked and groomed trails on the ranch and 24 miles of trails on adjacent Forest Service lands. Snowshoeing, ice fishing, dogsledding, ice climbing, and sleigh rides pulled by Daisy and Diamond, a team of Belgian draft horses. Steamboat Springs is a center of downhill skiing, including national and international ski jumping competitions.

FOR CHILDREN: Children over 6 participate in the general riding program with adults, although special programs, games, and rides are offered if there are many children present.

Children from about 3 to 6 have their own program, which includes an introduction to the care and feeding of farm animals, from ducks and chickens to goats and lambs. They are familiarized with horses and their care with the cooperation of Minnie and Tony, two miniature horses that they can saddle and halter lead.

Additional activities such as fishing, gold-panning, hiking, scavenger hunts, and rides in an antique fire engine keep kids happy. At dinner one night, you're likely to find that your children hand-cranked the ice cream!

Baby-sitting for younger children can sometimes be arranged with advance notice. There is an imaginative children's playground, Fort Smiles, with a play house, slides, and swings located within easy distance and sight of the cabins.

NICETIES: Hummingbird feeders hang from the front porch of the Main Lodge, and there are rope hammocks hung near the cabins so you can enjoy the gurgle of the nearby stream.

Small bags of potpourri in the cabins give them a woodsy smell.

Each cabin has cooking facilities and a small refrigerator. Coffee, tea, and hot cocoa are provided.

OF INTEREST NEARBY: The ranch is 45 minutes from Steamboat Springs, a major ski center in the winter and a popular western-flavor tourist stop in the summer. Steamboat Springs has many art galleries, shops and restaurants, as well as a large hot-springs swimming pool and giant water slide. In the summer, the Repertory Theatre, Strings in the Mountains festival, and the Perry-Mansfield School of Dance offer public performances, and the Fourth of July Rodeo is considered one of the best in the West. The ski area's gondola operates year-round.

Golf, tennis courts, boating, and sailing are available nearby at Steamboat Lake.

FOR MORE INFORMATION: Write Vista Verde Guest and Ski Touring Ranch, Box 465, Steamboat Springs, CO 80477, or call (303) 879-3858 or (800) 526-RIDE.

Averill's Flathead Lake Lodge and Dude Ranch
Bigfork, Montana

The setting is idyllic: 2,000 acres on the shoreline of Flathead Lake, North America's largest natural freshwater lake west of the Great Lakes, with the Swan River National Wildlife Refuge as a backdrop. The activities are endless: riding, boating, fishing, swimming, hiking, and tennis. The food is hearty, the staff energetic, the guests friendly, and the ambience totally conducive to relaxation.

All in all, Averill's Flathead Lake Lodge offers everything anyone could want in a western family vacation, unless your wants extend to glamorous nightlife and a fast pace. There's none of that here, and there never will be. The closest thing to nightlife one can find is the summer stock production at the nearby Bigfork Summer Playhouse. And the only devotees of a fast pace are a few of the horses.

The Averill family has been operating this first-class dude ranch since 1945, and their formula for hospitality remains unchanged. The ranch is now in the hands of a second-generation Averill, Doug, a former rodeo rider, and his wife, Maureen, and they make their home here, as well as their livelihood. Their own children move from activity to activity and provide welcome reassurance to guests that children aren't just tolerated here.

This AAA four-diamond ranch is so popular with guests that it's frequently booked more than a year in advance. The return rate is on the order of 90 percent plus. That kind of loyalty from guests—and the 4-star rating from Mobil—prove indisputably that the Averills are doing something right.

ACCOMMODATIONS: $$$$ The 125 guests at the ranch are assigned to 22 cottages and 20 lodge rooms, depending upon the size of their families and availability. The two- to three-bedroom cottages are rustic and furnished with handmade beds.

Rates include all meals and many activities. Children's rates rise with age. All guests arrive and leave on a Sunday. The season extends from May through September, with families accounting for most of the business in July and August.

DINING: All the cooking is done by college students, most of whom are studying for degrees in the hotel and restaurant management field. The food is hearty and the servings ample. Meals are served family style in the Main Lodge, which was built by the Civilian Conservation Corps in 1932 and features larch walls and floors, a dozen or so trophies of past hunting expeditions, and a huge stone fireplace. Old saddles line the balcony railing, and there's a piano for sing-alongs (and sheet music, too).

Breakfast, at 8 A.M., typically features a local favorite, such as huckleberry pancakes (much better than blueberry, as any bear will tell you). Lunch, at 12:30 P.M., is usually served outdoors on the terrace overlooking the lake. Dinner, at 6:30 P.M., is a one-entrée offering, ranging from prime rib to crown roast of pork to Cornish game hens. Children are served a half hour before adults, and then a staff member takes them to the game room or the swimming pool so that their parents can enjoy a leisurely meal. (Families may, however, choose to eat together.)

A highlight of each week is the Wednesday night steak fry in the mountains, which guests ride to either on horses or a hay wagon.

The ranch has no liquor license, but guests who enjoy a cocktail before dinner or a nightcap before bed may bring a bottle and place it in the cozy Saddle Sore Saloon, which is off limits to kids. Mixers are available there.

ACTIVITIES

 Four Plexi-Pave courts.

Privileges at an 18-hole course on the other side of Bigfork.

 Large outdoor pool.

Flathead Lake, clear and deep blue, offers water-skiing, sailing, fishing, and even scuba diving. Guests are free to check out a rowboat, canoe, or motorboat anytime at no charge or sign up for a short sail on the 51-foot *Questa*, a sailboat built for the America's Cup trials in 1929 by industrialist J. P. Morgan. A charter fishing boat is also available for half-day trips on the lake. And once or twice a week, a 200-passenger ship operated by the Averills from the other side of the lake comes over to the lodge to take guests on an evening cruise. (Watch out for the powerboats that chase the boat. They're filled with kids armed with water balloons!) The lodge's own full-time outfitter organizes several white-water rafting or tubing excursions weekly.

Several professional fishermen on the lodge's staff can serve as guides or simply direct guests to proven holes. Fly-fishing equipment, including waders, is available for the asking. A scenic fishing trip on a raft is offered on the upper Swan River for adults and children 6 and over (extra charge).

Several outings are planned weekly to Wildhorse Island State Park, a nature preserve accessible only by boat. Rocky Mountain sheep and wild horses roam the island. On the 20-mile boat ride there, passengers can see an old Indian site. Some rock paintings from prehistoric times are still visible.

Riding is decidedly the favored activity here. The lodge maintains a string of about 60 horses and schedules two rides daily, as well as special day-long, breakfast, and luncheon rides.

Barn dances with a bluegrass band, steer roping in the arena by professional ropers, or a bonfire on the lakefront in the evenings. Many guests go to the summer theater in Bigfork on one evening; it's a pleasant walk there, and the lodge will arrange return transport in its 1913 white open-air limousine.

FOR CHILDREN: Separate children's rides are offered in the morning and afternoon. A high point of each week for many children is the overnight campout in the two teepees by the lake. There's also a game room that serves as a hangout for children (located, conveniently, next to the guests' laundry room).

Each of the activity areas on the lodge property is staffed at all times, so you need not worry about your children being unsupervised. The Averills say that staff members are alert to the needs of children and keep an especially watchful eye on the waterfront.

Because of the special allure that horses hold for children, an extra effort is made to acquaint children with all aspects of their care. Those who are interested can be assigned a horse for which they are responsible for the week. They'll learn all about feeding and grooming and exercising—and cleaning out stalls.

Near the stable is a "bucking bronco" made out of a suspended barrel. Kids love sitting on this and pretending that they're out on the range.

The ranch has between 30 and 35 children as guests in any given week, most of them 8 or older. With advance notice, the management will be happy to arrange regular baby-sitting for a younger child for the entire week, or on an as-needed basis.

NICETIES: The Averills will provide a portable intercom so you can keep an ear tuned to a sleeping child while sunning yourself on the lawn.

Cars are available free for local use and at a competitive rental rate for longer trips to Glacier Park or other nearby attractions.

There's a bookcase full of old classics, western novels, spy thrillers and science fiction in the main lodge.

OF INTEREST NEARBY: Glacier National Park is about an hour's drive from the lodge, and most guests schedule at least a day's outing there. For a more intimate look at the park, plan to spend a few days there after your stay at the ranch. The park offers numerous ranger-led activities for children and endless hiking opportunities. The scenery is spectacular.

FOR MORE INFORMATION: Write Averill's Flathead Lake Lodge, Box 248, Bigfork, MT 59911, or call (406) 837-4391.

Lone Mountain Ranch

Big Sky, Montana

There's a reason Montana calls itself Big Sky country, and why the community where the Lone Mountain Ranch is located is called Big Sky. The sky really does seem bigger here. The mountain peaks also seem higher, the wildflower colors more vivid, the drinking water fresher and colder, the air crisper, the whole environment more invigorating.

Lone Mountain Ranch occupies a spectacular setting on the edge of the Lee Metcalf Wilderness Area, which encompasses the rugged Spanish Peaks range. In the background towers Lone Mountain, which is often snow covered, even in August. The area surrounding the ranch is protected from development and hence offers boundless opportunities for undisturbed trail rides or hikes on which one can view elk, moose, coyote, mountain sheep, mountain goat, deer, and eagles—and sometimes even a bear. Yet it's just 75 minutes from the airport at Bozeman, Montana.

After a multi-state search for an ideal site for a guest ranch, Vivian and Bob Schaap bought the ranch in 1977 and set out to transform it into one of the West's premier guest ranches and cross-country ski-touring centers. It is one of the few ranches in the West that operates year-round.

ACCOMMODATIONS: $$$$ The ranch has about 20 log cabins that range in age from brand-new to more than 50 years old; they accommodate a total of about 60 guests. Some cabins sit by the North Fork River; others perch on a hillside, affording panoramic views. All have electric heat and modern bathrooms, as well as front porches, and most have fireplaces or wood-burning stoves (with a large stock of wood and kerosene-soaked fire starter). Much of the furniture is made from lodgepole pines, which lends the cabins a truly rustic air. The large family-size cabins typically have two bed-rooms and a large living room with fireplace.

Rates are set according to the number of people in a cabin; there are discounted rates for children between 2 and 5. Children under 2 are free. Several of the larger log cabins are well-suited to sharing by two families. The rate includes all meals, riding instruction, an organized children's program, transportation to and from the Boze-man airport, and all regular ranch activities.

DINING: Eating at the Lone Mountain Ranch is akin to eating in someone's home—except that the food is likely to be better here. The ranch has an excellent chef in Neil Navratil, who has made it his permanent home. All meals are served in a western-style dining hall, replete with cowboy and Indian art and a huge rock fireplace. The ranch management calls the cuisine "ranch cooking with a gour-met flair," which is appropriate.

Breakfast is served buffet style from 7 to 10 A.M.; lunch is also served buffet style, from 11:30 to 2 P.M.

Dinner is a sit-down affair, with a hostess directing guests to different tables each night to ease mingling. Four entrées are served; wine and beer are available. Each week, weather permitting, several meals are served outside: a steak barbecue and sing-along are held one night a week by the Schaaps's house on top of a hill with glorious views. Another night is the dinner ride (non-riders and children take a hayride to the cook site). Highlights of the week are a breakfast and hamburger barbecue on the Schaaps's hill.

The dinner menu is posted a week in advance so that you can arrange an alternative entrée if the chef has planned something you are unable to eat. With advance notice, the chef will prepare special meals that meet specific dietary guidelines.

ACTIVITIES

 White-water rafting on the nearby Gallatin and Yellowstone rivers. The ranch arranges at least one rafting excursion weekly (extra charge).

Daily walks guided by naturalists, which provide a great way to learn about the greater Yellowstone ecosystem, local wildflowers and birds, and Indian lore. Excursions each week into Yellowstone National Park, for an additional charge.

Superb trout fishing on the nearby Gallatin River, a blue-ribbon trout stream, or on the Madison, Firehole, Yellowstone, Gibbon, and Henry's Fork rivers, somewhat longer drives. Lone Mountain is one of only a few resorts in the country to win the designation Orvis Endorsed Lodge from the Orvis Co., premier manufacturers of fishing equipment. An Orvis shop in the ranch's main building arranges guided fishing trips and instruction. Orvis rental equipment is also available.

The ranch maintains a stable of 115 horses and offers two rides daily to guests (except Sunday, the horses' and wranglers' day of rest). Rides are guided and limited to seven guests each. Each guest is assigned a horse and saddle for the week. Children ride separately from adults, although older children are allowed to accompany their parents on some trail rides. Children under 6 are not permitted on the trails, but are taken on rides around the property.

One of the original ranch buildings, the B-K, serves as the comfortable guest lounge. It's a great place for reading, relaxing, and gathering for a drink before or after dinner. (The kids have their own "Sasparilla Saloon" there.) The building also houses "The Hideout," a favorite gathering place for kids.

Talks on the area's wildlife, square dancing, and slide shows about Yellowstone are offered in the evenings.

FOR CHILDREN: The ranch offers a daily children's program for children between 6 and 12, and supervised activities for younger children. But the focus is really on older children, and families with younger children are gently forewarned by the management that they may feel tied down if they choose this ranch for a vacation.

For children over 6, the program features overnight camp-outs (in a teepee or old sheepherder's wagon!), cookouts, trail rides, rodeos, arts and crafts, nature walks, and outdoor games. The activities coincide with the adult trail rides.

One night a week, the children have a special nature walk and party at the North Fork Cabin. The cookout and camp-out on

Wednesday nights are something your children will remember for years to come. An 8-year-old boy we met here talked excitedly for the rest of the week about the seven shooting stars he had seen from his berth in the sheepherder's wagon!

The ranch has a well-designed playground.

NICETIES: There's a coin laundry for guests' use.

The Schaaps send out a newsletter twice a year to former guests to acquaint them with changes at the ranch.

The cabins all have an eclectic collection of paperback books, and board games can be borrowed to help while away evening hours. The office maintains a small library of historical novels and natural history works about Montana, Yellowstone guide books, and diaries of trappers.

OF INTEREST NEARBY: Yellowstone National Park is only an hour away. It's hard to imagine being this close to the nation's oldest national park and not taking time to visit.

Bozeman, an old cowboy town, is about an hour's drive. If it rains during your week at Lone Mountain, you'll probably be offered an outing to Bozeman, with a visit to the Museum of the Rockies, which has interesting exhibits on dinosaurs and western history.

The Big Sky ski area is just above the ranch (Lone Mountain is the peak that provides the most challenging skiing there). During the summer months, you can ride a gondola up the mountain.

FOR MORE INFORMATION: Write Lone Mountain Ranch, Box 69, Big Sky, MT 59716, or call (406) 995-4644.

Mountain Sky Guest Ranch
Emigrant, Montana

The Mountain Sky Guest Ranch is the oldest guest ranch in Montana, but in some ways it may also be the most modern. Founded in the 1880s as a working cattle ranch, it began welcoming guests (under a different name) in the mid-1930s, and some of its most sought-after log cabins date to that era. But you can't find much more modern facilities anywhere than the ranch's heated outdoor swimming pool, sauna, and hot tub, or its mirror-walled dance and exercise studio, or its more recently built guest units, complete with all the comforts of home.

The 5,000-acre ranch in the Gallatin National Forest, a 75-minute drive from Bozeman, Montana, has been owned by the Brutger family since 1980 and has been substantially improved since Alan and Mary Brutger took over as resident managers a few years later. The ranch experience here reflects what the Brutgers themselves have always sought for their own family vacations: good food, comfortable accommodations, spectacular surroundings, and a variety of activities for all age groups, but no pressure to participate.

Situated on the eastern slope of the Gallatin Mountains, the ranch is a roaming ground for moose, deer, elk, and an occasional bear. Every trail is more scenic than the one you took yesterday, whether on horseback or on foot. You'll feel like you're a million miles from anywhere, alone among the towering lodgepole pines and the Milky Way. There are no highway noises, buzzing power lines, or airplanes passing overhead to disturb your solitude—only the bubbling of Big Creek and the call of a passing coyote. And if it's companionship you seek, there are always the other guests. Guest ranches seem to attract nice people.

ACCOMMODATIONS: $$$$ Mountain Sky has accommodations for about 80 guests in two dozen cabins or motel-type units. You can choose from a half dozen or so wonderfully rustic old log cabins, with either a fireplace or wood-burning stove, or from among 19 newer units.

Our preference is for the older cabins, which have large screened-in porches, one, two, or three bedrooms, and a living room—and plenty of atmosphere. But the modern cabins are also lovely. Those appropriate for families have a sitting room with a hide-a-bed and a separate bedroom; the largest have two bedrooms, a sitting room, and two baths. All cabins have refrigerators and coffee pots that come with a selection of coffees and herbal teas.

The rate structure is based on both the size of the cabin and the number of occupants. Children receive a nominal discount from adult rates. The ranch is open from June through October.

In the summer, cabins are rented on a weekly basis, beginning on Sundays, but shorter stays can occasionally be arranged.

DINING: The bell rings 10 minutes before mealtime to summon guests to the rustic dining hall in the main ranch building, where most meals (except lunch) are served. The chef here is exceptionally good. For early risers, a continental breakfast is served at 7 A.M. The regular breakfast is served between 8 and 9 A.M. and alternates between a bountiful buffet and sit-down, order-from-a-menu meals. Lunch is served at 12:30 P.M., outdoors.

Dinner is served at 6:45 P.M. Sunday night, the day of arrival, is a get-acquainted night, with a family dinner served buffet style (lots of good, hearty food, but nothing fancy). Children eat with their parents at this meal, and over coffee and dessert Alan Brutger explains the ranch's rules (safety first) and routines.

Thereafter, special children's dinners are served most nights at 5:30 P.M. in a separate children's dining room, while parents have their cocktails nearby. After dinner, the children are taken up to the activities center for a few hours of games, songs, and storytelling while parents enjoy their meals alone.

Tuesday night is gourmet night, featuring haute cuisine accompanied by a group of Austrian accordion players. Wednesday night is country music night, with an outdoor barbecue by the pool (children eat with their parents) followed by a sing-along. Friday night is another family night, with the menu featuring seafood (flown in from the Pacific Northwest. Saturday night is another adventure in gourmet cooking.

The chef will gladly prepare special meals for guests with food allergies or special diet requirements.

ACTIVITIES

 Two tennis courts and a staff member who loves to pick up a game now and then or provide some instruction.

Heated pool, sauna, and hot tub. A poolside bar serves up favorite drinks from 11 A.M. to 5 P.M. daily.

The fishing is fabulous in the nearby Yellowstone River or the Armstrong or Nelson creeks, two nearby blue-ribbon trout streams. Big Creek flows through the ranch property and has been known to reward anglers for just an hour of effort. The ranch also has a trout pond stocked with whoppers.

Excursions by van are offered once or twice weekly to Yellowstone National Park, less than an hour away (there's an extra charge). Rafting on the Yellowstone River is offered once each week to ranch guests by the Yellowstone Raft Co. Children as young as 5 are welcome on the trips, which offer a nice diversion from the ranch routine and a spectacular way to see the scenery in the Yellowstone Valley (extra charge).

 The ranch has a string of 85 horses. Twice-daily rides are offered at 9:30 A.M. and 2 P.M. Monday through Saturday; on Sunday, the horses and wranglers have the day off. An all-day ride is offered Thursday to those guests who feel comfortable enough in the saddle for such a test of endurance, and on Tuesday and Friday there are breakfast rides, beginning at 7 A.M. The ranch's trails feature spectacular views of the surrounding Absaroka and Madison mountain ranges. Be sure to take a ride up into the ranch's overnight pasture, where you'll have a panoramic view of Big Sky country, with Emigrant Peak (elevation 10,960 feet) in the background.

Mary Brutger offers almost-daily aerobics programs (at 7 A.M.!) in the modern dance studio next to the pool.

Evening activities are frequently scheduled following dinner, ranging from softball games open to all ages, to square dancing, to an impromptu pool tournament. A popular gathering place for adults before and after dinner is the Mountain View Lounge, next to the dining room, where homemade hors d'oeuvres and a full selection of cocktails (and 25 or so different beers) are served up.

FOR CHILDREN: Mountain Sky has something to offer children of all ages, from attentive baby-sitting for the very youngest to an active, outdoors-oriented program for those 3 and over. The Brutgers themselves have two young boys who are fixtures in the children's program. The program is usually run by a young woman with a degree in early childhood education and extensive preschool experience.

A wooden playground structure outside the activities room has a gigantic, shaded sandbox, swings, a wide slide, and climbing equipment, and serves as the focal point for the children's activities. The children's program meets from 9:15 to 11:30 A.M. and 1:45 to 4:30 P.M., and for dinner and after-dinner activities on three or four evenings a week.

The log-walled activities center is a favored hangout for teens, who like the pool and Ping-Pong tables. There's often someone banging out a song on the piano, or looking for a partner for chess or checkers. Younger children also use this building for arts and crafts and games.

Children 7 and over are permitted to go on trail rides. A special children's wrangler first assesses their skills and provides whatever instruction is needed. Two wranglers accompany each children's ride. For younger children, an old gentle horse is frequently saddled up for rides around the playground area.

NICETIES: A basket of fresh fruit is placed in your cabin daily, which helps tide children over between meals.

The children's activity center has a variety of baby equipment available—a backpack carrier for hikes, a stroller, car safety seats, and a playpen—that you can borrow.

There's a laundry, complete with iron and ironing board, in the pool area.

Water coolers filled with the tastiest—and coldest—water imaginable are placed strategically around the property so that guests don't get dehydrated in the dry mountain air.

Arriving guests are given a list of all the other guests in residence that week, and their hometowns. In your cabin, you'll also find a Who's Who on the staff, with anecdotal information about all the employees who will help make your week enjoyable.

OF INTEREST NEARBY: Yellowstone National Park is only an hour or so away, and you shouldn't miss an opportunity to visit it. It's too vast to be appreciated in the one-day outing offered by the ranch, so plan to add on a few days to your vacation and experience it at your leisure.

FOR MORE INFORMATION: Write Mountain Sky Guest Ranch, P.O. Box 1128, Bozeman, MT 59715, or call (406) 587-1244 or (800) 548-3392 for reservations or information. The number at the ranch (June through October only) is (406) 333-4911.

Bishop's Lodge

Santa Fe, New Mexico

Two centuries ago, this land was a farm worked by Spanish colonials, who borrowed irrigation techniques from nearby Pueblo Indians and turned the dry soil into fields of wheat, corn, beans, and fruit trees.

Then came the property's most famous resident, Bishop Jean-Baptiste Lamy, who used this corner of the Little Tesuque Valley, which he named the Villa Pinctoresca, as a retreat from the dust and disorder of Santa Fe.

Then came some private owners—among them a local dairy farmer and the Pulitzer newspaper publishing family of St. Louis. But since 1919, this wonderful 1,000-acre spread in the "Land of Enchantment" has been the province of private paying guests, coddled and cared for by the Thorpe family. It has earned four stars from the *Mobil Travel Guide* for the last 12 years.

Bishop's Lodge is in a category all its own. Its adobe-style architecture lends a distinctly regional flavor, and its beautifully landscaped site in the pink and orange foothills of the Sangre de Cristo Mountains ensures peace and quiet and magnificent views. Yet it is only a 10-minute drive from Santa Fe, arguably the most interesting and beautiful small city in the United States.

ACCOMMODATIONS: $$ to $$$$ Bishop's Lodge has 74 rooms or suites that can accommodate about 150 guests. The rooms range from modest, hotel-type rooms to luxurious suites. Some of the standard doubles have separate sleeping alcoves that can easily accommodate a child or two. All deluxe rooms have fireplaces and balconies or patios. Suites can accommodate a family of six.

During the summer, a Modified American Plan package is available that includes breakfast and lunch or dinner daily and the children's program.

The lodge closes from January until mid-April.

DINING: A week of dining at Bishop's Lodge is guaranteed to send you home with a tummy bulge. The day begins with an elaborate breakfast buffet served from 7:30 to 10 A.M. The luncheon buffet, served from noon to 1:30, is an extravaganza that should be sampled at least once (there is an extra charge for guests on the MAP). The lodge's Sunday brunch draws diners from throughout New Mexico.

Dinner is cooked to order and features some regional favorites and continental dishes. Children's portions are available, as are hamburgers, chicken, and peanut butter or cheese sandwiches.

In the summer and at Christmas, children in the children's program can dine together, with their counselors, in a separate children's dining room. The cowboy trailside breakfasts are popular in the summer.

A limited room service menu is available. Cocktails are served each evening; during the summer, a trio provides background music on the patio outside the main dining room, which has a lovely view.

ACTIVITIES

Four tournament-grade Omni-Court tennis courts. Resident pro, round-robins, tournaments, and private, semi-private, and group lessons. Special instruction for "shorty swatters," ages 6 to 11, is offered three times a week. Court fees.

Privileges at the nearby Santa Fe Country Club, the Los Alamos Country Club, and the Cochiti Lake course on the Cochiti Indian Reservation.

Heated swimming pool and cabana, with an indoor sauna and whirlpool nearby.

 New Mexico offers some of the finest white-water rafting and kayaking opportunities in the nation, including the famous Taos Box on the Rio Grande River. Day outings are easily arranged.

A picturesque fishing hole chock-full of hungry trout is popular with children, who can borrow equipment from the counselors. Nearby stream and lake fishing for adults.

The Santa Fe National Forest and the Pecos Wilderness Area abut Santa Fe. There are scenic and rugged mountain trails, with good fishing. Families will enjoy a drive through the Santa Fe National Forest up to the Santa Fe Ski Basin, where they can ride the chairlift to the summit. The temperature drops about 30 degrees as you work your way to the top along a winding, scenic drive.

 The lodge has a string of about 65 horses for guests' use. You won't want to miss the opportunity to ride up into the foothills of the Sangre de Cristo Mountains for the panoramic view. There are two daily two-hour rides; children over 7 are welcome. Breakfast rides and picnic rides are offered each week during July and August. Pony rides for children are offered.

Skeet and trap shooting are available at an automatic range on the lodge's grounds for a charge; minimum age 12.

FOR CHILDREN: During the summer, Bishop's Lodge offers a fun-filled, well-supervised children's program free of charge to Modified American Plan guests (European Plan guests pay a fee). Children between 4 and 12 are supervised by a staff of four college-age counselors in planned activities and games seven days a week.

A typical day begins at 8:30 A.M. with a group breakfast in the special children's dining room, just behind the main dining room, followed by play on the playground, which has an authentic Indian teepee and standard playground equipment, as well as a nearby kids' fort (a sign proclaims "No Grown-ups Allowed"). After that, it's pony rides in a ring for younger children or a trail ride for those over 7. By then it's time for lunch, which the children eat together.

Then they're off on a hike, followed by arts and crafts and a swim at the pool. After their afternoon snack, they're returned to their parents at 4 P.M. But the group convenes again at 6:15 P.M. for dinner, followed by games, arts and crafts, or a movie that lasts until 8:45 P.M., which allows parents ample time for a dinner alone.

Your child is welcome to take part in all or some of the activities each day. There are typically 15 to 30 kids in the program.

The lodge tries to help teenage guests get to know each other by reserving a special table for them in the main dining room and organizing pool parties and pizza parties.

For children too young to take part in the children's program, the lodge will arrange for a local baby-sitter, usually a teenage girl. Many families with very young children reserve a baby-sitter in advance for the duration of their stay.

NICETIES: Kindling and firewood are laid out every morning in guests' fireplaces in the event that they want to light a fire to take the chill off a cool evening.

A topographical map showing the main trails through the lodge's property and a bird-watchers' field checklist are available at the front desk.

Early-risers' coffee is available each morning in the lobby.

The lodge has a small library off the lobby, where guests can grab a quiet moment or check out some bedtime reading. Lots of recent-issue magazines also are available.

OF INTEREST NEARBY: In 1987, Santa Fe was judged the most livable small city in the United States because of all its cultural amenities. It is truly a culture lovers' paradise—as well as a nature lovers' dream—with more to see and do than is possible in a week.

The heart of the city is the Plaza, which bustles with activity day and night. During the day, three or four dozen Native American merchants set up shop under the portico at the adjacent Palace of the Governors, built in 1609; beautiful silver and turquoise jewelry and pottery are offered for sale.

Each of the streets bordering the Plaza is lined with interesting little shops that sell everything from souvenirs to fine art.

Santa Fe is also rich is museums. Children will especially enjoy the International Folk Art Museum, which has folk art from over 50 countries and a scale model of an old-fashioned rail-car circus.

For tourists with an interest in Indian art, the nearby Wheelwright Museum has a rotating collection of Indian objects in a stunning building. The Museum of Fine Art, on Palace Avenue, has a reputation as one of the country's leading centers for the arts.

There are several dozen Indian pueblos near Santa Fe. Most are simply sleepy little villages, but a few are of interest to tourists. The Taos Pueblo is famous for its pueblo-style architecture and is worth a visit; it's a full day trip, but you can combine it with lunch in Taos, a visit to the nearby Millicent Rogers Museum, which has a fantastic Indian art collection, and a stop at the Rio Grande Gorge Bridge, which will give you a stomach-churning view down into this famous gorge.

Bandelier National Monument is less than an hour from Bishop's Lodge and has remnants of ancient cliff dwellings that children will love exploring. You can combine a visit there with a stop in Los Alamos, the atomic research center, which has a fascinating museum. A little farther are the Puye Cliff Dwellings.

FOR MORE INFORMATION: Write the Bishop's Lodge, P.O. Box 2367, Santa Fe, NM 87504, or call (505) 983-6377. FAX: (505) 989-8739.

Flying L Guest Ranch
Bandera, Texas

Bandera, a tiny western town about an hour northwest of San Antonio, boasts that it's the "Cowboy Capital of the World." You'll see hitching posts outside the general store on Main Street, though there are more pickup trucks than ponies parked there these days. And a souvenir shop reserves one whole wall for the autographs of rodeo winners in a town that has been called home by seven world champion rodeo riders.

The Flying L, about a mile south of town, is the area's most luxurious ranch for families who want to vacation in the wide open spaces. Unlike most of the area's other dude ranches, Flying L was never a working ranch. A San Antonio businessman founded the ranch in the 1940s when he was looking for somewhere to entertain friends, many of whom were pilots. He constructed some simple bungalows and built a private landing strip. Then his guests flew in for weekends of real Texas fun—barbecues, horseback riding, and camp fires. The ranch was sold in the 1970s and redeveloped as a 542-acre resort.

ACCOMMODATIONS: **$$$** Don't expect bunkhouses here. Guests bed down in bungalows, condominiums, and villas clustered around the main house, some equipped with frills that cowboys never even dreamed of—including whirlpool baths and wet bars.

The ranch's 38 units fan out from the main clubhouse to form a small compound where it would be hard for children to get lost. There are three types of rooms, all with a western flair. The Golfview suites, bordering the ninth fairway, are ideal for guests who want to be within putting distance of the golf course. Each two-room condominium suite has a refrigerator, cooking unit, wet bar, color television, and private balcony.

The Ranchview suites, the resort's most deluxe and spacious accommodations, can comfortably sleep a family of four. The suite's enormous kitchen is a perfect gathering place, with built-in banquettes and every convenience of home. There's even a washer and dryer in the kitchen. The living room has a stone fireplace as the focal point and a sofa that opens to a queen-size bed. The suite also has a large bedroom with a king-size bed and a Texas-size bathroom. The Ranchview suites are only a horseshoe pitch from the swimming pool and dining hall. Each one also has a covered patio, equipped with lawn furniture and a big barbecue pit.

The original guest houses are bungalow-style units, nestled under huge live oaks. They have color televisions, refrigerators, and even some fireplaces. Each of the larger units sleeps up to six people, with two double beds in the bedroom and a sofa with a double bed in the living room.

The ranch features an all-inclusive rate that covers the room, three meals a day, use of all facilities, including golf and horseback riding, and maid service. Children between 3 and 11 are charged a small flat daily rate, and there are reduced rates for children 12 to 17.

DINING: Meals are served family style in the cozy dining room in the main house, and they're more than ample.

The breakfast menu changes daily, but on a typical day you'll find stacks of butter-soaked pancakes, platters of fluffy scrambled eggs, toasty English muffins, spicy sausages, sweet rolls, and all the milk, orange juice, and coffee you can drink. If you miss breakfast in the main dining room, head for the pro shop, where a wrangler will fix you à la carte selections off a menu.

Lunch features salad and sandwich bars, soups, fresh fruits, and wonderful desserts.

Guests are summoned to dinner by a cowhand ringing a metal triangle. Every night of the week there's a different theme—Mexican Fiesta, Back to the 50s, Hawaiian Luau, German/Polish night, and everyone's favorite: Get Western. On Sundays, the spread is the kind of food you'd expect to find on a farm—oven-baked ham, turkey, roast beef, and fried fish with stuffing, homemade rolls, and baby carrots.

When weather permits, the buffets are served outside with all the food piled on long tables covered with red-checked tablecloths. You can eat on nearby picnic tables.

ACTIVITIES

Two lighted hard-surface courts; racquets and balls available.

Eighteen-hole course (6,787 yards, par 72), which is usually so uncrowded that the kids can caddy or come along for the ride in the cart. Pro shop, rental equipment.

Outdoor swimming pool, adjacent hot tub. Tubing in nearby creek.

Cane fishing poles available for use at the San Julian Creek, about three-quarters of a mile away.

The ranch has miles of established hiking trails.

The ranch has a stable of 25 horses. And there's plenty to see on the miles of private trails, along which wild cactus bloom in fields blanketed with wildflowers, deer slip in and out of bushes, and ducks waddle to the creek. There are morning and afternoon rides.

Volleyball, Ping-Pong, shuffleboard, bingo, movies, card games. In the evening you can swap trail stories in the Branding Iron Saloon, a small bar in the main lobby. There's nightly entertainment, including musical shows, twilight hayrides, marshmallow roasts, softball games, square dancing, hoe-downs, country-western dancing, and performances by a snake handler and expert trick roper.

FOR CHILDREN: The ranch's free formal children's program runs from Memorial Day to Labor Day and over school holidays.

Activities are held daily from 10 A.M. to noon and 1 to 3 P.M. for children age 3 and up. The daily schedule varies depending on the weather, the children's ages, and what the kids want to do. They can choose from horseback riding, fishing, hiking, movies, swimming in the pool and spring-fed creek, having sack races, going on fossil hunts, and learning rope tricks or western crafts. A low adult-child ratio is maintained.

Even if you visit when the children's program is not operating, the ranch will provide a list of sitters so parents can get away for several hours of golf or horseback riding.

NICETIES: Each guest unit has a clock-radio in the bedroom, and larger ones have a second in the kitchen. But you won't find any telephones in the units; they've been deliberately omitted to make your vacation as relaxing as possible. If you must make a call, there are pay phones at the main house, pro shop, and service room of the Golfview condominiums, where you'll also find coin-operated washers and dryers.

The kids will get a kick out of the sheep grazing in front of the main house. There's a Shetland pony available for the pint-size cow-boys to ride around the ring.

OF INTEREST NEARBY: A goat farm just across the entrance from the ranch on Highway 173 is a great destination for a 10-minute after-dinner walk. Also popular with families are the Frontier Museum in Bandera; dinosaur tracks at a creek bed in Tarpley; Medina Lake, a nearby boating, fishing, and recreational area; and Sea World, 45 minutes away in San Antonio.

FOR MORE INFORMATION: Write Flying L Guest Ranch, HCR1 Box 32, Bandera, TX 78003, or call (800) 292-5134 from anywhere in the U.S. or (512) 796-3001 from out of the country.

Paradise Guest Ranch
Buffalo, Wyoming

Paradise, defined by Webster's as "any place of great beauty and perfection," was not chosen lightly as the name for this ranch in north-central Wyoming. Nor was the ranch's brand, FUN, which hangs from the gate as you cross over French Creek.

This former cattle ranch is surrounded by close to two million acres of Bighorn National Forest—some of the most remote and scenic territory to be found in this arid country. To the west are the snowy peaks of the Bighorn Mountains. Bull moose, deer, and other wildlife graze against a backdrop of ponderosa pine and aspen.

The ranch has taken in paying guests since 1905 and is one of the oldest ranches in the West. Author Owen Wister, who stayed at the ranch in the 1920s, is said to have drawn on his experiences here for his Western epic *The Virginian*. Since Denver-based Apache Oil Co. bought the ranch at auction in 1981, it has been totally renovated and expanded to accommodate about 70 guests at a time. Its congenial managers are Jim and Leah Anderson.

The ranch buildings are attractively clustered at the foot of a hill.

A two-story bar-lodge with open loft is the center of evening activities. A few steps away is the dining hall, which has been built around the ranch's original registration center. Parked outside is an antique chuck wagon that is called into use each week to deliver the victuals to an upper meadow for a cookout dinner. Down the road (and downwind) is the corral, where guests saddle up each day.

ACCOMMODATIONS: $$$$ Eighteen log cabins with inviting front porches and stone chimneys are perched on a hillside overlooking the ranch buildings and, in the distance, the grazing meadows.

The authentic log cabins have rustic appeal but have been fully updated with modern bathrooms and kitchenettes. Four of the cabins have one bedroom, 11 have two bedrooms, and three have three bedrooms to suit larger families. As at many other ranches, no keys are issued.

The ranch's season runs from Memorial Day through the second week of September. With few exceptions, guests are booked for week-long visits, beginning each Sunday. Children's rates are available, including a greatly reduced rate for children under 6 who do not take part in trail rides. Besides lodging, the rates include all food, riding, the children's program, and entertainment. The only extras are alcoholic beverages, fishing licenses, an optional 3-day pack trip, and gratuities.

DINING: Exceptionally tasty meals are served at tables long enough to seat several families. Breakfast is a hearty affair, designed to tide you over if you're taking a morning horseback ride. Lunch features a choice of two entrées.

Dinners are special. Sometimes, they're planned around an activity like a late-afternoon ride to a high meadow called Bald Eagle Park, culminating in a chuck-wagon supper of barbecued ribs, potatoes, corn on the cob, and sourdough bread. There's a gourmet dinner each Thursday night for adults only. Saturday night's dinner features thick, juicy steaks barbecued on an open grill.

All breads and desserts are made fresh each day. The pastry chef's repertoire includes baklava, carrot cake, ice cream in a meringue shell, lemon pie, and strawberry flan.

ACTIVITIES

 Heated outdoor pool, whirlpool.

 French Creek is stocked with 12-inch rainbow trout, and fishing gear can be borrowed.

The ranch has 90 horses from which to choose; you can stick with the one you're assigned for the whole week or, if you prefer, switch daily. You'll want to do lots of riding here to cover as much of the varied terrain as you can. One trail may lead you along French Creek, another through thick groves of aspen and pine trees, and yet another between steep mountains. You can ride as a family or split up according to your level of experience.

Volleyball, horseshoes, pool, Ping-Pong. In the evenings: bonfire, sing-alongs, marshmallow roasts, slide shows, guest talent shows, rodeos and square dancing.

The ranch has designed a three-day guided pack trip into a base camp at Frying Pan Lake. Tacked onto the end of the week-long ranch stay, the pack trip carries an additional charge. Horse, sleeping bags, cots, food, and cook are supplied. The trip takes you to a 9,700-foot elevation, where you can catch cutthroat, brook, or rainbow trout in one of several lakes or rushing streams.

FOR CHILDREN: The ranch offers a free children's program directed by a warm-hearted college student with child-care experience.

Each morning after breakfast, she calls the children together for circle time to talk over the day's activities. Those who aren't riding that morning will do crafts developed around nature themes: watercolor mountains, grass rubbings, or pine-cone and dried-flower pictures. And they'll spend some time in active play, like relay races, badminton, or floating boats in the creek.

After lunch, an activity like Capture the Flag or a scavenger hunt is planned before the older kids trot out for their afternoon ride. Some time is spent on a second art activity or on a special event like learning roping from a wrangler or throwing a fishing line in the creek. Ping-Pong and horseshoe tournaments are often scheduled.

Each child's art treasures are kept in a folder during the week and are bound together in book fashion on Saturday.

One of the highlights of the week for children is an overnight camp-out in a walled tent in the woods across French Creek on Thursday night, planned to coincide with the adults' gourmet night. The kids hike up to the woods with the activities director and some of the ranch hands for a weenie roast and s'mores, followed by relay races and camp-fire songs.

But the favorite event surely is the rodeo, in which all but the smallest children demonstrate their skills in handling horses, under the direction of their favorite wranglers.

Among the sad farewells the kids will say on Sunday will be to the ranch pets that have become their friends. Buford is a bloodhound that sports a red neckerchief and howls whenever the lunch and dinner bells sound. His shadow is Bart, an Irish setter.

NICETIES: In your cabin you'll find coffee and herbal tea. You also can ask the kitchen staff to stock your small refrigerator with snacks and soft drinks.

Each day, the fireplace is serviced and the wood bin outside the door is replenished with firewood and diesel-soaked sawdust.

Some of the cabins are equipped with washers and dryers. For those that aren't, guests may use the laundry machines in the recreation hall after 3:30 P.M., at no charge.

When you check in, you'll get a list of the other guests' names, hometowns, and their children's ages, along with a "horse sense" handbook to give novices tips on how to handle their horses and a booklet on the ranch's history.

OF INTEREST NEARBY: There are few attractions in the vicinity of Buffalo, but many people combine a ranch visit with a trip to Yellowstone National Park, four hours west of Buffalo, or to the granite presidential images at the Mt. Rushmore National Monument in the Black Hills National Forest in western South Dakota, about four hours to the east.

Cody, Wyoming, the home of Buffalo Bill Cody, is about three hours to the west and has a wealth of memorabilia from the American West in four museums under one roof.

And 125 miles away in southern Montana, you can visit the Custer battlefield monument in Little Bighorn, where Custer made his last stand against the Indians.

FOR MORE INFORMATION: Write Jim and Leah Anderson at Paradise Guest Ranch, P.O. Box 790, Buffalo, WY 82834, or call (307) 684-7876.

WEST COAST

The Alisal Guest Ranch
Solvang, California

At any time of year, but particularly during holidays, guests of the Alisal include family groups in which three generations (sometimes four) gather to renew ties and enjoy a first-class dude ranch. Many families return year after year. Children grow up here and bring their children and, eventually, their grandchildren.

The Alisal is an ideal mixture of setting, facilities, activities, service, and hospitality. The setting is a working cattle ranch in the horse country of the Santa Ynez Valley 40 miles north of Santa Barbara. The Alisal property was one of four 18th-century Spanish land grants awarded to José Raimundo Carrillo, and the Alisal brand is one of the oldest registered brands in this country.

Comfortable accommodations, an excellent dining room, heated swimming pool, a fishing and sailing lake, golf course, tennis courts, and, of course, a corral and 70 horses provide the raw material for family fun here. Group activities abound.

The hospitality of the Alisal is legendary. Its staff members take pride in the service they provide and the friendships that grow with the families that come to the Alisal each year. Some of the current employees have been here for nearly half of the four decades that the Alisal facilities have been operating. They delight in seeing children grow up at the Alisal and have amazed more than one young adult by recalling events from visits that person made years ago.

ACCOMMODATIONS: **$$$** Guests are housed in 73 studios and suites. Studios generally have one room, two beds, and one bath. Suites usually have two rooms, three beds, and one and a half baths. All units have wood-burning fireplaces. Furnishings are unpretentious and very comfortable. Telephones and television sets are located in various public areas, but not in the guest rooms.

The Alisal is on the Modified American Plan, with breakfast and dinner included in accommodation rates; children occupying the same room as their parents pay a flat daily rate. The minimum stay is two nights.

Golf, tennis, and riding packages are available in certain periods of the year. A Round-Up Vacation Package offered in some weekday periods from mid-September through mid-June includes all horseback riding, tennis and golf.

DINING: The Ranch Dining Room serves breakfast from 8 to 9:45 A.M. and dinner from 6:30 to 8 P.M. At breakfast you choose between buffet and à la carte service.

Lunch is also available in the Dining Room and at the swimming pool and golf course snack bars. Before dinner cocktails are served in the Oak Lounge, adjacent to the Dining Room, and at the Waggin' Tongue Lounge in the recreation building. Dinner attire is dresses or pant suits for women and jackets for men.

Families take a table in the Dining Room when they arrive and return to the same table through the rest of their stay.

The food is ample, delicious, and far more sophisticated than typical dude ranch fare. Dinner menus offer a choice of entrées, including a fish or poultry dish. California wines are available to complement your meal. The standard children's favorites are always available as off-menu items.

ACTIVITIES

Seven year-round, hard-surface courts, professional instruction, clinics, tournaments.

A challenging 18-hole golf course (6,434 yards, par 72) designed by William P. Bell; clubhouse, pro shop, cart and club rentals, instruction.

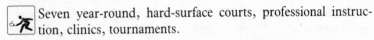

Large, heated outdoor pool with a shallow arm that ranges from two to three feet in depth, perfect for young children. The pool and adjacent hot tub are open until 10 P.M.

Rowboats, sailboats, and wind-surfing equipment available at 96-acre Alisal Lake during the summer season.

 Lake fishing for largemouth bass, catfish, and bluegill. Equipment provided. A ranch van shuttles to the lake.

 Ten thousand acres of both wooded and open country for horseback riding. Trail rides leave at 10 A.M. and 2 P.M. each day. Riders are grouped according to ability. Children must be 7 to go on trail rides, but wranglers are happy to put younger children on a horse for a corral ride. Private rides and riding lessons can be arranged. Breakfast rides or evening steak-fry rides to the Adobe are on the Alisal schedule during the summer and holiday periods. Good food, group sing-alongs led by the tuneful wranglers, and a tall tale or two are part of the Alisal experience.

A half-mile jogging course is available on the Alisal grounds. The nearby country roads are also good jogging territory.

Pool and Ping-Pong tables in the recreation building. Croquet, horseshoe, shuffleboard, badminton, and volleyball equipment can be found near the swimming pool or checked out at the office. A separate library building provides a wide selection of books and newspapers.

Family activities offered on each evening of the week during the summer include talent shows, square dancing, barbecues at the lake or pool, professional storytellers, and family bingo. The Oak Room Lounge has live music for dancing until midnight.

FOR CHILDREN: At the Christmas and Easter holidays and during the summer, the Alisal has a free children's program headed by a teacher from a nearby school, who is assisted by college students. The program is geared to children 5 to 12 and is held daily from 10 A.M. to 4 P.M. Younger children are allowed to participate if they seem mature enough. There is a playground for toddlers.

Arts and crafts are done in the recreation building. New projects are initiated each day and include nature banners, bean bags, name badges, and T-shirt art. Afternoon outdoor activities include hikes, ball games, swimming, and scavenger hunts.

Children receive special attention at the Alisal. The servers in the

Dining Room make a special point of learning children's names. Separate children's activities are organized at most evening events. Special evening programs for children include talent shows and storytelling by a professional storyteller. And the summer schedule includes two supervised children's dinners each week.

Golf and tennis clinics and private lessons are available for older children and teens for a fee.

Baby-sitting can be arranged through the ranch office.

NICETIES: A coin-operated laundry is located in the convenience center next to the tennis courts.

A call to the ranch office gets firewood delivered to your door.

Santa presents gifts to every child at Christmas.

OF INTEREST NEARBY: The Santa Ynez Valley is the southernmost wine-producing area in California, with a dozen or more wineries. Organize your own wine-tasting tour.

Solvang, only two miles from the Alisal, was settled by a group of Danes early in this century and is now a shopper's paradise with scores of quaint shops. Solvang's Theaterfest offers repertory theater in the summer months.

Your children will delight in a visit to the little red schoolhouse at Ballard, just a few miles beyond Solvang. The school has been in continual use since 1883.

The Camino Real, the route the Spanish missionaries used in the 18th and 19th centuries, crosses the Santa Ynez Valley. Santa Ynez Mission is located in Solvang. Mission La Purísima Concepción, 25 miles from the Alisal at Lompoc, is restored to the condition of a mission at the turn of the 19th century, right down to the furnishings and the vegetable garden. This mission provides a lesson in the early history of the West Coast and is well worth a half-day visit.

Nojoqui Falls Park is a few miles from the ranch down Alisal Road. Order box lunches from the Dining Room and come here one day for lunch.

FOR MORE INFORMATION: Write The Alisal Guest Ranch, 1054 Alisal Road, Solvang, CA 93463, or phone (805) 688-6411.

1. The "Star Kids" ski program at Northstar-at-Tahoe, Lake Tahoe, teaches children 5 to 12 the basics of skiing. *(Photo: Northstar-at-Tahoe)* 2. Beginners and experts alike will find challenges on the many slopes of Colorado's Telluride Ski Resort. *(Photo: Telluride Ski Resort/© Linde Waidhoffer)* 3. Not all activities are outdoors on a skiing vacation—a magic show is one of many treats kids enjoy at Mount Snow Resort Center in Vermont. *(Photo: © Bob Perry)* 4. Horse-drawn sleigh rides are one of many outdoor activities offered at Copper Mountain Resort in Copper Mountain, Colorado. *(Photo: Jeff Andrew/Copper Mountain Resort)* 5. The Children's Center at Killington Ski Area offers a wide variety of instruction programs to young skiers 3 to 15. *(Photo: Killington Photo/© Bob Perry)* 6. Along with sledding, Lake Tahoe South Shore offers a variety of outdoor activities, including snowmobiling, sleigh riding, and skiing, both alpine and cross-country. *(Photo: Lake Tahoe Visitors Authority)* 7. The Copper Mountain Resort's Our Youth programs cater to children ages 2 months to 14 years and includes professional ski instruction as well as baby-sitting. *(Photo: Jeff Andrew/Copper Mountain Resort)* 8. Gold panning along the Blue River is one of the summer activities that beckon families to the Breckenridge Ski Area. *(Photo: © Carl Scofield)*

5

6

7

8

NORTHEAST

Mont-Tremblant
Gray Rocks
Mont-Tremblant, Quebec, Canada

Americans can experience the ambience of European skiing by driving just 75 miles north out of Montreal into the world of French Canadian hospitality. After a one and a half-hour ride into the Laurentian Mountains, skiers can find themselves at any one of about 30 picture-book, snow-covered hostelries—with ski tows, runs, and trails rising behind them.

Getting there is part of the experience. Driving up the Laurentian Autoroute brings a delightful vista with every turn—a small village clustered in a valley, a steeple pointing high above the white rooftops, a chalet perched on a mountainside with ski trails converging behind it.

This is where recreational skiing is said to have begun in North America, when, in 1932, the world's first rope tow was installed in the village of Shawbridge. In 1951, a young man named Réal Charette furthered the industry by instituting the ski week at a resort named Gray Rocks. Even today, most of the skiers who come to the Laurentians sign up for ski weeks, at all-inclusive prices.

Whether staying at an intimate chalet, an inn, or a larger resort, guests find themselves basking in their hosts' courtesy and warmth, comfortable accommodations, French-influenced cuisine, and the *joie de vivre* of the Quebec lifestyle.

Students of French can even try out the language with the comfort of knowing that if they can't make themselves understood in French, someone nearby will understand English.

ACCOMMODATIONS: **\$\$** to **\$\$\$** The Mont-Tremblant area has numerous chalets, inns, and hotels, several with their own ski schools on the mountain. Prices at all are highest during Christmas and New Year weeks, the week including Presidents' Day in the United States, and the school holiday week in Ontario in March. Most provide package plans that include meals and skiing.

Gray Rocks Inn, the granddaddy of them all, is a large, rambling lodge and cottage complex with 208 spacious rooms, each with a picture-window view of either Lake Ouimet or Sugar Peak.

Station Mont-Tremblant Lodge, at the base of the Mont-Tremblant ski area, offers the advantage of skiing right to the door of your chalet or the main lodge. The 235 accommodations range from cozy, rustic rooms in the main lodge to multiple-bedroom luxury units with lounges and fireplaces to one- and two-bedroom condominium-style efficiency apartments.

DINING: Meals at Gray Rocks are served in an inviting dining room, with the tables dressed in white linen and freshly cut flowers. Each family or group is assigned a table for the duration of their stay.

Breakfast and dinner at Station Mont-Tremblant are eaten in either La Canadienne or L'Elizabeth dining rooms.

For lunch, skiers can remain at the mountain and eat in one of several cafeterias or at Station Mont-Tremblant Lodge. Choices include La Canadienne or Bon Vivant steak house in the lodge or one of the cafeterias at the mountain—Chalet des Voyageurs, Fourche du Diable, or Rendez-Vous.

THE SKIING: Above the sweeping valleys and the gently rounded mountaintops of the Laurentians rises Mont-Tremblant, at 3,000 feet the highest skiable peak in eastern Canada. Abundant natural snowfall—170 inches a year—provides for skiing from mid-November until mid-April. In addition, 75 computer-controlled snowguns spray forth each night to cushion the trails evenly. The manufactured snow provides a minimum base of 46 inches.

Gray Rocks has its own ski area on Sugar Peak, and most Gray Rocks guests do most of their skiing there. The area is also open to non-guests.

Mont-Tremblant: Four novice, 14 intermediate, eight advanced. *Gray Rocks:* Five novice, eight intermediate, seven advanced.

 Mont-Tremblant: One quad chair, two triples, four doubles, one single, one T-bar, two J-bars.
Gray Rocks: One quad chair, three double chairlifts.

Mont-Tremblant: 2,130 feet.
Gray Rocks: 620 feet.

Mont-Tremblant: Three and one-half miles.
Gray Rocks: One mile.

At the Mont-Tremblant Ski School, the 80 instructors are members of the Canadian Ski Instructors Alliance. For the ski week, guests are organized into classes of similar skill levels; groups stay together for the duration. Gray Rocks' Snow Eagle Ski School has 65 full-time instructors; all but advanced classes are taught on Sugar Peak.

The area has a network of 69 miles of regularly groomed cross-country ski trails. The trails wind up and around hills, through vales, and across frozen lakes. Numerous lodges sit along the trails; skiing to one for a leisurely lunch makes for a delightful day.

ACTIVITIES FOR NON-SKIERS: Gray Rocks offers ski movies, fashion shows, wine and cheese parties, a piano bar and sing-along, a weekly beer festival, dance contests and a talent night. An attractive and spacious indoor sports center has a heated swimming pool, hot tubs, saunas, massage and tanning rooms, aerobics classes, and Nautilus and Global equipment.

After skiing or after dinner, Station Mont-Tremblant Lodge offers conversation and drinks in La Catalogne lounge or a rousing good time at Disco Tremblant Express downstairs.

FOR CHILDREN: Gray Rocks offers ski classes for all children over 3, and from 4 to 11 P.M. daily there's an après-ski program featuring cider and cheese parties, swimming, sleigh rides, games, and dances. There is a recreation room in which kids can gather and a snack bar. The Snow Eaglet Day Care Service offers child care for 1- to 6-year-olds in the Eagle's Nest Lodge.

Garderie pour les Enfants, on the edge of the Mont-Tremblant ski slope, offers child care for 3- to 5-year-olds. There children can learn to ski, participate in indoor and outdoor group activities, and eat lunch. Each class has about five children. The classes ski on terrain appropriate to the children's ages and levels of skill. The cost includes lift tickets.

Children 7 and older who are in classes get priority access to all lifts at Mont-Tremblant. The older group of children and adults must buy lift tickets in addition to their ski school tickets.

Child-care options for younger children are a day-care center in Tremblant Village or private baby-sitting; hotels will help make arrangements.

The après-ski children's activities at Station Mont-Tremblant Lodge include movies in the solarium, broomball games on the ice rink, parties in the play room, bingo, cartoons, tobogganing, magic shows, crafts, and recreational games.

IN THE SUMMER: All the lodges offer extensive activities in the summer—boating, swimming, water skiing, and wind surfing on the numerous lakes; tennis; golf; horseback riding; hiking; and other outdoor recreation. Special children's activities are also offered.

FOR MORE INFORMATION: For more information about Gray Rocks, write the inn at C.P. 1000, St.-Jovite, Quebec, J0T 2H0, or call (800) 567-6767.

For more information about Station Mont-Tremblant Lodge, write to the lodge at Mont-Tremblant, J0T 1Z0, Quebec, Canada, or call (819) 425-8711.

For general information about tourism in the Laurentians, call (514) 436-8532.

Sugarloaf USA Resort
Kingfield, Maine

Sugarloaf USA refers to itself as "The Skier's Mountain," and that it is. But for all its reputation as a great spot for the accomplished skier, it also manages to be an ideal spot for families and beginner skiers. There's a term for the atmosphere at Sugarloaf: *Gemütlichkeit*, the German expression for warmth, friendliness, and good feelings. When you combine such a feeling with a village modeled after a European ski village, and top it all off with a beautiful mountain (Maine's highest ski mountain), you've got an ideal family destination resort.

Sugarloaf has long had a local reputation for excellence. In recent years, its reputation and following have widened so that it attracts a good number of return visitors from throughout the U.S., Canada, and several foreign countries.

Sugarloaf's annual White, White World Week celebration, a full week of on-snow events, nighttime theme parties, and concerts, is one of the best snow festivals offered by any ski resort. Scheduled the last week of January each year, it is capped by a dazzling display of fireworks over the mountain.

ACCOMMODATIONS: **$$** to **$$$$** No matter where you wind up within Sugarloaf's Alpine Village, you'll have easy access to the slopes, shops, and restaurants. Choices in accommodations abound —from the ultimate in luxury at the new Sugarloaf Mountain Hotel to the very comfortable and deluxe Mountainside Condominiums. The Sugarloaf Mountain Corporation manages most accommodations on the mountain. Most of the accommodations offer package plans that include lift tickets, ski school, and even meals.

Among the accommodations best suited for families are the following:

Sugarloaf Mountainside Condominiums offers spacious condos with large, fully equipped kitchens and fireplaces or wood stoves for which firewood is provided. Most are located right on a trail or at the base of a lift, so you have easy access to skiing. In addition, the on-mountain shuttle service can take you anywhere else in the vicinity that you might want to go.

The elegant Sugarloaf Mountain Hotel is located in the heart of the village, with direct access to all 63 ski trails. The hotel offers over 10 different types of accommodations, all of which include daily maid service, ski lockers, and access to the Sugartree Health Club, which has facilities for swimming and racquetball. Rates are in the **$$$** category; children 6 and under are free. Suites that can sleep up to six are also available.

Peter Webber's 36-room Sugarloaf Inn combines the ambience of a traditional New England country inn with all the amenities of a modern hotel. The inn is also in the heart of things, and its guests have privileges at the Sugartree Health Club.

DINING: Dining opportunities on the mountain are diverse and plentiful. With over 10 eateries to choose from, you may find you never leave the mountain for a meal.

The Bag, located in Village West, serves moderately priced meals and can't-clean-your-plate-size portions. The Whistle Stop is good for a quick breakfast or lunch. Weather permitting, Bullwinkle's on the Mountain, located at the top of the Bucksaw Chairlift, offers hot and hearty foods and beverages along with breathtaking views.

THE SKIING: In addition to an average of 168 inches of snowfall annually, a sophisticated snowmaking system provides supplementary snow on over 50 percent of the skiable terrain. Grooming is also emphasized, for just the right combination of snowpack and powder. The season here runs from mid-November to late April or early May, depending on the weather. There are low-season and peak-season lift ticket rates; multi-day tickets available at a substantial discount; and half-day tickets.

Twenty-seven novice, 19 intermediate, 24 advanced. Sugarloaf offers the only lift-serviced snowfield skiing in all of the East. From the 4,237-foot peak runs a network of 67 trails that provides 40 miles of skiing.

Seven double chair lifts, one triple chair lift, one T-bar, two quads, and a four-passenger gondola.

 2,637 feet.

 Over three miles.

The American Teaching Method is used by the 30 full-time instructors in the ski school, and classes are kept small. Special learn-to-ski packages provide discounts on lift tickets, equipment rentals, and lessons. First-time skiers can get a group lesson, equipment rentals, and an all-day lift ticket on the lower one third of the mountain for a modest charge. It contains a money-back guarantee that you'll be skiing with confidence at the end of the day.

Just one mile from Sugarloaf Mountain is the Carrabassett Valley Ski Touring Center, with almost 70 miles of groomed trails. You can ski over from Sugarloaf and relax in the solar-heated lodge or enjoy an outdoor barbecue on the sun deck.

ACTIVITIES FOR NON-SKIERS: Everyone in the family will delight in a ride on a dogsled. The guest services desk at Sugarloaf can provide information about departure times and prices.

There's an Olympic-size outdoor skating rink, with skating offered daily and nightly, at Carrabassett Valley Touring Center. Skate rentals are available.

FOR CHILDREN: Sugarloaf is a great place for children to learn to ski. All children under 6 get free lift tickets and equipment rentals (a real rarity) if enrolled in ski school. The program for 4- to 6-year-olds is called "Mountain Magic" and provides fairly intensive instruction, with a low student-teacher ratio.

Children between 7 and 14 can enroll in "Mountain Adventure," which provides two-hour classes, with skiers grouped by ability, not age.

Infant and toddler care is available in Sugarloaf's nursery; reservations are required; call (207) 237-2000. Special night care is offered at the center from 6 to 11 P.M. Monday through Saturday.

The day-care center is located on the lower level of Gondola Village. Infants and toddlers are separated from children over 2½. The nursery is bright and cheerful, with plenty of equipment and toys, and staff members seem to be chosen for their cheerfulness and love of children. The adult-to-child ratio is 1-to-5 or -6. You can purchase either a morning of care, enroll your child in the afternoon session, or keep him or her there all day (lunch included). There's a discount for a five-day stay.

The villagelike setting at Sugarloaf means that it is possible to give older children relatively free rein. The hot night spot for teenagers is Rascals, which is located in the Base Lodge. Rascals serves pizza and ice cream in an arcade, with video games all around.

During periods when many children are present, the Sugarloaf Mountain Corporation sponsors special movies and dances for teenagers, as well as fireworks and torchlight parades.

NICETIES: There's a separate Kids' Corner for rental equipment, which eliminates waiting in long lines with cranky kids.

The lift operators go out of their way to be helpful; they'll gladly slow down a lift so that a hesitant child can board.

OF INTEREST NEARBY: Nearby towns offer plenty of opportunities for shopping, dining in country inns, and nightlife.

The Stanley Museum in Kingsfield and the Dead River Museum in Stratton offer walks through America's past with emphasis on the history of the logging industry.

IN THE SUMMER: Summer and fall are popular times for visitors to Sugarloaf because of the numerous opportunities for outdoor recreation—white-water rafting on the Kennebec River, horseback riding, hiking on the Appalachian Trail, foliage-viewing gondola rides to Sugarloaf's summit, fishing, canoeing, and golfing on the beautiful 18-hole Sugarloaf golf course designed by Robert Trent Jones, Jr. Golf school is offered every weekend.

Visitors may enroll their children in one of the local summer day camps.

FOR MORE INFORMATION: Sugarloaf's general information number is (207) 237-2000. You can write Sugarloaf at RR 1, Box 5000, Carrabassett Valley, Kingfield, ME 04947-9799. For reservations and information call (800) THE-LOAF from the United States or Canada.

The Sugarloaf Area Chamber of Commerce, at (207) 235-2500, can provide general tourist information.

Killington Ski Area
Killington, Vermont

Killington is a vast ski area of six mountains laced with more than 100 trails and 721 acres of skiable terrain. Killington has skiing for every member of the family, from the mogul maniac to the slightly bewildered novice.

Killington also offers a lot of activity off the slopes, with scores of restaurants and shops, dozens of night spots, and ample entertainment for every family member.

Although Old Man Winter has smiled on Killington and provided an average 250 inches of snow a year over the last decade, Killington leaves nothing to chance. The ski season is extended at both ends— from October to June—with the use of snowmaking equipment on trails from all 18 lifts and on intermountain connecting trails, a total of 107 trails altogether. Come April, when other eastern ski areas are closing down, Killington skiers greet the spring skiing season with T-shirts and suntan lotion. Those long, sweeping vistas from the top of the mountain include views of the Killington golf course greening up at the base. In fact, the golfing season is well under way when the last skiers leave the slopes.

ACCOMMODATIONS: **$$** to **$$$** The Killington area offers a staggering variety of accommodations, with a choice of over 100 lodges, country inns, motels, and condominium groupings. Some offer no meals as part of the basic rates; others have Modified American plans or breakfast plans. Some are at the foot of the slopes, others are 10 or more miles away.

The Killington Lodging Bureau helps you find your way through this maze of options by providing a single source of information on accommodations. A wide variety of packages is available that offers lessons, lifts, equipment, and lodging in almost every combination. Ask the Killington Lodging Bureau for its brochure on accommodations and packages.

Killington Village has seven condominium complexes, a swimming pool, a health club, restaurants, and shops. There is no extra charge for children staying in a unit with parents.

DINING: There are so many options for dining in the Killington area that you couldn't possibly sample them all in several family vacations here. Everything from fast food to fine New England country inn fare is a few minutes' walk or drive from your room.

Killington offers five cafeterias and one full-service restaurant at the slopes and one mountaintop restaurant.

THE SKIING: Killington has one of the longest ski seasons in the east, thanks to good snowfalls and snow-making equipment that cranks all winter long. The six mountains feature an interconnected system of trails and lifts and offer what is widely regarded as the greatest diversity of ski terrain in the eastern United States and the highest lift-serviced skiing in New England.

 Forty-eight novice, 21 intermediate, 38 advanced. (Outer Limits, the steepest mogul slope in New England, has vertical drops and pitches up to 62 degrees.)

 One gondola, five quad chairs, four triples, six doubles, two Pomas.

 3,175 feet.

 Ten miles.

Group lessons, private lessons, lesson packages, and family workshops are available at both Snowshed and Killington Base Lodge. Intermediate and advanced skiers can sign up for the Mountain Ski Week. In this five-day program you, your instructor, and two other skiers at your ability level ski together for three hours a day on all kinds of terrain and receive intensive instruction. Killington's four acres of Mountain Training Stations are included in accelerated learning programs and Mountain Ski Week programs. Here instructors give individualized on-the-spot instruction on a wide variety of skiing terrains.

Touring centers at Killington itself, and the nearby towns of Chittenden, Stockbridge, and Woodstock.

ACTIVITIES FOR THE NON-SKIER: Killington has all the traditional winter activities of a quality ski resort, including ice-skating, snowshoeing, and sleigh rides.

You'll find racquetball facilities at the Killington Health Club and at Summit Lodge. Both indoor tennis and racquetball are available at Great Expectations and Racquetball in Rutland, 20 miles away.

The bowling alleys and the multi-screen cinemas in the Killington area are possibilities for family evening entertainment.

FOR CHILDREN: The Killington Children's Center offers child care for children from 6 weeks to 8 years. Excellent facilities include a reading corner, block area, science and music areas, jungle gym and large toy area, a housekeeping area, and games, puzzles, and arts and crafts area. The program is divided between structured and individual activities. Outdoor activities are scheduled, weather permitting. A lunch and two snacks are included in the charge.

The "Introduction to Skiing" program for 3- through 8-year-olds gets children skiing in short order with two one-hour lessons each day. These lessons can be combined with the enrollment of your child in the Children's Center child-care program so that your child gets day care and skiing from 8 A.M. to 4 P.M.

The "Superstars" all-day skiing program caters to children 6 through 12, with unlimited use of the lifts, ski instruction, ski videos, and indoor activities. Lunch is included.

Your teenage child, 12 through 15 years, can participate in the "Killington Teen Ski" program, offered during certain peak winter vacation weeks. The program includes two hours of lessons per day, ski races, movies, and social activities.

NICETIES: Complimentary "Meet the Mountain" tours provide a two-hour introduction to Killington's mountains by Killington guides. Tours leave daily from Snowshed and Killington Base lodges.

Killington provides *Your Ski Week*, an excellent pocket-size guidebook to the area, with maps and information on lifts, trails, lodging, restaurants, and services. The guide includes skiing courtesy and safety tips.

OF INTEREST NEARBY: Vermont is a patchwork of small shops and handicraft makers and vendors. It is roadside shopping at its best.

In addition to the shopping, consider visits to the New England Maple Museum near Rutland, which will give your family the complete low-down on maple sugar and other maple products. The Vermont Marble Exhibit, also near Rutland, tells the story of the rock for which Vermont is known.

IN THE SUMMER: When the snow finally does leave the slopes at Killington, summer activities are already under way. In summer the rates on Killington condominium units plunge, making Killington a very affordable summer family vacation destination.

Ten golf courses within 10 miles of Killington Village offer a new golfing challenge on every day of a golfing vacation. Killington's 6,300-yard, par 72 course is one of New England's most scenic.

From mid-May through mid-September the highly acclaimed Killington School for Tennis offers two-day and five-day tennis programs, which include five hours of daily instruction, tennis videos, ball machines, and all meals and lodging.

Killington is on the straw-hat trail, with Broadway-quality theater each July and August in the Killington Playhouse at Snowshed

Lodge. And the fine arts get their due in the annual Killington Musical Festival, the Summer Showcase, and the annual residency of the Hartford Ballet.

Horse riding is another summertime Green Mountain favorite. The Killington Mountain Equestrian Festival, held each July, brings in hundreds of top hunters and jumpers to compete.

FOR MORE INFORMATION: Write Killington Lodging Bureau, 203 Killington Rd., Killington, VT 05751, or phone (802) 773-1330.

Mount Snow Resort
Mount Snow, Vermont

That 8-year-old skiing down the mountain with a teddy bear strapped to his back isn't eccentric. Nor is the 7-year-old clutching her Barbie doll (all decked out in ski wear) or the 10-year-old with a threadbare stuffed dog tucked into his belt. They're all skiing Mount Snow during Teddy Bear Week, one of the most attractive family-aimed promotions of any ski resort. They're skiing free and then going on to have fun at the special activities that await them at the end of the ski day.

Mount Snow, long a favorite destination for day-trippers from Boston and smaller New England cities, has gone after the family business in a big way in recent years, offering five weeks during the winter—the Teddy Bear Weeks—when children under 12 who bring along their stuffed animals ski free for five days, and also get to take part in lots of special activities.

But Mount Snow is a good place for families anytime during the ski season. The atmosphere is unpretentious, and there's a wide variety of terrain. And there are plenty of restaurants nearby to sample at night.

Mount Snow is one of the most accessible of the New England ski resorts. And its part of southern Vermont has all the ambience you expect—charming country villages dominated by Victorian-era architecture, antiques shops galore, and inviting country inns.

ACCOMMODATIONS: $$ to $$$$ Mount Snow Vacation Services is a one-call service that handles reservations at all the on-site facilities and about 60 nearby country inns, motels, condominiums, and guest lodges as well. The reservation clerks can assess your needs and resources and recommend the place that's most appropriate.

Snow Lake Lodge, owned and operated by the Mount Snow Corporation, is a 103-room lodge on Snow Lake at the base of Mount Snow, a short shuttle ride from the slopes. It features lakeside dining, a cocktail lounge with nightly entertainment, indoor hot tub, outdoor Jacuzzi, a game room, a library, and a fitness center. The **$$** rates include two meals.

Snowtree Condominiums has 115 units, ranging from efficiencies to town houses that can accommodate 10. Guests here have the use of a sports center with whirlpool, sauna, and exercise room. Rates are in the **$$$$** category.

Seasons on Mount Snow offers ski-in–ski-out accommodations, in the **$$$$** range. There are 165 units, ranging from two to four bedrooms, with a sports center with an indoor pool, platform tennis, exercise and game rooms, and whirlpool and sauna.

DINING: During the day, quick meals are available at the main base lodge, which has a cafeteria, a Mexican food outlet, a pastry counter, and the Tavern, a full-service restaurant on the fourth floor. On nice days, outdoor barbecues provide a convenient, tasty alternative.

There's also a cafeteria and lounge at the Sundance and Carinthia base lodges, and the Summit Lodge, which has a gorgeous view of four states.

Snow Lake Lodge and several of the other private lodges near the area all have dining rooms. And restaurants on the road to nearby Wilmington and in Wilmington itself welcome families. A fun place for both adults and kids is Poncho's Wreck on South Main Street in Wilmington, which features idiosyncratic Mexican foods in a casual, rustic atmosphere. TC's Tavern is a good pizza and spaghetti place just a short drive from Mount Snow; kids can keep themselves occupied with the Junior Trivial Pursuit cards that fill a coffee mug on each table.

THE SKIING: Mount Snow is a big 3,600-foot mountain, with trails ranging from narrow, tree-lined runs (beginners, beware) to 100-yard-wide "highways." Mount Snow has four interconnected mountain areas, each with a different character. It boasts the greatest variety of terrain from one summit in the East and the greatest summit lift capacity in New England.

 Twenty-two novice, 49 intermediate, 13 advanced.

 Six triple chairs, eight doubles, one T-bar, two rope tow, one high-speed quad, one quad.

 1,700 feet.

Two and one-half miles.

 Mount Snow has a large ski school staff and offers a special Introduction to Skiing package to encourage novices to take a lesson before they hit the slopes. For intermediate and advanced skiers, Mount Snow offers EXCL, 45-minute workshops for small groups.

Four cross-country skiing centers in the area. A directory is available at the front desk of most lodges. The top of the southern Green Mountain range is the site of a 3.1-mile cross-country skiing trail called the Ridge Trail, which connects the summits of Mount Snow and Haystack Mountain and offers gorgeous vistas from six peaks.

ACTIVITIES FOR THE NON-SKIER: There are numerous shops and night spots in nearby Wilmington, as well as a nice skating rink.

Sleigh rides are offered several times a week at the Matterhorn (464-8011) and Adam's Farm (464-3762).

Guided snowmobile tours through the Vermont countryside can be arranged through Wheeler Farm Snowmobile Tours; call 464-5225.

FOR CHILDREN: For children between 6 weeks and 8 years, the state-licensed Pumkin Patch Day Care offers a variety of indoor activities and attentive caregivers. The center operates daily from 8:30 A.M. to 4:30 P.M. and from 5:30 to 9:30 P.M. Wednesdays; parents must provide lunch, drinks, and snacks for children under 3. The staff is caring and competent; a ratio of one adult to 3 or 4 children is maintained at all times for children under 1. Children between 18 months and 3 years are segregated from the babies and cared for in slightly larger groups.

The center is in the Vacation Center, next to the Main Base Lodge. Reservations are required. Multi-day discounts are offered.

Children ages 3 and 4 are offered a daylong program that balances ski instruction and indoor and outdoor activities. Mount Snow helped develop the SKIwee teaching method. Lessons for this age group, called PeeWee SKIwee, are held on a separate slope a short walk from the Pumkin Patch; a rope tow helps them get up the slope. Between the two daily ski lessons, children enjoy arts and crafts, songs, games, cooking, and free play with toys. Two snacks and lunch are served.

Six- to 12-year-olds can enroll in a six-hour program that includes five hours of ski instruction and lunch. Beginning lessons are conducted on the children's slope, but those children with intermediate or above skills use the whole mountain as their classroom.

NICETIES: There's a protected box of tissues at the entrance to most lifts, a real godsend to snifflers.

Mount Snow issues a daily newsletter that lists special activities and offers tips to save time at lunch.

FOR MORE INFORMATION: Call Mount Snow Vacation Service, at (802) 464-8501; (800) 245-7669 from outside New England, New York, and northern New Jersey.

Stratton
Stratton Mountain, Vermont

It's no accident that this ski area, New England's premier four-season resort, has the look of a Tyrolean village. Many of the principals involved in its development since the 1960s were Europeans attracted to the picturesque charm of Vermont's Green Mountains and the skiing terrain of Stratton Mountain, the highest mountain in southern Vermont. Even today, a few members of the top management are Europeans, as well as many of the instructors. They lend the area an international air.

Stratton is a top-quality ski resort and planned community. Nothing looks out of place; there's no chance of a honky-tonk joint opening down the street from the base lodge. The architecture looks like it all came out of the same shop—and, in large part, it did, $60 million worth since 1984. It attracts many families because of its fine ski school and its easy accessibility to the slopes. There may be no closer-to-the-slopes accommodations anywhere.

And after the day's skiing is done, you have the wonderful small towns and country inns of southern Vermont just a short drive away. Although you can easily spend your time cloistered in the Stratton Village, it also provides a nice base from which to explore.

ACCOMMODATIONS: $$ to $$$$ The Stratton Corp. operates a one-call lodging service that handles reservations for the Stratton Mountain Villas and two dozen other lodgings, from lodges to country inns.

The Stratton Mountain Inn offers 125 beautifully decorated rooms just a short shuttle ride from the slopes. Better suited to families is the newer Stratton Village Lodge, right behind the base lodge, which has 91 rooms, some with lofts and each with a kitchenette (children are free in the same room).

The Stratton Mountain Villas have one- to five-bedroom condominium units that you can ski in and out of.

Special package rates are available at all Stratton Corp. lodgings, which can reduce the nightly rate.

Also very close to the mountain are two European-style lodges, the Birkenhaus and the Liftline Lodge, which have a cozier ambience. They are suitable for families with older children.

DINING: Stratton has a busy, but friendly, slopeside cafeteria, and another cafeteria at the Sun Bowl Base Lodge; there are outdoor barbecues in spring. A wine bar café, open only on weekends, serves specialty cheeses and smoked meats and wine and imported beers. The base lodge also has a sit-down restaurant, the Bear's Den, which provides good cooked-to-order food at lunchtime. The Mid-Mountain Restaurant at the base of the North American lift offers complete cafeteria service, as well as a special fast-food kiosk.

Many skiers at Stratton make dinner a real event, trying a different restaurant each evening. For families with children, the best bets on the premises are the BreakPoint Restaurant, upstairs at the Stratton Sports Center, with tableside views of the lovely indoor swimming pool, and Sage Hill, Birkenhaus and Liftline Lodge or Mulligans and La Pizzeria in The Village Square. In the nearby town of Bondville, four miles from the slopes, the River Café is a nice place for dinner, and it welcomes children. Three of the area's finest restaurants, Bear Creek, Waterside Cafe, and Jamaica House, are in nearby Jamaica.

THE SKIING: Stratton is situated in the middle of Vermont's snow belt and receives an average of 170 inches of snow a year, guaranteeing reliable skiing from late October until well into April. Stratton also makes its own snow; 60 percent of the terrain can be covered with machine-made snow.

 Thirty-two novice, 35 intermediate, 25 expert.

 Four quad chairs, one triple, six doubles, one gondola.

 2,003 feet.

 Four miles.

Stratton's Ski School has 175 professional instructors, many of them European, who use the American Teaching Method. Group lessons last 1¾ hours each and are held daily at 9:45 A.M. and 1:15 P.M. Individual lessons available.

Eleven miles of tracked and groomed trails at the new Sun Bowl Cross-Country Ski-Touring Center. Guided moonlight tours along the trail are offered Wednesday nights. Skating trails and 50 kilometers of back country skiing trails available.

ACTIVITIES FOR NON-SKIERS: Stratton offers a full range of alternate activities each day, including sleigh rides, snowboarding, shopping in The Village Square, après-ski entertainment, and movies in the Bijou Theater.

The Stratton Sports Center is a fully equipped exercise center and spa that offers facilities for aerobics and water exercise classes, badminton, golf lessons, Ping-Pong, indoor tennis, and racquetball. Massages and tanning beds are available.

Numerous social activities are offered each week at the base lodge. The Stratton Mountain Boys provide lively après-ski entertainment—yodeling and Tyrolean folk dancing—a few days a week in the Bear's Den. On other days, there's rock and jazz music.

The Stratton Village Square has 30 shops and restaurants.

Kids will enjoy a sleigh ride. Several are scheduled daily from the Sun Bowl Base Lodge.

FOR CHILDREN: Stratton is serious about putting kids on skis at an early age; it operates one of the first bona fide ski schools for children in the United States, using the SKIwee system.

From 8:30 A.M. to 3:45 P.M., children between 4 and 6 can attend the "Little Cub" all-day program, which includes between four and five hours of skiing, lunch, and some indoor play. Unlike most other ski areas' programs for children this age, much more time is spent skiing than playing. Children under 7 do not need lift tickets.

Children between 6 and 12 go into the "Big Cub" program, running from 8:30 A.M. to 3:45 P.M., which provides all-day supervision and lunch. At 10 A.M. and again at 1:15 P.M., they join the

Junior Ski School for lessons. Reservations for both programs are strongly suggested at the time you make your lodging reservations.

For children younger than 4, Stratton operates a state-licensed day-care program in the bright, new Base Lodge Childcare Center. About 80 children can be accommodated; reservations are suggested.

The child-care center operates from 8:30 A.M. to 4:30 P.M. and takes children as young as 6 weeks. With advance notice, extra hours also can be scheduled before the regular program and from 4:30 to 11 P.M. The charge is by the hour (minimum of two hours). The center provides a variety of activities for infants and toddlers, including arts and crafts, games, storytelling, and songs. There's a separate sleeping room for infants. Lunch and two snacks are served.

NICETIES: The Villager Lift, which provides access to a nice, gentle beginners' slope, is free at all times. That's nice for parents who want to do some skiing with their children—or for a beginner who wants to put in a lot of practice on turns.

A shuttle van and buses operate between all of the on-property lodging, the ski-touring center, the sports center, and the slopes.

Stratton has a multi-level parking garage that is a great alternative to the mud flats at many other New England ski resorts.

OF INTEREST NEARBY: Stratton is about a 20-minute drive from Manchester, Vermont, a charming New England community with dozens of Victorian mansions, lovely country inns and restaurants, and The Equinox, a famous old hotel. It's also a major center for factory outlets; ski wear, sportswear, designer clothes, and kids' clothes can be had for a song.

A cross-country touring center is operated on the grounds of the estate of Abraham Lincoln's son in Manchester Village, just beyond the Equinox. The home is operated as a museum in the summer.

IN THE SUMMER: Stratton is a full-service golf and tennis resort in the summer months, with one of the nation's finest golf schools and plenty of other activities for families, too, including horseback riding, expert tennis instruction, carriage rides, wind-surfing, and gondola rides.

FOR MORE INFORMATION: Call (802) 297-2200 for general information or (800) 843-6867, outside Vermont, for reservations, or write the Stratton Corporation, Stratton Mountain, VT 05155.

SOUTHWEST AND MOUNTAIN STATES

Aspen Area Ski Resorts
Aspen Mountain
Buttermilk Mountain
Snowmass
Aspen Highlands

Aspen, Colorado

It seems as though the silver mines of Aspen had just fallen silent when adventurers began clearing trees so they could streak down the snow on Aspen Mountain. Its slopes now offer a skiing experience that many consider among the best in the world—and an après-skiing experience that is definitely unparalleled in the United States.

Aspen is an area of high fashion and cowboy boots. It is, as its promotional literature says, at once "rustic and cosmopolitan, tranquil and trendy, historic and futuristic." People go there to ski, and also to be seen.

But that doesn't mean that Aspen isn't for families. Since it was a real town before it became a ski resort, it has lots of inherent charm. Its streets are lined with colorful Victorian houses, and its sizable year-round population means that it has such real-town amenities as playgrounds and good supermarkets and a library.

The Aspen area offers four separate ski areas, each with a different atmosphere and clientele. Aspen Mountain, sometimes called Ajax, overlooks the city of Aspen. Aspen Highlands is located on Maroon Creek Road, southwest of Aspen. Buttermilk Mountain is located just down Highway 82 from the Highlands. And Snowmass, one of North America's largest mountains, is just a 20-minute drive down Highway 82 south of Aspen.

ACCOMMODATIONS: **$$** to **$$$$** Aspen Central Reservations Travel (800-26-ASPEN) offers a convenient, one-stop reservations service. Prospective visitors can book lodging alone or ski packages that include lodging, lift tickets, airfare, ground transportation, and ski lessons. The agency is a subsidiary of the Aspen Chamber Resort Association and represents a wide variety of lodgings, from hotels and condominiums to private homes and bed and breakfasts.

The heartbeat of Aspen can be felt at the magnificently restored Hotel Jerome; call (303) 920-1000. Originally opened in 1889, the Belle of the Roaring Fork Valley regained her crown in the mid-1980s after a $30 million renovation and addition.

For something off the beaten track, consider staying at the moderately priced T Lazy 7 Ranch on Maroon Bells Road, just up the road from Aspen Highlands. The ranch offers cabins ranging from rustic to very rustic; many have fireplaces, and all have kitchens. There's a hot tub and sauna and a bar for après-ski gatherings. Transportation is available to the slopes. Phone (303) 925-4614.

Snowmass has 650 comfortable guest rooms in modern lodges ranging from luxurious to the casually simple, including the newly renovated Silvertree Hotel (303-923-3520), with its own day-care center, and Hotel Wildwood (303-923-3550). And there are more than 1,250 spacious condominiums, many with ski-in–ski-out convenience.

DINING: You can easily dine somewhere different every night. Restaurants like the Copper Kettle and Abetone Ristorante offer cuisine of international reputation. Most restaurants require reservations.

Families on a budget will like the Hickory House Restaurant and the Home Plate. The Aspen Grove Café is a charming restaurant serving breakfast, lunch, and dinner at moderate prices. The Asia, formerly Arthur's, is a Chinese restaurant specializing in gourmet Mandarin and Hunan cuisine. The Red Onion is a popular local spot serving fine homemade American food.

And no trip to Aspen is complete without a meal at Little Annie's, which serves home-cooked foods, such as ribs and chicken. Aspen also has a McDonald's, directly across from Wagner Park (which has an excellent children's playground).

In Snowmass there are the Mountain Dragon, the village's only Chinese restaurant; Mama Maria's Pizza & Subs, and La Piñata, famous for double Margaritas and great Mexican food. For elegant mountaintop dining try the High Alpine Restaurant, located at the top of the Alpine Springs lift in the Snowmass ski area.

THE SKIING: Three areas—Aspen, Snowmass, and Buttermilk— are operated by the Aspen Skiing Co. The fourth area, Aspen Highlands, is operated by the Aspen Highlands Skiing Corp. The skiing season at all four areas typically extends from Thanksgiving weekend through the first or second week of April. A coupon book is available for skiing at all 4 areas.

Aspen Mountain: 35 percent more difficult, 35 percent most difficult, 30 percent expert.
Snowmass: 10 percent easiest, 62 percent more difficult, 21 percent most difficult, 7 percent expert.
Buttermilk: 35 percent easiest, 40 percent more difficult, 25 percent most difficult.
Aspen Highlands: 25 percent novice, 50 percent intermediate, 25 percent advanced.

Aspen Mountain: One gondola, one high-speed quad chair, two regular quads, four doubles.
Snowmass: Three detachable quad chairs; two triple chairs, nine doubles.
Buttermilk: Six double chairs.
Aspen Highlands: Nine double chairs, two Pomas.

Aspen Mountain: 3,267 feet.
Snowmass: 3,615 feet.
Buttermilk: 2,030 feet.
Aspen Highlands: 3,800 feet.

Aspen Mountain: three miles.
Snowmass: four miles.
Buttermilk: three miles.
Aspen Highlands: three and one-half miles.

Ski schools at all areas.

The largest free cross-country system in the country, with more than 40 miles of groomed trails radiating from the heart of Aspen through forested hillsides to Snowmass Village.

ACTIVITIES FOR NON-SKIERS: Just a few blocks from downtown Aspen is the municipally operated Aspen Ice Garden. Public skating sessions are scheduled throughout the week.

A year-round program of theater, dance, music, and film classics is offered in the historic Wheeler Opera House. Aspen also boasts two public museums, the Aspen Historical Society Museum and the Aspen Art Museum. The Aspen-Snowmass area has more than 30 art galleries and an assortment of eclectic shops.

Snowmobiling is an ideal way to explore the mountains above the Roaring Fork Valley. The T Lazy 7 Ranch on Maroon Creek Road has nearly 50 miles of groomed trails ready for exploring by competent snowmobilers. The trail to secluded Maroon Lake is about seven miles long through towering stands of willowy white aspen trees. The ranch also offers a snowmobile caravan up Independence Pass to the gold-mining ghost town of Independence.

Sleigh rides and guided evening dinner ski tours are available at Pine Creek Cookhouse (303-925-1044) at nearby Ashcroft.

If you'd like to experience the Jack London life-style, you can contact Krabloonik Kennels (303-923-4342) in Snowmass and arrange for a sled and team of dogs. Teams of 13 dogs and a crack guide take guests on two-hour tours of the winter wilderness.

Hot-air balloons ascend each morning for voyages over the Roaring Fork Valley. Several balloon companies offer regular flights.

FOR CHILDREN:
Aspen Mountain: Kidstime Childcare Referrals (303-925-KIDS) offers daytime and nighttime baby-sitter services. It's best to book in advance of your arrival.
Snowmass: "Snowmass Snowbunnies" is a state-licensed children's ski-and-play school for children ages 1½ through 6. Children under 3 receive attentive indoor care, and 3- to 6-year-olds can learn to ski. The daily fee includes lunch. Call (303) 925-7126.

"Snow Cubs Play School," a program with both indoor and outdoor activities, is for children 18 months to 4 years. It operates from 8:30 A.M. to 4 P.M. daily and provides hot lunches and snacks.

"Big Burn Bears" is a ski program for children ages 4 to 6. It offers ski instruction in small groups of similar abilities, and provides hot lunches and snacks.

A special Kids' Ski Week package includes five days of lessons, lifts, races, picnics, and group activities for 7- to 12-year-olds.

Teens-only groups meet from 10 A.M. to 3:30 P.M. daily, and the Teens' Ski Week fee includes lessons, lift tickets, races, and picnic lunches.

Buttermilk: "Power Pandas" is a learn-to-ski program from 8:30 A.M. to 4:30 P.M. daily for children between 3 and 6. The fee includes lunch and lift tickets. For older children, the Kids' Ski Week and Teen Ski Week programs are similar to Snowmass's.

Aspen Highlands: "Snow Puppies" is the ski school for 3½- to 6-year-olds. Supervised by specially trained and very patient instructors, children are taught skiing safety, etiquette, and basic skills. The program operates from 9:30 A.M. to 3:30 P.M. daily, and the fee includes lift tickets, lessons, and lunch. Baby-sitting for younger children can be arranged only on an individual basis (ask the Snow Puppies staff for referrals). Children 12 and under ski free with a paying adult.

Aspen Highlands also offers the "Kids Camp" for kids 7 to 12. It meets daily from 10:15 A.M until 3:30 P.M. The charge includes lifts, lessons, and a variety of fun activities.

NICETIES: Many winter visitors find car rental is unnecessary because of frequent free shuttle buses connecting the town with the slopes.

IN THE SUMMER: Aspen is a terrific summer destination for families, with boundless opportunities for hiking, fishing, whitewater rafting, ballooning, and just plain sightseeing. The nearby Maroon Bells Wilderness Area is also a wonderful place for hiking, fishing, and camping. In the summer Aspen becomes Colorado's cultural arts center, with a dizzying schedule of performances by the

Aspen Music Festival, the DanceAspen Summer Festival, the Aspen Theatre Company, and the Snowmass/Aspen Repertory Theatre.

FOR MORE INFORMATION: Call Aspen Central Reservations at (800) 262-7736 or (303) 925-9000. Call Snowmass Central Reservations at (800) 332-3245.

For information about all programs at Aspen Mountain, Buttermilk, and Snowmass, call the Aspen Skiing Co. at (303) 925-1220. For information about Aspen Highlands, call (303) 925-5300.

Crested Butte Ski Area
Crested Butte, Colorado

Crested Butte isn't a ski area you just stumble upon. It's at the end of a paved road, nowhere near an interstate highway, 230 miles from Denver, and decidedly not on the way to anywhere else. You have to set out for Crested Butte in order to end up there.

Yet tens of thousands of skiers make it their chosen destination every year. The reason? There are many: the charm of an authentic Old West town whose downtown area is a National Historic District; locals who love living here year-round; a spectacular setting amidst six mountain peaks that exceed 14,000 feet, and absolutely free skiing for children who are accompanied by a paying adult.

And from just after Thanksgiving to mid-December, *everybody* skis free at Crested Butte (no kidding).

ACCOMMODATIONS: $ to $$$$ The area offers lodging for 6,000 visitors in condominiums, lodges, bed, and breakfasts, and a luxury hotel, the Grande Butte Hotel. Crested Butte Vacations offers a one-call booking service (800-544-8448).

For a family of intermediate to expert skiers, secluded Irwin Lodge, North America's highest-year-round, full-service resort, provides the most unique skiing experience in the area. Snocats gives skiers access to untouched powder and natural terrain with a thrilling 2,000-foot vertical drop; after skiing, you can retreat to one of the 25 cozy guest rooms atop a convivial lodge with a gourmet restaurant. Call (800) 2-IRWIN-2.

DINING: When you get there, pick up a copy of Menu Magazine for a quick look at the offerings (and prices) of almost all of the area's restaurants.

The Bakery Cafe has wonderful breads, pastries, soups, sandwiches and natural food offerings. The Slogar Bar & Restaurant is famous for its skillet-fried chicken and family-style service.

In the evenings, families will feel welcome at the Powerhouse Bar & Grill, which serves Mexican food in the town's old water-driven powerhouse, and the IdleSpur, a restaurant and micro-brewery that serves sandwiches and steaks in surroundings with a western motif.

THE SKIING: Over the last three decades, Crested Butte has had the highest average snowfall of any ski town in Colorado: 229 inches a year, compared with 172 at Steamboat, 153 at Aspen, and 145 at Dillon. The expert-only North Face contains some of the most daring ski terrain in the country.

 Eighty-five trails, 13 percent beginner, 30 percent intermediate, nine percent advanced, 48 percent expert (double black diamond ungroomed terrain).

 Three triple chairs, six doubles, four surface lifts.

 3,062 feet.

Almost three miles.

Group and individual lessons, workshops and clinics for beginning to expert skiers. Readers of *Rocky Mountain Sports and Fitness Magazine* have voted Crested Butte Colorado's best ski school. The ski school, founded by Robel Straubhaar, incorporates such concepts as relaxation and body awareness in its teaching. Nastar races and clinics Wednesdays through Sundays; coin-operated, self-timed race courses.

On an 18-mile groomed track system at the downtown Nordic Ski Center at the Crested Butte Club; rentals, instruction. Guided backcountry tours through Elk Mountains and Paradise Divide, including overnight excursions utilizing wilderness huts. Periodic Nordic races through the winter.

ACTIVITIES FOR NON-SKIERS: Until you've ridden a horse over a snow-packed trail, you've no idea what a special experience that can be. Call (303) 349-5425 to arrange.

Hot-air balloon rides are available year-round from Bighorn Balloon, the highest altitude balloon company in North America; call (303) 349-6335.

Adventurers will enjoy snowmobiling through the Elk Mountains, including lunch and dinner tours (303-349-5031) or special Snocat powder tours from Irwin Lodge (303-349-5308.)

FOR CHILDREN: Crested Butte's big lure for families is free skiing almost every day of the season for each child, 12 and under, accompanied by a ticket-purchasing adult.

The Crested Butte Mountain Resort Children's Ski Center, in the Whetstone Building right on the mountain, offers half- or full-day nursery care for children between 6 months and 3 years in a cheerful setting; reservations are mandatory (303-349-2259.)

Children ages 3 to 6 can be enrolled in either day-care (no skiing) or the "ABC's on Skis" program. Graduates of the ABC program and children who are experienced lift riders can take half- or full-day group lessons. One-on-one lessons for 2 to 6-year-olds are also offered. (For a small extra fee, parents can tag along with the private lessons and learn how to coach their child on basic skills.)

For children between 7 and 12, the "Butte Buster" program offers half- and full-day instruction.

NICETIES: There's a free shuttle bus between Mt. Crested Butte and the downtown area.

For intermediate skiers, there's a free two-hour guided tour of the mountain three times a day; advanced skiers can sign on for a free tour of the Extreme Limits of the North Face and Phoenix Bowl twice daily.

IN THE SUMMER: Crested Butte is the official Wildflower Capital of Colorado, and in the summer the ski slopes, roadsides, and mountain meadows are ablaze with millions of blooms, including the protected Colorado columbine.

The famed Rocky Mountain Biological Laboratory (303-349-7231) in nearby Gothic offers special adult nature walks, family field tours, and children's nature workshops through the summer.

For a moderate daily rate, the ski area's Sports Afield Family Adventure package provides families with accommodations at the Plaza Hotel, sports equipment, and a selection of adventure-oriented outdoor activities: trail rides, raft trips, four-wheel-drive tours of mountain passes, mountain bike rentals, canoeing, fishing, riflery, trapshooting, archery, fly-fishing instruction, overnight camping, tennis, and chairlift rides. The rate includes enrollment in the Mountain Day Camp for 1- to 6-year-olds. All activities are also available a la carte. Call (800) 544-8448.

There's golf at the Skyland Country Club on a 7,200-yard course designed by Robert Trent Jones Jr.

FOR MORE INFORMATION: Call Crested Butte Mountain Resort at (303) 349-2281.

Steamboat Ski Area
Steamboat Springs, Colorado

Steamboat has been playing host to skiers since 1962, when local developers built a ski lift and modest A-frame warming house on Storm Mountain in northern Colorado. The area's commitment to family skiers was evident almost from the start; the nursery building was added just 2 years after the opening.

It wasn't until 1969 that the development of Steamboat Village Resort began in earnest, but a series of regular improvements nearly every year since then has resulted in one of the nation's premier ski resorts. The ski area boasts that it has Colorado's biggest lift system, "trails so long you have to stop to catch your breath, and mountain panoramas so vast they will leave you breathless."

Steamboat has the feel of a family resort; fancy furs and Ferragamos are few and far between, and in the parking lots, station wagons and Wagoneers win out over sports cars and imported sedans.

ACCOMMODATIONS: $ to $$$$ The selection is eclectic. The area offers everything from the inexpensive downtown Alpine Motel to expensive mountainside luxury condominiums like The Lodge at Steamboat and Bearclaw. Less expensive condominium accommodations are available at Ptarmigan House, Storm Meadows, and Thunderhead Lodge.

The Steamboat Reservations Service (800-922-2722) can match you with a place that suits your needs.

DINING: A range of food, with an emphasis on western specialties, is available in more than 60 restaurants on and around the mountain and in town. On one of the nights when the stars came out with a special brilliance, we took the ski area's 8-passenger high-speed gondola to a place called Hazie's. The menu offers everything from steak to sushi. The view of the setting sun and, later, the twinkling lights of Steamboat Springs and the sprawling Yampa River basin were spectacular. It's a special place for a parents' night out. Reservations are necessary.

Also at the ski area, the Thunderbird facility at the upper terminal of the Silver Bullet has a cafeteria and a barbecue sun deck. The Rendezvous Saddle facility, in the Priest Creek area, offers fine dining, with unusual Norwegian specialties at Ragnar's. There's also a barbecue deck and a cafteria on the second and third floor.

For those who choose to prepare some or all of their meals in a condominium kitchen, there are food shops aplenty and two supermarkets near the mountain (and on the bus loop).

THE SKIING: Steamboat's season normally runs from late November to mid-April, with the regular season beginning around mid-December. The ski area covers a mountain range that includes Sunshine Peak, Storm Peak, Thunderhead Peak, and Christie Peak, and encompasses 2,500 acres, of which 1,400 are groomed. The elevation is 10,500 feet at the top; 9,080 midway, and 6,900 at the base. Snowfall ranges from 325 to 350 inches per season. Steamboat's snow is famous among skiers; it is among the best in the West.

 106 cut trails, plus glades: 15 percent novice, 53 percent intermediate, 32 percent advanced.

 One gondola, one quad chair, seven triples, 10 doubles, two surface lifts.

 3,600 feet.

 Three miles.

Fully staffed ski school, all levels of instruction. NASTAR Racing Clinics for youngsters and grown-ups Tuesday through Sunday (two hours of coaching and a videotape analysis). There is also a coin-operated race course open from 10 A.M. to 3:30 P.M. daily called the Marlboro Ski Challenge. Billy Kidd is the head counselor at two-, three- and five-day race camps for recreational racers throughout the season.

The Steamboat Ski Touring Center maintains 33 miles of trails, with guided tours and moonlight journeys by appointment. Some area inns offer their own cross-country programs.

ACTIVITIES FOR NON-SKIERS: The ski area's promoters put together a series of special events every year, including torchlight parades and the popular Winter Carnival, which features ski racing and jumping, hot-air balloon racing, parades, and fireworks.

Regular offerings at Steamboat include hot-air balloon rides, bobsledding, sleigh rides, Snocat rides, ice-skating, bowling, and movies. There is also a a run on Howelsen Hill in downtown Steamboat that is lighted for nighttime skiing from 6 to 9 P.M. Tuesday through Friday. Don't miss a soak in one of the area's hot springs, either downtown or at Strawberry Fields.

FOR CHILDREN: Except over the Christmas–New Year holidays, kids under 12 ski free at Steamboat if their parents stay a minimum of five nights at a Steamboat Springs Chamber/Resort Association member lodge and if they purchase lift tickets for themselves for five or more days. Children also stay free in the same lodging room with their parents and have free ski rentals when their parents rent skis for the same period of time.

All-day lessons are available for children 3½ and up. The "Kiddie Corral Ski School" gives 2½- to 6-year-olds all-day or half-day classes that include instruction, games, and lunch. Children must be out of diapers in order to participate. The Kiddie Corral Child Care facility at the lower Silver Bullet terminal operates from 8 A.M. to 5 P.M. daily, with half-day care available, morning or afternoon. The facility welcomes children as young as 6 months, but food for children under 2 years must be supplied by the parents. Evening care is offered for children from 6 months through 12 years on Tuesdays through Saturdays during the ski season.

"Rough Rider Ski School" is open to children from 6 to 15.

NICETIES: Steamboat operates a "host and hostess" program in which employees are stationed on the mountain and in the information center to give directions, inform visitors about activities, help reunite parents with lost children, and generally keep the peace.

The resort puts out the "Steamboat SKIDS Newsletter" to acquaint families with all the amenities the area offers. It lists the two dozen or so restaurants in the area that either offer children's menus or special price meals for kids 12 and under.

IN THE SUMMER: Summertime here is marked by vigorous hikes into the surrounding Routt National Forest; horseback rides through Aspen groves; llama trekking; rafting on the Colorado and Yampa rivers; the Friday night rodeo; golf at two public courses, including Robert Trent Jones Jr.'s 18-hole course at the Sheraton Steamboat; fishing for mountain trout; boating on Steamboat Lake and Stagecoach Reservoir; bicycling on the new trail system along the Yampa River or on mountain-bike trails, gondola or balloon rides, and thrill-filled voyages down the municipal waterslide.

Steamboat is also known for its summer festivals: Cowboy Roundup Days in July; Strings in the Mountains Chamber Music Festival in July and August; Steamboat's Summer Children's Jubilee; Rainbow Weekend, a ballooning competition, and the annual Vintage Auto Race & Concours d'Elegance.

FOR MORE INFORMATION: Call Steamboat at (303) 879-6111 or write 2305 Mt. Werner Circle, Steamboat Springs, CO 80487. For reservations, call (800) 922-2722.

Summit County Ski Resorts
Breckenridge
Copper Mountain
Keystone

Summit County, Colorado

Summit County, Colorado, has one of the greatest concentrations of world-class ski resorts, skiable terrain, diverse accommodations and après-ski activities of any county in the nation.

Just 75 miles west of Denver's international airport via Interstate 70, Summit County offers skiing conditions that will please skiers of any ability. And through "Ski the Summit," the ski areas' joint marketing program, skiers can purchase coupons that entitle them to ski at any or all of the areas for less than the price of a lift ticket at a single area. On a week-long ski vacation, you may find you never have to ski the same trail twice!

Each area has its own appeal and an army of diehard loyalists who proclaim it their favorite. Breckenridge, the largest and most popular of the county's ski areas, has the charm of an old Victorian mining town, complete with a 350-building historic district.

ACCOMMODATIONS: $** to **$$$$ You can stay at any one of dozens of condominium complexes with one- to four-bedroom units, quaint bed and breakfasts, cozy country lodges, or the Keystone Lodge, which has been given a four-diamond rating by the AAA. Each of the ski areas offers its own central reservations service.

At Breckenridge, accommodations are found both in town and at the Village at several slopeside hotel complexes; Breckenridge boasts more ski-in–ski-out lodgings that any ski resort in North America. Call Victoria Vacations at (800) 877-5437 or the Breckenridge Resort Chamber at (800) 221-1091 (800-822-5381 within Colorado.)

All of Copper Mountain's accommodations are within walking distance of the ski slopes. Guests who stay anywhere at Copper Mountain have privileges at the Racquet and Athletic Club, which offers year-round tennis, hot tubs, saunas, steambaths, exercise classes, and therapeutic massage. For Copper Mountain reservations, call (800) 458-8386.

Keystone Lodge, a member of Preferred Hotels Worldwide, offers luxury hotel rooms right next to the Keystone slopes; in addition, Keystone Resort has almost 1,000 rental condominiums and private homes. For lodge reservations, call (800) 541-0346; for Keystone condominium reservations, call (800) 222-0188. A cozy alternative is the rustic Ski Tip Lodge, which offers 22 quaint rooms decorated with antiques in a restored stagecoach stop next door to the cross-country center (303-468-4202.)

DINING: Breckenridge alone has more than 100 restaurants, including 14 on its three ski mountains and their bases. Many others are in the lovingly restored Victorian-era bulidings in the downtown historic district.

Copper Mountain has about 20 eating establishments, ranging from O'Shea's Copper Bar at the base of the American Eagle Lift to the elegant Pesce Fresco restaurant in the Mountain Plaza.

Keystone has about 20 restaurants, ranging from very casual to highly elegant. The Edgewater Cafe in the lodge, the Alpentop Deli and Bentley's in the Village, and the Pinebridge Cafe at River Run Plaza are popular for breakfast. Lunch is usually a quick bite at one of the base lodges. At night, the Last Lift Bar at the mountain and the Last Chance Saloon in the village are popular watering holes. Garden Room Restaurant in the Lodge, the mountaintop Outpost, and Ski Tip Lodge are nice places for dinner.

THE SKIING: Breckenridge offers three distinct ski mountains, each with its own personality. Copper Mountain is widely regarded as a "skier's mountain," with an award-winning trail system that features naturally separated terrain for beginning, intermediate and expert skiers. And Keystone offers four distinct ski experiences: the groomed boulevards of Keystone Mountain, the moguled challenges of North Peak, the exhilaration of Arapahoe Basin (the continent's highest lift-served ski area), and the untamed ski experience of The Outback, above timberline. With many of its trails lighted, Keystone can guarantee 13½ hours of skiing every day.

 Breckenridge: 112 trails; 20 percent beginner, 31 percent intermediate, 49 percent advanced.

Copper Mountain: 76 trails; 25 percent beginner, 40 percent intermediate, 35 percent advanced.

Keystone: 51 trails; 25 percent beginner, 50 percent intermediate, 25 percent advanced. (At *Arapahoe Basin:* 29 trails; 10 percent beginner, 50 percent intermediate, 40 percent advanced.)

 Breckenridge: four quad superchairs, one triple, eight doubles, three surface.

Copper Mountain: two quad superchairs, six triples, eight doubles, four surface.

Keystone and Arapahoe: two gondolas, four quad superchairs, four triples, 10 doubles, four surface.

 Breckenridge: 3,400 feet.
Copper Mountain: 2,760 feet.
Keystone: 2,340 feet; *Arapahoe Basin:* 1,670 feet.
The Outback: 1,520 feet.

 Breckenridge: Three and one-half miles.
Copper Mountain: Almost three miles.
Keystone: Three miles; *Arapahoe:* One and one-half miles.

Ski schools at all areas. Breckenridge offers special "women only" lessons with female instructors upon request, and Copper Mountain offers several Women's Skiing Seminars throughout the season. Breckenridge also has one of the most complete programs for disabled skiers anywhere.

In the county, a total of 73 miles of groomed cross country and ski-skating trails, plus more than 320,000 acres of skiable backcountry terrain. Breckenridge has 13 miles of double-set cross country trails next to the ski area; the Breckenridge Nordic Center offers torchlight skiing and a nordic program for disabled skiers. Copper Mountain's Trak Cross Country Center has 15 miles of groomed trails. Keystone has 16 miles of groomed trails, plus guided tours into national forest lands. Helicopter skiing can be arranged in the backcountry.

ACTIVITIES FOR NON-SKIERS: There's ice-skating on the largest outdoor rink in the country (at Keystone) and the West Lake at Copper Mountain. Romantic horse-drawn sleigh rides depart in the evening for swings through the village at Copper Mountain and historic Breckenridge. You can take Keystone's gondola to the summit for a candlelit fondue dinner. The Keystone Science School (303-468-5824) offers talks by naturalists on Friday nights from January through mid-April. For the adventuresome, there's snowmobiling in the backcountry and even dogsled rides. Theatrical performances and tours of Breckenridge's Historical District are also offered through the winter.

FOR CHILDREN: At Breckenridge, the "Fanta-Ski Kingdom" program offers a full day of skiing instruction, supervised skiing, and just plain fun for children 6 to 12. Three-year-olds can take an introductory skiing course, with lessons no more than 90 minutes in length; 4- and 5-year-olds can be enrolled in the Junior Ski School for 90-minute lessons. The resort's specially designed terrain gardens make learning fun. (Parents must provide the skis and boots.) Two daycare centers, at the Peak 8 and Peak 9 base areas, provide child care for non-skiing children as young as two months. Half-, full-day, and hourly rates available. Up–to–date immunization records must be provided for children under 12 months. Reservations are essential; call (303) 453-2368.

At Copper Mountain, the "Belly Button Nursery" at the base of the mountain provides care for children from 2 months on up. The center has special areas for arts and crafts, reading, story-time, creative play, and outdoor snow play. Children 3 and older can try to ski. A highlight of each day is the baking of cookies, cakes, pizza, and other goodies, which are presented to parents at the end of the day. The Junior and Senior Ranch skiing programs meet on the ground floor of the center.

Copper Mountain's "Junior Ranch," for ages 4 to 6, enjoys its own ski lift close to indoor facilities that have games, cubbies for storage, and overnight ski storage. The "Senior Ranch," for ages 7 through 12, give children easy access to the entire mountain with a small group of children of similar age and ability. Children stay with the same instructor all day, eat lunch with their class, and ski as much as time allows.

The Keystone children's programs operate out of two Children's Centers, one at Keystone Mountain and the other at Arapahoe Basin, from 8 A.M. to 5 P.M. At Keystone Mountain, care is provided for children ages two months on up; at Arapahoe Basin, the minimum age is 18 months. Call (303) 468-4182 for reservations. The "Mini–Minor's Camp," for 3- and 4-year-olds, and the "Minor's Camp," for 5- to 12-year-olds, include lift tickets, lessons, lunch, and equipment rental in the fee. Call (303) 468-4170 for reservatons.

Teens will want to find the teen center on the lake, which has plenty of electronic games and pinball machines and serves snacks and soft drinks.

NICETIES: Getting around the Summit County ski areas is made easy by the Summit Stage, the free shuttle service that runs from early morning until late evening.

Breckenridge offers free skier evaluations every day from 12:30 P.M. to 1:15 P.M. at the mountaintop restaurants.

IN THE SUMMER: The Breckenridge Golf Club features the only public course in the world designed by Jack Nicklaus. Bicycling is popular along miles of country roads or the paved two-lane bicycle path that links Breckenridge with Copper Mountain. Tiger Run Tours (303-453-2231) offers backcountry jeep tours, gold-panning, and whitewater rafting. The Breckenridge Music Institute's summer festival runs from late June through July, with numerous chamber orchestra concerts, workshops, and lectures. Other special summer events include fishing contests, arts and crafts fairs, a water toy festival, mountain-bike races, and a jazz festival.

Copper Mountain lures summer vacationers with paddleboat and chair-lift rides, 40 miles of smooth bike paths, whitewater rafting, fly-fishing in Ten Mile Creek, a mid-mountain nature center, a special kids' fishing pond, boundless hiking opportunities, and guided horseback rides. The Copper Creek Golf Club, designed by Pete Dye, has the highest altitude championship course in the United States. The Belly Button Nursery operates through the summer.

Keystone has one of the most comprehensive summer activity programs of any ski resort. Many summer visitors don't even think of it as a ski resort; to them, it's a mecca for golf, sailing, tennis, hiking, and just relaxing. It is famous for its Keystone Tennis Center and for its championship 7,090-yard golf course designed by Robert Trent Jones Jr. The 90-piece National Repertory Orchestra performs through the summer. For children, Keystone offers all-day or half-day summer programs, beginning at 2 months of age. Activities include hiking, swimming, boating, arts and crafts, and pony rides.

FOR MORE INFORMATION: Write Ski the Summit, P.O. Box 267, Dillon, CO 80435, or phone (303) 468-6607.

Telluride Ski Resort
Telluride, Colorado

The secluded town of Telluride is as attractive a ski resort as you'll find anywhere in Colorado. Nestled in a valley deep in the San Juan Mountains, this old mining town turned resort, with its brightly painted Victorian houses and cosmopolitan atmosphere, exudes charm. With the awesome beauty of the surrounding mountains as a backdrop, the skiing here is a special experience too. The slopes on the San Juan mountains rise up on the very edge of town, and the views from the ski trails are spectacular enough to prompt a skier to pack a camera on a sunny day. Ski round a bend on a trail on the mountain and you will find Telluride almost straight down, several thousand feet below you, literally at your ski tips.

Named for a kind of ore in which gold is found (tellurium), the town itself is tiny, about six streets wide by 12 streets long, with a year-round population of about 1,200. You will find no Dairy Queen here; Telluride's strict zoning codes ensure the town's quaintness. The downtown area is a National Historic District.

But Telluride and the ski resort are expanding to meet the growing number of skiers that come here. And there is no shortage of après-ski activity, with a number of interesting restaurants, shops, and pubs to try out after the day's skiing is done.

Telluride opened in 1972 with five lifts and 20 ski trails. In 1979, the resort was purchased from the original developer by Benchmark Companies, which also developed property at Avon, Colorado. Millions have since been spent on new lifts and trails, and the development of Mountain Village Resort, where the $68 million Doral Telluride Resort and Spa opened in 1991.

ACCOMMODATIONS: $$ to $$$ Telluride's accommodations are concentrated in the town, where 80 percent are within walking distance of the base facilities, and at Mountain Village Resort, where 95 percent are ski-in–ski-out. You can choose from condominiums, bed and breakfasts in old Victorian homes, and rooms in the luxurious Doral Telluride Resort and Spa.

The staff answering the central reservation number (800-525-3455) can direct you to accommodations that best suit your needs and budget. You can also use this number to arrange lift tickets and air or ground transportation.

DINING: Telluride has about 25 restaurants, many of them with interesting interiors and menus, ranging from ethnic cuisine to continental cuisine and seafood.

At the Meadows base lodge, the Day Lodge Restaurant offers a full-service cafeteria and bar with a large outdoor sun deck. The Cactus Cafe offers Mexican food at the base of lifts 3 and 4 in Mountain Village Resort, and Cassidy's serves snacks and meals at the base of the Coonskin lift. At mid-mountain, the Gorrono Ranch and Saloon offers a full cafeteria, self-service deli, barbecue, and full-service bar. Once the site of an old ranch, the Gorrono Ranch has magnificent mountain views.

Giuseppe's Restaurant is at the top of Telluride's expert slopes, and offers pizza, Italian sandwiches, soup, beer and wine.

THE SKIING: With an average snowfall each year of 300 inches, Telluride usually has snow when other ski resorts may not. The mountain has a summit of 11,890 feet and a base of 8,735 feet.

 Forty-three trails: 24 percent novice, 51 percent intermediate, 25 expert.

 One quad chair, two triples, six doubles, one surface lift.

 3,165 feet.

 Almost three miles.

Ski school with 75 instructors. Beginners learn the basics at the Meadows and Sunshine Mountain. The Meadows has gentle glades and broad, well-groomed trails for the beginner and the "never-ever" skier.

Thirty miles of groomed trails and backcountry skiing maintained by the Telluride Nordic Center, which is west of the Meadows base facility. Equipment rentals, private and group lessons and guided backcountry tours.

Experience helicopter skiing over spectacular scenery in the Uncompahgre and San Juan national forests. A high Alpine tour designed for skiers of all abilities includes a gourmet lunch and ground transportation (728-4904).

ACTIVITIES FOR THE NON-SKIER: Deep Creek Sleigh Rides will take you on a dinner ride on a 16-passenger sleigh; call (303) 728-4142. Another option is snowmobiling around the high country meadows of Alta Lakes and Beaver Park; call Telluride Outside at (303) 728-3895. Telluride Outfitters offers trail rides in the foothills of the Black Canyon even in the deep of winter; call (303) 728-3895. San Juan Balloon Adventures offers dawn and brunch rides; call (303) 728-3895.

Telluride's Town Park Ice Rink offers free ice-skating parties every Wednesday night in the winter, with hot refreshments, music and a roaring fire in the warming shelter. Rentals, instruction; call

(303) 728-3851. You can take a self-guided walking tour of the Telluride National Historic District using a map available at the Visitor's Center. Or visit the San Miguel County Historical Museum at 317 N. Fir St.

Indulge yourself at the Doral's full-service spa, which offers an indoor lap pool (with a slide down to an indoor/outdoor pool), a circuit weight-training facility, squash and racquetball courts, steam baths, sauna, indoor and outdoor whirlpools, and massage and skin therapies.

FOR CHILDREN: Telluride offers a variety of children's programs, starting with the Village Nursery for children 2 months to 3 years old. Day care is provided from 8:30 A.M. to 4:30 P.M. in Le Chamonix Complex near the Mountain Village base facility; lunch is included. The adult-to-child ratio is one-to-two for children under 2.

The resort's "Snowstar" program introduces 3- to 5-year-olds to skiing with a combination of snow play, ski lessons, and indoor play. Children learn the parts of the ski and the basic movements indoors in front of a mirror; the emphasis is on fun. The adult-to-child ratio is one-to-three. For information and reservations, call (303) 728-8000.

The "Telstar Ski School" offers lessons to children age 6 to 12. Lunch is included in the daily fee.

NICETIES: A free shuttle bus to the ski resort operates every 12 minutes during the ski season from the city of Telluride. Another free shuttle bus takes skiers from Telluride to the Mountain Village Resort.

There are protected tissue boxes at each of the chair lifts.

IN THE SUMMER: Summer is special here. The mountain meadows are ablaze with wildflowers, and the town hops with festivals, special events, and seminars. Among them: the Telluride Balloon Rally, Bicycle Classic, and Bluegrass Festival in June; the Telluride Wine Festival, Firemen's Barbecue, Alpine Wildflower Photography Workshop, and Rotary 4 × 4 Rally in July; the Telluride Jazz Festival and Chamber Music Festival in August, and the Film Festival, Hang Gliding Festival, and Bicycle Tour of the San Juans in September.

The Telluride Institute (303-728-4981) offers special interest camps, seminars, and retreats through the summer.

A new lure to golfers: the 18-hole, high-country golf course with a 7,009-yard championship tee, which opened in July 1991 at the Telluride Mountain Resort Village. Summer also offers horseback riding, tennis, fishing, hiking, horseback riding, mountain biking and kayaking.

FOR MORE INFORMATION: Call the Telluride Ski Resort at (303) 728-3856 or write Box 11155, Telluride, CO 81435. For ski school, child care, and rental equipment reservations, call the Telluride Ski Resort at (303) 728-4424.

Vail/Beaver Creek
Eagle County, Colorado

It can't be just good luck that continually earns Vail the highest ratings by readers of national ski publications. Skiers vote with their feet as well, and more choose to ski at Vail than at any other Colorado ski resort (and all but one other in the nation.)

One reason for its phenomenal allure is that Vail has the country's largest ski mountain, with 3,834 acres of runs. It also has perhaps the best children's ski programs anywhere, and some of the most impressive nursery and day-care facilities we've seen. Add to that its easy accessibility by major airlines and automobile; a natural, gladed bobsled run; a snowboarding park; plenty of breathtaking upper-mountain intermediate ski areas, a dazzling array of après-ski activites and a world-famous reputation, and it's easy to understand why many families return to Vail year after year.

For the last decade, part of the draw has also been Vail's nearby sister ski area, Beaver Creek, a beautifully designed resort that is particularly attractive to families because of its self-contained, intimate feeling.

ACCOMMODATIONS: **$** to **$$$$** Vail offers accommodations in every price range, from motels affiliated with most of the national chains to on-mountain condos to in-town guest houses and bed and breakfasts. The Westin Resort-Vail (303-476-5031) has its own ski lift direct to the top of the mountain. For all reservations in Vail, call (800) 525-2257.

There are 4,700 beds within the Beaver Creek Resort, all luxurious and all quite close to the slopes. Among the hotels are the Hyatt Regency Beaver Creek, with its year-round outdoor pool and its own children's program; the Beaver Creek Lodge, an all-suite hotel, and the Park Plaza, which offers elegant two to three-bedroom apartments, many with a family-sized Jacuzzi in the master bath. For all reservations in Beaver Creek, call (800) 622-3131.

DINING: Vail and Beaver Creek together have more than 100 restaurants, with cuisines ranging from haute French to Malaysian to Mexican to Western.

At Vail, the Two Elk Restaurant, new in 1991, offers Southwestern, Western, and American food in a beautifully decorated cafeteria-style facility, elevation 11,200 feet, overlooking the majestic China Bowl.

Spruce Saddle, at Beaver Creek, is a mid-mountain restaurant that serves skiers coq au vin, red or green chili, and fresh deli sandwiches. Its upstairs adjunct, Rafters, serves pastas, salmon, salads, and hearty stews in a clublike atmosphere.

A very special dining experience is offered at Beano's Cabin on Beaver Creek Mountain. For a fixed price, visitors can enjoy a sleigh ride from the mountain base to the log restaruant, followed by an elegant dinner in front of a blazing fire. (In the summer, the restaurant is reachable by van, horseback, or horse-drawn wagon.)

THE SKIING: Only the front side of Vail's mountain is visible to skiers at the base. There are runs there suitable for skiers of all levels of expertise. But it's the back side, with its expansive bowls, that has made Vail truly legendary among skiers.

Beaver Creek's newest terrain, Grouse Mountain, was opened to skiers in 1991 on a ridge on the western section of the mountain. It features undulating terrain and long, sweeping expanses, with enough steep, gladed parks to thrill any expert.

 Vail: Front side, 32 percent beginner, 36 percent intermediate, 32 percent advanced; back side, 36 percent intermediate, 64 percent advanced.
Beaver Creek: 18 percent beginner, 39 percent intermediate, 43 percent advanced.

 Vail: Seven high-speed quads, two fixed-grip quads, one gondola, two triples, six doubles, two surface lifts.
Beaver Creek: Two high-speed quads, five triples, four doubles.

 Vail: 3,250 feet.
Beaver Creek: 3,340 feet.

 Vail: Four and one-half miles
Beaver Creek: Almost three miles.

Vail's 700 ski instructors and Beaver Creek's 400 offer classes that aim to make any skier better, from the novice to the black-diamond connoisseur. Among the tools: video analysis with on-slope viewing centers, SyberVision role-model tapes, and express lift-lanes for ski-school participants. Expert skiers can sign on for a session with a "super guide"; in this program, small groups receive light coaching as they explore seldom-skied areas of the mountains.

The Vail and Beaver Creek Cross-Country Ski School (303-476-5601) offers instruction for every level of Nordic skier, including telemarkers. Also offered are all-day nature tours in the White River National Forest, gourmet tours, and overnight hut tours along the Tenth Mountain Trail.

Vail's Nordic Center has 11 miles of groomed trails. At Beaver Creek, McCoy Park, reachable by its own lift, offers 18 miles of machine-set double track that meander through aspen groves and alpine glades.

ACTIVITIES FOR THE NON-SKIER: You needn't ever put on skis to have a good time at either of these resorts.

Among the options for the adventuresome are snowmobile tours at secluded Piney River Ranch, backcountry tours by a 12-passenger heated Snocat, horsedrawn sleigh rides and guided snowshoe walks. All arrangements can be made through the Adventure Co. (303-949-9090.)

The free Hot Winter Night ski shows, generally on Wednesday nights at Vail, combine synchronized skiing, technical displays, comedy demonstrations, and aerials with a light show, music, and fireworks. On Thursday nights at Beaver Creek, the torchlight ski-down is a must-see. The best viewing spot is on the Hyatt Regency patio.

For shoppers, Vail and Beaver Creek offer dozens of interesting shops.

FOR CHILDREN: Both Vail and Beaver Creek take children's ski instruction very seriously, but one of their goals is to ensure that children also have the time of their lives. At both ski areas, instruction takes place on a Children's Adventure Mountain, which integrates a taste of Colorado's colorful history with the teaching of skiing skills as children ski through attractions like a "gold mine," an "Indian village," or a "frontier town." Most days, ski school children will be delighted by a visit from Sport Goofy, the resorts' ambassador of skiing and good sportsmanship.

All-day classes are offered for 3- to 12-year olds at the children's skiing centers at Lionshead and Golden Peak in Vail and at the base of the mountain at Beaver Creek. There are special children's rental shops in the Golden Peak and Beaver Creek Children's Skiing Centers.

For non-skiing children between 2 months and 6 years, the on-mountain Small World Play Schools provide licensed day-care with low adult to child ratios (evening care for an hourly fee is available at Beaver Creek.) Advance reservations are required for the nursery: call Golden Peak at (303) 479-2044 and Beaver Creek at (303) 949-2306.

Teenagers will be attracted to the special snowboarding and racing programs.

Special activities include Family Night Out on winter Tuesdays, featuring dinner and a performance by the Beaver Creek Children's Theatre; Kids' Night Out Goes Western, on winter Thursdays at Golden Peak Children's Skiing Center; K2/Sport Goofy Challenge on Fridays at Vail's Gitchegumee Gulch and Beaver Creek's Buckaroo Bowl, and Après-Ski with Sport Goofy. Call the Family Activity Line at (303) 479-2048 for details.

NICETIES: Parents with infants in the nursery can borrow a personal beeper so that they can be reached in an instant.

At Vail, there's a free intra-resort bus system. At Beaver Creek, there's a free "dial-a-ride" service. Regular bus service also links the two ski areas.

Cindy Nelson, an Olympic medalist, offers free pointers every Wednesday at Beaver Creek and every Thursday at Vail. Other free extras include daily ski trips for intermediate to expert skiers and a "Meet the Mountain" tour several days a week.

IN THE SUMMER: Vail and Beaver Creek are wonderful family vacation destinations in the summer. Marked hiking trails and separate mountain-biking trails crisscross both mountains, and hundreds of miles of trails meander through the nearby White River National Forest and the Eagle's Nest Wilderness as well. Vail's Lionshead Gondola and Beaver Creek's Centennial Express chairlift operate throughout the summer. There are five 18-hole golf courses in the valley.

At Piney River Ranch, 13 miles north of Vail, families can rent rowboats or canoes and take horseback rides in the shadow of the Gore Ranch (there's even a supervised play area for children too young to ride.) One night each week, there's a special Western night for families featuring a performance by the excellent Beaver Creek Children's Theater.

Beaver Creek's children's programs operate through the summer. Visiting children can be enrolled in several short overnight camps, run by the resort, that are exceptionally well-planned: Winona's Art Camp, Chief Passamaquoddy's Fishing Camp, and Camp Matawin, where campers dress, live, and sleep like Indians (the teepees are spectacular!)

"Bravo! Colorado," the state's summer music festival, offers a program of music and dance from early June through early August at the amphitheater in Vail. The Vail Nature Center (303-479-2291) offers guided walks, campfire talks, and nature discovery programs for families in the summer.

Also possible: swimming, jeep adventures, hot-air balloon rides, whitewater rafting, guided fishing expeditions, tours of ghost towns, and overnight pack trips.

FOR MORE INFORMATION: Write Vail Associates, Inc., P.O. Box 7, Vail, CO 81658 or call (303) 476-VAIL or (303) 949-5750.

Winter Park Resort
Winter Park, Colorado

Winter Park calls itself "Colorado's favorite ski resort," and with good reason. It's the place Colorado skiers choose to ski more than any other, partly because of its proximity to Denver, but also because of its good mixture of slopes and its friendly family atmosphere. People come to Winter Park to ski, not to gawk at celebrities, bar-hop, or shop for designer clothes. Skiing is first and foremost, and whether you're a 3-year-old putting on skis for the first time or a middle-aged pro, the skiing is fabulous.

Winter Park is unique among large-scale ski areas in that it is owned by the city of Denver and operated by a volunteer board. Denver's civic leaders had the good sense several decades ago to see the potential for a major playground just a 90-minute drive from downtown. All of the profits are plowed back into improvements.

Clearly the most important addition for families in recent years was the construction in 1986 of a $3.5 million, 32,000-square-foot Children's Center, which consolidated all of the resort's children's programs under one roof and created one of the largest and most impressive ski-area children's centers in the nation.

Other recent improvements include the opening of 200 acres of intermediate and expert terrain on Mary Jane's Backside, with service on the new Sunnyside triple chairlift, and the opening of the resort's third mountain, Vasquez Ridge.

All of this development has been imposed on a gorgeous and challenging landscape. Just over the Berthoud Pass (elevation 11,307 feet) through the front range of the Rockies, the resort's three distinct skiing areas provide breathtaking views from every trail.

ACCOMMODATIONS: $ to $$$ Winter Park offers a range of accommodations, from basic motel rooms, to rooms with meals in mountainside lodges, to condominiums. A central reservation service operated by the resort can direct you to accommodations that best suit your needs and budget. One phone call also arranges lift-ticket purchases, ski school registration, and reservations for the children's programs.

Hi Country Haus offers studios to three-bedroom condominiums, most with huge stone fireplaces, just a short drive or bus ride from the slopes. The complex includes an indoor swimming pool.

The Iron Horse Resort Retreat offers luxurious ski-in–ski-out accommodations near the base.

A group of charming mountain inns (the central reservations service can make referrals) provides rooms with breakfast and dinner daily at reasonable rates. One of our favorites is Arapaho Lodge, which has a cozy living room, a great kitchen, and good children's rates.

The Timberhouse Ski Lodge is close enough to the slopes so that you can ski there.

DINING: The Winter Park–Fraser area has about 35 restaurants, ranging from standard American fare, to Cajun cuisine, to German cooking, to fast food. All welcome families.

In the base lodge, the Derailer Bar and Club Car Restaurant serve good food and drinks with great views of the slopes. A cafeteria is available for those in a hurry.

The mid-mountain Snoasis serves sandwiches, snacks, and light meals cafeteria style.

THE SKIING: The Winter Park Resort offers three separate but interconnected skiing mountains: the main mountain, Mary Jane

Mountain, and Vasquez Ridge. The latter two are favored by intermediate and expert skiers and offer glade and near-treeline skiing.
Winter Park gets more frequent snowfalls than other parts of the
Rockies and averages 360 inches annually. Snowmaking equipment
extends the ski season from mid-November to mid-April.

 Twenty-five percent beginner, 51 percent intermediate, 24
percent expert. Some of "the Jane" is considered the most
exciting expert terrain in the nation.

 Four quads, four triples, 11 doubles.

 2,220 feet.

 Four miles.

Winter Park has one of the largest ski schools in the state and
boasts that it has taught more Coloradans to ski than any other;
group or private lessons available. The instructors are especially
skilled at dealing with children and disabled individuals; the resort
has the largest disabled skiers' program in the world. Each year, it
provides 29,000 free ski lessons to about 2,500 disabled people.

Dozens of miles of cross-country skiing trails nearby. Equip-
ment can be rented at Beaver Village and Idlewild Touring
Center in Winter Park, Devil's Thumb, and at the YMCA's Snow
Mountain Ranch.

ACTIVITIES FOR NON-SKIERS: Several different outfitters provide moonlit sleigh rides through the snowy woods; some end with
a gourmet dinner around a warm bonfire. Jim's Sleigh Rides go
through the forest and meadows by the Fraser River. The Dinner at
the Barn Sleigh Ride ends with an elegant dinner in a heated homestead barn.

Snowmobiles can be rented for touring through mountain meadows.

The Fraser Tubing Hill is a local landmark. Kids will love riding a giant inner tube down a snow-covered hill (for a fee).

FOR CHILDREN: Winter Park was one of the pioneering ski areas in the provision of child care to skiers' children.

Child care is provided from 8 A.M. to 4 P.M. daily in the ski season for children between 2 months and 8 years, with skiing experience available for all children 3 and over. The infants and toddlers are kept apart from the older children and spend their days playing with a large supply of toys; the adult-to-child ratio is one-to-five or better. Children 18 months and older are fed two snacks a day and lunch; parents must feed infants. A separate nap room, gaily decorated has private cubicles with cribs. At the end of the day, parents are given a written report about the child's naps, diaper changes, and meals.

Three- and 4-year-olds are dubbed "Penguins" and alternate indoor play with skiing. Lunch and snacks are served, and a separate room is available for napping. The adult-to-child ratio ranges from one-to-five or -eight, depending upon the activity. Most children in this group are on skis for the first time and don't venture farther than the rise just outside the center; an observation deck is available from which parents can watch. A 3- or 4-year-old with more extensive ski experience can join the SKIwee program and go on the slopes. Children 5 and under ski free.

"Ski Scouts" is the name given to the 5- through 7-year-old group. These children spend more time skiing, using the SKIwee program. A large playroom is used for indoor activities.

"Ski Rangers," the 8- through 13-year-olds, spend most of their days on the slopes and sometimes even eat lunch on the mountain. They ski as a group, but with parental consent older children can be released on their own at the end of the lesson.

NICETIES: The Lift, a free bus with several different routes, transports skiiers to and from their accommodations throughout the day and evening.

Mary Jane has a free beginners' lift—the Galloping Goose— which is perfect for parents who want to take their beginner children skiing without the expense of a lift ticket.

IN THE SUMMER: Winter Park offers innumerable opportunities for water sports such as boating, fishing, rafting, and wind-surfing. Golfers can play at the Pole Creek Golf Course, rated the best new public course by *Golf Digest* (in 1985), and mountain-bikers will enjoy the best trail system in the nation. Children gravitate to the 3,000-foot-long Alpine Slide, which has a 650-foot vertical drop. Numerous festivals are held throughout the summer, and there are rodeo performances every weekend.

FOR MORE INFORMATION: Call Winter Park Central Reservations at (800) 453-2525.

Park City Area Ski Resorts

Deer Valley Ski Area
Park City Ski Area
ParkWest Ski Area

Park City, Utah

A common criticism of ski resorts is that they are colorless, high-tech recreation machines, providing interchangeable slopes to ski on by day and indistinguishable accommodations by night. Park City, Utah, is a different story.

Its three ski areas are located in a landscape enriched by landmarks from its century-old mining days, and the lively town itself is no monochromatic "concept," but rather a colorful jumble of independent businesses. It offers a combination found only in the West —spectacular natural scenery, old mining buildings and Victorian homes, and snow, 300 inches of it a year. Another major selling point is that it's only an hour's drive from Salt Lake City's airport.

Deer Valley is the newest, poshest, ski area. It offers the best intermediate skiing and on-site child care, as well as incomparable restaurant fare. Not surprisingly, everything costs a little more.

Then there is ParkWest, at the other end of the spectrum; uncrowded, catering more to local skiers, but with tough, long runs down the mountain, and a very relaxed, unpretentious atmosphere.

Finally, there is the granddaddy of the three, Park City Ski Area, old by ski resort standards. Local skiers looking for challenges still lean toward the Park City Ski Area. Park City also offers night skiing and says it has the longest lighted night run in the Rockies, Payday.

What many visitors like best about Park City is that it still feels like a town, a place where people live and where there is more to life than shuttling to the ski slopes.

ACCOMMODATIONS: $ to $$$$ A broad range of accommodations is available: Victorian-style, but recently constructed, homes just west of the ski areas—contact Park City Management Services at (801) 545-7669; inexpensive motel rooms just a short walk from the Park City lifts—try Acorn Chalet Lodging at (800) 443-3131 or Budget Lodging at (800) 522-SNOW; quaint bed-and-breakfasts like the Washington School Inn at (800) 824-1672 or the more affordable Imperial Hotel on Main Street at (801) 649-1904.

If you don't have to ask the price, try Stein Eriksen Lodge, with two restaurants and a health spa, at (800) 453-1302. It's a gorgeous lodge with a rustic look, providing such niceties as tea in the lobby every afternoon.

The Prospector Square Hotel, (801) 649-7100, offers $ to $$$$ rooms, with an excellent athletic club that offers free baby-sitting while you work out. A pleasant alternative would be to stay at the old Homestead resort, located 20 miles south of Park City, with a hot spring-fed pool and relaxing ranch atmosphere; call (801) 654-1102.

DINING: It would take several vacations to thoroughly explore the more than 45 dining rooms of Park City. Cisro's on Main Street offers inexpensive pasta dinners and a selection of veal and chicken dishes at moderate prices. Adolph's, at the Park City Golf Course, serves international cuisine at high prices. The restaurants in the various lodges at Deer Valley are top of the line, with prices that reflect their reputation. The Snuggery at Silver Lake Lodge offers a sumptuous buffet; also good is the more casual Stew Pot at the Deer Valley Plaza and the two fine European-style restaurants at Stein Eriksen Lodge.

The oddly named Irish Camel, on Main Street, is renowned for its Mexican dishes. There are numerous steak and seafood restaurants, among them the Brand X Cattle Company on Park Avenue and the Columbine at the Park City Resort Center.

THE SKIING: There's a wide range of skiing opportunities at the three ski areas. Many skiers regard the snow in this part of the country—light, dry powder—as the greatest on earth. Excellent skiing conditions are guaranteed from mid-November to May. The average annual snowfall is more than 300 inches.

 Park City: 14 novice, 40 intermediate, 29 advanced, 650 acres of open bowls.

ParkWest: 11 novice, 15 intermediate, and 15 advanced nine expert.

Deer Valley: 54 runs, with 15 percent novice, 50 percent intermediate, and 35 percent advanced.

 Park City: one gondola, two quads, five triple chairs, five doubles.

ParkWest: seven double chairs.

Deer Valley: one high-speed detachable quad, seven triple chairs, one double.

 Park City: 3,100 feet.
ParkWest: 2,800 feet.
Deer Valley: 2,200 feet.

 Park City: Three and one-half miles.
ParkWest: Two and one-half miles.
Deer Valley: Two miles.

 All three ski areas offer ski lessons for adults and children.

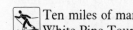 Ten miles of marked, maintained trails on a golf course at the White Pine Touring Center, one mile from town.

Try backcountry hut skiing in the High Uintas; contact White Pine Touring in Park City at (801) 649-8710.

Helicopter skiing is available in the mountains around the ski resorts.

ACTIVITIES FOR NON-SKIERS: There's a lot more to do in the winter at Park City than ski. You can ice-skate at the Park City Ski Area Plaza. And several outfits offer sleigh rides, usually in the evening, with dinner and entertainment following the ride.

The Norwegian School of Nature Life—call (801) 649-9321, ext. 63—offers touring and lessons, as well as dogsled adventures.

The ultimate thrill may be to lift off one bright morning in a gondola attached to a hot-air balloon and view the mountains and valley from that perspective. Contact Balloon Affaire at (801) 649-1217 or Park City Balloon Adventures at (801) 649-3866. Children older than 5 are generally allowed on the flights.

Nightlife is plentiful. Live theater at the Egyptian, on Main Street, is an unusual diversion for a ski area (the Brickyard Playhouse offers more serious plays).

There are several nightclubs in town; to enjoy them, Utah's liquor laws require you to buy a club membership. Favorites on Main Street are the Alamo, popular with local residents, and the Club, next door, which attracts more high-lifers.

FOR CHILDREN: Probably the most convenient system for skiing families is at Deer Valley, where a licensed day-care center is located in a roomy facility at the resort center (they take children in diapers and can accommodate 48 non-skiers). Children from cradle age on up seem well cared for. Reservations are a must for infants, particularly during the holiday seasons. Call (800) 424-DEER.

For children between 3 and 5, Deer Valley offers a combination of ski instruction and supervised play; children between 6 and 12 have their own program, with a heavier emphasis on skiing. Both programs include lunch.

Park City Ski Area and ParkWest have "Kinderschule" programs (3- to 6-year-olds at Park City, 18-month-olds to 9-year-olds at ParkWest), and youth lessons for older kids. Neither provides infant care. The Park City facility is in a basement, but parents who have used it praise it for its equipment and activities. It can handle 140 kids and is extremely crowded during holidays. It is much less expensive than Deer Valley's facility.

ParkWest's "Kids Central" offers a full day of lessons for children for the lowest cost in the area.

There are some off-slope alternatives for infants and young children if you're not going to ski at Deer Valley. One of the best is Miss Billie's Kid's Kampus, located near ParkWest on Highway 224. Kid's Kampus has a big outdoor play area, an upstairs nursery, and well-equipped playrooms downstairs. It's open seven days a week, from 9 to 5. Baby food must be brought by parents; the school serves hot lunches to older children. Billie Koleman, the owner, also coordinates ski lessons at the Park City Ski Area. Call (801) 649-KIDS for more information and reservations.

Another option is K.I.D.S. Hotel (Kid's Individualized Daycare and Skiing Hotel) at the Ramada Hotel in Park City, (801) 649-2900. It offers full day care at a daily rate, and nighttime care for an hourly fee from 7 P.M. to midnight.

Baby-sitting service in your motel or condominium can be obtained through Merry Pop-ins in Park City at (801) 649-1701.

NICETIES: Free bus service is offered throughout the town, and a free chair lift carries you from downtown to the Park City Ski Area.

Cars can be rented in town for just a day if you want to go on an excursion elsewhere.

Utah ski resorts have joined forces to offer multi-area ticket books containing ski checks usable for all-day lift passes at the three Park City resorts, as well as Brighton, Alta, Snowbird, and Solitude in the Cottonwood Canyons, an hour's drive away.

OF INTEREST NEARBY: Both children and adults will enjoy a ride on the Heber Creeper, an old steam engine that takes travelers up into the mountains 18 miles south of Park City. You can dine on the train in the evening, or take a day trip. For schedules and information call (801) 534-1779.

IN THE SUMMER: Park City has a crowded summer calendar, and its proximity to Salt Lake City permits promoters to stage events that are unthinkable in other towns with only about 3,000 summer residents. ParkWest stages a series of outdoor jazz, pop, and country music concerts throughout the summer at the ski area, and Deer Valley holds a jazz festival, a bluegrass festival, and symphony concerts. The city of Park City offers a Shakespeare festival.

The historic feeling of the town makes it a pleasant place to base oneself for summer vacations that feature hiking in the Uintahs, golfing at the Jeremy Ranch Golf Course of the Park Meadows Country Club, horseback riding, and virtually any other outdoor activity imaginable. Summer accommodations are quite inexpensive. And many provide amenities like swimming pools, racquetball courts, and health clubs. Fishing at nearby Echo Reservoir is popular, and many cycling competitions are held. The valley ballooning industry is in full flower in September, when the annual Hot Air Balloon Festival is held.

FOR MORE INFORMATION: The Park City Area Chamber of Commerce/Convention and Visitors Bureau is an excellent source of general information; call (800) 453-1360.

Write the Park City Ski Area at Box 39, Park City, UT 84060, or call (801) 649-8111. Write ParkWest at 4000 ParkWest Drive, Park City, UT 84060, or call (801) 649-5400. Write Deer Valley at Box 3149, Park City, UT 84060, or call (800) 424-3337.

WEST COAST

Lake Tahoe Area Ski Resorts

Squaw Valley
Alpine Meadows
Northstar-at-Tahoe
Heavenly Valley
Kirkwood

Lake Tahoe, California

The Tahoe area is home to the biggest concentration of ski resorts in the country—15 within a 100-mile radius. Most ring the north or south shores of Lake Tahoe and some, particularly Heavenly Valley, offer top-of-the-world views of this turquoise-blue, 22-mile-long lake. The offerings range from small "Mom and Pop" resorts with a couple of lifts to the mammoth Heavenly and Squaw Valley U.S.A. ski areas, the latter the home of the 1960 Winter Olympics. Because of the array of choices, many skiers—particularly more experienced ones—choose to sample several different areas if they're going to be here for more than a few days.

Probably best known among the Tahoe ski resorts are "the Big Five"—Squaw Valley, Alpine Meadows, and Northstar on the North Shore and Heavenly Valley and Kirkwood on or near the South Shore. Though South Lake Tahoe tends to be a fast-paced vacation spot, North Lake Tahoe offers a quiet and relaxed atmosphere.

A still-burning Olympic flame at the entrance to Squaw Valley reminds visitors of the resort's venerable past. Squaw is a skier's paradise because of the sheer variety and number of slopes. The beginner's area is set apart, so novices can enjoy wide open runs without worrying about faster, more aggressive skiers whooshing by.

Just a few minutes down the road is Alpine Meadows, the favorite of locals and the home of the area's ski school for the disabled. Less than a half hour away is Northstar-at-Tahoe, which prides itself on being an all-in-one ski area, with lodging, restaurants, and entertainment all wrapped into its tidy boundaries. All three are close to the folksy, lakeside town of Tahoe City, which is chock-full of specialty shops, delis, restaurants, condos and bed-and-breakfast lodges.

At the other end of the lake sits Heavenly Valley, which claims to have more acres of skiable terrain—21,000—than any other resort in the country. It is also the area's big city resort, with 20,000 hotel beds lying below. Off the beaten track is Kirkwood, which has the highest base elevation in northern California and a complete cross-country ski center.

ACCOMMODATIONS: $ to $$$$ On the North Shore, the busy little resort town of Tahoe City has lodging ranging from relatively inexpensive motel rooms to posh condominiums.

Granlibakken is a charming resort that was the site of the 1932 Olympic ski jump trials. A former lodge for alumni of the University of California, Granlibakken, phone (916) 583-4242, has been transformed into a pleasant bed-and-breakfast resort and conference center. For very young or novice skiers, Granlibakken also offers an added plus: it has its own free mini–ski slope, which is served by a rope tow. Adjoining it is one of the area's few sanctioned "snow play hills." An overnight stay in a two-bedroom town house at Granlibakken includes a buffet breakfast.

Also on the North Shore, Northstar-at-Tahoe (800-533-6787) is a completely self-contained ski resort, with 220 rental units ranging from hotel-style rooms to fully equipped four-bedroom homes. The Ski Trails condos here are within 100 yards of the Northstar slopes, providing ski-in–ski-out convenience.

Squaw Valley's accommodations are pricey, but within walking distance—or a short shuttle ride—of the slopes. Among them are the Squaw Valley Lodge (800-922-9970), which has apartment-type units with kitchens, and Olympic Village Inn (800-VILLAGE), which served as housing for the 1960 Olympic athletes.

Skiers using Heavenly Valley can select from such accommodations as the inexpensive Flamingo Lodge (800-544-5288) and the expensive Tahoe Chalet Inn (800-821-2656). Kirkwood has six different condominium complexes within walking distance of the lifts; call (209) 258-7000.

DINING: On the North Shore, Tahoe City offers hungry skiers everything from Texas-style barbecue to more elegant steak and seafood dining.

Hearty and tasty German meals are served up in a cozy family atmosphere at Pfeifer House. Jake's on the Lake specializes in seafood and steaks, and, as its name suggests, has lakeside views. A favorite among local residents is Rosie's Café. Tahoe House has Swiss and California cuisine. And in the old railroading town of Truckee, O.B.'s Pub and Restaurant is recommended.

On the South Shore, the Beacon has a great view of the lake, the 89th Street Bar and Grill features live jazz and blues with its steaks and chops, and Sweet Inspiration is a '50s-style deli with nostalgia to spare.

Northstar-at-Tahoe has about a half-dozen restaurants, delis, and bars either in the mid-mountain area or in the little village below.

THE SKIING: Skiing ranges from the thrills of Squaw and Heavenly to the tamer, more family-oriented slopes of Northstar and Kirkwood. Alpine Meadows considers itself a compromise—big enough to offer variety, but not so large as to be overwhelming. Because of its sheer size and variety of slopes, Squaw Valley is the best known of the Tahoe ski resorts. Yet local residents caution that, because of the crowds, it is not the place for families looking for a quiet day of skiing. Northstar-at-Tahoe, built on 1,700 acres on the hips of 8,600-foot Mt. Pluto, limits the number of daily ski passes it sells to minimize waiting time in lift lines.

Multi-day passes, as well as interchangeable passes good at all 5 resorts, are available at all the resorts.

 Alpine Meadows: 100 runs, six open bowls; 25 percent novice, 40 percent intermediate, 35 percent advanced.

Heavenly Valley and Northstar-at-Tahoe: 25 percent novice, 50 percent intermediate, 25 percent advanced.

Kirkwood: 15 percent novice, 50 percent intermediate, 35 percent advanced.

Squaw Valley: 25 percent novice, 45 percent intermediate, 30 percent advanced.

 Alpine Meadows: one high-speed quad, two triple chairs, eight doubles, two Pomas.

Heavenly Valley: one aerial tram, detachable quad, seven triple chairs, nine doubles, six surface lifts.

Kirkwood: six triple chairs, six doubles, one surface lift.

Northstar: one gondola, two high-speed quads, three triple chairs, three doubles, two surface lifts.

Squaw Valley: one aerial tram, one gondola, two detachable quad chairs, five triples, 16 doubles, two surface lifts.

 Alpine Meadows: 1,797 feet.

Heavenly Valley: 3,600 feet.

Kirkwood: 2,000 feet.

Northstar: 2,200 feet.

Squaw Valley: 2,850 feet.

 Alpine Meadows: Two and one-half miles.

Heavenly Valley: Seven miles.

Kirkwood: Two and one-half miles.

Northstar: Almost three miles.

Squaw Valley: Three miles.

 Ski schools at all areas.

The North Lake Tahoe area has eight cross-country ski areas offering almost 400 miles of groomed trails. A nordic ski center is located in a clearing just behind the mid-mountain lodge at Northstar; there are 25 miles of groomed and tracked courses that wind through woods on logging roads. Kirkwood's Nordic Center has 45 miles of groomed trails.

ACTIVITIES FOR NON-SKIERS: Non-skiers can take in stunning views by riding the trams and gondolas at most resorts.

Strolling through quilt and handicraft shops in Tahoe City is a pleasant way to spend a few hours. Along the way, kids can drop some bread or crackers to the rainbow trout swimming under the Fanny Bridge at Highways 28 and 89.

And, of course, there are the casinos in South Shore and Reno, which routinely present big-name entertainers and shows. Harrah's on the South Shore has a supervised, check-in and check-out arcade for youngsters aged 6 to 14 and a movie room and video games.

Sleigh rides can be arranged through the Hilltop Lodge in Truckee at Kirkwood, Richardon's Resort and next to Caesar's Tahoe.

Mountain Lake Adventures in Kings Beach has guided snowmobile tours of the backcountry along the North Shore. Phone (702) 831-4202 for more information.

Mountain High Balloons has hot-air balloon trips that lift off, weather permitting, during the winter. Phone (916) 583-6292.

For a different kind of commute to the slopes, skiers staying on the South Shore can hop aboard a Mississippi-style stern-wheeler and ride across the lake to the North Shore resorts. A shuttle then takes skiers to either Squaw Valley, Alpine Meadows, or Northstar. On the way home, there's dancing to a live band, plus appetizers and cocktails. For more information, call the Tahoe Queen Ski Shuttle at (916) 541-3364.

FOR CHILDREN: All "Big Five" resorts offer full-day ski schools for children from age 3 or 4, but little child care is available yet for younger children.

One exception is Squaw, which in its 1986–87 season began caring for tots as young as 6 months at its "10 Little Indians Snow School." The fee includes lunch and snacks. Ski lessons are available starting at age 3.

Alpine Meadows emphasizes learning to ski in its snow school for kids aged 3 to 6, open from 8:30 A.M. to 4:30 P.M. For youngsters aged 6 to 12, a day of lessons and lift tickets at the children's ski school is available.

Northstar has an especially attractive nursery program, called "Minors' Camp," which includes low-key ski lessons, for potty-trained children aged 2 to 6. It's in the Village Mall and operated from 8 A.M. to 4:30 P.M. daily. The adult-to-child ratio is one-to-six. An all-day ski program, "Star Kids," also is available for children aged 5 to 12.

Heavenly Valley's ski school is for children 4 to 12 years of age.

An entire slope festooned with balloons and dubbed "Mighty Mountain" has been set aside for children at Kirkwood. There's an all-day ski school for youngsters 4 to 12, and day care is available for children as young as 3.

NICETIES: Free shuttle service is widely available to and from the bigger condo complexes and ski resorts.

A parking spot can be reserved ahead of time at Sugar Bowl.

OF INTEREST NEARBY: The tragic tale of the Donner Party, a group of pioneers who got trapped in these mountains during the winter of 1846–47, is detailed at the Donner Memorial State Park in Truckee. Open daily from 10 A.M. to noon and 1 to 4 P.M., the museum includes displays on the pioneer movement, railroading local Indians, and geology. Call (916) 587-3841.

The history of skiing from 1860 to the present is covered at the free Western American Ski Sports Museum off Interstate 80 near Boreal Ridge. Phone (916) 426-3313.

IN THE SUMMER: The Lake Tahoe area provides innumerable recreational opportunities in the summer, from boating to fishing, golf, tennis, hiking, horseback riding, sightseeing, jet skiing, windsurfing, bicycling, river-rafting, miniature golfing, hot-air ballooning and seaplane rides. There are also such special events as the Lake Tahoe Summer Music Festival, Music at Sand Harbor, Shakespeare at Sand Harbor, Truckee Tahoe Airshow, Truckee Championship Rodeo, and Concours d'Elegance Wooden Boat Show.

There are seven golf courses in the area, including the 18-hole, 6,897-yard, par 72 course at Northstar-at-Tahoe designed by Robert Muir Graves.

In fact, Northstar-at-Tahoe is an especially attractive summer destination for families. Ten acrylic tennis courts and an Olympic-size pool are available, and the Northstar stables offer guided rides along mountain trails. Children between the ages of 4 and 10 can take part in a summer day camp that features swimming lessons, storytelling, nature walks, tennis, arts and crafts, and horseback riding from 10 A.M. to 5 P.M.

FOR MORE INFORMATION: The Tahoe North Visitors and Convention Bureau is a great source of information. The bureau makes reservations for lodging, ski packages, and car rentals. The phone number is (800) 822-5959 inside California, (800) 824-6348 from other states.

On the South Shore, the Lake Tahoe Visitors' Authority, at (800) 288-2463, provides general tourist information and a referral service for lodgings.

The direct numbers for each of the five ski areas are as follows: Squaw Valley, (916) 583-6955; Alpine Meadows, (916) 583-4232; Northstar-at-Tahoe, (916) 562-1010; Heavenly Valley, (916) 541-1330; and Kirkwood, (209) 258-6000.

1. At Plimoth Plantation in Plymouth, Massachusetts, families can observe faithful re-creations of everyday Pilgrim life. *(Photo: Plimoth Plantation)* **2.** In Harrodsburg, Kentucky, visitors can explore the restored community of Shaker Village and watch 1850s-era craftsmanship up close. *(Photo: Shaker Village at Pleasant Hill)* **3.** Children can dress up in period clothing in the Children's Discovery Room at Fort Mackinac. *(Photo: Mackinac State Historic Parks.)* **4.** At the Pliny Freeman Farm, a working historical farm at Old Sturbridge Village, Massachusetts, visitors can observe daily chores from another era. *(Photo: Robert S. Arnold)* **5.** Families can observe craftsmakers as well as take part in workshops at Old Sturbridge Village. *(Photo: Robert S. Arnold)* **6.** During the three-day living history program at Norlands in Livermore, Maine, families learn about the real flavor of 19th-century life. *(Photo: James Bliven)*

4

5

6

NORTHEAST

Mystic Seaport Museum
Mystic, Connecticut

Today's children may associate boats with pleasure—boarding an ocean liner for a long vacation cruise or paddling in a canoe on a camping trip. But long, long ago, boats were a way of life for entire communities, whose residents built them at a local shipyard and then went to sea to catch fish and whales and even fight wars.

Nowhere is the adventure, romance, and hard work of the high-seas life experienced more vividly than at the Mystic Seaport Museum, a picturesque 17-acre historic village in Mystic, Connecticut, located on the Mystic River 50 miles northwest of New Haven.

One day is sufficient to stroll through the seaport, see a movie on whaling and a show in the planetarium, and even visit the nearby Mystic Marinelife Aquarium, operated by a separate non-profit organization. But to really steep yourself in the rhythm of a 19th-century maritime village, plan on staying for a few days and participating in one of the programs offered for adults and children by the Seaport's Education Department. You can even learn to sail.

Mystic Seaport owns 400 sailing vessels, making it the largest maritime museum of its kind in the country. Ships are maintained through a working preservation shipyard. Usually 150 ships are on view, and visitors can board four.

The seaport also contains approximately 60 old frame buildings that house shipbuilding activities and vestiges of 19th-century life. Some of the buildings are original; others were moved there.

Exquisite examples of scrimshaw, portraits of famous sea captains, and elaborately carved ships' figureheads are among the exhibits. Also worth visiting are the buildings that display machinery and photographs showing how the 19th-century division of labor made seagoing life possible. For example, in the oyster house, moved to Mystic from New Haven, oysters were sorted by size and shipped to markets as far away as California. In the ropewalk building, rope was made to rig boats. In the cooperage, barrels were assembled to hold provisions for long journeys.

Among the biggest attractions for children are the "role players," who dress in period outfits and demonstrate activities from another era, such as squeezing lemonade by hand.

Mystic, which numbers 9,000 full-time residents, was first settled by fishermen and farmers in the 1600s. Shipbuilding was important from early days and fueled the growth of the area. The War of 1812 further spurred its growth.

Other 19th-century events necessitated building other types of boats. For example, the California Gold Rush of 1849 called for clipper ships, which could sail quickly around Cape Horn. Many of the clippers built at Mystic set speed records. The Civil War required steamships for moving men and arms. Demand for wooden boats decreased after 1870, and many shipyards were shuttered. World Wars I and II revived demand briefly.

Mystic was founded as the Marine Historical Association, a non-profit maritime museum and educational institution, by three Mystic residents in 1929. In addition to charming visitors, it houses the G. W. Blunt White library, with more than 350,000 manuscripts and 56,000 ships' plans and charts for study.

Seaport hours are 9 A.M. to 5 P.M. daily, May through October, and from 9 A.M. to 4 P.M. daily, November to April. The museum is closed Christmas Day. The aquarium is open daily from 9 A.M., except Thanksgiving, Christmas, and New Year's Day.

ACCOMMODATIONS: $ to $$ Mystic offers at least 10 different places to stay, including several large chain-affiliated motels.

Locally owned hostelries include the Old Mystic Motor Lodge on Interstate 95 ($); the Inn at Mystic on Routes 1 and 27 ($ to $$); and the Red Brook Inn, a bed-and-breakfast house on Route 184 and Welles Road, with nine rooms ($ to $$).

Families that like to camp can pitch their tents at Seaport Campgrounds on Route 184; Rocky Neck State Park on Route 156;

Camp Niantic by the Atlantic on Route 156; or Ponderosa Park and Campgrounds on Chesterfield Road, Route 161.

DINING: The Galley on the grounds of the seaport, near the South Gate, offers cafeteria-style New England fare.

The Seamen's Inne, a full-service restaurant near the North Gate, offers lunch and dinner. It has an oyster saloon for snacks and drinks and a terrace for warm-weather meals.

Ten miles west of Mystic is the Lighthouse Inn in New London, which has an elegant restaurant for lunch and dinner.

ACTIVITIES: Take your time to explore the Seaport's buildings. In the Aloa Meeting House, you can see a black-and-white movie about whaling, with footage from the 1920s. In the planetarium, you can learn how knowledge of the stars, moon, and sun helped sea captains and their crews navigate safely.

Special activities abound, especially from May through October. On Memorial Day the seaport stages a lobster fest near Lighthouse Point. In June, the Sea Music Festival brings together 50 musicians from both sides of the Atlantic to play popular sea and folk music. On July 4, the seaport holds a parade with a 19th Century wreath ceremony and country dance. At Christmastime, the seaport decks the hulls with fresh evergreens and lights. Costumed guides lead evening tours and caroling expeditions with kerosene lanterns.

In addition, the seaport offers numerous classes throughout the year in woodcarving, blacksmithing, fireplace cooking, boatbuilding, and sailing. Subjects vary from year to year.

FOR CHILDREN: A Children's Museum allows kids to try several popular 19th-century pastimes, such as walking on stilts, rolling hoops, or sleeping in a child's bunk.

Four of the museum's old ships can be explored: the 1841 111-foot-long wooden whale ship *Charles W. Morgan*, whose whaling days ended in 1921; the 1882 square-rigged training ship *Joseph Conrad*, which was moored permanently at Mystic in 1947; the 1921 fishing schooner *L. A. Dunton*, which had been used to catch haddock and halibut; and the 1908 57-foot S.S. *Sabino*, the last coal-fired steamboat still in operation. The *Sabino* makes 30-minute daytime and 90-minute nighttime cruises from the seaport every day from mid-May through mid-October, which children will love. Music enlivens its nighttime cruises.

Other boats to look for—the 1891 oyster sloop *Nellie*, the 1866 Noank smack *Emma C. Berry*, and the *Estell A.* sloop, which had been used as a lobster boat. It's fascinating to children to pick out the differences among the boats.

Plan to take the one-mile side trip to the aquarium, where you can see 6,000 specimens of marine life in 45 exhibits, including sharks and performing dolphins and sea lions.

Through the year, Mystic offers special activities for children; write the Education Department and ask for the schedule. In recent years, they have held Family Days over Thanksgiving weekend; a children's winter program in mid-February, the highlight of which is an overnight program aboard the tall ship *Joseph Conrad*; games and special children's tours daily through the summer; two-week summer day camp sessions; a children's field day in late fall; and Victorian Christmas activities.

For children between 12 and 16, the Seaport Sail Education Program is offered through the summer, with accommodations on the *Joseph Conrad*. This program offers children a crash course in the fundamentals of sailing, rowing, small boat safety, weather prediction, marlinspike seamanship, and aspects of maritime history. Children 15 to 19 who have completed the program can cruise the New England waters for a week on the schooner *Brilliant*.

OF INTEREST NEARBY: New London has an impressive historic district with many buildings dating from the late 18th century. Old Lyme, Stonington, and Norwich also are pleasant towns to visit.

FOR MORE INFORMATION: Write Mystic Seaport Museum, P.O. Box 6000, Mystic, CT 06355-0990, or call (203) 572-0711.

Washburn-Norlands Living History Center

Livermore, Maine

"It is 1870, Ulysses Simpson Grant is President. The United States has just purchased Alaska. . . . "

So begins the letter you will receive from the Washburn-Norlands preparing you for your visit. You and your family are participating in a three-day living history program at Norlands, the home of the Washburns, one of the nation's most prominent families in the mid-19th century. Here you'll spend a weekend living as people lived in the latter part of the last century.

A Norlands live-in experience catapults you back more than 100 years—not only into the physical surroundings of the late 19th century, but into the ideas, language, mores, and customs of people who lived four and five generations ago.

Washburn-Norlands is a living history center about 30 miles west of Augusta (a one-hour drive from Portland). The Washburn-Norlands Foundation was established as a center for history programs for schoolchildren. The program was later expanded to adult live-ins, and there are now a limited number of spaces for families as well. Unlike some historic villages that are creations that never were, Norlands existed in the past and continues today. No other program in the nation is quite like it.

Israel and Patty Washburn settled this farm in the early 19th century. They raised two daughters and seven sons. Among this single generation of Washburn sons there were two governors, four congressmen, a senator, a navy captain, a general, a secretary of state, two diplomats, and some prominent businessmen (some had several careers). The original house burned in 1867, and the sons built a Victorian mansion in its place which they named Norlands.

As you are escorted from your 20th-century vehicle by a Norlands staff member in authentic period dress, you are given the identity of a 19th-century neighbor of the Washburns—a member of the Pray family or the Waters family—who has come to visit. You are addressed as Simeon Waters or Eliza Pray or some other Waters or Pray relative throughout your stay. So are your children. No lectures, no museum exhibits with titles or explanations. It's all role playing.

ACCOMMODATIONS: $ Live-ins are limited to 14 participants. They usually last three days and are scheduled on selected weekends through the year. The rate includes three nights' lodging and all meals. Children's rates are available; children younger than eight are discouraged.

The house is in a traditional interconnected New England style of front house/middle house/back house/barn. The front house is now a Washburn museum. The middle house is living quarters for some of the Norlands staff. The back house, once the hired men's residence, is your abode for the live-in.

The back house has no running water, no electricity, and no central heating (wood stoves suffice for heating and cooking). The icebox is cooled by ice cut from the local pond. Your bed in one of the upstairs bedrooms has a corn husk mattress that rests on ropes stretched between the frames. The outhouse is at the back of the barn, about 100 feet away. (There is modern toilet paper in the outhouse, along with the traditional corn cobs.) As you pass through the barn to the outhouse in the middle of the night, the tethered cows, oxen, and horses fidget a bit, the chickens stir. (There's a chamber pot under the bed for intrepid guests who don't want to make the hike.) This is the way people lived 100 years ago. And that's the adventure in Norlands.

DINING: Today, as yesterday, the kitchen is the center of activity, where every family member gets a chance to help the Norlands staff prepare food. The food is plentiful and delicious. All of it is prepared using equipment and recipes from the late 19th century.

The days starts early on a farm. Some live-in participants help the farmhand with the chores in the barn—feeding the livestock, milking the cows, mucking out the animal stalls—while others help prepare breakfast. Breakfast is a hearty meal of pancakes, freshly churned butter, New England maple syrup, and fried ham or bacon.

The midday meal, called "dinner," is the main meal of the day, as it still is in many rural communities in this country. Everyone sits down to a family-style meal of roast pork, smoked ham, or chicken and dumplings; in summer, there are fresh vegetables from the garden, and in winter, vegetables that have been "put up." Every main meal includes potatoes or homemade bread, and a pie or cake for dessert. There is milk fresh from the cows.

Supper is light. It might consist of a chowder with meat and vegetables, leftovers from the noon meal, cheese and cookies.

Neighbors from the local community sometimes join you at meal-time—Aunt Clara or Grandma Smith or Martel, the farmhand. Brother Stevens sometimes visits. He is a self-taught circuit preacher who might offer a blessing before the meal, concluding with a plea that the community be spared from the "terrible diphtheria that's going around." Miz Lovejoy, the widow and town pauper who has recently been auctioned off to a local family, might come and recount her many misfortunes. The mealtime conversation could include a political discussion about an upstart suffragist in New York or some gossip about local characters.

In the clean-up after the meals, all the scraps go into the slop bucket in the kitchen, later to be fed to the pig. There are no waste-baskets at Norlands. These are the days before plastic, paper, and glass packaging. Nothing is wasted; everything is recycled.

ACTIVITIES: The major activity in 19th-century farm life was work. Norlands is a working farm that uses 19th-century methods for most tasks. Live-in guests share in some of the work.

In addition to preparing the meals and cleaning up afterwards, the live-in participants might churn butter, spin wool, weave cloth, help with quiltmaking, or participate in any of dozens of other jobs that were part of daily life in an earlier era.

Others help with the firewood, plow the fields with oxen, weed the main garden (the Norlands women have their own smaller "kitchen garden"), hand harvest and shuck corn, or cut ice.

But life is not unremitting work, even in the 19th century. After evening meals there are stories and parlor games. The games are authentic 19th-century amusements—word games like "Our Old Grannie Doesn't Like Tea" or "Shout a Proverb" and counting games. One evening the live-in group might light the kerosene lanterns and walk down the road to a neighbor's for a visit. Or a fiddler might scratch out some traditional tunes at a barn dance. Or the neighbors might come over for a quilting bee.

If Brother Stevens is in the community, he will give a church service on Sunday morning with traditional hymns and a sermon that reflects the religious temper of the day. Grannie Fuller might hold a session in the community schoolhouse. Men and women will please sit on opposite sides of the room and "keep their manners." Every student will recite when called upon. Lessons are written on slates or on paper with quill and ink.

Live-ins also spend some time in the library at Norlands, looking through the letters and diaries of the Washburn family. These primary materials lend more insight.

Sometime during your stay, you will visit the community cemetery on the hill above Norlands. Somewhere on the tombstones you'll find the name of your character in the Norlands drama. The people are real. They lived, worked, and died here. It is quite a moving experience.

FOR CHILDREN: Norlands is a fascinating experience for children. The staff constantly engages them in history and in rural life. What would this kitchen implement be used for? How will we cool the butter? Is the milk from the cow warm or cool? Children love the farm animals and take up the chores as play. They experience social events unlike any they have ever known—a barn dance, or a quilting or cornhusking bee.

The learning is fun, but the lessons are profound—how different life was in the 19th century, when children played a vital economic role. Children are expected to role play alongside adults. Your child should be 8 years old before you undertake this vacation experience.

OF INTEREST NEARBY: Consider a stop at Sabbathday Lake Shaker Village on Route 26 in New Gloucester. Sabbathday Lake is the oldest religious community in the nation and home of some of the few remaining Shakers. Walking tours of the village buildings, gardens, and orchards are available, and there is a small Shaker museum.

Rock hounds will want to head for Perham's of Paris at the crossroads town of West Paris. Browse the rock and semi-precious stone collection and get a map to one of five nearby quarries where you can do your own prospecting.

FOR MORE INFORMATION: Write Washburn-Norlands Living History Center, R.D. 2, Box 3395, Livermore Falls, ME 04254, or phone (207) 897-2236.

Old Sturbridge Village
Sturbridge, Massachusetts

Life in the 1830s had its share of daily surprises, so don't be surprised if, while walking the paths of Old Sturbridge Village, you encounter a farmer rolling a broken wagon wheel to the blacksmith's shop. Walk along with the farmer on his errand and you might discover that blacksmiths in the early 19th century did not shoe horses; they primarily used their iron-making skills to forge tools and farm implements.

Most of the "villagers" you encounter at this living museum won't have time to recite any long, memorized speeches about life in the 1830s; they are much too busy making cheese or candles, fixing the split rail fence, and grinding corn at the mill. But they gladly respond to questions as they go about their chores.

Old Sturbridge Village is an outdoor living history museum set on 200 acres in Sturbridge, Massachusetts. The museum comprises more than 40 structures, most of them restored buildings brought from other areas. Each building is staffed by costumed men and women who are well versed in the details of daily life in a New England town during the early part of the last century.

Visitors will need at least a day to get around to all parts of Old Sturbridge Village. Starting at the Village Common, where sheep are often seen grazing, one can visit the bank, the law office, the parsonage, and various other residences or meeting houses. Your children might enjoy taking their places on a wooden bench in the small district school, where the schoolmaster or mistress explains the daily lessons. Wander down the dirt roads or take a detour onto one of the quiet, wooded trails, and eventually you'll find yourself near the Pliny Freeman Farm, a complete, working historical farm. By the time you work your way through the Mill Neighborhood and see the large bellows working in the blacksmith shop or the grist mill grinding a variety of grains, your family will be ready for a horse-drawn ride along the edge of the millpond.

Throughout each season, various demonstrations are held at different spots in the Village, so be sure to check the daily schedule when you enter.

Old Sturbridge Village is open year-round, with the seasons determining the special events and demonstrations.

ACCOMMODATIONS: $ to $$$ The Sturbridge area offers a variety of accommodations that are convenient to both the highways and Old Sturbridge Village. The Old Sturbridge Village Lodges and Oliver Wight House, phone (508) 347-3327, are adjacent to the Village entrance. The restored house, which is listed in the National Register of Historic Places, has 10 moderately priced rooms furnished in the style of the Federal period and two detached luxury suites. The Lodge has inexpensive first-floor rooms with private entrances. Restaurants are nearby.

Across from the entrance to Old Sturbridge Village is the Sheraton Sturbridge Resort and Conference Center, phone (508) 347-7393, which offers accommodations in the **$$ to $$$** range. The resort, located on the edge of a lake, has a private sand beach for swimming, boat rentals, and plenty of hungry ducks. Rooms overlook the lake or a lovely indoor pool. A miniature golf course, outdoor tennis courts, and a health club with racquetball courts and Nautilus equipment are also on the resort grounds.

DINING: Visitors to Old Sturbridge Village may dine at the Bullard Tavern, which has a Buffet and Tap Room serving lunch and a cafeteria serving a continental breakfast and lunch. The Buffet serves a variety of traditional hot foods, such as chicken pot pie and Indian pudding. There are also two snack bars on the Village grounds, and the Miner Grant Store and Bake House sells freshly made cookies. Picnic tables are available.

Outside the Village grounds there's a wide variety of dining choices, ranging from the typical assortment of fast-food stops to full-service restaurants. An unusual eating experience can be found about 25 minutes from Sturbridge at the Salem Cross Inn in West Brookfield, Massachusetts. Several times a year, the Inn serves a traditional 1700s drover's roast, which features "traditional American fare recalling the hearty Massachusetts trailside meals of John Pynchon, the nation's first cattle drover."

ACTIVITIES: The seasons dominate life at Old Sturbridge Village, much as they dominated life in the 1830s. Demonstrations and exhibits, as well as special events and workshops, vary as the chores necessary for each season change. Write ahead and ask for the calendar of events, which is issued in both the spring and the fall. Some programs require reservations and extra fees.

Your family could enjoy a special New England fall by attending the Village's Harvest Weekends, when the farmers bring in the crops and the Village women start storing food for the coming winter. Thanksgiving week is a wonderful aroma-filled time to visit and observe all the open-hearth cooking leading to the holiday; Thanksgiving Day itself is celebrated with services at the Center Meetinghouse, and a traditional holiday dinner is available at the Bullard Tavern with advance registration.

Seeing the Village under a fresh blanket of snow would be a special winter experience, particularly when combined with Christmas shopping in the lovely gift shop and bookstore. February brings a weekend birthday celebration for George Washington, complete with speeches and toasts. Maple sugaring in late winter is a sure sign that spring is just around the corner. Spring brings new arrivals in the barnyard, as well as Wool Days, which offers an opportunity to watch sheep shearing and wool processing, plus a chance to see the sheep washed in the brook. Militia Day and Garden Days are other examples of spring and summer events.

Independence Day is grandly celebrated with speeches, a parade, games, and picnic. Or you might arrange to visit the Village during the Female Charitable Society Fair and Picnic, when the Village ladies hold their annual meeting and fair to raise money and make plans to help the poor.

Workshops, evening programs, and concerts are offered throughout the year. These activities change from year to year and generally require advance registration. One that is especially appealing is Crafts at Close Range, a program offering hands-on experiences in a variety of 19th-century crafts and activities, such as spinning, hearth cooking, and blacksmithing. These workshops, for adults and children 14 years or older, are offered from November to May.

FOR CHILDREN: Everything that goes on at Old Sturbridge Village is designed with children in mind, but there are several programs operated periodically during the year that focus even more on children's interests.

Summershops are week-long workshops, providing time travel back to the 19th century for children ages 8 to 14. The children, wearing costumes, learn firsthand about life during the period. Eight- to 10-year-olds can experience fireplace cooking, spinning, and woodworking. They observe the Village in action and make their own souvenirs in craft workshops. Older children learn about printing, blacksmithing, basketmaking, and farming. All the children spend time in the Village with the other "villagers." The sessions, directed by the Museum Education Department, run Monday through Friday from 9 A.M. to 2 P.M.; there's a fee.

Old Sturbridge Village offers several programs designed for the entire family. The first, called Explorations, is offered during the week between Christmas and New Year, and consists of a variety of hands-on activities. The other programs offered are winter Fun and Family Weekend in January and Summer Fun and Family Weekend in June.

FOR MORE INFORMATION: Write Marketing Department, Old Sturbridge Village, 1 Old Sturbridge Village Road, Sturbridge, MA 01566, or call (508) 347-3362.

Plimoth Plantation
Plymouth, Massachusetts

To most people, Plymouth Rock means Pilgrims, and Pilgrims mean Thanksgiving, with a huge feast featuring turkey and cranberries on the side. A trip to Plymouth, Massachusetts, an hour south of Boston, can provide families with a much deeper understanding of the annual holiday and early American history.

Plymouth bills itself as "America's Hometown," and nearly everything ties into the Pilgrim theme in one way or another. Most of the Pilgrim Americana here is in good taste and is either authentic or has been re-created to make your visit seem like a trip back through time, more than 360 years ago, when people seeking a better way of life braved a treacherous trip across the ocean.

The centerpiece for this Old World atmosphere is Plimoth Plantation, a living museum set on a 105-acre site along the Eel River. In the 1627 Pilgrim Village, Pilgrim "townspeople" who have been steeped in the customs and the way of life of their 17th-century counterparts are available for questions and demonstrations of how things were done then. The adjacent Wampanoag Homesite presents the history and culture of the Indian natives whose friendship and support were so important to the new settlers in their early days.

Also available to satisfy your curiosity about the lives of the Pilgrims is *Mayflower II*, a modern-day version of the type of ship that brought the voyagers to Massachusetts in 1620. Nearby is the famous Plymouth Rock, now only a fraction of its original size but still suitably enshrined, with a seasonal guide to tell the story of the Pilgrims' crossing and to answer questions.

Other attractions include authentically restored buildings and museums to deepen your knowledge of Pilgrim lore, and the cemetery high atop a hill where names such as Carver and Bradford adorn many of the tombstones, giving a somewhat eerie reminder of the town's importance in early American history.

Plimoth Plantation is open daily from 9 A.M. to 5 P.M., April 1 through November 30. Children under 5 are admitted free.

ACCOMMODATIONS: $ You can either commute from Boston or choose from several bed-and-breakfast accommodations, motels, and campgrounds in the area.

If you prefer a motel, the choices include the Sheraton Plymouth at Village Landing, phone (508) 747-4900, which is right on the waterfront, and a pair of inns known as the John Carver and the Governor Bradford. The Sheraton offers a heated indoor pool, saunas, whirlpool, and exercise room, as well as an attractive, glassed-in restaurant with a view of Water Street.

The Governor Bradford Inn, phone (508) 746-6200, overlooks the harbor and has a small outdoor swimming pool. The John Carver Inn, phone (508) 746-7100, on the town square, was redecorated in the mid-1980s and also has a pool and restaurant.

DINING: Plimoth Plantation offers a snack bar for a midday break. Reservations are required for the 17th-century dinner and many other special theme dinners. Picnic tables are available in summer.

There are numerous family restaurants in the town of Plymouth.

ACTIVITIES: After a visit to the orientation center at the plantation, including a multi-media presentation, you will go to the Pilgrim Village. There, interpreters portray individual pilgrims such as William Bradford and John Alden.

As much as possible with visitors swirling about them, the residents of the Pilgrim Village go about their normal daily lives. If no one approaches them, they carry out their daily chores—cooking, cleaning, and tending to the variety of duties that their forebears had to take care of as well. If someone asks them a question, they will answer with knowledge that stops in the 1620s. One young visitor, for example, asked why there weren't any kids in the area. A village resident, pretending to be momentarily befuddled, quickly pointed out that there were many baby goats all around.

The sights, sounds, and smells of the village are accurately re-created, down to the heavy clothes that the residents wear even in the heat of the summer. Asked why he would not doff some of his clothing to cool off, one of the residents, who was wearing wooden shoes, replied, "We've come to an uncivil place, but we did not come to uncivilize it, just because of its warm climate."

When one young visitor came up with a case of the hiccups, two village residents began an earnest consultation of the best way to cure the affliction they called "the hikkets." Their prescription: sassafras bark or root.

After wandering around the Pilgrim Village, visitors can go to Hobbamock's Indian Homesite, the re-created Indian encampment. Inside a dome-shaped home *(wetu)* made of bent saplings and woven reed mats of bark, they can sit on a bed covered with beaver pelts and listen to tales of the history and culture of the Wampanoag people.

The homesite does not carry over the Pilgrim Village premise of role-playing; instead, it features members of the Wampanoag tribe plus trained guides explaining native ways. The guides explained that the Indians used to play-act as the Pilgrims do, but visitors couldn't understand their native language as easily as visitors could make out the Pilgrim's English.

FOR CHILDREN: School-age children will delight in imagining that they are back in "the olden days." A favorite game is trying to trick the guides into answering a question with knowledge gained since the 17th century.

The Education Department schedules special activities for children periodically during the summer and holiday tourist seasons and on weekends.

OF INTEREST NEARBY: The *Mayflower II,* is located on the Plymouth waterfront, about three miles north from Plimoth Plantation. As at the plantation, the *Mayflower II* is staffed by costumed workers who speak the language as it was spoken in the Pilgrims' time. They describe the long voyage across the ocean and talk about why they left their known world for a new land where they could worship as they wished.

The full-scale reproduction was built in England and sailed across the Atlantic in 1957. Visitors first see a dockside exhibit that introduces the passengers who sailed for 66 days on the ship's namesake. Aboard the ship, there are both the sailors (hired hands who are looking forward to returning to England) and Pilgrims, faced with the challenge of building a new colony.

The original *Mayflower* did not first touch land at Plymouth. Instead, it reached the tip of Cape Cod at Provincetown, which was deemed an unsuitable spot for settlement. Plymouth Rock, now surrounded by a Parthenon-like structure on Water Street, is only about a third of the size of the original rock; over the years people have chipped away at it, removing thousands of pounds. A guide gives a brief talk on the history of the site.

A walk along Water Street should also include a visit to Ocean Spray's Cranberry World, where not only admission but small samples of juice and other cranberry delicacies are available free of charge. Also on hand are exhibits on the life and times of a cranberry bog, showing how the berries are grown, harvested, and processed.

FOR MORE INFORMATION: Write Plimoth Plantation at P.O. Box 1620, Plymouth, MA 02362, or call (508) 746-1622.

Write the Plymouth County Development Council, P.O. Box 1620, Pembroke, MA 02359, or call (508) 826-3136.

SOUTHEAST

Colonial Williamsburg
Williamsburg, Virginia

Families come to Williamsburg to learn about an important time in history. In this small, restored town in tidewater Virginia, once a colonial capital, they see for themselves what life was like in the 18th century. They gain a different perspective on democracy in the Hall of the House of Burgesses where the patriots—Patrick Henry, George Washington, and Thomas Jefferson—came together to discuss and debate the inalienable rights to life, liberty, and the pursuit of happiness. Williamsburg inspires children to look at history in a new way.

In 1926, the Reverend Dr. W. A. R. Goodwin, rector of the Bruton Parish Church in Williamsburg, persuaded John D. Rockefeller to help in the restoration of Colonial Williamsburg. Eighty-eight 18th-century buildings were restored; 19th- and 20th-century buildings were torn down, and, in their place, more than 50 reconstructions of their 18th-century predecessors were built, including the Governor's Palace, the Capitol, and the Public Hospital.

When children think about "the olden days," they often focus on what people didn't have—electricity, modern plumbing, telephones, computers. At Williamsburg they're made aware of what the people did have, as well as how they worked and played. Artisans and costumed interpreters bring the 18th century to life.

On a walk down Duke of Gloucester Street, you'll see the printer and bookbinder at work. You'll learn who subscribed to the *Virginia Gazette* and how many books the average person owned. The wigmaker will show you how a wig is made and explain why wigs were a status symbol. The apothecary will give you a lesson in the medicinal use of leeches.

The costumed interpreter at the Geddy House will tell you about 18th-century family life. You'll see the toys the children played with and maybe watch an 11-year-old do needlework. Outside, your children will play the same games children played 200 years ago.

You can participate in an auction, dine in a colonial tavern, attend a service at the Bruton Parish Church, see the public "gaol" where prisoners were given "salt beef damaged, and Indian meal," or tour the Capitol, where the House of Burgesses met. A visit to Williamsburg will show you how people from many walks of life lived—the craftsman, the innkeeper, the slave, and the governor.

ACCOMMODATIONS: $ to $$$$ Colonial Williamsburg operates a variety of accommodations. The Williamsburg Inn is the most elegant, furnished in the Regency style. The Williamsburg Lodge, right next to the Historic Area, has comfortable rooms.

Williamsburg Woodlands, located next to the Visitor Center, has a more casual atmosphere and offers several recreational opportunities—3 swimming pools, a putting green and miniature golf course, shuffleboard, table tennis, and a playground. The Governor's Inn is located 3 blocks from the Historic Area and has inexpensive rooms.

If you're looking for the total "colonial experience," you may enjoy staying in one of several buildings in the Historic Area. These range from a 16-room tavern to a small cottage.

A range of motels, not operated by Colonial Williamsburg, offers other lodging options. Most national chains have affiliates here.

DINING: Dine in the colonial manner at one of the 4 taverns that offer traditional southern cooking, served by costumed servers. Choose from the King's Arms Tavern, which has an excellent chicken pot pie; Shielde's Tavern, perhaps the most authentic; Christiana Campbell's Tavern, where George Washington ate; and Chowning's Tavern, known for its Welsh rarebit and Brunswick stew. Chowning's Gambols (colonial games and entertainment) begin at 9 P.M. These taverns are open for lunch and dinner, and children's menus are available.

The Williamsburg Inn Regency Dining Room is open for breakfast, luncheon, and dinner. If you go for Sunday brunch, you'll hear the Williamsburg Chamber Players. Friday and Saturday evenings, the Williamsburg Lodge features the Chesapeake Bay Feast.

One block from the Visitor Center, you'll find the Cascades, which offers a reasonably priced and hearty Hunt Breakfast Buffet (with scalloped oysters, grits, and hotcakes). Right across from the Visitor Center, you'll see the Williamsburg Woodlands, where you'll find quick service, good food, and reasonable prices.

ACTIVITIES: The "Visitor's Companion" provides a calendar of special events and a map of the Historic Area. Here's just a sampling of what you might find in any given week.

- Take a carriage or stage wagon ride through the Historic Area.
- Hear the Fife and Drum Corps or attend a militia review.
- Visit selected crafts shops on an evening Lanthorn Tour.
- Take another special tour led by a costumed interpreter. "According to the Ladies" portrays women of 18th-century Williamsburg. "The Other Half" explores slave life.
- Enjoy "Bruton by Candlelight," a recital at Bruton Parish Church.
- Attend an 18th-century play in the Williamsburg Lodge.
- Take in evening entertainment at the Capitol, which may include a "Musical Diversion," or "An Assembly" (an evening of dance and music), or "A Capitol Evening" (with political debate, court drama, and period music).

A separate admission is charged for most of these events.

FOR CHILDREN: Special two-hour programs for young people are available in the summer at a nominal cost. These include "Once upon a Town" for ages 4 to 6, a walking tour of the Palace Green neighborhood with an emphasis on the lives of children in 18th-century Williamsburg; "Stepping into the Past" for ages 7 to 9, a walking tour of the historic area, and "Young Apprentice Tour" for ages 10 to 12. Costumed interpreters lead the sessions. Tickets are on sale at the Greenhow Lumber House.

Special tours are offered for families at Benjamin Powell House, where interpreters representing 18th-century family members (including children) act out the relationships between family members and household slaves.

OF INTEREST NEARBY: Visit the College of William and Mary adjacent to the Historic Area. The main building of the college, called the Wren Building, dates from 1695 and is the oldest college building in the United States.

Take the seven-mile Country Road, passing by woodlands, marshes, and ravines, to Carter's Grove, a beautiful 800-acre estate with a 200-year-old mansion. There you'll find reconstructed slave quarters. As you look out at the James River from the mansion, you'll see the 17th-century remains of Wolstenholme Towne. The archaeological history of this small village is fascinating. The six sites, which date from between 1619 and 1710, were excavated between 1976 and 1981. An archaeological museum displays artifacts. Admission fees for Carter's Grove are included in the Patriot's Pass.

Jamestown, Williamsburg, Yorktown—historians say that it is here that the British Crown acquired a vast empire, debated it, and lost it. Try to include a visit to both Jamestown and Yorktown while you're in the area. At Jamestown, see the statues of John Smith and Pocahontas and the Old Church Tower (the only standing ruin of the 17th-century town), visit replicas of the James Fort and Powhatan's Lodge, and board replicas of *Susan Constant*, *Godspeed*, and *Discovery*, the vessels that brought the first English settlers to Virginia.

Visit the battlefield at Yorktown; you'll find the auto tours well marked. Also plan to stop at the National Park Service Visitor Center and the Yorktown Victory Center for interesting films and exhibits.

FOR MORE INFORMATION: Write Colonial Williamsburg, P.O. Box C, Williamsburg, VA 23187, or call (804) 220-7083.

For information and reservations for accommodations operated by Colonial Williamsburg, write to the Reservations Manager, Post Office Box B, Williamsburg, VA 23187, or call (800) HISTORY.

MIDWEST

Living History Farms
Des Moines, Iowa

Unlike most historic restorations that re-create only one time period, Living History Farms takes the visitor on a walk through 300 years of farming and rural life in Iowa. From the gardens of an Indian village to a futuristic look at the agricultural promise of genetic engineering, Living History Farms tells the story of farming in the rich, black soil of the American Heartland.

The Farms are organized in five historic areas. The walking trail begins with a visit to an Ioway Indian village in the year 1700, where a low cooking fire heats stew simmering in an iron pot. The Ioway still depended on traditional ways in 1700, but they were beginning to enjoy such conveniences as iron knives and pots, which they received from traders in exchange for their furs. Their lush gardens provided corn, beans, squash, and pumpkins to sustain them through the harsh winters.

Just up the trail is the 1850 Pioneer Farm. In the corner of a one-room log cabin stands a bed frame with ropes, which supports a straw mattress covered by a simple but attractive quilt. Using Dutch ovens and kettles hung in her open fireplace, the pioneer farmwife turns out cakes, pies, and delicious stews. The pioneer husband plows his corn and wheat fields with a team of oxen and keeps his hogs and sheep penned behind split-rail fences. Chickens dart in and out of bushes and through the garden fence.

The 1875 Frontier Town of Walnut Hill has craft shops, professional offices, a general store, a church and cemetery, a school, and a Victorian mansion. "The Walnut Advocate," printed each week from handset type on a flatbed press, records society items, farm conditions, and local news. The carpenter doubles as the undertaker, and the potter hawks his stock of salt-glazed crocks, pitchers, and cups. You can smell the coal smoke from the blacksmith's forge and hear the ring of his hammer on an anvil as he mends a plough-share or a link of chain. And in the Flynn Mansion, you'll see the Victorian finery fancied by a rising young railroad contractor.

At the 1900 Farm, visitors learn how work horses, windmills, the treadle sewing machine, and the parlor pump organ eased turn-of-the-century rural life. Here the farmwife bakes bread and pies in her giant wood stove, cans dozens of jars of fruits and vegetables, washes on Monday, irons on Tuesday, feeds the chickens, gathers the eggs, and still finds time to put in a few stitches each day on her next quilt.

The Henry A. Wallace Crop Center features displays on recent developments in American agriculture, including the miracle of hybrid corn. Outside are small plots of crops that were important in America's farming past or that may become major cash crops in the future.

ACCOMMODATIONS: $ No overnight accommodations are available at Living History Farms, but there are numerous motels in the vicinity. A Sheraton Inn (515-278-5575) is located directly across the road from the Farms' entrance; it has heated indoor pool, wading pool, sauna, and whirlpool. The Holiday Inn University Park (515-223-1800) is about a mile away; it, too, has a heated indoor pool, sauna, and whirlpool, as well as an exercise room.

DINING: At The Farms, the Cellar Door Deli offers hearty sandwiches, side dishes, fresh-baked brownies and filling soups. The Deli is open daily from the beginning of May to the end of October. Picnic facilities are on site, and there are numerous fast-food outlets nearby.

From November to April, the 1900 Farmhouse serves a farm supper on selected evenings for up to 10 guests. Visitors enjoy a horse-drawn hayrack ride to the farm house and a mug of hot cider on their arrival. A family-style meal is served at the kitchen table in the soft glow of kerosene lamps. The fare is hearty Midwestern farm food—roast beef, vegetables, and mashed potatoes and gravy, along with homemade rolls and butter, jams, jellies, and pickles topped off with delicious pie and cake. After the meal, guests retire to the parlor to play turn-of-the-century games, peruse the Sears & Roebuck catalogue and play the organ. Reservations are necessary.

ACTIVITIES: Thirty to 40 interpreters staff the historical sites every day, each clad in period clothing. Their jobs are to re-create the daily routines and chores of their time.

The potter, cabinetmaker, blacksmith, and broommaker demonstrate some of the historical crafts that sustained frontier life. The pioneer farmer plows his fields with oxen, plants corn by hand, and cuts wheat shocks with a scythe. The 1900 farmer harnesses Percheron workhorses to the sulky plow and cultivator, blasts the whistle on the steam engine that powers the threshing machine, and picks corn by hand.

The Folk Trades Summer School offers classes in toymaking, woodcarving, basketmaking, embroidery, quilt-making and beekeeping for adults, children, and whole families. Master craftsmen from around the Midwest teach these classes on weekends each June. Classes last about two hours; there's a small fee.

FOR CHILDREN: The farm animals, particularly the spring lambs, pigs, calves, and chicks, are an appealing attraction for children.

Children are invited to join in and help with the chores they would have had to do if they had lived a century ago, such as gathering firewood or eggs. The Farms encourages "hands on" experiences whenever possible.

Special activities at Easter, Halloween, Christmas, and the Fourth of July and most summer weekends are of interest to children; they include storytellers, craft classes, and traditional music and games.

The Farms also offers an extensive selection of educational programs in the winter months. One of the most popular with children is spending a half-day in the 1875 school house where they learn lessons from the McGuffey Reader and practice penmanship on slates.

OF INTEREST NEARBY: The State Historical Society Museum in downtown Des Moines houses excellent exhibits on Iowa history, including one of the few remaining Conestoga wagons, a 1909 Bleriot airplane, and the Van Allen satellite.

The Des Moines Art Center, designed by Eliel Saarinen and I. M. Pei, and the Science Center of Iowa are not far from the Farms. The Science Center has a miniature railroad exhibit that traces 100 years of railroad history, and an animal area that houses animals native to Iowa.

FOR MORE INFORMATION: Write Living History Farms, 2600 N.W. 111 Street, Urbandale, IA 50322 or phone (515) 278-5286.

Conner Prairie
Noblesville, Indiana

The year is 1836, only 20 years after the state of Indiana was carved out of the old Northwest Territory. President Andrew Jackson's term is coming to an end, and in the small frontier village of Prairietown, Indiana, the residents are talking about the upcoming election that pits Martin Van Buren against William Henry Harrison.

Mrs. Zimmerman, the proprietress of the Golden Eagle Inn, is preparing the noonday meal for the Inn's guests, who pay 12½ cents a night to sleep in the common sleeping chamber.

Outside the inn, a traveling gunsmith and his son have set up shop under a canvas awning beside their wagon. They are in the village for a week or two repairing the rifles and muskets of the men of Prairietown and nearby villages. On this day, they expect business to be good because Mr. Whitaker, the storekeeper, is staging a shooting match in Prairietown.

You and your family head toward the shooting match over the dirt streets of Prairietown, a historically accurate re-creation of a 19th-century frontier village. You stop on the way and knock on doors, enter houses or workshops, and chat with Prairietown "residents" and listen in on their conversation and gossip.

A visit to Conner Prairie is a visit into the daily lives of Indiana's first-generation settlers. Prairietown villagers, by their dress, mannerisms, food, speech, and interactions with the social, religious, political, and economic issues of 1836, convey history in the first person. You and your family participate in the everyday events of Prairietown. This is living history at its best.

The Conner Prairie settlement grew out of the keen interest in Indiana history and archaeology of pharmaceutical magnate Eli Lilly. In the 1930s, Lilly purchased and restored the 1823 home of William Conner, a prominent resident and key player in the early development of Hamilton County, Indiana. The land and buildings were eventually given to Earlham College to develop as a museum. In the 1960s and 1970s, more authentic 19th-century buildings were moved to Conner Prairie and grouped into the fictional, but historically accurate, Prairietown. Funds from the National Endowment for the Humanities and other sources allowed Conner Prairie historians to do research on frontier life in Indiana and create the characters who now inhabit Prairietown.

Prairietown at Conner Prairie is open from early April to late November. But programs take place elsewhere at Conner Prairie throughout the year.

ACCOMMODATIONS: $ to $$ Conner Prairie has no regular overnight accommodations. But on selected weekends in the winter, spring, and fall, you and your family can rent a pioneer log cabin for Friday night, Saturday night, or both. The Lilly Cabin is a genuine one-room log cabin furnished with all the amenities available to Indiana pioneers—a double bed with a straw-stuffed mattress, a simple table and benches, a fireplace with 19th-century cooking equipment, candle lanterns, and an ample supply of firewood. You bring your own food, blankets or sleeping bags, and other necessities. A modern conference facility with rest rooms (but no showers) is a short walk from the cabin.

Two package options are available through Conner Prairie at local hotels. The Quality Inn in Castleton, just six miles away, is annually named one of the top Quality Inns in the country. Choose between a king and queen size suite, each with a wet bar and refrigerator. A full breakfast is included in the rate.

Or choose the Waterfront Inn overlooking Morse Reservoir, just a 20-minute drive from Conner Prairie. Rooms are available with and without fireplaces. All rooms have kitchenettes, a dining area, and a sundeck. A continental breakfast is provided.

Overnight packages at both hotels include accommodations for two adults, two days of touring at Conner Prairie and Saturday lunch at Governor Noble's Eating Place at the museum.

DINING: During the winter months, Conner Prairie offers special dinners for groups of up to 12 people in the dining room of the William Conner home. The menu for Hearthside Suppers includes 19th-century items like fricassee of chicken, pickled beets, and green beans, hearth bread, and Everlasting Syllabub. Costumed interpreters prepare your dinner on the kitchen hearth using traditional recipes and cooking implements. Guests can help with some of the meal preparation. The dinner is served by candlelight on a table in front of the fireplace in the Conner dining room. Nineteenth-century parlor games and a tour of the Conner home conclude the evening. Reservations are required.

Throughout the year, Governor Noble's Eating Place in the Conner Prairie Museum Center serves daily lunches and Sunday Brunch. Picnic facilities are also located on the grounds.

ACTIVITIES: Conner Prairie offers four windows into the early 19th century. The first is Prairietown, the living history village; the second is the restored Federal-style home of William and Elizabeth Conner; the third is the Pioneer Adventure Area; and the fourth is the Weaver Gallery.

Fifty Conner Prairie staff members re-create the roles of Prairietown residents each day from early April through late November. In addition to the Golden Eagle Inn, the village contains a pottery, blacksmith's and carpenter's shops, a village store, a school, and a number of homes, including the doctor's house. Special events like weddings, temperance society meetings, and local elections are part of the daily program.

The Conner home is listed in the National Register of Historic Places. In the home and its outbuildings, interpreters recount the life and times of the Conner family and explain the origins and function of the estate's furnishings and equipment. Cooking demonstrations take place in the kitchen. At intervals throughout the year, interpreters demonstrate spinning, weaving, and dyeing in the loom house. The barn contains farming equipment from the early 19th century. Candlelight tours of the Conner home are conducted at Christmas time.

The Pioneer Adventure Area is the hands-on aspect of the Conner Prairie experience and is appealing to children and adults alike. Here you and your family can spin, weave, cook, make soap, split logs, or play frontier games. Perhaps a spelling bee is in progress or an itinerant violin-maker is in residence. Special theme weekends focus on one particular aspect of frontier life. Other special events are scheduled from time to time. Your visit might coincide with a hay-ride, a pig roast and picnic, or a barn dance. The Sleepy Hollow legend is reenacted in the Halloween season.

At intervals throughout the year, a two-hour nature program is available by reservation only and for a modest additional fee. The Conner Prairie naturalist tells stories, demonstrates simple cooking procedures on a hearth, gives an introduction to Indian sign language and pictographs, and leads your family in animal tracking or role plays about trading between trappers and traders.

FOR CHILDREN: Children on the staff of Conner Prairie play roles in the reenactment of history in Prairietown. Seeing how children lived more than 150 years ago provides your own children with a fascinating lesson in cultural history and one they can relate to.

The Pioneer Adventure Area is the focus of activities for children. The schedule of events changes weekly and includes naturalist programs as well as history-related activities.

Conner Prairie will appeal to children over 4. Since much of the mission of Conner Prairie involves working with schools, the staff is skilled in relating to children and their interests.

OF INTEREST NEARBY: The Children's Museum of Indianapolis is the largest children's museum in the world. Galleries focus on the physical and natural sciences, history, foreign cultures, and the arts. This is one of the best children's museums anywhere.

The Indianapolis Museum of Art is located in a park with a botanical garden designed by Frederick Law Olmsted, the designer of Central Park in New York. In the park you'll find restaurants, shops, a wildlife refuge, lakes, and a greenhouse.

Union Station is Indianapolis's train station, which has been restored and converted into a "festival marketplace" with shops, restaurants, nightspots, and entertainment. The Holiday Inn, located in the original train shed, features 26 suites in fully restored Pullman cars from the 1920s.

White River State Park houses the Indianapolis Zoo, with its cageless design and excellent exhibits on marine life.

FOR MORE INFORMATION: Write Conner Prairie, 13400 Allisonville Road, Noblesville, IN 46060, or phone (317) 776-6000.

Historic New Harmony
New Harmony, Indiana

On the banks of the Wabash River, near Indiana's border with Illinois and Kentucky, lies a small town of 1,000 that is unlike any other in the United States. New Harmony is a living history village in the most literal sense, for modern-day folks go about their daily tasks in the midst of a setting that is steeped in history. A two or three-day visit here imparts such a sense of tranquility and well-being that many visitors begin to daydream about moving here.

New Harmony served as the sites of two of the most ambitious utopian experiments in the nation. It was founded in 1814 by a Lutheran separatist group called the Harmonie Society. Its charismatic leader, Father George Rapp, devised a plan for the construction of a model town in what was then the wilderness of the Indiana Territory, and within a year the community housed 800 people in 150 structures. It thrived for 10 years, exporting more than 20 products throughout the South and Midwest, and its per capita income and cultural amenities rivaled those of many long-established cities in the East.

The entire town was bought in 1825 by a Welsh-born industrialist, Robert Owen, of New Lanark, Scotland, after the Harmonists decided to move back to Pennsylvania. Owen had his own vision of a model community where education and social equality would serve as the watchwords. William Maclure, the nation's most eminent geologist, joined Owen's venture a year later, and brought with him a group of pre-eminent thinkers. Owen stayed for only two years, and his vision was never fully realized. But his sons stayed behind, and from 1830 to 1860 New Harmony was one of the most important training and research centers for the study of geology in America. Its residents also made pioneering contributions to education, women's rights, science, architecture, and the arts.

The visonary focus of the town weakened over the next century, but in 1959 a trust established by one of Owen's descendants began a restoration process that led to the re-emergence of New Harmony as a center of progressive thought and innovative design.

Today, many of the original buildings have been restored and furnished with period pieces, and Historic New Harmony, Inc., which is affiliated with the University of Southern Indiana, operates a series of year-round cultural programs and historic tours. A visit here is both a step back in time and a look towards the future, for the spirits of the Harmonists and the Owenists hover over the town, inspiring visitors in the belief that a better life is possible.

ACCOMMODATIONS: $ The New Harmony Inn, on the edge of the historic district, was built in 1974 according to a design that captures the Harmonist spirit. There are 90 lovely rooms, ranging from doubles to unusual bi-level suites with sleeping lofts. Three rooms have kitchenettes, and 18 have working fireplaces. Furnishings feature original designs crafted by an artist in Posey County. The hotel, which is featured in many country inn guides, has a glass-enclosed heated swimming pool for year-round use, a sauna, a Jacuzzi, and several tennis courts. Call (812) 682-4491 for rates and information.

Campsites, both primitive and modernized, are available in Harmonie State Park, which has an Olympic-sized swimming pool with a 110-foot water slide, a picnic area and nature trails.

DINING: The Inn has two restaurants, the famous Red Geranium, which draws diners regularly from three states, and the more casual

Bayou Grill. The Red Geranium serves regional and continental cuisine for lunch and dinner (except Mondays, when it is closed). Its memorable baked goods are available to take home.

ACTIVITIES: Tours of New Harmony are self-guided, but tickets are required. The historic district is open daily from April through October, and weekends only in March, November, and December (the historic buildings are closed in January and February). Tours start at the Atheneum, a striking building designed by architect Richard Meier, which houses an excellent gift shop, an 1824 model of New Harmony, an observation deck, exhibition space, and a theater in which a 20-minute orientation film is shown. A tram links most of the historic sites and runs continuously from 9 A.M. to noon and from 1 to 5 P.M. Many visitors, however, like to bring their bicycles.

There are almost 20 historic buildings or points of interest that are open to visitors. Among them are the David Lenz House, where children will marvel over the outdoor baking oven; the West Street Log Cabins, where there are frequent rope making demonstrations; the Salomon Wolf House, which houses an automated model presentation of 1824-era New Harmony, the John Beal House, which has exhibits on natural science and education from the Owen era; the Victorian-era doctor's office, which has one of the most complete collections of medical and apothecary objects in the Midwest; and the Lesueur American Indian Museum, which traces the history of the region's earliest inhabitants.

The town's famous Roofless Church, opened in 1960, is an inter-denominational church designed by the noted architect Phillip Johnson, with bronze entrance gates and sculpture by Jacques Lipchitz. Nearby is Tillich Park, where German theologian Paul Johannes Tillich is buried.

The New Harmony Theatre, produced by the University of Southern Indiana, is the home of professional theatrical productions in the summer.

FOR CHILDREN: The costumed guides stationed at many of the historic buildings take care to explain things in a way that children can understand. Most children will be fascinated by the frequent demonstrations of crafts and early machinery.

Children will also love visiting the Labyrinth, a restored garden maze, which to the Harmonists symbolized the twists and turns along life's pathway.

Throughout the year, special events are held with particular appeal to children. Among them are the traditional Easter egg hunts in Harmonie State Park and the Harmonist Cemetery; Heritage Week in April, during which 19th-century crafts are demonstrated; the annual storytelling festival in May; the Kunstfest in September, and a series of Christmas candlelight tours in December.

FOR MORE INFORMATION: Write Historic New Harmony, Inc., P.O. Box 579, New Harmony, IN 47631 or call (812) 464-9595.

Shaker Village at Pleasant Hill
Harrodsburg, Kentucky

Utopian movements are a distinctive part of American history. Groups that held divergent religious beliefs and practiced nonconformist life-styles flourished on the American frontier in the 1800s. These movements typically dispersed and died within a few generations, but their achievements in agriculture, science, architecture, design, and commerce were out of all proportion to their numbers and their life spans.

One such group was the Shakers, followers of a messianic woman who immigrated to the United States from England about the time of American independence. A dissident Quaker group whose name evolved from the writhing, whirling body movements used by the faithful in worship, the Shakers expanded from a single colony near Albany, New York, to 18 colonies scattered from New England to the Ohio valley.

The Pleasant Hill community in what is now Mercer County,

Kentucky, 25 miles southwest of Lexington, was one of the western-most colonies. Founded in 1805, it grew to about 500 members at its zenith in 1840, and then gradually faded away.

The history and achievements of the Shakers are celebrated here in a faithful restoration of 30 of the nearly 300 buildings the Shakers built, in the display of more than 2,000 items crafted and used by the Shakers, and in demonstrations of early-19th-century Shaker crafts like broom making, spinning, and weaving. Pleasant Hill has been designated a National Landmark and is listed on the National Register of Historic Places.

ACCOMMODATIONS: $ The Village has 79 guest rooms located in 15 original Shaker buildings. Pleasant Hill is the only historic village in the United States that has located all its guest services in original buildings. Concessions to modern times include central heating and air-conditioning, ice machines, telephones, TV sets, and bathrooms with each guest room. But otherwise, your room at Shaker Village is furnished and decorated much like the rooms the Shakers inhabited 150 years ago.

Furniture is in the simple Shaker style, with high beds, hard wooden chairs and rocking chairs, a simple writing table, a high bureau, and a fireplace. Some rooms have a trundle bed for a child. Broad plank floors are covered with rag throw rugs. The only wall decorations are candles (now with electric bulbs) and a single mirror. (The Shakers took mirrors down immediately after use to avoid the sinful thoughts that vanity might engender.) There are no closets. The Shakers ringed the walls of their rooms with pegs and hung many things from them, including chairs. In all of Shaker Village there are more than 30,000 pegs.

In addition to large single rooms with baths, there are some two-bedroom combinations, and some two-bedroom suites with sitting rooms. Most guest rooms are located in the East Family House and the West Family House. These buildings have common lounges for guests with reading lamps and ice and soda machines.

There is no extra charge for children up to the age of 18 who stay in the same room as their parents. Shaker Village does not accept credit cards.

DINING: The Village dining room occupies the first floor of the Trustee's Office, a building completed in 1839 as the administrative center for Shaker business with the outside world. Guests are seated in low-back Shaker-style chairs at plain wood tables. Hurricane lamps are the only table decoration. In this simple setting, wonderful southern food is served at breakfast, lunch, and dinner.

An afternoon tea is offered between November and February. Special dinners are presented in the Thanksgiving and Christmas periods. A children's menu is available.

There are three seatings for lunch and two for dinner year-round; make reservations at the time of your arrival. The dining room has a no-tipping policy. Mercer County, Kentucky, is a dry county. No alcoholic beverages are served in the dining room.

ACTIVITIES: Exploring the restored community is the major activity here. Shaker Village is best seen at a leisurely pace.

Start your tour in the Centre Family House. Guides in 19th-century dress will orient you to Shaker beliefs and way of life; the house itself serves as the museum of Shaker Village. With original articles made and used by the Shakers, various rooms depict how the Shakers cooked, ate, slept, cared for the sick and infirm, and raised orphaned and abandoned children to recruit new members. There are exhibits on the industries the Shakers created in vegetable seeds and personal and household articles manufacture.

From Centre Family House you might go directly across the road to the cantilevered Meeting House that was the site of worship services. Or you could turn in either direction down the Old Turnpike road that was the main street of Pleasant Hill to watch demonstrations of furniture making, medicine making, spinning and weaving, barrel making, quilting, or broom making set up in a half dozen other restored buildings. In each exhibit, well-informed guides demonstrate how the Shakers worked using tools from the last century. They also point out the many inventions of the Shakers, including a washing machine, clothespins, and circular saws.

Every day from April through November, a demonstration of some aspect of Shaker domestic life takes place at Pleasant Hill. These events include candle dipping, hearth cooking, beehive-oven baking, natural dyeing, silk culturing and butter churning.

Buildings and exhibits are open from 9 A.M. to 6 P.M. daily from April through November. Winter hours vary and not all exhibits are open during winter months. Children under 6 are free.

Special events throughout the year feature visiting artisans and artists, and performances of Shaker music and dances. Winter weekends are available in a one-price package that includes lodging, meals, and programs.

FOR CHILDREN: Any child with an interest in history will be fascinated by Pleasant Hill. Shaker Village may not be appropriate for children under 4, depending on their individual interests and attention spans, although many will enjoy sleeping on a trundle bed, playing with door latches and bolts, or exploring spiral staircases. Children also enjoy the horse-drawn wagon rides in summer and sleigh rides in winter.

OF INTEREST NEARBY: From late April through October, the paddle-wheel riverboat *Dixie Belle* leaves Shaker Landing below Shaker Village for 1-hour excursions on the Kentucky River. The captain comments on the importance of the river to the Shaker economy and the natural history of the Kentucky River valley. Special extended excursions are held from time to time, including nature cruises and a cruise through Lock and Dam No. 7 on the Kentucky River. Box lunches can be arranged at the Inn. Guided nature walks in early spring and winter are a special feature.

Harrodsburg is the nearest community to Pleasant Hill. The town dates from the frontier days of the 18th century and bills itself as Kentucky's oldest town. A replica of the 1775 fort stands in Old Fort Harrod State Park. Beaumont Inn dates from 1845 and is renowned for its traditional Kentucky fare. From late June through August, outdoor dramas on the lives of Daniel Boone and Abraham Lincoln are presented in the James Harrod Amphitheater. Harrodsburg is also a crafts center with many shops.

FOR MORE INFORMATION: Write Shaker Village at Pleasant Hill, 3500 Lexington Road, Harrodsburg, KY 40330, or phone (606) 734-5411.

Mackinac State Historic Parks
Mackinac Island and Mackinaw City, Michigan

When visitors disembark from the ferry on Mackinac Island, Michigan, they have three choices for getting around: foot, bicycle, or horse-drawn carriage.

That's right. Horse-drawn carriage. There are only three vehicles with internal combustion engines on the whole island: a fire engine, a police car, and a maintenance truck.

Instead of cars, Mackinac Island has the largest fleet of radio-dispatched horse-drawn taxis in the world. There are so many horses on the island—600 at last count—that the city's small staff of employees includes several whose sole job is cleaning up after them.

It is this quaint insistence on maintaining some of the vestiges of 19th-century life that brings thousands of visitors to the island every day through the spring, summer, and fall.

Most visits to Mackinac Island start off in Mackinaw City, Michigan. This was where French settlers in 1715 established Fort St. Philippe de Michilimackinac (pronounced MISH-ili-mack-i-naw) as a trading post and fort guarding the Straits of Mackinac, which link Lake Michigan with Lake Huron.

Now called Colonial Michilimackinac, the old fort today is one of three living history museums in the area that are operated by Mackinac State Historic Parks. (A combination ticket admits you to all three.) The fort's buildings have been painstakingly reconstructed and authentically refurnished so that 20th-century visitors can get a sense of early life in what was once the greatest fur trading center in North America.

A few miles down U.S. 23 is Mill Creek, another state historic park. Here, in 1790, settlers built a water-powered sawmill that provided much of the finished lumber for Fort Mackinac.

Fort Mackinac, on Mackinac Island, was the successor to Fort Michilimackinac, built largely from limestone in 1780. Today, period displays and costumed interpreters impart a sense of military life in the 1880s, about 10 years before it was decommissioned.

Mackinac Island is reached by ferry from Mackinaw City or St. Ignace; there are scores of departures every day.

ACCOMMODATIONS: $ to $$$$ There are 1,400 tourist beds on the island distributed among 11 hotels and eight bed-and-breakfasts. The most famous is The Grand Hotel (800-334-7263), which has become synonymous with the island and represents one of its most lasting images. The expansive white frame structure occupies a post-card-perfect perch overlooking Lake Huron, and the hotel's public rooms and guests room are decorated with period furniture and Victorian era-inspired wallpapers and rugs.

Although the atmosphere here is sedate and reserved, The Grand Hotel is a great place for families to stay. There's a fabulous serpentine-shaped pool where Esther Williams once swam. And the hotel's youth counselor supervises a special children's barbecue lunch and nature walk almost every day, as well as a separate children's dinner at night.

The Mission Point Resort (800) 833-7711, on the opposite end of the downtown area from the Grand, is as unlike the Grand as possible, but no less inviting. Its lobby, with a cathedral ceiling crafted from gigantic rough-hewn logs, gives it the look of a northwoods lodge. The atmosphere here is casual and the emphasis is on relaxation and fun.

There are special children's activities here, too, three hours of games and arts and crafts for 5- to 12-year-olds on Tuesdays, Thursdays, and Saturdays and a free half-hour story-time for children every morning. Mission Point has a heated outdoor pool, tennis courts, a fitness center, and the island's only movie theater.

A number of inexpensive motels and bungalow colonies can be found in Mackinaw City.

DINING: The Grand Hotel is famous for its cuisine, especially its luncheon buffet. The hotel also operates the Tea Room at Fort Mackinac; the terrace there has some of the best views on the island.

Zach's Delicatessen, on Huron Street, packs excellent picnic lunches for bicyclists, and even provides a backpack!

ACTIVITIES: Every day through the summer, employees of Colonial Michilimackinac dress as villagers, soldiers, traders, and priests and perform tasks out of the 1770s—horseshoeing, cooking over a fireplace, tending farm animals, paddling a birchbark canoe, and even taking part in a wedding (performed in French, the settlers' language).

At Mill Creek, visitors can watch informative sawmill and sawpit demonstrations and a slide show about the area's historic significance, and hike several trails through the surrounding 625-acre wooded park. A staff naturalist leads nature discovery tours five days a week.

At Fort Mackinac, there are guided tours, musket shoots, cannon firings, soldiers on parade, and even re-enactments by a local family with five children, ages 1 through 12, of the chores of 19th-century family life.

Taking one of the carriage rides operated by Mackinac Island Carriage Tours is a great way for families to get a sense of Mackinac Island. Two Belgian draft horses pull a 16-seat, roofed carriage along the island's streets while the driver provides a running commentary about historic sites and what island life is like for the 600 permanent residents.

Bicycling the eight-mile length of State Highway 185, which hugs the Lake Huron shoreline, is another must-do for vacationers. Bring your own bicycles, or rent them from any of the outfitters along Huron Street. They have everything from tandems with a rear seat specially adjusted for a child's short legs to adult bikes with trailer attachments for toddlers.

FOR CHILDREN: At Colonial Michilimackinac, separate tours are offered for children that emphasize what it was like to be a child in the 18th-century.

At Fort Mackinac, there's a children's discovery room where children can pretend to be soldiers or laundresses (pretty much the only options for islanders in the 1880s) and press buttons to hear such sounds of history as a horse clopping down the street, a steamboat arriving from the mainland, or a laundress scrubbing on a washboard.

The interpreters at all three sites are attuned to children's interests and draw them into their activities, whether it is sawing a log, playing a drum, dancing a jig, or firing a cannon.

FOR MORE INFORMATION: For information about the state parks, call (906) 847-3328 or write Box 370, Mackinac Island, MI 49757. For general tourist information about Mackinac Island, call (906) 847-3783. For general tourist information about Mackinaw City, call (800) 666-0160.

Crow Canyon Archaeological Center
Cortez, Colorado

For more than 14 centuries the Anasazi Indians inhabited the Four Corners region of the United States. They built pueblos of magnificent masonry on a scale unequaled anywhere in the United States. Their settlements spread from the Grand Canyon in the west to the Great Plains in the east, and from central Arizona and New Mexico north into southern Utah and Colorado.

Then, suddenly, in the 13th century, the Anasazi abandoned the Four Corners area. Why? No one knows for certain. The mystery of the Anasazi has fascinated archaeologists for decades.

Crow Canyon Archaeological Center, a not-for-profit organization, is dedicated to investigating the Anasazi civilization. Its scientists are attempting to answer questions concerning how the Anasazi lived, how they were organized socially, and why they abandoned their magnificent dwellings.

In addition to its exacting research and scholarship, the center has pioneered a unique program of public archaeology and education in which families can learn about the Anasazi and participate in archaeological field work. This is not a stuffy, boring college course in disguise, but a fun and challenging vacation adventure in which you help unearth the past and solve the mystery of the Anasazi.

ACCOMMODATIONS: $ to $$$$ Accommodations are provided in the Crow Canyon Lodge and in comfortable log hogans, patterned on the eight-sided Navajo ceremonial house. The hogans are located on a pinon and juniper-covered hillside above the lodge, with doors that face the rising sun, as Navajo tradition prescribes.

The lodge has dormitory-style rooms that sleep two to 11 people in bunk beds. Hogans contain four beds each. Both lodge and hogans have shared bath facilities. The toilets and showers for the hogans are in a separate building in the hogan complex. Guests bring their own linens or sleeping bag.

During family week, Crow Canyon attempts to house each family together, but it is sometimes necessary to separate families and provide accommodations in the sex-segregated dormitory rooms.

Housing is only available for participants of week-long programs. Participants in shorter programs stay in motels in nearby Cortez.

DINING: The Crow Canyon dining room serves three delicious homestyle meals a day. The food is quite a few cuts above typical camp cuisine. Breakfasts always include fresh fruit and when egg dishes are served, a low-cholesterol egg substitute. Box lunches are provided when your schedule takes you away from the center on field trips. Dinners often feature Southwest-inspired dishes. Tea, coffee, and lemonade are available throughout the day.

ACTIVITIES: Crow Canyon offers a wide variety of educational programs, including excavation archaeology, environmental archaeology, workshops, seminars, cultural explorations, Family Week, and one-day programs.

The week-long excavation and environmental archaeology programs are centered on field work and laboratory analysis of artifacts found in the field. The area surrounding Crow Canyon has one of the highest concentrations of Anasazi sites anywhere in the Four Corners region. The center always has several excavations in progress.

Cultural explorations and seminars take the form of both travel within the Four Corners area and on-site workshops and are led by Native Americans and other specialists. The themes for cultural explorations range over a wide variety of topics, including traditional crafts, Native American culture, and archaeology.

Each evening finds amateur archaeologists sitting in the rockers on the lodge porch watching the sun set against the La Plata mountains in the distance and swapping stories of experiences in the field that day. At the end of the week, every participant receives a certificate at a farewell party and awards ceremony.

Families who can't schedule a full week at Crow Canyon can experience the excitement of archaeology and the richness of Anasazi culture through a day program. The one-day programs include an examination of Anasazi artifacts in the laboratory, experience in Anasazi lifestyles, and a visit to a working archaeological site. One-day visits are available Tuesday through Thursday from late May to early October. The program fee includes lunch. Reservations are essential.

FOR CHILDREN: Crow Canyon is as dedicated to its educational mission as it is to research. Its staff is especially skilled in relating to children. Children learn through hands-on activities which include handling artifacts and relating them to the lives of an ancient people.

Family Week, held each August, is geared to parents or grandparents with children in fourth grade or above. Children in grades four through six take part in a simulated excavation program; students in grades seven and up excavate in the field with adults and the Crow Canyon research staff. The week-long program includes an introduction to Southwest prehistory, an ecology hike, experience in handling and classifying aritifacts in the laboratory, a visit to Mesa Verde National Park, and such Anasazi activities as grinding corn on a stone metate, throwing a spear with an atlatl, and starting a fire with a fire bow.

Adults and older students help excavate an Anasazi site and work in the lab washing, sorting, analyzing, and cataloguing artifacts. Younger students visit the Anasazi Cultural Center in nearby Dolores, visit an Anasazi site under excavation, do simulated lab and excavation work, make pottery, and play pueblo games. Families come together for the evening meal and an evening program, which can include stories, Native American music, and making arrow heads and spear points.

Children 12 years and older can participate with adults in the other excavation and environmental programs.

Crow Canyon will obviously appeal mostly to children who have an interest in Indians or archaeology. The Crow Canyon experience gives them an appreciation of prehistoric culture, an understanding of the continuity of the human experience through time, and a sense of their place within that experience.

OF INTEREST NEARBY: Crow Canyon is located in the heart of the Four Corners area, near numerous national parks and monuments, including Mesa Verde, Hovenweep, Chaco Canyon, Canyonlands, Arches, Natural Bridges, Black Canyon, and Canyon de Chelly. It is a day's drive from the Grand Canyon and five hours from Sante Fe.

Nearby are Navaho and Ute Indian reservations, which offer various cultural events throughout the summer. In Cortez and Durango, many vacation activities are offered, including hiking, mountain biking, horseback riding, rafting, fishing, swimming in pools fed by hot springs, and llama trekking. The famed Durango-Silverton narrow gauge railway is popular with families.

Both Durango and Cortez are located on the San Juan Skyway— a highway loop through some of the most scenic mountain country in Colorado.

FOR MORE INFORMATION: Write Crow Canyon Archaeological Center, 23390 County Road K, Cortez, CO 81321 or phone (800) 422-8975.

1. The M.S. *Starward* offers supervised programs for both teenagers and younger children, with activities such as swimming pool games, scavenger hunts, and relay races. **2.** As part of the ShipShape program on the *Song of America*, families can participate in golf driving and putting, walkathons, aerobics classes, basketball tournaments, and more. **3.** Two "keikis" make friends with the captain aboard American Hawaii Cruises' S.S. *Independence*. **4.** On the *Starship Oceanic*, scheduled kids' activities run all day and include arts and crafts in the ship's Club House. *(Photo: Premier Cruise Lines)* **5.** The waiters on Carnival Cruise Lines' ships all take a special interest in the younger passengers. *(Photo: Martha Shirk)* **6.** Ring toss is one of the many planned activities that are part of Royal Caribbean Cruise Line's "Kid/Tween/Teen" program.

CRUISES

4

5

6

THE CARIBBEAN AND THE BAHAMAS

Song of America
   Royal Caribbean Cruise Line
Western Caribbean

When the *Song of America* departs from Miami, Florida, on Sundays for its seven-day cruises to the Caribbean, a band plays and streamers fly. The departure is every bit as exciting as it was when steamships were the only means of transport across the Atlantic and "making the crossing" was only within the reach of the upper class. Before you know it, you'll have left Miami behind and be out in the middle of the deep blue sea. During your seven days at sea, you'll sail through tropical waters, discover new territory, feast on elegant meals, walk the Promenade deck, and feel the sea breeze.

Song of America, one of the newest ships of the Royal Caribbean fleet, made its maiden voyage in 1982, and the ship still glistens from fore to aft. The third-largest of the Royal Caribbean ships—it's 705 feet long and weighs 37,584 tons—*Song of America* can accommodate 1,390 passengers, a small town's worth. You'll find sun decks at several levels, an outdoor café, two swimming pools, and the Viking Crown Lounge—the Royal Caribbean hallmark. This glass-enclosed lounge rises 10 stories above the sea, cantilevered from the ship's funnel stack.

The staff of 500 includes Norwegian officers and employees of dozens of nationalities, which gives the ship an international flavor. The passenger list also usually contains names from all over the world; your children are as likely to make friends from Canada and France as from New Jersey or Missouri. And it's not uncommon to have more than 200 passengers under the age of 18, especially during the summer and holiday periods.

   In one week, *Song of America* will take you to Playa del Carmen and Cozumel, popular tourist stops in Mexico; Grand Cayman Island; Ocho Rios; and Labadee on the northern coast of Haiti.

If some other ports in the Caribbean interest you more, check the itineraries for the line's other ships: *Nordic Prince, Sun Viking, Song of Norway, Sovereign of the Seas,* and *Monarch of the Seas,* which made its maiden voyage in 1991. Nearly identical children's programs are offered on all of the ships. The *Sovereign of the Seas* has two youth centers on board and year-round children's counselors.

ACCOMMODATIONS: $$$ to $$$$ All of the 695 staterooms are comfortable, well designed, and attractive. You'll find ample closet and drawer space, a tabletop that can be used as a desk or dressing table, and single beds, most of which convert to double beds. In many of the standard staterooms, Pullman upper beds are available for families of three or four. Larger families will have to reserve two cabins.

During the day, beds in the standard staterooms are made up into sofas. Each stateroom has a private bathroom with shower, a telephone, a three-channel radio, and 110-volt outlets, standard American voltage, for small appliances.

A cabin steward will make up your room, keep your fruit basket full, place chocolates on your pillow at night, and distribute the Cruise Compass, a daily listing of activities, as well as the Ship & Shore News Bulletin, taken from the Associated Press wire service. You'll find the cabin stewards friendly and attentive.

Children sharing a stateroom with their parents qualify for third- and fourth-person rates, which are substantially lower than double rates. Rates include round-trip air transportation to Miami from most major cities, all meals, services, and entertainment. The fares do not include gratuities, shore excursions, and port taxes.

DINING: You can start out with Early Bird Coffee at the Verandah Café on the Sun Deck and end up with the Midnight Buffet in the Madame Butterfly Dining Room. You'll be amazed by all the choices available morning, noon, and night.

For breakfast, you can choose from a modest continental breakfast served in your cabin, a served breakfast in the dining room, or a buffet breakfast outside at the Verandah Café.

The Verandah Café is also a popular spot for lunch. You'll find a hot entrée, barbecued hamburgers and sandwiches, as well as salads and desserts. If you'd like a more formal luncheon, you can always retreat to the Madame Butterfly Dining Room for a five-course meal. Afternoon tea is served in the Verandah Café. The *pièce de résistance* for kids is serve-yourself ice-cream sundaes.

Dinner is always an event, complete with music, costumed waiters, and flaming desserts. One night, the theme is French; another night, it's the exotic cuisine of the Caribbean. As a band plays, waiters parade with dessert cakes balanced on their heads. The passengers cheer and twirl red napkins above their heads.

There is no printed children's menu, but hamburgers, hot dogs, and pizza are always available.

Passengers request one of two sittings (6:30 or 8:30 P.M.) and receive table assignments. High chairs are available.

Dress for several evenings is casual (men won't even need a jacket) but on at least two occasions, very fancy.

ACTIVITIES

 Two saltwater pools. When the ship's in the Cayman Islands, Royal Caribbean throws a beach party at Buccaneer Beach.

Children and their parents can join in the ShipShape program, where you earn ShipShape "dollars" that can be redeemed for a ShipShape T-shirt and sun visor. Activities include a walkathon, aerobics classes, golf driving and putting, Ping-Pong and basketball tournaments, and aquacize.

A mind-boggling array of daily activities, including cash bingo, Trivial Pursuit, gambling (slot machines, blackjack, or American roulette), movies.

Dancing, star-gazing, cruise staff shows and cabaret shows with professional singers and dancers can be enjoyed in the evening. One night each week there's a masquerade ball, a country and western night, and a passenger talent show.

FOR CHILDREN: During the summer months and over the Christmas, New Year's, and Easter holidays, an organized children's program called "Kids/Tweens/Teens" is offered for children 5 and over. Trained counselors supervise activities that will keep your children busy (and happy) all day and evening. Participation is voluntary, and kids can drop in and out as they please.

On a typical day, children meet their counselor for breakfast at the Verandah Café and then join in the morning activities, which might include a walkathon, golf-putting tournament, shuffleboard, or pool games. In the afternoon, a scavenger hunt, kite flying, or a special kids' tour might be offered. After dinner, kids frequently play bingo, see a special movie, or join the masquerade parade. Older kids will enjoy the Disco Dance Parties in the Guys and Dolls Lounge, or an 11 P.M. Pizza Party at the Verandah Café.

Free shore excursions for children are offered.

Children under 5 are welcome to participate in the children's program as long as they're accompanied by a parent or older sibling. Many families bring infants and small children with them on the ship, and hire private baby-sitters as needed. The purser or hotel manager will arrange for a baby-sitter with a 24-hour notice.

NICETIES: If you arrive in Miami the day the *Song of America* departs, you will be met at the airport and taken to the ship. There are no luggage worries either. If you attach a yellow *Song of America* tag to your bag before you check in at the airport, you'll find your luggage in your cabin that evening.

The Bell Station provides cabin service 24 hours a day. Coffee, drinks, sandwiches, and continental breakfast are available.

On the last day of the cruise, the youth counselors distribute autograph books and pens to all the children.

OF INTEREST IN PORT: Playa del Carmen, on the Yucatán peninsula, is the departure point for tours of Tulum, the only known Maya seacoast center of any importance. The ruins are awesome and an adjacent beach is a wonderful place for a dip in the Caribbean. Follow that with a snorkeling expedition to Xel-ha, a natural lagoon.

Cozumel, just a short sail from Playa del Carmen, is a diver's paradise, with clear blue waters unrivaled in the Caribbean. Located about 12 miles off the east coast of the Yucatán peninsula, the island has only 50 miles of paved road, best explored by bicycle or taxi.

Grand Cayman is another diver's paradise, almost completely surrounded by coral reefs. Excursions by small boats are offered to the reef, or you can don a mask and fins and snorkel from the beach. Grand Cayman is a British colony, and the atmosphere is distinctly British. For non-divers, the shops of George Town offer duty-free bargains. A side trip of interest to children is to the Cayman Turtle Farm, about seven miles north of George Town.

Not too long ago, Ocho Rios was a sleepy fishing village on the unpopulated north coast of Jamaica. It's still a small town, but it bustles when the cruise ships are in port. Skip the crafts market and commercial shopping area, where you'd be besieged by some of the most aggressive hawkers in the Caribbean, and go instead to Dunn's River Falls, a 600-foot waterfall that cascades in wedding cake–like tiers down into the sea. Climbing it is fun for all ages. Take a taxi to beautiful Shaw Park, a botanical Garden, or just lounge on the public beach.

Labadee, *Song of America*'s last port of call, is a secluded 260-acre private resort on the north coast of Haiti. You can walk for miles on white sand lined with palm trees or swim and snorkel in clear blue water. You can have lunch under a thatched roof and explore a market full of Haitian paintings and metal figurines sculpted from oil drums. Haitian musicians and dancers also stage a show.

FOR MORE INFORMATION: For more information, see your travel agent.

Star/Ship Oceanic

Premier Cruise Lines

The Bahamas

From the moment you step off the gangplank onto the gleaming *Star/Ship Oceanic*, there's no doubt what this cruise ship is all about. If you have children in tow, the first thing you're handed are schedules of all the activities the ship's youth counselors have planned for the next three or four days. There's something to do for children until midnight the night before they get off.

The *Oceanic* makes three- and four-day cruises each week from Port Canaveral, on Florida's east coast (the three-day cruises leave on Fridays, the four-day cruises on Mondays) to Nassau and a private out-island, Salt Cay, in the Bahamas. A West-Coast-based cruise ship with a Disneyland tie-in is planned for 1992.

Premier Cruise Lines has been operating these Bahamas cruises since 1984. Two smaller sister ships, the *Atlantic* and the *Majestic,* operate concurrently, with the *Majestic* calling on the Abacos, a group of secluded islands in the northern Bahamas. Premier is the official cruise line of Walt Disney World, and the tie-in is evident throughout the cruise. Characters such as Mickey Mouse, Donald Duck, Goofy, and Pluto roam the ship looking for youngsters and creating photo opportunities. All three ships underwent refurbishment in 1991 and 1992.

The *Oceanic* is a beautiful ship, built in 1965 and overhauled in 1986 when Premier began using it. Its hull is a deep red and its upper decks white. At 40,000 tons and 782 feet long it is one of the largest ships in the Bahamas cruise market. The ship has a capacity of 1,500 passengers; on a cruise during the summer or some school holidays, there are likely to be about 250 children aboard, which makes cruises on this ship decidedly family affairs.

ACCOMMODATIONS: **$$** to **$$$** The ship has about 550 passenger cabins, ranging from tiny inside cabins with one double bed to suites with private patios that can easily accommodate extended families. The majority of cabins can accommodate third, fourth, or fifth passengers; there are cabins of this size in most price categories.

The cabins all have private bathrooms and ample closet and drawer space. Many of the four-passenger cabins use upper bunks for the third and fourth passengers. Cribs can be arranged. Children are charged a flat rate if they occupy the same cabin as their parents.

Premier offers a package that includes the cruise, airfare, hotel accommodations at Walt Disney World, admission fees, a rental car and tours of Spaceport USA.

DINING: As on most cruise ships, meals are an experience. You can begin your day at 6 A.M. with early-risers' coffee and pastries and end it with the midnight buffet, with in-between stops for a hearty sit-down breakfast, late-morning coffee, a luncheon buffet or sit-down lunch, afternoon tea and cakes, cocktails, an elegant dinner, and the midnight buffet. On the night you're docked in Nassau, there's an additional repast—French onion soup and made-to-order eggs Benedict from 1 to 3 A.M.

The food on the ship is exceptionally good and beautifully presented. There are two seatings for each dinner, at 6 and 8:15 P.M. Special children's menus ensure happy children.

Each night of your cruise, dinner is organized around a different theme. The first night out is usually "A Stop in the Italian Riviera." On the second night, it's "An Evening in Paris." The night in Nassau is, appropriately, "The Caribbean Isles." The last night at sea is "A Salute to America the Beautiful."

ACTIVITIES

Two saltwater pools on the pool deck. When at Salt Cay, a beautiful spit of land where opening scenes for the old television show "Gilligan's Island" were filmed, a guided snorkeling expedition is available for an additional charge.

Health club with exercise equipment and a jogging track. Exercise classes are offered every morning. Once or twice during the cruise, the health club staff organizes a passenger Olympics.

Bingo games, scavenger hunts, pretend horse-racing competitions, trivia quizzes, talent shows, shuffleboard, costume parties, dance classes, ice-cream sundae socials, special teas for grandmothers and beer bashes for grandfathers, vegetable carving demonstrations, lectures about the Bahamas, and movies. Casino with slot machines, several blackjack tables, and a roulette wheel.

At night, the lounges hop with a variety of entertainment.

FOR CHILDREN: There are separate indoor play areas for children between 2 and 12 and teenagers, as well as a private open deck with great playground equipment, cute stationary riding toys, and a popular splash pool.

Scheduled kids' activities begin at 9 A.M. and end at 9:30 P.M., with breaks for meals with parents; group baby-sitting is available in Pluto's Playhouse from 9:30 P.M. to 1 A.M. for an hourly fee. Most parents use the program for just a few hours at a time.

The ship has up to 13 youth counselors, most of them cheerful young women who have had previous experience in child care. Children are usually divided into groups by age: "First Mates" for children 2 to 4; "Kids Call" for ages 5 to 7; "Starcruisers" for ages 8 to 12; and "Teen Cruisers" for ages 13 to 17.

The program begins with a "Coketail" party for parents and kids shortly before the ship embarks. The first evening, younger kids get acquainted with all the treats Pluto's Playhouse has to offer: hundreds of Lego blocks, waffle blocks, stuffed animals, puzzles, games, a video casette player, and arts and crafts materials.

The morning of the first full day often begins with cartoons, followed by a tour of the bridge. Then come "Disneycises" to use up energy, a scavenger hunt, kite flying, pool games, sundae building, movies, and a "Coketail" party with the captain.

Older children have video game competitions, go on scavenger hunts, play water basketball, make crafts and play games. Supervised beach activities are offered on Salt Cay.

Around 9:00 P.M., the counselors dim the lights, lay out mats, and give each child a blanket and a pillow to curl up with in front of a Disney video. In-room baby-sitting is available.

A separate lounge for children over 12 has a dance floor, jukebox, and video games, and is off limits to adults (the kids like it that way). There are some organized activities for this age group as well, particularly in the mornings and evenings. There's also a separate video game room near the casino.

NICETIES: All kids have a bagful of chocolate "ship" cookies awaiting them in their cabin.

The entire staff is extremely attentive and congenial. If your child doesn't like what he's ordered for dinner, another selection is brought to try to appease him.

The ship's doctor will make cabin calls.

OF INTEREST IN PORT: The ship is usually in Nassau for less than 24 hours on a three-day cruise, but with a little advance planning you can get a good taste of the city and visit attractions with special appeal for children. Should you wish to leave the children behind, the children's lounge remains open for supervised free play.

Private taxis can be hired rather inexpensively for a personal sightseeing tour. If you prefer to set out on your own on foot, a walking tour map is available at the tourist information office on the wharf. Children will enjoy walking up the 65 steps of the Queen's Staircase, which leads to another popular historical site, the ship-shaped Fort Fincastle.

Ardastra Gardens, a short taxi ride from downtown, is Nassau's private zoo; it features the only flamingos in the world that have been trained to march.

Coral World is a marine park and underwater observatory on Silver Cay. Children will enjoy watching the shark, stingray, and turtle tanks and observing action in the reef tank 20 feet under the sea.

Many passengers spend the only night in port at the casinos on Paradise Island; the children's playroom remains open late.

FOR MORE INFORMATION: See your travel agent.

M.S. *Starward*

Norwegian Cruise Line

Lower Caribbean Islands

Norwegian Cruise Line is one of the masters in the Caribbean cruise business. Its three- to seven-day cruises crisscross the Caribbean from the Bahamas to South America, and from Mexico to the West Indies, calling at 20 different ports. The line's ships range from a group of smaller ships in the 12,000- to 16,000-ton range—the *Skyward, Starward, Sunward, Southward,* and *Seaward*—to a mid-size ship, the *Westward*—to the *Norway,* the world's largest cruise ship and the flagship of the fleet.

We cruised out of San Juan, Puerto Rico, on the *Starward* for one week to the lower Caribbean islands of Barbados, Martinique, Antigua, St. Maarten, and St. Thomas. The line's other cruise ships begin in different ports, cruise for different lengths of time, and visit different islands. But the on-board amenities and programs of all the ships are similar.

The attractions of this particular cruise for families are the varied ports of call (there's a little bit of France, England, and the Netherlands to be experienced at these Caribbean stops, besides the exotica of the Caribbean itself); the extensive range of shore excursions and opportunities; the active children's program; and the luxuries and amenities that this quality cruise line provides to all passengers on all of its ships.

ACCOMMODATIONS: $$$ to $$$$ Norwegian Cruise Line has "one class" ships, with the staterooms varying very little in decor and amenities. All staterooms are above the water line. But rates reflect differences in location and whether there are portholes. Deluxe suites are much larger than standard rooms.

Rates include round-trip airfare from about 100 American cities to the port of embarkation. Passengers who do not require air transport can deduct $250 from the rates. Children occupying the third or fourth bed in a cabin are charged a flat rate.

The standard cabin on the *Starward* has a double bed or twin beds and a bunkbed that is stowed away during the day. The bunks are suitable for children, but a large teenager or adult would find them cramped. All cabins have private baths, with shower, and 110-volt electrical service to handle hair dryers, electric razors, and small travel irons.

Cabin service is excellent. Your steward will straighten up during the day, provide turn-down service at night, and make sure you have a constant supply of fresh towels for bathroom and pool.

DINING: The *Starward*, like most cruise ships, offers more food each day than any rational human would ever consider consuming: early-morning wake-up snacks, six-course breakfasts, luncheon buffets, afternoon teas with pastries and finger sandwiches, marvelous dinners, and a sumptuous midnight buffet.

Food quality on the *Starward* is excellent, and the variety astounding. Among the courses offered at every meal are "light options" for calorie watchers. Buffet breakfasts and lunches are always available in a poolside café.

Room service is available on all ships. When the ship is in port, you may take your meals in restaurants on shore (at your own expense) or return to the ship.

ACTIVITIES

 Two pools. Snorkeling instruction. The "Dive-In" program of snorkeling and scuba diving provides an underwater exploration of coral reefs on every stop. Fees include snorkeling equipment and diving vests. Persons who have never snorkeled receive instruction. Families with children aged 5 and up are welcome.

Early-morning fitness program, workout facilities. Basketball, Ping-Pong equipment.

Backgammon tournaments, beauty demonstrations, perfume and cosmetics seminar, lectures on the sightseeing possibilities in the next port of call, tours of the ship's bridge, arts and crafts classes, card and Ping-Pong tournaments, movies, trapshooting.

After dinner, the ship's nightclub starts up with a variety show of music, comedy, and magic, or the ship's entertainment staff puts on a comedy review. Casino, disco, movies.

FOR CHILDREN: The *Starward* offers supervised programs for both teenagers and younger children throughout the summer vacation months and over Thanksgiving, Christmas, and Easter holiday periods. The daily "Kid's Cruise News" or "Teen Cruise News" will keep you informed of activities for children. The stated minimum age for participation is 6, although the staff can sometimes be persuaded to allow mature 4- and 5-year-olds to participate. As many as 100 children are aboard during holiday periods.

While at sea, children's activities start after the second breakfast seating ends, at about 10 A.M. Activities include a tour of the captain's bridge, swimming pool games, bingo, scavenger hunts, drawing contests, movies, word games, ice-cream sessions, stories, and masquerade parties. On most cruises, children practice songs, dances, and magic tricks and perform a "Circus at Sea" for parents on one of the last nights of the cruise.

On some days, children eat lunch with parents; on others they eat with the children's program coordinators. Parents collect children at about 4 P.M. to prepare for dinner. Another one-hour session of the children's program usually meets later in the evening, between the two dinner sittings.

Teens have their own on-board program, with games, sports, and social events.

When the ship is in port, the children's program frequently goes ashore to spend a day at a beach or to do a half-day tour of a turtle farm or coral garden (fees charged).

Baby-sitting is not available.

There are no special facilities for children on the *Starward*. However, the S.S. *Norway* has a playroom specifically for children, Trolland, which is outfitted with play equipment, arts and crafts materials, and games. (The *Norway* also has a year-round children's program.)

NICETIES: Passengers can charge all drinks in the bar and dining room and settle up with the purser at the end of the cruise.

Every ship has a physician and nurse to handle medical needs that may arise. You'll also find a beauty salon–barbershop.

Let your dining room waiter know about birthdays and anniversaries in your family. A chorus of waiters will present a cake and sing for the honoree.

With the combined air/sea package, NCL staff members meet your flight, whisk away your baggage, and place it at your cabin door a few hours later. On the way back home, NCL takes your bag to customs and then puts it on your homeward flight.

OF INTEREST IN PORT: NCL offers up to a half dozen shore excursions in every port of call; separate fees are charged.

In each port, you always have the option of doing your own exploration. The excursion your family plans for itself may have a better mix of activities family members can enjoy together. Things we would have missed if we hadn't done some exploring on our own include: fun and games with the monkeys at the Wildlife Reserve in Barbados and the excellent history museum; a delightful swim in a freshwater pool, followed by a seafood lunch at the Leyritz Plantation, a hotel surrounded by fields of bananas high on the shoulders of Mount Pelée in Martinique; a tour of the Antigua History Museum led by Judi, a very knowledgeable 10-year-old; a delightful morning on strikingly beautiful and deserted Runaway Beach in Antigua.

FOR MORE INFORMATION: Contact your travel agent.

S.S. *Jubilee*
Carnival Cruise Lines
Mexican Riveria

More than any other American cruiseline, Carnival Cruise Lines has mastered the art of mass-market cruising. In 1991, the year its ninth "Fun Ship" entered service, the line sent more than one million happy campers off to sea. Its ships carry nearly twice as many passengers as the nearest competitor; fully one-fourth of all the North Americans who cruise in any given year go on a Carnival ship. Carnival must be doing something right.

What Carnival does for its passengers is to pack a 24-hour day with nearly 24 hours of activities. Its ships are sleek and well-maintained, its staff professional and friendly. Families are present on nearly every sailing. Over Christmas, the staff doesn't even blink at the prospect of having 500 chldren aboard.

The S.S. *Jubilee* is one of the few ships that ply the gorgeous waters of the Pacific off the coast of California, Baja California, and mainland Mexico. The other lines that cruise this route are Commodore and Princess (March through early May only.)

Part of the reason for Carnival's overwhelming success is that it maintains an even standard of quality of all its ships, from the older two—the *Mardi Gras* and *Carnivale,* which sail on three- and four-day cruises from Port Canaveral, Fla. to the Bahamas—to its new generation of seven superliners, which, in addition to the Pacific Coast itinerary, offer seven-day cruises to nearly every port in the Caribbean.

ACCOMMODATIONS: $$$ to $$$$ The *Jubilee* has 743 staterooms with a total capacity of 1,896 passengers. Most of the staterooms have twin beds that convert to king-size beds, and some also have one or two upper bunks that are perfect for children. Ten outside suites are available. The cabins are compact but not unpleasantly confining. A big plus are the large picture windows in most outside staterooms.

Children sharing a stateroom with their parents pay a flat rate that amounts to about half the lowest published, cruise-only full fare. Special "Fly Aweigh" rates include round-trip airfare to Los Angeles and transfers to the ship.

DINING: The food is topnotch and ample. There are only a few hours a day during which there's no scheduled eating, and even then, room service is available.

Early risers will find coffee and sweet rolls in the Funnel Bar & Grill. For breakfast, passengers can choose from a full menu in the dining room or go through the cafeteria line in the Funnel Bar & Grill, where an abbreviated menu is served and bathing suits are acceptable attire.

Coffee, tea and bouillon are served from 10 to 11 A.M. daily, followed a half-hour later by a buffet lunch in the Funnel Bar & Grill and sandwiches and chips by the main pool. Sit-down lunch is also served in the dining rooms.

Afternoon tea—sandwiches, cakes, and hot drinks—is served in the Speakeasy Lounge; for the younger set, there are ice-cream sundaes and cookies in the Funnel Bar & Grill. There's just enough time to dress for happy hour and the main sitting dinner. If you're still hungry after all this, you can try to stay awake for the late-night (around midnight) buffet, followed an hour later by the mini-buffet.

Both dining rooms—the Burgundy and the Bordeaux—are luxuriously appointed, and the menus are identical. Children are welcome to choose from the regular menu, but the waiters will offer sure-fire child-pleasers—hamburgers, hot dogs, and pizza—as well. High chairs and boosters are available.

Low-calorie alternatives are available at all meals, and some special diets can be accommodated with advance notice.

ACTIVITIES

Two saltwater pools on the Lido deck, one with a popular water slide (children must be 7 to use it). The saltwater wading pool on the Promenade Deck is a favorite spot with toddlers.

Gymnasium with exercise equipment, separate men's and women's saunas; exercise track. Daily aerobics classes and "walk-a-mile" activities while at sea. Carnival says its Nautica Spa program, which features such exotic body and facial treatments as ionothermie and cathiodermie therapies, is the most elaborate at sea.

Days at sea are filled with organized activities, from volleyball to bingo to travel and shop talks to lotto drawings to galley tours to pool games. At night, Las Vegas-style entertainment is offered in the Atlantis Lounge; sometimes, there's dancing to live music in the Terraces in the Grove Lounge. There's also a lot of organized silliness: pillow fights (between adults), male nightgown contests, and beer-drinking contests.

For some solitude, stake out a deck chair on one of the open decks and watch the sea pass by. If you run out of reading material, you can borrow a book from Churchill's Library.

FOR CHILDREN: The *Jubilee*, like all the Carnival ships, offers supervised children's activities on all sailings year-round, whether there are 10 kids on board or 500. It also has a special playroom, well-stocked with games and toys, where many children's activities are held.

The line's "Camp Carnival" is staffed by 22 permanent counselors or children's coordinators, who rotate among the ships as bookings demand. During the summer and school holidays, they are augmented by temporary employees with child-care experience.

Separate activities are offered for 4- to 7-year-olds, 8- to 12-year-olds, and teens. On a typical day at sea, the younger children will meet for an hour in the morning for a ship-drawing contest and a video game competition. After lunch with their parents, the kids will reconvene for a half hour of games, followed by a scavenger hunt and some more play time in the playroom. After dinner, there's a spirited hour-long game of "Win, Lose or Draw," a movie, or a kiddie disco.

Teens are kept busy with "Name that Tune" contests, Ping-Pong tournaments, bingo (for crazy prizes), and disco parties.

Baby-sitting can be arranged in the playroom for a fee in the evening and during days when the ship is in port. No baby-sitting can be arranged during scheduled children's activities.

Children under 4 may join in the children's activities if accompanied by an adult. Babies under 4 months are not permitted on the ship.

NICETIES: The dining room waiters and busboys will delight your children by creating comical animal puppets out of napkins. They are also great about serving children quickly.

Complimentary hors d'oeuvres are served during the cocktail hour on most of the nights at sea.

OF INTEREST IN PORT: The *Jubilee*'s first stop, after two days at sea, is Puerto Vallarta, where it docks from 8 A.M. to 10 P.M. The ship offers a four-hour tour, for a fee, to the picturesque town of Mismaloya, where "Night of the Iguana" was shot. On your own, you can stroll Puerta Vallarta's stone-paved streets, stopping in a cantina for a margarita and bargaining for handicrafts in the town market, which is at the northern end of the upstream bridge over the Rio Cuale. Or you can just spend the day at the beach.

The next day, after turning northward, the ship pulls into Mazatlan at 9 A.M. for a nine-hour stay. The ship offers a three and a half hour city tour and beach and shopping expedition. Or you can visit the Mazatlan Aquarium on your own or loll on the beach (Playas Norte, Sabalo Camarones, and Las Gaviotas are the most popular).

After an overnight voyage, the ship anchors offshore at Cabo San Lucas, for a five-hour stop, tidal conditions permitting. Here, if you're lucky, you'll see whales and sea lions at play in the water.

The ship offers a two-hour glass bottom boat trip and restaurant tour. You can also amble around the village on your own, if you like.

It's a full day-and-a-half sail back to Los Angeles, where the ship docks at 9 A.M. Sunday.

FOR MORE INFORMATION: Contact your travel agent.

ALASKA

M.S. *Westerdam*
Holland America Line
Inside Passage from Vancouver to Alaska

In the Alaska cruise market, one cruise line is pre-eminent: the Holland America Line. One of the oldest cruise lines in the world, Holland America was the first to introduce tourists to Alaska, the last frontier, in 1947, and it's been operating cruises through the Inside Passage ever since. More than 100,000 travelers, including 2,000 children, see Alaska every year under the auspices of Holland America or its land-tour subsidiary, Holland America Westours.

The M.S. *Westerdam* leaves Vancouver on Saturdays for seven-day cruises through the Inside Passage to Ketchikan, Juneau, Glacier Bay National Park, and Sitka, and then back to Vancouver. Some passengers disembark in Juneau for extended land excursions, but most families stay on board to complete the round-trip.

On a cruise to Alaska, the scenery is the thing. You may find it difficult to leave the deck for meals, let alone bingo games, for fear of missing a sighting of a humpback whale, or yet another glorious fjord. Holland America recognizes that travelers who choose an Alaska cruise for their vacation have a special interest in the state's flora and fauna, so a naturalist is on board every one of its Alaska cruises.

The *Westerdam* and its sister ships, the M.S. *Nieuw Amsterdam*, M.S. *Noordam*, and the S.S. *Rotterdam*, make 69 cruises to Alaska from May to September. The *Westerdam*, *Nieuw Amsterdam*, and *Noordam* cruise the Inside Passage, the intracoastal waterway protected from the open Pacific Ocean by a multitude of scenic islands. The *Rotterdam* generally makes seven- and 14-day cruises along the

Glacier Route, which passes by some of Alaska's most magnificent glaciers. The line's officers are all Dutch and the crews Indonesian and Filipino.

Other lines that offer cruises along these routes are Princess, Costa, Cunard, Regency, Royal Caribbean, Royal Viking, and World Explorer. Holland America also offers cruises to the Caribbean in the winter.

ACCOMMODATIONS: $$$ to $$$$ At 52,000 gross tons, the *Westerdam* is a large ship, with about 750 staterooms and a capacity of about 1,500 passengers, not counting those occupying upper berths. Staterooms range from compact cubicles to suites. All are equipped with televisions, telephones, multi-channel music, and private bathrooms. Those suitable for families have either sofa beds or Pullman beds. Adjoining cabins are available.

Up to two children sharing a stateroom with two adults pay the third and fourth person rates. A child sharing with one adult pays half the regular fare. Children under 2 sharing with two full-fare adults sail for $199 each.

Discounted airfare to Vancouver is available through Holland America.

DINING: Meals are served in the Amsterdam Dining Room or the more informal Lido or Verandah restaurants. There are open seatings for breakfast, which is served at 8 A.M., and lunch, which is served at noon, and two seatings for dinner: 6 and 8 P.M. Families can request to be seated alone or in a larger group.

Children will enjoy eating some meals at the Lido buffet restaurant or at the portable buffet bars outside on the Lido deck. There they'll find make-it-yourself pasta dishes, tacos, nachos, hamburgers, sandwiches, and gourmet sausages.

The ship's chef is a member of the exclusive *Confrerie de la Chaine des Rotisseurs*, so the meals are excellent. You'll find such tried and true favorites as prime rib and Cornish game hen as well as seafood from Pacific Northwest waters, including Alaskan king crab legs.

ACTIVITIES

 Two outdoor pools, one with a sliding glass roof.

 Health spa and fitness center with exercise equipment; aerobics classes. Two tennis courts.

The ship's naturalist gives at least two lectures during the week and provides an interesting narrative over the ship's public address system when the ship is passing particularly scenic points. Between sightseeing stints on the deck, you can play shuffleboard or jackpot bingo, feed the ship's slot machines, or stop by classes on topics ranging from bridge to blackjack.

At night, you can be entertained by world-class singers, dancers, comedians, and illusionists or dance to the music of big bands, orchestras, or combos. Current hit movies are shown in the ship's theater. The ship library, with a good selection of books on Alaska, provides a quiet spot for reading or card playing.

FOR CHILDREN: Because of the high historical, scenic, and cultural content, a cruise to Alaska is usually wasted on very young children. But school-age children will be very interested in the geology, geography, history, and wildlife of Alaska and can be taken to the naturalist's talks and included in the scenery-watching on deck.

Children are welcome on almost all the shore excursions and receive discounted rates.

During the three days when the ship is at sea, the youth counselor organizes about three hours of activities a day for children, custom-tailoring them to the ages and interests of the children on board. The activities include games, sports contests, scavenger hunts, a pizza party, a "Coketail" party, coloring contests and show-and-tell time.

The *Westerdam* has a children's video arcade, "The Big Apple," with a small dance floor for evening parties. Baby-sitting by staff members can be arranged.

High chairs, booster seats or cribs should be reserved at the time of booking. Freshly made or commercially prepared baby food can also be requested in advance.

NICETIES: In addition to the ship's naturalist, a ranger from the National Park Service is on board during the cruise through Glacier Bay National Park.

The ship has both a self-service laundry and professional dry-cleaning and laundry services.

OF INTEREST IN PORT: The ship departs Vancouver at 5:45 P.M. and arrives in Ketchikan at 8 A.M. on its second full day out for a seven-hour stay. Ketchikan began as a Tlingit Indian summer fishing camp and now makes its living from mining and forestry as well as commercial fishing. Shore excursions include a chartered fishing trip, a flight on a float plane to Misty Fjords National Monument, and a mountain lake canoe trip. On a walking tour of the city, you can visit Creek Street, where the houses are built on pilings, the Ketchikan Historical Museum, with its display of pioneer memorabilia and early Indian artifacts, and the Totem Heritage Cultural Center, which has preserved totem poles from Tlingit and Haida Indian villages.

On Day four the ship docks in Juneau, Alaska's capital, at 8 A.M. You'll have time before the midnight departure for a helicopter excursion to the Mendenhall Glacier, which is well worth the expense, or a five-miles raft trip down the Mendenhall River. Another alternative is a cruise up Lynn Canal to Skagway, with a return by plane over the Tongass National Forest. And the Gold Creek salmon-bake offers good food and a chance to explore an abandoned gold mine.

After leaving Juneau, you'll spend a day cruising Glacier Bay. Be sure and stake out a good viewing spot on the deck, because the scenery is fantastic. The ship will pass by spires, pinnacles, and pillars of ice, with seals sliding in and out of view and eagles soaring overhead.

Then it's on to Sitka for a six-hour stop. There you'll see the Russian influence everywhere—in the 18th-century icons of St. Michael's Cathedral, in the Russian Bishop's House, and in the performances of the New Archangel Dancers. You can also watch Tlingit artists demonstrate totem carving at the Sitka National Historic Park and view the collection of Indian and Russian artifacts at the Sheldon

Jackson Museum. The adventuresome will want to take the Zodiac raft tour of the offshore islands.

After leaving Sitka, the ship will turn back toward Vancouver. You'll spend a day-and-a-half cruising the Inside Passage. Again, a good spot on the deck is imperative for the best views of the rustic lumber camps, fishing villages, and majestic fjords that you pass.

FOR MORE INFORMATION: Contact your travel agent.

HAWAII

S.S. *Constitution* and S.S. *Independence*
American Hawaii Cruises & Land Vacations
Hawaiian Islands

The waters surrounding the Hawaiian islands are perfect for cruising. The climate is, of course, deliciously tropical, and every island is attractive and unique. The smell of frangipani wafts through the air. Humpback whales can even be spotted from the ship's deck at times.

American Hawaii Cruises & Land Vacations is the major cruise operator in the Hawaiian Islands. Its sister ships, the S.S. *Constitution* and the S.S. *Independence*, have been cruising Hawaii since the early 1980s and are the only major cruise ships sailing anywhere under the American flag with all-American crews.

The ships themselves are a treat for anyone interested in the history of water travel. Both were launched in the early 1950s for the trans-Atlantic passenger trade. Each longer than two football fields and with graceful lines, these former North Atlantic speed demons carried politicians, movie stars, and tourists between New York and Southampton until sidelined by the rise of jet travel. Both ships have been completely refurbished for the cruise trade, but they retain their historical allure.

The ships travel the same route, but in opposite directions. They depart Honolulu on Saturday evenings and visit ports on Maui, Hawaii, and Kauai.

The major Hawaiian islands are relatively close together, so there is only one full day at sea (Sunday) in a seven-day itinerary. The ships travel between islands at night, dock first thing in the morning, and depart for the next port between 6 P.M. and 9 P.M.

ACCOMMODATIONS: $$$$ Each ship's capacity is 798 passengers. Staterooms range from deluxe outside suites to budget inside cabins, each with a private tub or shower and toilet. Sleeping configurations include double, king, and twin beds, and upper berths. All are decorated in light pastels. Many of the outside staterooms have large picture windows. Some two-room suites have king-sized beds and marble bathrooms. Cribs should be requested in advance.

Among the packages American Hawaii offers are the seven-day cruise, three-day cruise and four-day hotel, and four-day cruise and three-day hotel combinations. The cruise line also offers optional vacation extensions in luxury hotels at special rates.

From mid-June through mid-September, children 16 and under travel for free when staying with two full-fare adults in certain cabin categories; free children's fares are also sometimes offered during Easter and Thanksgiving week sailings when booked by July 31. At other times, children pay a flat rate equal to less than half the lowest adult published fare. Reduced airfares are available from most U.S. cities.

DINING: Cruises are famous for food, and the *Constitution* and *Independence* are no exceptions. The feasting begins with an early buffet breakfast on deck and continues through regular breakfast, lunch, late afternoon tea, dinner, and a late-night buffet.

At each meal there's a choice of traditional American and continental favorites, plus at least one Polynesian-influenced offering, such as Kona coffee lamb noisette, mahi-mahi Polynesian style, and chocolate macadamia nut cream pie. The Hawaiian pupu plate, offered on Polynesian night, includes smoked marlin, Hawaiian prawns, and scallops. Fresh papaya and pineapple are always available. Kona coffee is served at every meal. Each dinner revolves around a different theme.

The options at every meal include a selection of health-conscious items that are clearly marked.

ACTIVITIES

 Two fresh water pools on two different decks. While in port, you can swim at a beach.

▨ The ships' health and fitness centers open at 6 A.M.; each has state-of-the-art exercise equipment, free weights, and workout mats. Staff members lead early risers in a mile walk around the deck at a brisk pace. Aerobics and water exercise classes; massage available.

▨ The daily newsletter, "Tradewinds," lists a panoply of traditional cruise activities (except for gambling): cards, reading, games, crafts, films, quizzes, trivia contests, musical reviews, comedians, talent shows, and dancing. A nice extra is the emphasis on Hawaiian culture and heritage. Passengers can learn the hula, take ukulele lessons, make their own leis, weave with coconut palms, and take Hawaiian language lessons. The nightly entertainment is frequently Polynesian as well. On selected cruises, a naturalist travels along and lectures on the native flora and fauna, including whales.

FOR CHILDREN: Both the *Constitution* and *Independence* have children's and teens' programs. Each also has a video arcade and Youth Recreation Center.

The program for 5- to 12-year-olds begins at 8 A.M. with breakfast and includes beach parties and games at the swimming pool, scavenger hunts, Ping-Pong, putt-putt golf, bingo, hula lessons, movies, crafts, dancing, shuffleboard, and parties. Thirteen- to 17-year-olds have pool parties, dances, mystery games, talk shows, and a junior olympics. Activities in both programs end at 10 P.M. Parents pick up children for lunch and dinner.

NICETIES: The lava flow that has been active on the Big Island of Hawaii since 1983 may be visible as your ship glides by in the dark. The Purser's office will be happy to arrange a wake-up call so that you may view it.

Children receive pictures of their group prior to docking in Honolulu at the end of the cruise.

OF INTEREST IN PORT: You might try a mix of organized shore excursions (each ship offers 45, for an extra charge) and your own family explorations. The kitchen staff will pack a picnic lunch.

Rental cars can be arranged at the ship's shore excursion office or on your own at each port of call.

The outdoor-loving family will find many good hiking trails on every island. On the island of Hawaii, the most interesting walks are in Volcanoes National Park. On Maui, the best walks are on the flanks of Haleakala in Haleakala National Park. On Kauai, the legendary Kalalua Trail traverses the Na Pali Coast; you'll also find good hiking trails in Waimea Canyon in Kokee State Park.

Temple sites, the only vestiges of ancient native Hawaiian architecture to survive, dot the islands. One of the most interesting is at Puuhonua O Honaunau National Historical Park on the Kona coast of the Island of Hawaii.

On Oahu, don't miss the Bishop Museum in Honolulu, which houses one of the world's best collections of artifacts from the Pacific Islands, and Brigham Young University's Polynesian Cultural Center. At Sea Life Park you can learn about the undersea world. The Arizona Memorial in Pearl Harbor is a sobering reminder of the price of war.

Among the ships' shore excursions that are of most interest to families are Zodiac raft adventures off the coast of Kauai, snorkeling and sailing near Kona, and bicycling down Haleakala. Children's rates are available.

FOR MORE INFORMATION: Contact your travel agent or phone (800) 765-7000 for a brochure.

1. On a white-water raft trip on the New River in West Virginia, children can accompany their parents on the calmer sections. *(Photo: Dept. of Commerce, Charleston, WV)* **2.** Children of all ages will love the thrill of a family sailing adventure in the Apostle Islands. *(Photo: Martha Shirk)* **3.** The wagon train trips through the Flint Hills of Kansas give families a sense of life as 19th-century pioneers of the Old West. *(Photo: Kansas Division of Travel and Tourism)* **4.** Families on a raft trip with Dvorak Expeditions take a break in a natural hot spring along the Colorado River. *(Photo: Martha Shirk)* **5.** Llama trekking in the Big Horn Mountains in Sheridan, Wyoming, allows families to explore the wilderness of the Bighorn National Forest. *(Photo: Wyoming Travel Commission)*

ADVENTURE
TRIPS

3

4

5

NORTHEAST

Chewonki Wilderness Trips
Wiscasset, Maine

The Chewonki Foundation is a leader in natural history and conservation education, having shaped the environmental commitment and leadership skills of four generations of American youth. The Chewonki summer camp for boys, begun in 1915, still thrives as the oldest ecologically oriented camp in the country. Its alumni include Roger Tory Peterson and Kingman Brewster; Rachel Carson sent her nephew there. Happily, in recent years the Chewonki program has expanded in many other directions with workshops, wilderness trips and expeditions, school semester and outreach programs, and environmental education programs for families.

The Chewonki experience has as its starting point an encounter with nature, whether on a canoe, sailing or hiking trip, or in a natural history workshop. One outcome is a greater understanding and appreciation of our natural environment. But the Chewonki experience is more. Through the skill of the Chewonki staff, these encounters with nature challenge participants individually and as a group through observation, problem solving, communication, and decision making. The result is a sense of community and a growth in personal insight and self-confidence.

Chewonki programs operate in every month of the year, but the programs specifically designed for families are scheduled during summer months. Participants range from elementary students to retirees, and include individuals as well as family groups.

Chewonki takes the great out-of-doors as its classroom. Headquarters are 400 acres of beautiful, heavily wooded peninsula not far from Wiscasset, Maine. Chewonki's wilderness trips start here, but Chewonki utilizes all of Maine for its outdoor adventures. Various trips explore the spectacular coast, mountains, forests, and streams of Maine. Chewonki trips vary in length, type, degree of challenge, and emphasis. Groups of 8 to 12 are encouraged to organize themselves and approach Chewonki to design a trip of length, type, challenge, and emphasis, that will serve that particular group. Trips can be tailormade to the needs of a particular group of individuals or families. Samples of trips scheduled in recent years include the following:

- Ten days on the Allagash River in the Allagash Wilderness Waterway, with both lake and river paddling, from Telos Lake to the town of Allagash.

- Seven days on the St. Croix River from Vanceboro to Grand Lake, Big Lake, and West Grand Lake.

- A seven-day lake and river-paddling trip in the Penobscot West Branch including Lobster Lake, Black Pond, and Caucomgomac Lake.

- A sailing and rowing trip among the Maine islands in traditional boats built at Chewonki.

- A six-day hiking trip in beautiful Baxter State Park, including a climb of Mt. Katahdin.

- A seven-day sea kayak trip from Chewonki Neck downeast to Muscongus Bay or beyond, depending on weather conditions.

THE OUTFITTER: The Chewonki Foundation is a tight-knit community made up of people with shared values and beliefs. Of the full-time staff of 42, 20 are environmental educators. Most have formal training in ecology or environmental education, and all are experienced educators and skilled in the ways of the out-of-doors.

THE ITINERARY: Each Chewonki trip is unique, but with some common themes. One theme is environmental education. Throughout each trip, Chewonki leaders teach trip members about the local ecology, through both formal lectures and hands-on observation. For example, the leaders will include a night walk for children. The group walks with a leader to a spot in the woods, then sits quietly in the dark and listens. Children hear a porcupine walking nearby, flying squirrels jumping from branch to branch, bats in search of insects, an owl's hoot, the distant cry of gulls, and some rustling sounds that can't be identified.

Every Chewonki trip produces a journal that represents the combined efforts of the group. Group members take responsibility for recording a day's activities or a special event. Poems, recipes, drawings, and short essays are included. Children too young to write contribute drawings. Finally, names and address are added, and the resulting record of the trip or workshop is photocopied and distributed to all group members.

A journal entry from a week-long sailing/rowing trip from Jonesport to Northeast Harbor tells of the camaraderie the group feels with a group of curious dolphins that circled the boat so closely that their breathing could be heard.

The journal is not just a souvenir, but another mechanism for learning. In addition to recording the details of the environment around them, group members record their personal reactions to the environment, their reactions to the trip or workshop as a group process, and their reactions to other members of the group.

The idea of sharing carries over into the daily chores involved in setting up camps, preparing meals, and cleaning up. Chewonki counselors do not take on the role of outdoor servants who do all the grunt work. Rather, work that supports the welfare of the group is a shared responsibility.

Another important part of a Chewonki experience is the food. Good nutrition is part of the Chewonki creed. Rather than load up backpacks and boxes with highly processed dehydrated foods, Chewonki trips carry the real thing—vegetables, whole-grain cereals, flour, and fresh meat for the first day or two of the trip. Chewonki staff members show group members how to cook in the out-of-doors over open fires, and everybody shares in the cooking chores. The results are gratifying: pancakes for breakfast, delicious sandwiches for lunch, stir-fry dishes for dinner, and a cake from the reflector oven or biscuits from the Dutch oven.

Each night the group gathers around a fire to exchange experiences and reflections on the day and sing. On every trip a staff member brings a musical instrument of some sort.

FOR CHILDREN: The canoeing, hiking, and sailing trips are suitable for any capable age. The guiding rule for all Chewonki activities is capability. No one is excluded from any activity by age or lack of previous experience. Chewonki requires only that participants be physically capable of engaging in the activities that are necessarily part of a trip.

RATES AND PERSONAL GEAR: $ Costs vary based on the itinerary and each group's special needs. Rates include meals and all general camping equipment, such as tents, cooking equipment, saws, axes, and the special equipment required for any trip, such as canoes, paddles, life jackets, and the like. Families bring their own sleeping bags, packs, and clothing. Detailed equipment lists appropriate for anticipated trip conditions are sent to all participants well ahead of departure. Reservations are advisable four months in advance.

Since all Chewonki trips involve close encounters with nature, appropriate clothing is a must—good shoes for hiking, shoes for wading, warm clothes for cool Maine nights, and good rain gear.

FOR MORE INFORMATION: Write Chewonki Foundation, RR 2, Box 1200, Wiscasset, ME 04578, or call (207) 882-7323.

Maine Windjammer Cruise
Penobscot Bay, Maine

Since the early 1970s, the jagged coast of Maine has become one of America's favorite summer playgrounds. Water, sun, delightfully cool summer weather, great scenery, and marvelous seafood all contribute to the Maine experience. But popularity has its price. In the summer invasion of the Maine coast, tourists fight monumental traffic jams on U.S. 1 to crowd into hotels and restaurants.

A cruise on a windjammer is the answer for families who want to get away from it all on the Maine coast. A vacation on one of these great sailing ships combines solitude, history, adventure, relaxation, good food, and wonderful scenery in half-week or full-week sails among the islands off the coast of Maine.

America's rich maritime history comes alive on an authentic coastal schooner. Many of the ships in the Maine Windjammer Association fleet date from the turn of the century—the golden age of sail when "coasters" dominated the eastern seaboard, engaged in the work of fishing and hauling cargo and passengers.

Most Maine windjammers are schooners—an American sailing craft specially rigged to accommodate the variable winds off American coasts. Schooners have great maneuverability, allowing the craft to change course quickly and to sail equally well on either tack without lowering or resetting sails.

The oldest ships in the Maine windjammer fleet were built more than 100 years ago. The newest were inspired by the traditional boats and were built as recently as the 1980s specifically for the Maine vacation trade. Every boat in the fleet is U.S. Coast Guard inspected and carries a ship-to-shore radio. The boats range in length from 64 to 132 feet.

THE OUTFITTER: The Maine Windjammer Association got its start in the 1930s, when steamships and railroads were putting schooners out of business. The idea of windjammer cruises for pleasure was conceived on Maine's Penobscot Bay. Thus began the tradition of renovating historic vessels for safe, comfortable passenger travel. Today the Maine Windjammer Association is made up of individual and family owners of 12 ships.

Originally designed for fishing or cargo hauling, the renovated boats in the Maine windjammer fleet have been completely refitted below decks with galleys, comfortable guest cabins, and heads (toilets). Each boat accommodates 22 to 44 passengers in cabins that sleep one to four persons. Electric lights and portholes are standard features in the cabins of most boats in the fleet. Galleys are warm cozy spaces with varnished tables close by the cook's area.

Windjammer accommodations are comfortable, but not luxurious. The food is first rate. The crew rises long before first light to bake a breakfast treat for you to enjoy when you climb to the deck in the morning. On most of the windjammers the cooking, including fresh-baked breads and pastries, is done on wood-burning stoves.

From the ovens and the frying pans and pots on the wood-burning stove come breakfasts of pancakes, blueberry muffins, eggs, and bacon; lunches of chili, chowders, corn bread, and cookies; and dinners of fresh fish, turkey, breads, pies, and cakes. A lobster feast or roast turkey dinner are the culinary highlights of the week.

Meals are served family style. The "buffet deck" is the choice in good, warm weather. The long varnished tables in the galley are the scene for breakfast, special dinners, and for all meals in cool or rainy weather.

THE ITINERARY: Before sailing, the captain holds an informal meeting to familiarize all passengers with the ship and with safety procedures; a welcome-aboard get-together follows. Sailing time is usually set for late morning. Your ship is slowly towed out of the harbor at Camden or Rockland past rows of smaller boats. As your vessel clears the channel markers, the motor of the tug is silenced. The sails are raised, and you move backward in time. The shapes of modern society—buildings, cars, and such—recede and disappear into the beauty of the Maine coast.

This is not like a cruise on an ocean liner; there are no schedules with a half dozen activities to choose from every hour, nor is there a staff of social directors. On a windjammer, there are no pressures, schedules, or deadlines, no phones, no television sets. Instead, you can lie on the deck and watch clouds drift above the wind-tautened sails. Stand at the rail as your vessel silently treads the narrow passage between uninhabited islands. Watch and listen to the sea as it constantly changes with the weather and time of day. Soak up the sun. Read the books you've been storing up. Play chess or Scrabble or cards. Get to know the other passengers on the boat.

A chance pass by another windjammer results in a flurry of picture taking and perhaps a spontaneous "race." Fishermen can troll from the stern of the boat. Nature lovers will be on the lookout for eagles, diving cormorants, and the occasional minke whale. The captain will let you take the helm and show you how he or she navigates among the islands sprinkled along the Maine coast. The crew needs help each morning in raising the nearly half-ton anchor and in hauling up the sails (if you're a late riser, you'll get a second chance to help in the evening). The cook always has vegetables and salad ingredients to prepare and cookie batter to mix.

In the late afternoon, the captain consults the charts and selects a safe anchorage in an island cove or small village harbor. When the sails are down, but before the air temperature drops, the hearty swimmers in the party will do laps around the boat. The dinghy will be lowered into the water so that photographers and sightseers can row out to explore the surrounding shores and take photographs of the windjammer against the setting sun. The general store at the nearby village may be the objective of others.

After dinner, passengers either gather to tell stories and sing to the accompaniment of instruments that passengers and crew have brought on board or sit on the deck talking quietly or gazing upward at an unrivaled display of stars.

FOR CHILDREN: The relaxed pace of shipboard life and the desire on the part of most guests to experience the quiet and solitude of sailing mean that windjammer trips are most appropriate for families with older children. If you want to take a windjammer trip with children less than 14 years of age, check with the captain first. The *Nathaniel Bowditch* (800-288-4098) accommodates children over 8 years old, accompanied by an adult.

RATES AND PERSONAL GEAR: $$$ Rates are comparable on all boats in the fleet. The peak season is July and August. Rates are somewhat lower in June and September, when wind and weather are often ideal for sailing. Rates include all meals and parking for your car.

Dress on the ships is casual, with no dress-up clothes required. Some guests like to bring along small musical instruments so they can contribute to the entertainment at night. Passengers wishing to drink carbonated beverages, beer, wine, or liquor must bring their own; large ice chests are provided. You'll certainly want to bring a camera and a pair of binoculars.

OF INTEREST NEARBY: En route to the Penobscot Bay area (a two- or three-hour drive from Portland), consider visiting some of the attractions of coastal Maine. Wiscasset has one of the finest groups of colonial era buildings in the country. The Maine Maritime Museum and Sewall House Mansion in Bath recall the age of sail in the United States. Boothbay is the site of the Railway Village and the Marine Resources Aquarium, with its touch tanks and tidepools. Pemaquid, near Bristol, was one of the earliest settlements in North America and is still one of the most picturesque; its small museum is worth a visit. Rockport has Shore Village Museum, a transportation museum, and historic Owls Head Light. Camden Hills State Park near Camden boasts Mount Megunticook, the highest point along the Atlantic seaboard.

FOR MORE INFORMATION: Write the Maine Windjammer Association, P.O. Box 317P, Rockport, ME 04856, or phone (800) 624-6380.

Hiking Inn to Inn
Vermont's Long Trail
Brandon, Vermont

For generations, families of hikers have been able to hike through the mountains of Europe, stopping in strategically placed huts overnight and resuming their trek the next day. In the early 1970s, the innkeepers of Vermont found a way to improve on the European system. They began offering custom-planned hikes through Vermont's Green Mountains with overnight stops not in rustic huts, but in quaint country inns. For a family that is enthusiastic about hiking —but not about carrying tons of gear or pitching a tent and eating freeze-dried food at the end of a long day—the Hiking Inn to Inn program offers a marvelous opportunity to hike in relative luxury, while someone else does most of the work.

The Hiking Inn to Inn program is characterized by personal attention, good food, and flexibility. The inns provide elegance and comfort after a day's hike. And the variety of hiking trails in the Green Mountain National Forest, as well as the Long Trail, and other activities available in the area—bicycling, canoeing, fishing, and horseback riding, for instance—make the program suitable for almost all ages.

The Green Mountain region, once part of a vast inland sea, is rugged, with sharp crests and generally steep slopes. The lower slopes of the Green Mountains are covered with northern hardwoods, with sugar maple and beech the dominant species. Between 2,400 feet and 3,000 feet, red spruce and balsam fir dominate, with the concentration of balsam fir increasing with the elevation. There are many mountain summits that reveal views that make the climb invariably worthwhile.

The inns, 12 in all, are located along a 100-mile section of Vermont's Long Trail, which runs on a north-south axis along the ridge line of the Green Mountains. The trail extends some 265 miles from the Massachusetts state line to the Canadian border. In addition, there are some 100 side trails that add about 175 miles of hiking opportunities, making the entire trail system about 440 miles long.

As an alternative to hiking inn to inn, you might want to consider bicycling or cross-country skiing inn to inn.

THE ITINERARY: All hikes are self-guided and custom-tailored to your hiking ability, energy level, and time commitment. As soon as you sign up for the program, the organizers begin to plan your route. Trips can be of any desired length, starting with several days. For casual hikers, the organizers suggest spending two nights at each inn, which lessens the daily chore of packing up and moving on and also allows time for more sightseeing.

Each day, hikers are presented with several alternative hiking routes, oriented to hazards on the trail, and given trail maps.

Each inn is assigned a segment of the trail; a daily car shuttle travels to specified points to enable hikers to move their baggage. Early in the morning, hikers pack everything that they will not need for the day's hike and drive their cars to the day's trail-end. The innkeeper returns them to the inn for breakfast, and later takes them to the beginning of the segment of the trail they will hike that day. In some cases, the trails can be picked up at the back of the inns.

For the most part, the Long Trail is a wilderness trail, and some of it is steep, boggy, and rugged. Hiking on the southern portions of the trail is the easiest, quite manageable even for 12-year-olds. Farther north, the trail becomes more challenging; at Camel's Hump, it reaches over 4,000 feet. By design, the Long Trail has been kept as a "footpath in the wilderness"; no artificial surfaces have been used, and no switchbacks built.

The inns vary in size and ambience; their variety is part of the fun. Mountain Meadows Lodge is the largest, with accommodations for 70 during the ski season and 45 during summer and fall. Long Run Inn (capacity 16) is an older lumberjack hotel in the small town of Lincoln, across the road from the New Haven River. Mountain Meadows Lodge overlooks a small lake; it was a working farm, and the barn and farmhouse have been converted into guest rooms. Churchill House, a century-old farmhouse, has a small pool and provides bicycles for rental. Blueberry Hill, which can accommodate 45 guests, is an exquisitely restored 1813 farmhouse. Waitsfield Inn, Pittsfield Inn, Tucker Hill Lodge, Chipman Inn, Camel Hump View Farm, Marble West, Silas Griffith, and Wallingford Inn also share similar reputations for pleasant accommodations, fine cuisine, and a congenial atmosphere.

All of the inns provide a gracious and personal welcome. There are no telephones, bedside radios, or private television sets. There are books and pleasant surroundings, and opportunities, after a gourmet dinner, to share the day's experiences with fellow hikers.

FOR CHILDREN: Children under 12 are not encouraged to hike the Long Trail, unless they are seasoned hikers. But there are plenty of other things for families with younger children to do in the area while one parent and the older kids hike: shorter, less demanding hikes, biking, canoeing, swimming, and horseback riding. Many local farms permit visitors.

Another attraction is the University of Vermont Morgan Horse Farm just outside of Middlebury, which provides guided tours of its stables. During the summer, Branbury State Park, at Lake Dunmore near Brandon, has a daily naturalist program with guided nature walks and a small nature museum.

The inns each have different minimum ages for guests.

RATES AND PERSONAL GEAR: $ to $$ The hiking season begins mid-May and continues through the third week of October. During peak periods, reservations are difficult to make at some of the inns. Rates include lodging, dinners, breakfasts, packed trail lunches, car shuttle, taxes, and gratuities. Lois Jackson at Churchill House Inn takes reservations and coordinates the program. Ask whether special rates can be provided for children.

Hikers are advised to bring a day pack, two pairs of sturdy hiking shoes (the trail can be boggy and wet, and the first pair may not dry out overnight); cushion socks, thin liner socks, lightweight rain gear, insect repellent, and a small water bottle or canteen. The inn-keepers advise against Vibram-soled boots because of the damage they do to the trails. We found long pants more comfortable than shorts because of the bugs and underbrush.

The inns are informal; dress-up clothes are not required.

FOR MORE INFORMATION: Write Churchill House Inn, R.R. 3, Box 3265-SFV, Brandon, VT 05733, or telephone (802) 247-3300.

SOUTHEAST

Cumberland Island Camping Adventure
Cumberland Island, Georgia

"Geologic Gussie," "Nudibranch Nancy," "Jungle Jim!" No, these are not endangered species, but participants in a Wilderness Southeast camping adventure as they introduced themselves on disembarking from a ferry at Cumberland Island National Seashore off the coast of Georgia.

This unusual round of introductions fits with the philosophy of Wilderness Southeast, a non-profit education corporation whose programs emphasize learning about the natural world in a fun, exciting, and non-stressful way. Wilderness Southeast runs trips for families and individuals that encourage participants to look at nature, the environment, and themselves in new ways.

Cumberland Island National Seashore, with its rich social and natural history, is a perfect destination for families. Cumberland is the southernmost and largest of Georgia's barrier islands. It is 18 miles long and three miles across at its widest point; the occasional sand dune reaches 50 feet above sea level. The land varies from beaches and dunes, to live oak forests, to freshwater ponds and salt marshes.

Although it has felt the impact of society's presence, most of the island is wild and uninhabited, with many distinct habitats. Congress guaranteed their preservation when it established the Cumberland Island National Seashore in 1972; 85 percent of the island is designated part of the national seashore.

THE OUTFITTER: Wilderness Southeast was founded in 1973 by ecologists Dick and Joyce Murlless as a not-for-profit "school of the outdoors," with the belief that learning about nature should be comfortable and fun. The organization's board of directors is sprinkled with naturalist writers and educators, and the staff is composed of naturalist educators.

Wilderness Southeast offers quality outdoor experiences throughout the Southeast for those who seek something beyond a luxury tour. Campers are made comfortable, but not pampered; they are invited to live with nature, not conquer or endure it. Trip leaders are experienced naturalists who put heart and soul into maximizing a camper's contact with nature while relieving him or her of the chores of wilderness travel.

Groups are kept small to allow group members to form closer bonds and to minimize the ecological impact of camping.

THE ITINERARY: On the Cumberland Island trip, the group gathers at the ferry terminus and Park Headquarters Visitors Center in St. Marys, Georgia. You then board the ferry for a 45-minute trip through the St. Marys River coastal marshes and Cumberland Sound to the island. After a round of introductions, gear is loaded into hand carts, and the group walks a half mile to beautiful Sea Camp campground, set in a live oak forest just behind barrier dunes and Sea Camp Beach on the ocean side of the island.

Sea Camp is a well-equipped campground with rest rooms and shower blocks built of attractive native oak. Not-so-seasoned campers will appreciate electric outlets in the rest rooms for hair dryers or electric shavers.

At the camp fire on the first evening, the leaders introduce the area and the activities that the group might undertake. Together the group and leaders set a tentative agenda for the next three and a half days, allowing ample free time for individual activities.

A typical day begins in a leisurely way. Early risers have the beach, the morning mist, and the sunrise to themselves. Breakfasts of fresh fruit, bagels and cream cheese, pancakes or omelets, hot chocolate, and tea or coffee are cooked by the leaders and guests.

Each day involves explorations of different parts of the island. On some days the group takes a lunch on a full-day trip; on other days the group returns to camp for lunch.

Explorations are leisurely walks to the beach, salt marsh, forest, dunes, and historical sites on the island. The group sets the pace.

Group members disperse to explore and collect shells, with members returning to the leader from time to time with interesting finds.

Leaders are schooled in the local ecology, and are fully capable of presenting an academic lecture on the subject. But the learning process is experiential, not pedantic. Leaders allow group members to engage nature, and assist them in the process. They explain the ecology of the island using the plants, animals, and land forms encountered on a walk. They also follow individual and group interests, expanding on any topic that the group finds interesting. Slowly a cumulative picture of the local ecology builds.

The beach is a magnificent stretch of white sand, always changing, seemingly untouched by society. The Atlantic Ocean beaches on Cumberland Island rival the best beaches in the world. Each high tide washes up millions of shells. Shore birds—sea gulls, terns, black skimmers, pelicans, sanderlings—can always be seen; more than 300 species have been sighted here. Female loggerhead turtles lay eggs here during the summer months.

Live oak and pine forests occupy the central part of the island. Freshwater ponds attract raccoons, deer, and feral horses (descendants of horses released by the Carnegie family). Armadillos waddle everywhere and are easily approached. Wild pigs are more elusive and harder to spot. Trails crisscross the forests, making access easy.

Salt marshes line the sound side of the island. These wetlands are among the most productive habitats in the world and are the home for ducks, fiddler crabs, wading birds, shrimp, and numerous fish. Walks to the marshes are some of the most interesting.

The remnants of society's history on the island may be the subject of another walk. Shell middens are reminders of the coastal Indian society. The 19th-century agricultural economy is represented by ruins of plantation buildings. And the ruins of the Carnegie Dungeness mansion evoke insights into the leisure activities of early industrialists.

Two Visitors' Centers are located at the south end of the island, with a half-mile trail between them along the St. Marys River and Cumberland Sound. Each has a museum. The museum at Sea Camp Dock illuminates the natural history of the island. Human history is the subject of the museum at Dungeness Dock.

After group activities, there is ample time for families or individuals to explore, or swim, or just relax.

Dinner is always an extremely appetizing and appealing culinary experience—nothing like the instant meals from freeze-dried food that some outfitters provide. A soup may begin the meal, followed by a chicken and vegetable casserole. Fresh corn bread baked at the camp fire in a Dutch oven and a tossed salad accompany the meal, with a pudding or strawberry shortcake for dessert. Fresh fruit is part of every dinner. Leaders do the cooking with the help of volunteer assistants from the group.

After dinner, the evening's entertainment begins around a camp fire and frequently ends with a game on the beach. The camp fire is a time for discussing that day's activities and planning the following day. Camp-fire games all have an ecological theme and are appropriate to all ages. "Emerald hunts" with flashlights reveal insect eyes and beach creatures that glow in the dark. In a guessing game, each group member uses "magic clay" to sculpt an animal found on Cumberland Island.

FOR CHILDREN: Each Wilderness Southeast trip varies in sleeping arrangements, activities, and strenuousness. The Cumberland Island trip is appropriate for children 8 and older. It is best that your child have some camping experience.

In addition to its regularly scheduled group trips, Wilderness Southeast will custom design trips for one or several families to any of its regular nature destinations or to other mutually agreeable destinations.

RATES AND PERSONAL GEAR: $ There's a 15-percent discount for children under 18 who are accompanied by one parent and a 25-percent discount for children accompanied by two parents.

Wilderness Southeast provides two-person tents, all food, and eating gear. You may bring your own tent, if you prefer. Sleeping bags, air mattresses, and a day pack may be rented. A list of recommended personal clothing and equipment is mailed to all group members. When trips involve canoes or snorkeling, Wilderness Southeast provides the equipment. The outfitter even brings a small "library" of field guides appropriate to the area and ecology.

Remember, there are no stores on wilderness camping experiences. Bring sun-block lotion, insect repellent, sunglasses, and comfortable walking shoes.

OF INTEREST NEARBY: Okefenokee National Wildlife Refuge is an hour's drive from St. Marys, Georgia, and is an ideal area for camping and canoeing adventures. Consider visiting Okefenokee before or after a Cumberland Island trip.

FOR MORE INFORMATION: Write Wilderness Southeast at 711 Sandtown Road, Savannah, GA 31410, or call (912) 897-5108.

White-Water Raft Trip on the New River
Fayette County, West Virginia

An outfitter on the New River in West Virginia has found a way to remove the barriers to white-water rafting for many families. Class VI River Runners of Lansing, West Virginia, provides a number of trip options that allow children to accompany parents on the calmer sections of the New River—and then take part in stimulating off-river activities while their parents run the more demanding sections.

The New River is a great white-water stream and a geological curiosity. It is one of the few rivers outside the Arctic region that flows northward; its headwaters are in North Carolina, and it flows into the Ohio River. It also has one of the deepest river gorges east of the Mississippi, well over 1,000 feet deep at points. The New's descent is gradual over much of its course, but a 16-mile stretch descends more rapidly with a gradient of 12 feet per mile.

The history of settlement along the New River adds to the fascination of a raft trip. The completion of the C & O rail line in 1873, linking the Ohio valley with the Eastern Seaboard, opened the valley to coal mining. New River coal was in great demand for its clean burning properties, and more than 20 coal towns sprang up on the riverbanks over the next 50 years—towns like Prince, Dunfee, Rushrun, Beury, and Nuttall. But the coal industry is depressed now, and as you raft down the New River you pass the ghost towns of that once-thriving coal economy.

The history and the scenic beauty of the New River led the federal government to designate it a National River in 1978; it is managed by the National Park Service.

THE OUTFITTER: Class VI is one of more than 20 outfitters on the New River. What sets Class VI apart is the quality of its services and the activities it offers families.

Class VI offers a large variety of raft trips on the New River and on the nearby Gauley. You can choose a casual one-day float down calm, scenic portions of the New River or a hair-raising ride down the most difficult sections of the New or the Gauley.

The most popular trip is the one-day raft trip down the most challenging section of the New River, which includes some good solid Class IV rapids and maybe a Class V, depending on how the water is running.

Class VI's headquarters and stylish reception building overlook the New River Gorge near the small town of Ames Heights, West Virginia. Its equipment is first rate. Rafts accommodate six to nine people. All rafts are guided by expert members of the Class VI staff, who have knowledge of the local history. No prior rafting experience is required of passengers; you need not even be a swimmer. Good-quality life jackets are provided, as well as instruction.

THE ITINERARY: The section of the New River from Prince to Thurmond is a good one-day family trip. When you assemble at the Class VI headquarters at 9 A.M., sweet rolls, coffee, and hot chocolate are available. Use the change rooms to don swimsuits or shorts, and then board the Class VI bus for the 45-minute ride to Prince.

Your guide fits you with a life jacket and explains procedures on your arrival at the put-in point. No alcoholic beverages are allowed on this or any other Class VI trip. A waterproof rubber bag is available for cameras.

Your trip will have one or more rafts. Inflatable kayaks, better known as "rubber duckies," are also used on this relatively calm portion of the river. They accommodate one adult or an adult and a child and are paddled using a double-bladed kayak paddle. The duckies are great fun. Even the novice can manage them on this portion of the river.

Near midday, the group stops for lunch. An upside-down raft serves as a table. For lunch you will be offered make-your-own sandwiches with appropriate relishes, and perhaps marinated mushrooms, potato salad, a salmon pasta salad, dessert, and cold drinks (there's also peanut butter and jelly for balky kids).

There are several Class II rapids in the afternoon. These are fun rapids that are easily run in the equipment provided. The trip ends around 4 or 5 P.M. at a take-out point just above Thurmond. Beer and soda pop are served before the bus departs for Class VI headquarters.

Class VI serves dinner on the upper deck of its reception building on Friday through Monday evenings during the summer. Charcoal grilled roast beef, turkey, ribs, or chicken are on the menu, along with a salad bar, fresh vegetables, potatoes, baked beans, and a homemade dessert. Reserve dinner places in advance during busy periods.

An alternate raft trip is from Thurmond to Fayetteville, the most challenging part of the New River. Your raft glides by the old railroad town of Thurmond, and a series of small rapids sharpen paddling skills in the first seven miles of this trip. Later in the day, you'll crash through the three Keeneys, with a total vertical drop of 45 feet from the top of Upper Keeney to the bottom of Lower Keeney. The Keeneys are the best known rapids on the New River.

FOR CHILDREN: The age minimum for children on raft trips in the popular Thurmond-Fayette Station section of the New River is 14 years until July 1 and 12 years afterward.

Other portions of the New are more appropriate for family trips. The 12 miles of river above Thurmond, starting at Prince, have calmer water, with Class I and II rapids, which is perfect for a family raft trip. The minimum age for children in the Prince-Thurmond section is 6 years. The section of the river above Prince is a little calmer.

Class VI will take children 5 and older on a raft trip on the calmer portions of the New River while you get your kicks in the heavy rapids. Both the adults' and children's trips depart and return to headquarters at approximately the same time. Or Class VI will take your children on a one-day van excursion to the children's museum and Exhibition Coal Mine in Beckley, West Virginia, while you plunge through the rapids. The van driver and the raft guides are in contact by radio, and they time the raft trip and the museum trip so that both return to Class VI headquarters within minutes of each other.

An alternative is to do a two-day trip by combining a one-day family trip on the upper New River with a second day in which the children take the excursion to Beckley and you continue the river trip. You can do the two days as a camping trip, or you can stay in a motel or hotel. A two-day camping expedition for the whole family is also a possibility with a trip that starts higher up on the New River and ends on the second day before the section with difficult rapids.

Class VI will attempt to arrange a schedule that will meet your needs and will even arrange baby-sitting for your younger children. The only limitation is that six or more people are necessary to make any trip go. Since weekends are peak periods for white-water rafting on the New River, the chances of placing your child on a day excursion while you raft are best on a Friday, Saturday, or Sunday.

RATES AND PERSONAL GEAR: $ Class VI runs New River trips from mid-March through October. In peak periods, and particularly on weekends, it is best to make reservations. Children under 17 are half-price.

The water is cold in March, April, and May and again in late September and October. You may need a wet suit then, which can be rented for a nominal fee. Windbreakers also can be rented.

Rain gear is not necessary for one-day trips. But it's a good idea to have sunglasses or a hat, sunscreen, and a windbreaker in all seasons on the river.

Class VI will send you a recommended personal gear list for overnight trips. You provide sleeping bags and a tent (or rent the latter). Class VI provides waterproof bags for packing your gear and all food for overnight trips.

OF INTEREST NEARBY: Highway 19 spans the New River Gorge over one of the longest arch construction bridges in the world.

Class VI headquarters is a short distance away. Stop at the Visitors' Center on the north rim of the gorge and walk to the observation platform for a good view of the bridge and a last look at the New River before returning home.

FOR MORE INFORMATION: Write Class VI River Runners, Ames Heights Road, P.O. Box 78, Lansing WV 25862-0078, or call (304) 574-0704 or (800) CLASS VI (252-7784.)

Canoeing on the Buffalo National River
The Ozarks, Arkansas

In 1972, as the last of America's free-flowing streams seemed destined for damming, Congress acted to protect some of those that were still untamed. The Buffalo River, one of the nation's finest streams, was the first to be designated a national river. Development was banned along its entire length of 132 miles, and most of the vestiges of previous development were removed. A float from the river's source in the Boston Mountains to its junction with the White River is truly a wilderness experience.

Unlike the rivers in the West, which are known for their thrills and spills, the Buffalo is very much a river for families, with long languorous stretches lined with hardwood forests and towering limestone bluffs. The scenery is lovely, with rushing streams, caves, natural arches, and feeder springs seemingly at every turn. Clear, deep pools, perfect for swimming, alternate with narrow sections that provide just enough challenge to make it interesting.

The river is perfect for day trips, with evenly spaced put-in and take-out points, but it also offers one of the few opportunities in the central United States for a canoe-camping trip of 10 days or more. While the primary activity is canoeing, self-guided raft trips are increasing in popularity. A trail along the river's entire length is currently under development, with about 26 miles completed between Ponca and Pruitt. Marked trails leading from many gravel bars and riverside campgrounds also offer opportunities for shorter hikes.

THE OUTFITTER: The Buffalo Outdoor Center is the largest authorized concessioner on the river, with 90 canoes based in Ponca and 150 more downriver in Silver Hill. Mike and Evelyn Mills, the owners of Buffalo Outdoor Center, met while at the University of Arkansas at Fayetteville, and spent their courtship exploring the Buffalo, even before it became a national river. In 1978, they started up their own river outfitting business with a goal of providing the best service on the river.

Since then, the Millses have been custom-designing float trips for thousands of canoeists each year from early spring through late fall. They have two young daughters of their own, so they are attuned to the kind of experience a family seeks on a river trip. Mike Mills is the author of a picture book, *The Buffalo, America's First National River*, which he dedicated "to the families who gave up their land so that all might enjoy it, and to the individuals that strove to protect this free-flowing stream forever."

THE ITINERARY: The Millses will suggest a stretch of river that suits both your canoeing ability and the depth of your desire to escape from civilization. Anything from a five-hour, 10-mile float to a 10-day, 132-mile voyage is possible. You can leave your car at the offices in Ponca or Silver Hill and have it shuttled, for a fee, to your destination.

The upper Buffalo above Ponca boasts some of the greatest white water in the region in spring, when it's suitable only for experts. Come late May, the level drops to levels more appropriate for amateurs, and by early summer it's unfloatable. The 11-mile stretch from the Steel Creek put-in near Ponca to Kyles Landing is an easy first-day float for families. It's particularly scenic, with landmarks such as 500-foot Big Bluff, the tallest bluff in the Ozarks; Hemmed-In Hollow, with the tallest waterfall between the Appalachians and the Rockies; and Bear Cave Hollow, which was carved out of the mountains by a scenic cascading stream.

Another nice stretch for families goes from Pruitt to Hasty. It's particularly good for rafting in the summer months, with many deep holes for swimming, lots of nice gravel bars for picnicking, and plenty of bluffs.

In July and August, the only reliably floatable stretches are on the middle and lower Buffalo, from Woolum Ford to White River. There are many good stretches for fishing and wildlife sighting. From Rush to the White River is the most isolated section of the river because it requires at least one or two overnights. Most of the area below Rush has been designated a wilderness area.

FOR CHILDREN: There are no special programs for children along the river, but they will enjoy the summer ranger programs at Buffalo Point, Lost Valley, and Still Creek. They include campfire programs, guided walks and hikes, guided canoe trips, and Ozark crafts and folk music demonstrations. For a schedule, call the National Park Service.

Children age 6 and over will find the whole canoeing experience wonderful if the pace allows plenty of time for swimming and exploring the riverside by foot. There are fossils to be found on most gravel bars, fish to be caught, and deer, turtles, and great blue heron to be spotted.

For a first-time canoeing experience, we recommend renting one of the Buffalo Outdoor Center's cabins at Ponca or Silver Hill and taking several day-long trips on the river. Families with canoeing experience may want to try canoe-camping, stopping overnight on isolated gravel bars or in the National Park Service campgrounds.

RATES AND PERSONAL GEAR: $ The Buffalo Outdoor Center's cabins (nine at Ponca, six at Silver Hill) are comfortably furnished and fully equipped for housekeeping. They sleep six in three double beds, two of them upstairs in a sleeping loft. Each of the log cabins has a massive stone fireplace, cathedral ceiling with ceiling fans, front porch (some with double swings), and barbecue grills. The cabins are situated in the wooded hills next to the river.

The National Park Service operates 14 campgrounds along the river, each about 10 miles apart. Thirteen are considered rustic (outhouses only) and are free. The campground at Buffalo Point, where fees are charged, has water and electrical hookups, restrooms, showers and trailer dump stations, group sites, and day-use pavilions.

Buffalo Outdoor Center provides paddles, lifejackets, and good-quality plastic canoes, which glide easily over the river's low sections. All you need to bring for day floats are a cooler, water bottles for all, sunscreen, hats, and a good hearty lunch. Put anything you need to keep dry in a dry bag (available for purchase at the center), and tie everything to the canoe. Wear bathing suits, because you'll surely want to swim.

For multi-day floats, you can either keep your camping and overnight gear in your car and have it shuttled to your destination, or carry it in your canoe.

OF INTEREST NEARBY: While off the beaten path, Ponca is a good base for a family vacation. You can alternate canoeing days with sightseeing forays into the countryside. Mike Mills was director of tourism for Arkansas in the mid-1980s, so he knows the state's tourist attractions intimately. Among those worth visiting:

Eureka Springs, about an hour away, drew visitors from all over America to its mineral-water baths in the 19th century, and today it is a charming enclave of former hippies, New Age devotees, folk art craftsmen, and artists. Its hilly streets are lined with beautifully renovated Victorian homes that now house bed-and-breakfasts, shops, and restaurants. Mineral baths, eucalyptus steam treatments, facials, and massages are still offered at the Palace Bath House (call 501-253-8400 for reservations). Children will enjoy a ride on the Eureka Springs and North Arkansas steam-powered train.

Somewhat further afield, the Ozark Folk Center State Park in Mountain View, Arkansas celebrates the culture and way of life of the Ozark mountain region before 1920, and its music before 1940. Here you'll find about two dozen craft demonstration buildings within which artisans practice lost skills—broom making, spinning, gun making, candle-dipping, and creating cornhusk dolls. Accommodations are available in 30 round cabins. Call (501) 269-3851 for a brochure.

Blanchard Springs Caverns, about 15 miles from the folk center in the Ozark National Forest, has two underground trails.

FOR MORE INFORMATION: Write Buffalo Outdoor Center, P.O. Box 1, Ponca, AR 72670 or call (501) 861-5514.

For park information, write Superintendent, Buffalo National River, P.O. Box 1173, Harrison, AR 72602-1173 or call (501) 741-5443.

MIDWEST

Wagon Train Trip Through the Flint Hills
El Dorado, Kansas

Here in the remote and rugged beauty of the Flint Hills, not far
from the old Santa Fe Trail, you can still find a vast expanse of tallgrass prairie that has changed hardly at all since the pioneers made
their way west.

The tallgrass prairie was once a great sea of grass that covered
400,000 square miles, stretching west from what is now part of Ohio
into Nebraska and Kansas, north into Canada, and south into Texas.
The grasses nourished the buffalo that fed and clothed Plains Indians
and provided them with many of their myths. In a relative instant,
civilization obliterated most of the prairie by plowing for crops,
bulldozing for cities, and clearing great tracts for suburban housing.
The Flint Hills are the continent's largest remaining swath of essentially undisturbed prairie.

Flint Hills Overland Wagon Train Trips wind through time and
place to an America that is accessible almost no other way. They
offer a chance to be a pioneer for 24 hours, to relive the experiences
of our ancestors, to take inspiration from unspoiled nature under a
seemingly endless prairie sky, and to get farther away from it all
than most people could ever imagine.

The landscape and the cowboys are right out of a western movie
without all the shooting. The trail riders who accompany the wagons
are about the closest facsimile of real cowboys that 20th-century
America offers. One octogenarian who sometimes makes the trip has
genuinely bowed legs, and his spurs jingle when he walks.

The century-old wagons are pulled by Belgian draft horses and
rumble along on high wooden wheels. Inside under the canvas cover

sit the weekend pioneers. Padded benches have been installed, but they do little to absorb the jolts that come from driving over unpaved trails without the benefit of rubber tires, springs, and shock absorbers.

The hills provide breathtaking vistas that are a bright and luminous green flecked with yellow, blue, purple, white, and orange wildflowers. The grass, moving in continuous rhythm with the wind, makes the hills seem alive. On a hot day in this landscape, cold water tastes so good it's worthy of the gods.

THE OUTFITTER: Flint Hills Overland Wagon Train Trips, Inc., offers five wagon train trips through the Flint Hills annually, usually as early as June and as late as September. Each trip can accommodate about 50 people. The trips begin at 10 A.M. on Saturday and end at noon Sunday. If you choose not to stay the night, you are returned to your car after the camp-fire dinner and entertainment at about 10:30 on Saturday night.

The outfitter provides the wagons and the teams of draft horses to pull them, a knowledgeable wagonmaster and trail boss, plenty of cold water, a campsite under a huge cottonwood tree by a small stream, wonderful meals cooked over an open fire, and good stories and western music around the camp fire after dinner.

Portable rest rooms are provided at rest stops and at the campsite. The price also includes limited individual medical expense insurance.

Perhaps the most important ingredient the outfitter provides is the friendly people who operate the tours. Most are members or friends of the family of wagonmaster John Hogoboom, a retired rancher whose collection of wagons makes the trip possible and whose good humor and expertise in the lore of the Flint Hills and of cowboy life provide grace notes for a beautiful experience. Because of the openness and good feelings Hogoboom and his family foster, by the time the weekend is over the outfitters and the tenderfeet are all one big family.

In case of weather problems, or any other emergency, the company will provide transportation to the outside world on nearby surfaced roads, day or night.

THE ITINERARY: The weekend pioneers gather at 10 A.M. Saturday in the parking lot of the Flint Hills High School in the little town of Rosalia, Kansas. No matter how old you are, the first things you get after arriving to start the trip are a bright red bandanna, a tin drinking cup, and a lecture about safety requirements around the horses and wagons. The pioneers' cars are led in a convoy to Glen Kirk's ranch headquarters northeast of town, the staging area for the wagon train.

You unload your gear so the crew can take it to the campsite for you, pile in the wagons, and head out. Right away the transition to the America of more than a century ago is palpable, as the old wagons jolt over the rough ground. The trail riders are the vanguard, opening fence gates to allow the wagon train access to the vastness of the grazing lands. Over a hill the weekend pioneers roll, and then another, ever so slowly, getting used to the experience of going at a pace slower than unhurried, until the chuck wagon comes into view. The lunch consists of sandwiches and cold lemonade, cookies, and fresh fruit.

Next the wagons set out for Lookout Point, where the land falls away to incredibly distant horizons. Hogoboom stops from time to time to describe what you are seeing—including the foundation of a house his grandfather built as a homesteader.

At midafternoon, there is a snack of chilled watermelon, and after that more rumbling along, and more interesting commentary. Before 5 P.M., you reach the campsite, which turns out to be very close to where you ate lunch. The wagon train has gone in a great circle, but in the Flint Hills vastness this is hard to discern.

For dinner, the crew cooks a superb stew, plus beans and corn bread, on a huge grill made from a 55-gallon drum split lengthwise. There are also cookies and fresh fruit, plus a mouth-watering cobbler baked in the coals. The coffee is ground fresh and brewed cowboy style (put in a sock and boiled in a huge pot over the coals). After dinner a singer or two perform western music. And then there is sleep, dozing off under multitudes of stars whose light is unimpeded by the maddening glow of cities. Sleeping arrangements are casual; you may unroll your sleeping bag in the wagons or under them, on the open ground, or in a tent if you choose to bring one.

Breakfast is also cooked over the coals, and is just as hearty as dinner. Scrambled eggs—four dozen go into one huge skillet—are accompanied by biscuits and gravy. After breakfast there is an informal open-air worship service. Then you board the wagons and rumble back to Kirk's ranch, where lunch is available and where many weekend pioneers trade addresses with the new friends they have made.

FOR CHILDREN: Children of any age are welcome. The trip is slow paced (about two and a half miles an hour), and the outfitter warns that 3- and 4-year-olds may tire easily or find the trip overwhelming.

Still, there is plenty to do and enjoy. For most city kids, just being around working horses in the great outdoors is a treat. There are the other kids to get to know, and a creek in which you can catch crawdads, toads, and frogs. There are lots of flat stones to skip, and entertainment such as sing-alongs.

It is not unusual to see three generations of a family on a trip, with all enjoying themselves. People in their 70s and 80s are not uncommon on the trips—indeed, Hogoboom and some of the trail riders are in that age bracket—but the outfitters discourage participation by people who need regular medication or special diets or who have physical difficulties that would make it dangerous to ride in the wooden-wheeled wagons or to walk up steep hills. Riders are occasionally asked to get out and walk so the teams and wagons can negotiate steep slopes or rough or rocky terrain, or to cross streams.

RATES AND PERSONAL GEAR: $$ If you elect to skip the camp-out and leave after dinner, you get a 20-percent discount. Reservations are mandatory and must be made and paid for at least 21 days in advance.

Fireworks, firearms, and noisemakers are prohibited. Use of alcoholic beverages is discouraged, and smoking is restricted to wagons equipped with butt buckets and to the campsite.

After you call about reservations, the outfitter will send you comprehensive information about what supplies you will need, such as your own tent and sleeping bag. If you are flying in and want to limit the amount of gear you bring, they will try to find a rental source. They also will suggest motels in the area if you need one.

OF INTEREST NEARBY: This is oil country, and the Butler County Museum in El Dorado is devoted to the oil boom days, including an old-time derrick.

The El Dorado Reservoir is an 8,000-acre lake with camping, boat rentals, and fishing.

These are wide-open spaces, and the most plentiful thing nearby is more Flint Hills. You can drive north for two and a half hours on scenic Kansas Highway 177 through Cottonwood Falls to Council Grove, a historic town on the Santa Fe Trail (now U.S. Highway 56). About two hours east is Independence, Kansas, where a log house has been erected on the site of the original Little House on the Prairie.

FOR MORE INFORMATION: Write to Flint Hills Overland Wagon Train Trips, Inc., P.O. Box 1076, El Dorado, KS 67042, or call (316) 321-6300.

Apostle Islands Sailing Adventure
Madeline Island, Wisconsin

The Apostle Islands are scattered off the tip of the Bayfield peninsula, the westernmost of the three large peninsulas that jut northward into the clear waters of Lake Superior, the largest of the Great Lakes. The 22 Apostles range in size from the three-acre dot of Gull Island to the 14,000 acres of Madeline Island. Twenty-one of the Apostles and a 12-mile-long strip of the mainland shoreline make up the Apostle Islands National Lakeshore.

What a wonderful place for family sailing! The Apostles are a vacationer's paradise of sunshine, clear water, and deep green islands edged with red sandstone cliffs, perfect for any family that loves sailing or has ever dreamed of taking a family sailing vacation. Many protected coves provide safe anchorages, and several marinas in the area also rent slips or anchorages for overnight stays.

The Apostle Islands are a dream spot for nature lovers, too. They have a mixed forest ecology with hardwoods and conifers that provide good habitat for bear, deer, beaver, smaller mammals, and a diverse population of birds, whose numbers and species swell with spring and fall migrations. Terns, herring, and ringbill gulls, loons, great blue heron, and the ruby-throated hummingbird are commonly seen here. From May to October, waves of wildflowers bloom in successively bolder hues. Orchids, bog laurel, and sand cherry are seen here, too.

The Apostles are also rich in history. Vestiges of human excursions through these islands remain in abandoned quarries and fishing camps, old lighthouses, and in the Ojibway cemetery on Madeline Island. Many of the Ojibway Indians, also known as the Chippewa, were driven from their home along the eastern Great Lakes by more aggressive tribes. They eventually made their way to the southern shores of Lake Superior and the Apostle Islands. The Madeline Island Historical Museum in La Pointe and the National Lakeshore Visitors' Center in Bayfield house historical relics of these eras and are worth visiting.

THE OUTFITTER: The Apostle Islands Yacht Charter Association (AIYCA) is a co-operative formed by individual boat owners at the Madeline Island Marina. AIYCA was the first charter fleet on Lake Superior to organize in this fashion. The association's offices are in the marina headquarters building on Madeline Island, accessible by car ferry from Bayfield, Wisconsin. Charter guests have full marina privileges, including use of bathroom and shower facilities.

Each boat in the fleet is owned by an individual co-op member, and each boat and skipper must pass stringent qualifications to be included in the charter fleet.

AIYCA offers a wide selection of boats, from day sailers to large yachts that sleep 6 or more people and can be sailed the length and breadth of Lake Superior. Interior appointments range from the spartan to the luxurious. Boats suitable for overnight cruising all have bunks with mattresses, a head, and a galley (sink, stove, and ice chest). An assortment of pots, pans, plates, cups, and flatware is provided.

If you opt for an AIYCA skipper, he or she will involve your family in sailing the charter boat and teach you some sailing and water safety fundamentals. But a family that wants to learn to sail, as opposed to being chauffeured, would do well to investigate the Blue Waters Sailing School. The school is headquartered at Madeline Island Marina and is directed by Captain Ann M. Larson, an AIYCA member. Larson and her staff of Coast Guard qualified instructors have 20 years of accumulated teaching experience.

To give its students extended sailing experience on big yachts, the Blue Waters Sailing School periodically offers a nine-day scheduled cruise on a 42-foot ketch from its base at the Madeline Island Marina around Isle Royale in Lake Superior. The sailing party is usually made up of unrelated individuals or several family groups, which makes it an excellent way to share the cost of a yacht-training experience. The Isle Royale training cruise spends four days at Isle Royale itself, circling the National Park, anchoring at night in protected coves, and allowing plenty of time during the day for sightseeing and hiking.

For bare-boat charters, the association requires a certificate from a recognized sailing school or appropriate references.

THE ITINERARY: Firm itineraries are not always possible in sailing. The winds and weather help determine where and when you go.

The best approach is to sit down with an AIYCA representative and a chart of the Apostle Islands and sketch a tentative route for your sailing adventure. Consider the amount of time you want to devote to sailing and land exploration, the places you might want to visit, the anchorages available in the islands, and the weather forecast, including wind speed and direction.

The Apostles are a good place for spur-of-the-moment stops. Camping, fishing, hiking, beachcombing, scuba diving, and animal watching experiences await the sailing family in numerous spots.

Before you start, mark the location of the 11 public docks scattered throughout the islands. These are prime locations for picnic lunches and the starting points for exploring many of the islands. Campgrounds with picnic tables and toilets adjoin many of these.

Also, come prepared with information on other facilities and programs provided by the National Park Service in the Apostle Islands. Rangers are stationed on some of the larger islands. Stockton Island has a National Lakeshore Visitors' Center with evening programs for campers in the summer months. The larger islands have trail systems linking historic sites like old lighthouses, quarries, or abandoned fishing camps with sand dunes, bogs, and lovely red sand beaches. Trails frequently follow the course of old railroad beds and logging roads.

FOR CHILDREN: Even young children will enjoy life on a boat if you remember to bring appropriate games and activities to amuse them. If there is one common mistake in family sailing, it is spending too much time sailing and not enough time having fun in the places you can reach by water. Allow for plenty of shore time and remain flexible enough to change schedules as the needs of family members dictate.

RATES AND PERSONAL GEAR: $$$ to $$$$ Charter rates vary with the size of boat. Hiring a skipper or crew member raises the cost considerably. Weekly rates are available.

You will probably want to stop at one or more of the towns and marinas in the Apostle Islands to replenish your food supply as your cruise progresses. You will find a supermarket in Bayfield and a small grocery store near the marina on Madeline Island. The Association will provide food, if you prefer, for a charge.

AIYCA charters are fully equipped with all the gear necessary to sail the boat, including a life jacket for each member of your party. A dinghy is provided with most boats, which allows you to get ashore at each of your anchorages. Your personal items should include deck shoes; foul-weather gear; warm sweaters, jackets, hats, and windbreakers; sunglasses, sunscreen, and sleeping bags or sheets and blankets for every member of your party.

FOR MORE INFORMATION: Write Apostle Islands Yacht Charter Association at P.O. Box 188, La Pointe, WI 54850, or call (715) 747-2983 May through October or (800) 821-3480 year-round.

Tourist information is available from the Apostle Islands National Lakeshore, Route 1, Box 4, Bayfield, WI 54814.

Wisconsin Bicycle Adventure
Madison, Wisconsin

Imagine riding down a quiet country road. There, in a field of yellow wildflowers that competes with the sun for brightness, stand a doe and her fawn, calmly eating breakfast. Unperturbed, they graze as you pause motionless, mouth open in wonder. With appetites finally satisfied, they walk away into nearby woods, turn for one last look at you, then vanish silently.

Such a serendipitous experience is a common occurrence when one travels by bicycle. Families seeking an exciting adventure at a leisurely pace should consider a cycling vacation. Bike touring allows intimate contact with nature and the environment; it is an excellent way to savor—up close—all the details of one's surroundings. And Wisconsin is an ideal place to pedal around, soaking up experiences and storing shared memories. Bike Wisconsin, Ltd., a cycling tour outfitter, makes a biking vacation easy to arrange and offers an opportunity for families to explore and enjoy the quiet beauty of country roads and small-town friendliness.

The state of Wisconsin has been a leader in governmental commitment to cycling, beginning in 1965 with the conversion of abandoned railroad right-of-ways into bicycle trails. The state's system of bicycle routes covers more than 10,000 miles and a variety of picturesque landscapes. With many rivers and trout streams, 15,000 lakes, and over 1,000 miles of shoreline along the Great Lakes and Mississippi River, Wisconsin offers cyclists plenty of chances to follow a winding stream, to relax on a sandy beach, or to enjoy the sunset over Lake Superior after a day's pedaling.

THE OUTFITTER: "Cozy lodges, hearty meals, and carefree backroads cycling." That's the motto of Bike Wisconsin, Ltd., which offers both novice and experienced cyclists the opportunity to explore and enjoy scenic country roads without worry. Based in Madison, Bike Wisconsin was formed in 1987 by Scott and Jane Hall, who together have over a decade of experience as international tour directors.

Bike Wisconsin's tours are non-competitive, with each person riding at his or her own pace. Cycling groups are small (25 or fewer), and the schedules allow plenty of time to get acquainted and to share experiences and biking stories.

Bike Wisconsin offers a variety of cycling options in Wisconsin, Minnesota, and Michigan. Weekend tours of two and three nights are ideal for families who want a short getaway or who want to try bik touring for the first time. These trips usually run from Friday evening to Sunday afternoon, with both nights spent at the same lodge.

Midweek tours of five nights provide a chance to explore a region more intimately as bikers ride from inn to inn. There is always one free day on the midweek tours for day trips or non-biking activities such as swimming, sightseeing, or attending one of the many summertime festivals and fairs held in Wisconsin's small towns. "Cycling Plus" tours incorporate sailing, hiking, or canoeing with bicycling.

Bike Wisconsin is a small, well-run outfitter. Both Halls work hard to make each trip special by researching routes, inns, and local attractions.

The Halls incorporate regional food specialties such as a Door County fish boil or a "taste of Wisconsin" gourmet picnic. Always available in shops and markets are wonderful Wisconsin cheeses and dairy products.

THE ITINERARY: A typical Bike Wisconsin cycling trip is the Pioneer, a weekend getaway that starts in Green Lake. This small resort community, one of the oldest in Wisconsin, is located on the deepest inland lake in the state.

Accommodations at the family-owned Oakwood Lodge are spacious and comfortable; some of the rooms have shared baths. Located on the lakefront, the lodge has a private pier for swimming and fishing and several verandas for socializing and enjoying the view. A family room with television and piano are available, and guests are encouraged to bring books, games, and musical instruments for their own entertainment.

Upon arrival at the lodge on Friday evening, tour members are greeted by the leaders, offered a cold drink, and given a folder with schedules, maps, and other information. In the guest rooms, each person finds a Bike Wisconsin T-shirt and a personal note welcoming him or her to the group. A wine (and soda) and cheese party and a delicious dinner at a local restaurant give tour members a chance to get acquainted. Back at the lodge after dinner, the tour leaders hold a mini-clinic to discuss safety rules, the itinerary, and general biking tips.

Saturday morning, over breakfast at Oakwood Lodge, the tour leaders review the routes and explain maps, reinforce safety rules, and mention items of interest that will be encountered along the way, such as a county fair, an antiques show, and a dairy farm that offers tours. On the first day of the Pioneer, cyclists ride a loop from Green Lake through the small towns of Berlin and Ripon, then back to Green Lake, a total distance of about 35 miles. Ripon is the birthplace of the Republican Party, and visiting its original headquarters makes a fascinating side trip. Dairy farms, fragrant fields of newly mown hay, and the songs of red-winged blackbirds provide a backdrop for the undulating country roads.

The second day's trip (approximately 40 miles) consists of biking around beautiful Green Lake, having lunch in Princeton with its antiques shops and memorable ice-cream parlor, then traveling on to the White River Marsh, a wetlands area that is home to a variety of birds, including sandhill cranes, osprey, and heron. On this morning, an optional before-breakfast ride gives cyclists a chance to tour the 1,100-acre grounds of Lawsonia, a retreat center owned by the American Baptist Assembly. Early morning is the perfect time to enjoy views of the lake, the cool quiet of the woods, and plenty of deer roaming the meadows.

During the day's biking, one leader rides with the group while the other drives a support van stocked with water, snacks, tools, and equipment, plus a bike rack. (On longer trips the van also transports luggage between inns.) Weary cyclists are encouraged to ride in the van whenever necessary.

Meals are a highlight of a Bike Wisconsin cycling vacation. Besides hearty breakfasts, dinners at local restaurants are delicious and substantial. On the Pioneer trip, the first night's meal is taken at a local restaurant; the next night, dinner is served aboard a yacht cruising Green Lake.

During the daily ride, frequent rest periods are scheduled, usually in shady village parks. Bikers eagerly munch fruit and home-made cookies, drink cold lemonade, and refill water bottles. Weekend tours include one lunch—a gourmet picnic prepared by the tour leaders.

FOR CHILDREN: Bike Wisconsin cycling vacations vary in location and duration, distance, and difficulty. Children age 10 and above are welcome when accompanied by a parent or guardian. Wisconsin State Trails are suitable for most bicyclists able to ride 10-speed bikes.

Children need some experience riding in light traffic situations and must be familiar with safety rules. Pre-vacation family bike rides allow practical application of these rules.

RATES AND PERSONAL GEAR: $ Included in the fees are all accommodations, breakfasts and dinners, one lunch, snacks, the welcome party, two experienced tour leaders, a support van, park and trail admissions, ferry or boat fares, and a Bike Wisconsin T-shirt.

Participants may use their own bicycles, although rental bicycles and equipment such as helmets, water bottles, and handlebar bags are available at reasonable rates.

Upon registration for a particular trip, each participant is sent a packet containing tips for bicycling safety, pre-trip physical conditioning, clothing, and equipment, plus information on the locale and any special events. All bicyclists must wear helmets.

FOR MORE INFORMATION: Contact Bike Wisconsin at P.O. Box 3461, Madison, WI 53704, or call (608) 249-4490.

Boat-Camping in Voyageurs National Park
International Falls, Minnesota

Voyageurs National Park is a 219,000-acre expanse of beautiful lakes set in towering forests on the Canada–Minnesota border. It is among the least well-known and used of our national parks.

These lakes and the narrow passages between them were once the highway of the *voyageurs*, the French-Canadian adventurers who paddled heavy canoes 12 to 16 hours a day to bring trade goods from Montreal into the vast northern wilderness. Life then centered on the waterways, and even today many of the ridges and hilltops in this region are without names. Fifty-six miles of the *voyageurs'* route lie within the boundaries of the park.

The park is made up of four major lakes—Rainy, Kabetogama, Namakan, and Sand Point—and more than two dozen smaller lakes. Almost a third of its 217,300 acres are covered by water. Only three small areas of the park are directly accessible by road, so boats are the only practical way to explore and enjoy its beauty.

THE OUTFITTERS: The Voyageurs area has many outfitters who can provide your family with the essential equipment for an outdoor adventure in the National Park. The Crane Lake Commercial Club is an organization of outfitters who serve the Crane Lake access area; call (218) 993-2346 or write the club in Crane Lake, MN 55725. The National Park Service can provide you with a list of authorized outfitters in all four access areas.

Outfitters will provide you with charts of the lake system, help you select an itinerary, and provide you with a well-maintained motorboat and all the equipment and provisions you might need. They will also teach those not familiar with power-boating how to read channel and hazard markers. They will alert you to Indian pictographs, rookeries, and particularly beautiful islands and coves along the way. Some outfitters can arrange for a guide to accompany your party and to help with fishing, setting up and striking of camp, and cooking.

Renting a houseboat is an alternative for families who want to experience the wilderness without roughing it.

THE ITINERARY: You can retrace the route of the *voyageurs* or just casually cruise the shallow bays and narrow passages between islands, ever on the lookout for deer, beaver, otter, moose, and bear. You're sure to see numerous species of birds, including bald eagles, loons, great blue herons, mergansers, and ducks of many stripes.

Your wanderings may take you to Kettle Falls at the juncture of

Kabetogama and Rainy lakes. A shuttle is available here to take your boat and belongings around the falls. Kettle Falls is an historic spot because all water-born commerce through the vast North had to pass this spot. Indians, *voyageurs*, loggers, gold miners, and fishermen all converged here. The historic Kettle Falls Hotel has been restored by the National Park Service. Located in the wilderness and accessible only by boat, its rooms and furnishings—especially the barroom with the nickelodeon and the uniquely slanted floor—all speak of the heritage of the great northwoods. Call (218) 374-3511 in advance to arrange a stay.

There are 120 designated boat-in camp sites in the National Park and countless other sites suitable for camping. Campsites are on a first–come, first–served basis (no charge). Each designated site is equipped with a picnic table, fire grate, pit toilet, and tent pad. Most of the campsites on the mainland and on larger islands are also equipped with "bear boxes" for storing food at night to protect against the infrequent visits of one of the park's 200 black bears.

FOR CHILDREN: Boat-camping has a natural appeal to children. If you rent a large boat, you will be able to take many camping luxuries—a comfortable tent, camp stove, lantern, ice chests, lawn chairs, fishing gear, extra fuel, and a hoard of food to tide you over until the fishing gets going.

Many campsites in the park have spectacular vistas, and some have sandy beaches nearby. Avoid camp sites with no room for children to play, and choose spots that have safe approaches to the water.

If camping is just not your thing, consider one of the many resorts near the national park that cater to families. Several resorts have children's programs and are particularly appropriate for families with younger children. Nelson's Resort on Crane Lake (phone 218-993-2295) has first-rate cabins, a gourmet dining room, a naturalist program for children, and one of the largest sand beaches in the Voyageurs area. Sandy Point Lodge and Resort, an informal family-friendly place on Kabetogama Lake, has a half-day nature-oriented children's program. It offers a choice of housekeeping cabins or full American plan dining with special children's rates. Call (800) 777-8595.

The National Park visitor centers at Rainy Lake, Kabetogama, and Ash River offer naturalist-guided activities such as canoe trips, puppet shows, and walks around a beaver pond. The "Kids Explore Voyageurs" program for children 7 to 12 years of age includes a ride in a 26-foot long "Duck" or birchbark boat, a chat with a "voyageur," and an exploration of a beaver pond.

RATES AND PERSONAL GEAR: $ to $$ Rates vary by outfitter and with the amount and kind of equipment and provisions you require. Contact several outfitters and compare services and rates.

Be sure to bring appropriate clothing. The summer weather here can range from very hot to very cool. Bring good rain gear and all the potions you'll need to ward off insects, which can be fierce.

ON INTEREST NEARBY: The Boundary Waters Wilderness Canoe Area is just east of the park. This western entrance is the preferred entrance for those who want the wilderness to themselves. Outfitters in Crane Lake can set you up for the Boundary Waters; they are prepared to shuttle your canoe right up to the area by power boat, if you like.

FOR MORE INFORMATION: Write Superintendent, Voyageurs National Park, Box 50, International Falls, MN 56649, or phone (218) 283-9821 for general information on the park and lists of outfitters and resorts. For general travel information, call the Minnesota Department of Tourism at (800) 657-3700.

SOUTHWEST AND MOUNTAIN STATES

Houseboating on Lake Powell
Glen Canyon National Recreation Area
Arizona and Utah

There are few more serene experiences than sitting on the deck of a houseboat and drifting by some of the most spectacular scenery in North America—the Glen Canyon National Recreation Area, with its multi-colored canyons and riveting mid-lake peaks.

Although Lake Powell has been a water playground for millions of Americans since it was opened to boats in the mid 1960s, it is so vast in size—161,390 acres and 186 miles long, with 1,900 miles of zigzagging shoreline—that houseboating vacationers not infrequently find themselves alone with the scenery, with only an eagle soaring overhead for company.

Renting a houseboat is the best way for families to experience the glories of the area, as well as an adventure unto itself. Children of all ages will delight in making themselves at home in these compact floating houses. A week or even just a few days spent here will present you with innumerable opportunities to fish for bass, crappie, walleye, channel catfish, and bluegills; swim in the crystal-clear water; hike into otherwise inaccessible canyons; spot wildlife; and visit ancient Indian ruins.

THE OUTFITTER: ARA Leisure Services, the largest concessioner in the National Park Service system, operates all facilities at Lake Powell, including 308 houseboats out of four marinas: Wahweap Lodge & Marina, on the south shore six miles north of Page, Arizona; Bullfrog Resort & Marina, in Utah, midway on the lake; Hall's Crossing Resort & Marina, across the bay from Bullfrog at mid-lake; and Hite Marina, on the upper lake.

399

All of the rental boats are in impeccable shape. Three sizes are offered: 36 feet, which sleeps six in three beds; 44 feet, which sleeps 10 in six beds; and 50 feet, which sleeps 12 in eight beds. Each size contains a fully equipped galley, a bathroom with shower, a 12-volt light system (no outlets), a gas grill, and an outdoor deck. The two larger sizes have a separate sleeping area.

Many renters also rent a small tag-along boat—a skiff or a powerboat—and tie it onto the houseboat while they traverse the lake. Families can then waterski or motor into the smaller canyons.

THE ITINERARY: The outfitter purposefully avoids handing out suggested itineraries to houseboat renters to avoid overcrowding particular areas of the lake. But the staff will make informal suggestions based on renters' interests.

No special skills are needed to operate a houseboat. Renters are given about an hour of instruction when they take possession of the boat. Instruction manuals are aboard each boat in case you run into problems after you leave shore.

The detailed "Boating and Exploring Map," available at all marina stores, is a good thing to pick up before you embark. Keep to a leisurely pace, and let a commitment to serendipity be your guide. Plan on anchoring frequently throughout the day to permit fishing, swimming, or hiking onshore.

With 96 major canyons ringing the lake, there's plenty of spectacular scenery to explore. Be sure to cruise by Rainbow Bridge, one of the seven natural wonders of the world. It is a designated national monument because it contains the largest known natural stone bridge. You'll also want to see Hole-in-the-Rock, where the Mormons crossed the Colorado River in 1879 and 1880.

Two of the most well known Indian ruins are off the Escalante River and in Forgotten Canyon. They are old Anasazi Indian dwellings that have been sheltered by cliff overhangs and stabilized by the Park Service.

Among the suggested hikes for families is an hour or two walk into Dungeon Canyon, just above Padre Bay. Along it you'll find a sliderock mound with remnants of Moki steps carved by Anasazi Indians 600 years ago, as well as the ruins of a Navajo hogan and its nearby rock sheep corral. Other hiker-accessible canyons include

West Canyon, with spectacular examples of erosion, Davis Gulch, with its impressive Bement Natural Arch, and the beautiful San Juan Arm's Alcove Canyon.

FOR CHILDREN: Houseboating is suitable for children of all ages, provided precautions are taken. State regulations require that anyone 12 or under wear a lifejacket at all times when on deck. (If parents set an example, there should be little resistance from children. By calling it a "magic jacket," one family we know got their 3-year-old to regard the lifejacket as a treat to wear.)

Children will enjoy frequent stops for fishing, swimming, and exploring the shoreline; looking for birds and other wildlife is also an adventure for them. Don't expect young children to be as enchanted with the scenery as you are; bring along plenty of their favorite toys to occupy them in the cabin.

You may want to plan to spend a night or two nights moored at a marina such as Wahweap, which has restaurants, a laundry, video games, gift shops, and other tourist facilities.

Most families rent houseboats in the summer; although the days are hot, the evenings are pleasant, and the water temperature can reach 80 degrees. But spring and early fall are the best times to visit to avoid crowds. Temperatures are moderate, and fishing is at its best.

RATES AND PERSONAL GEAR: $$ Rates depend on the size of boat you choose, the length of the rental (it's less expensive to rent by the week) and the time of year (summer rates are highest). Houseboating can be surprisingly inexpensive if two or more families share the cost.

It's a good idea to bring children's lifejackets from home to ensure that they fit properly and comfortably. The outfitter's promotional literature contains a detailed list of other items to bring. The actual necessities are surprisingly few, since the houseboats are completely outfitted, except for bedding, which can be rented. Food can be brought from home or purchased at the marina stores.

In spring and fall, with advance notice, the outfitter will provide a captain and cook (for an extra charge) if you want to have a completely hassle-free vacation. But be aware that opportunities for privacy then are minimal.

OF INTEREST NEARBY: You can make a houseboating adventure on Lake Powell the centerpiece of a tour of some of the seven national parks and seven national monuments in what's called the Grand Circle area. They include Grand Canyon, Bryce Canyon, Capitol Reef, Zion, Canyonlands, Mesa Verde, and Arches national parks and Natural Bridges, Hovenweep, Canyon de Chelly, Navajo, Rainbow Bridge, Pipe Spring, and Cedar Breaks national monuments.

Other points of interest include the Anasazi Indian village near Boulder, Utah, which contains an excavation of Indian ruins that date back to 1050 A.D. Newspaper Rock State Park, at Blanding, Utah, preserves a rock with 1,000-year-old petroglyphs. The Monument Valley Navajo Tribal Park, near Valley, Utah, preserves hundreds of acres of naturally carved red sandstone buttes and weather-carved arches. Canyon de Chelly National Monument, near Chinle, Arizona, memorializes the slaughter of Navajos by Kit Carson in the 1860s and preserves the spectacular 1,000-foot sandstone walls of the canyon. The Navajo National Monument, near Tonalea, Arizona, preserves three major ruins dating to 1274 A.D.

FOR MORE INFORMATION: Call Lake Powell Resorts and Marinas, at (800) 528-6154; from Phoenix, call (602) 278-8888.

Other tourist information is available from the Grand Circle Association, P.O. Box 987, Page, AZ 86040. Call (602) 645-3232.

Pontoon Boat Adventure Through the Grand Canyon
Georgie's Royal River Rats
The Grand Canyon, Arizona

There's nothing that can compare to the Grand Canyon for sheer beauty and splendor, and nothing quite like a raft trip to experience it. There is also no one quite like Georgie Clark, over 80 years old and still going strong, to guide it. Dressed in a fake leopard-skin outfit, Georgie still guides the Grand Canyon river trips that she pioneered 40 years ago.

Other river runners call her the "First Woman of the River," and with good reason. She made her first trip to the Grand Canyon in 1944 to join a Sierra Club member, Harry Aleson, in several river adventures—among them swimming 60 miles down the Colorado River and later floating down in an inflatable raft. In 1952, Georgie became the first woman to row the entire length of the Grand Canyon. Soon after that she started leading commercial trips using army surplus rafts. Georgie's been a river runner ever since, simply because she "likes to give people a good time."

Both first-time rafters and veteran river runners will find the Grand Canyon's rapids exhilarating. It's also a naturalist's nirvana. Some of the rock formations are more than a billion years old and many of the plants, insects, reptiles, and birds can only be found here. As you go downriver from Lee's Ferry to Lake Mead, tumbling over 160 rapids and dropping 1,900 feet, you will see one of the world's natural wonders from a unique vantage point. While you are down below looking up, time will seem to stop.

THE OUTFITTER: Georgia Clark drives a motor-powered boat of her own design. This "G-rig" ("G" for Georgie), as it is called, is made by tying three pontoons together to form one raft 27 by 35 feet, which holds 24 people. Depending on the size of the group, one or two smaller single boats are also used. The National Park Service regulates the number of trips Georgie's Royal River Rats and other concessioners can make each season, and also sets safety regulations.

Georgie is not only the guide for each river trip, but she pilots one boat, decides when and where to stop, and cooks and serves the meals. Motorman Al Korber pilots the second boat and offers passengers a short informal course in Grand Canyon geology. You'll soon learn to recognize Vishnu schist, Bright Angel shale, Navajo sandstone, Redwall limestone, pink granite, and lava rocks.

The crew members are all enthusiastic river runners. They may be firefighters or college professors in their other lives, but they all love the river—and Georgie.

THE ITINERARY: Most six- and eight-day rafters meet at the Showboat Hotel in Las Vegas, where they board a bus for Lee's Ferry at the eastern edge of the Grand Canyon National Park. The six-day trip ends at Whitmore, 188 miles downriver. From there you'll go by helicopter to Whitmore Lodge; at the end of the trip, you'll be taken by a small plane back to Las Vegas. If you opt for the eight-day trip, you'll go all the way to Pierce Ferry at Lake Mead (a total river journey of 279 miles) and then by bus back to Las Vegas.

If you'd rather avoid Las Vegas, you may drive to Marble Canyon through vast expanses of desert and rugged forbidding cliffs, with few signs of modern civilization. Spend the night at Marble Canyon Lodge (602-355-2225), where you can pick up last-minute supplies. You can join the group in the morning when the bus from Las Vegas makes a stop on its way to Lee's Ferry.

From the moment you first step foot on the boat, you will hear about Crystal. You don't reach Crystal until the third day, and by this time the crew will have shared so many Crystal stories that you will be thoroughly spooked. On a scale of one to 10 in thrills, Crystal rates a 10+.

Georgie will stop often for side trips to some of her favorite spots. On Day Two, you can swim in the Little Colorado River, where you'll find the turquoise water both other-worldly and inviting. On Day Four, you can make the steep hike to Deer Creek Falls. The view of the Colorado is splendid and a dip under the falls invigorating. On Day Five, wind your way over cliffs to the sparkling Havasu Creek on the Havasupai Indian Reservation. You can swim from one brilliant blue pool to the next.

Georgie also offers trip options for people with little time to spare. You can fly from Las Vegas to Whitmore Field and from there go by helicopter to the river and join the longer trip. You'll run medium-size rapids and see the Lower Granite Canyon. You return to Las Vegas by bus from Pierce Ferry after a three-day, two-night trip.

The river's campsites are filled on a first-come, first-served basis, so you won't know exactly where you'll stop. (This uncertainty will add to the sense of adventure.) When you do land, you find your own place to sleep in camp and then help unload the boats. Georgie makes dinner with a little help from the crew.

Dinner is served when Georgie blows her horn. This is always a four-course, one-bowl meal. You start with salad, follow with vegetables, top that with grilled meat wrapped in a tortilla, and end with canned chocolate pudding or fruit cocktail.

You retire soon after dark because you know you'll awake at dawn to the sound of Georgie's horn. As you struggle to the kitchen area, Georgie, wide awake, is busy serving breakfast—cereal, juice, and coffee or cocoa. Most mornings you'll stop for a second breakfast or "egg break." (Fill a tortilla with your own concoction—hard-boiled eggs, bacon bits, cheese, hot sauce—and you have "egg break.")

FOR CHILDREN: Children 6 and over may run the Colorado with Georgie, though the experience clearly isn't for every 6-year-old.

The favorite daily activity, of course, is running rapids—the bigger the better for most kids. In camp, they'll enjoy swimming, climbing on the rocks, and playing in the sand. When they go exploring, they may discover a cave, a lizard, or a handprint from an Anasazi Indian. Each side trip on shore is an adventure. The hikes are physically challenging and the views unbelievable. You may find yourself crawling on a rock ledge, standing under a waterfall, or playing frisbee in a cavern.

RATES AND PERSONAL GEAR: $$ to $$$$ Georgie's rates are considerably less than most other outfitters', but there is no discount for children. A 10% discount is available for May and September bookings. Georgie does not provide tents and discourages people from bringing them. Most children love sleeping out in the open (there are no mosquitoes).

You may bring your own tarps, sleeping bags, and waterproof bags or rent them from Georgie. Each rafter must bring a bowl, spoon, and cup, as well as raingear. (You'll wear the rain suit when you run rapids in the early morning.) Don't forget a waterproof camera and plenty of film.

Try to pick up a copy of Larry Stevens's guide, *The Colorado River in Grand Canyon,* at Marble Canyon Lodge. (You'll make a rest stop here on the bus trip from Las Vegas to Lee's Ferry.) Also of interest is *The River Runners,* a captivating history of Georgie Clark and all the other explorers since John Wesley Powell braved the rapids in 1869.

OF INTEREST NEARBY: If you want to experience the Grand Canyon from the top, plan to visit the North Rim. The view is breathtaking, and you'll find far fewer people here than at the South Rim.

You'll find great opportunities to hike amidst dramatic scenery at Zion and Bryce National Parks. If you go to Marble Canyon, you can visit the nearby Navajo reservation and the Painted Desert. The mesas of the Hopi reservation lie 100 miles to the east.

FOR MORE INFORMATION: Write Georgie's Royal River Rats, P.O. Box 12057, Las Vegas, NV 89112–0057 or call Lee McCurry at (702) 798-0602. Videos are available. For a list of all authorized river rafting companies in the Grand Canyon, write The Superintendent, Grand Canyon National Park, P.O. Box 129, Grand Canyon, AZ 86023.

Rafting on the Colorado River

Bill Dvorak's Kayak and Rafting Expeditions
Colorado and Utah

The Colorado River starts out high in the Rocky Mountains of Colorado, and 1,400 miles away it empties into the Gulf of California. Along the way, it drains one twelfth of the continental United States. It is the only significant source of surface water in the entire Southwest.

At its beginning, the Colorado is a free spirit, tumbling wildly through gorges and creating spectacular canyons. But as it heads south, it becomes much tamer, harnessed by 26 dams and encum-

bered since 1922 by volumes of court decrees and interstate com-
pacts that govern its use.

But where the river is still wild, it is awesome. Bill Dvorak's
Kayak and Rafting Expeditions, one of the most responsible outfitters in the Southwest, provides a wonderful opportunity to experience the Colorado's grandeur in a three-day trip from Loma,
Colorado, to Cisco, Utah, that takes in three of the river's most
spectacular canyons: Ruby, Horsethief, and Westwater.

Ruby Canyon is known for the red sandstone bluffs that tower
over the Colorado River, with some of the formations as high as
1,000 feet above the water. Horsethief Canyon once provided shelter
to horse thieves, bank robbers, and outlaws; now, the box canyons
serve instead as habitat for great blue heron, waterfowl, mule deer,
and desert bighorn. Westwater Canyon is marked by black, igneous
rock that is 1.7 billion years old, the oldest exposed formations in
eastern Utah. Along the entire route, heron soar overhead, swooping
down occasionally to fish; lucky boaters might also see golden eagles,
beavers, and deer.

THE OUTFITTER: Dvorak's Kayak and Rafting Expeditions
started in 1969 as Partners' River Program, a non-profit social service agency dedicated to bringing boating to special populations,
such as youths, families, and the disabled. Partners' became Dvorak's in 1984, and it has maintained its dedication in serving special
populations; approximately 40 percent of Dvorak trips are with
youth groups. Bill Dvorak, the owner, is also committed to making
the river accessible to the disabled through special services, adapted
boats, and substantial discounts.

Dvorak offers trips through 29 canyons on 10 rivers; they vary in
difficulty and include some of the most beautiful and historic regions
of the Southwest and West. Some trips are limited to children over
10; on other rivers Dvorak will take children as young as 5.

The basis of Dvorak's philosophy is participation. Unlike many
other white-water expedition outfitters, Dvorak prefers to take vacationers in paddle boats, which they paddle themselves, rather than
oar boats, which are paddled by guides. However, vacationers can
request to ride in an oar boat, if they prefer.

Dvorak employs only licensed professional guides who are trained in first aid and resuscitation, as well as lifesaving skills. All the guides are knowledgable about the flora, fauna, geology, and history of the canyons.

The rafting season on the Colorado, as on most western rivers, runs from May through September.

THE ITINERARY: The Ruby Canyon–Westwater trip is a three-day trip, with two days of flatwater and small rapids building up to the last day, when your raft passes through Class III, IV, and V rapids. Early in the spring, there is faster white water; later, the river is lower and calmer, perfect for a relaxed float through desert canyon.

Most participants schedule their arrival in Grand Junction, Colorado, the day before the raft trip embarks. Participants are taken from there in a 15-passenger van to the put-in point on the Colorado River, about a 20-minute drive.

The first day on the river, you learn paddle strokes and commands, and soon your crew is working together as a team, moving the boat backward and forward, left and right, as if you had been doing it all your life. High points on the first day are the trip through Ruby Canyon and the crossing of the Colorado-Utah state line. (Look for the line marked on the cliffs.)

Your boats will probably pull into camp early enough to allow you to take a swim or a walk before dinner. Watch for cougar tracks, old deer bones, and other signs of wildlife. You might want to just sit on the beach after unloading and look at the bluffs and the river. Or the crew will happily take you up on any offers of help in setting up camp and cooking dinner.

The camping is wilderness camping, following the "take only pictures, leave only footprints" philosophy. Tarps are provided for cover, though vacationers can rent or bring their own tents if they wish.

The food does not suffer from the primitive surroundings. Dvorak follows a long-established tradition of good eating among boaters.

Half of the fun of a river trip is listening to the staff tell tales (some of them tall) about the rapids they have run and those you can look forward to. There are nightly activities for children.

Most of the Dvorak trips have one side trip a day, often more, to a point of interest along the river. On the Ruby Canyon–Westwater trip, expect to hike in to see 14th-century petroglyphs left by the Indians who lived along the river. Everyone will enjoy the treat of a waterfall massage at an inlet a half mile up the Dolores River, which runs into the Colorado at the second day's campsite. Stepping into a prospector's soddy brings history home. The highlight, however, is an outlaws' cave, which you float to on the third day.

The third day of the trip also provides the greatest thrills. The rapids in Westwater Canyon are a chance to put what you have learned about boating to the test. After seven miles of successive rapids, everyone is ready for lunch and a few hours of easy boating to the take-out point near a ghost town. From there, it's a 90-minute ride by van back to Grand Junction.

FOR CHILDREN: Bill Dvorak has young children himself; the youngest took his first raft trip at the age of 7 weeks. He believes a river trip is especially suited for a family vacation, since boating allows families to come together on neutral ground with no distractions and no place to go except down the river. Dvorak caters to families with various discounts and custom trip planning.

Children are generally happier if there are other children in the group. Check with Dvorak's to see if you can book your trip when another family is signed up.

Children under 10 must ride in an oar boat; older children may ride in a paddle boat. The staff makes an extra effort to assure that children on the trip feel included and enjoy themselves.

RATES AND PERSONAL GEAR: $$ Dvorak's trips range in length from a half day to 12 days. Children's prices are approximately 10 percent less than adult prices, but substantial family discounts are offered on specified trips. To encourage family rafting, on some of the Dolores River trips each adult is allowed to bring along one child under 16 for free; this is also true on some of the six-day trips on the Green River. Early reservations are suggested for these trips.

Tarps, ground sheets, dry bags, water-resistant camera boxes, eating and cooking utensils, and food and wine are provided by Dvorak. He will rent you other equipment as needed and will mail you a checklist with packing suggestions before you leave home. You may bring your own beer or liquor.

OF INTEREST NEARBY: Grand Junction borders the Colorado National Monument, a national park with hiking and driving trails, picnic areas, and campgrounds. Evening camp-fire programs are offered by the National Park Service.

While in Grand Junction, you might want to stop at Dinosaur Valley at Fourth and Main streets, which displays dinosaur skeletons as well as one of the world's largest exhibits of animated lifelike dinosaurs. Then walk through the nearby "Rabbit Valley Trail Through Time Paleontological Area" to see the excavation sites.

Especially appealing to young children in Grand Junction is the Moon Farm, with farm animals, pony rides, an "international play-house," and the Doo Zoo, a miniature adult world and playhouse.

FOR MORE INFORMATION: Write Dvorak's Kayak and Rafting Expeditions at 17921 U.S. Highway 285, Nathrop, CO 81236, or call (719) 539-6851 or (800) 824-3795. FAX: (719) 539-3571.

Llama Trekking in the Big Horn Mountains
Sheridan, Wyoming

The old frontier town of Sheridan in central Wyoming has a natural appeal for adventurous families. Sheridan is just east of the Big Horn Mountains, called the White Rain Mountains by the Plains Indians, with fabulous outdoor recreation possibilities. Many fine dude ranches are scattered along the base of the mountain chain.

The Bighorn National Forest protects most of the scenic mountains in the area, and at its center is the Cloud Peak Wilderness

Area, a perfect place for an off-the-beaten-track family wilderness experience. While vacationing there, your family is likely to see mule deer, moose, and even elk. Small mammals and birds abound, including wild turkey. Trout fishing is allowed in most streams and lakes (rainbow and brown trout are the most common species). And the scenery is magnificent.

But to really enjoy the Big Horns you need to get out of your car, walk along a trail, and stay overnight beside a stream or lake, under a starlit sky. Not an easy thing to do with a family. Enter the llama, the perfect pack animal and a delightful trail companion. Llamas are now widely used in wilderness areas to carry the tents, sleeping bags, and food of families on outdoor adventures. Llamas won't bite or kick. They are easily handled, even by children, and their hoofs do far less damage to the terrain than those of horses and burros. They make a humming sound when they are contented and have the good grace to say nothing when they are not. No wonder everyone loves them!

THE OUTFITTER: Cloud Peak Llama Treks, in Story, Wyoming, organizes llama treks in the Cloud Peak Wilderness Area and throughout the Big Horn range. Owned by Dean and Barbara Coffman, the company specializes in trips for families; they know what it takes to provide a first-class outdoor experience with a mix of hiking, fishing, nature exploration, and relaxing. Experts in the natural history of the Big Horns accompany selected trips in the summer season, which adds a first-rate educational dimension.

The food provided by the outfitter is the kind of rib-sticking fare necessary to keep families going in the great outdoors. Pancakes and Dean's Breakfast Stew are specialties for the first meal of the day. Steak, chicken, or freshly caught fish, accompanied by fresh breads, biscuits, and cookies from the campstove, is served at lunch and dinner.

The trekking season extends from mid-May to mid-September. Early reservations are advised.

THE ITINERARY: Cloud Peak Llama Treks offers both regularly scheduled trips and custom trips tailored to fit a particular family's age range and physical abilities.

For all trips, Cloud Peak Llama Treks will meet trekkers at the airport or a hotel in Sheridan and transport them through the Bighorn National Forest to the trailhead. If you have your own car, you can follow the Coffmans to the trailhead and park your car there. At the trailhead, trekkers repack their gear into Cloud Peak's duffel bags for loading on the llamas. Scheduled trips range in length from two to 22 miles. On all trips, the pace is leisurely. Trekkers can stay with the llamas or walk at their own speed.

"Day Picnic Trips" include a short hike and a picnic lunch, some fishing, and a return to your car with no overnight stay. This is an ideal trip for families with very young children or those who want to sample a wilderness experience.

The "Scheduled Trip" will appeal to families who are beginning hikers and to more seasoned hikers who want to travel at an unhurried pace while enjoying the grandeur of the Big Horn Mountains. These two-night, three-day trips establish a base camp on the first day either two miles or four miles from the trailhead. Activities on the second day occur around the base camp. On the third day the group breaks camp and hikes back to the trailhead.

The two-mile base camp is set up on the East Fork of Big Goose Creek in the Bighorn National Forest. There your family can explore Big Goose Canyon, with its spectacular waterfalls and many natural swimming holes. Coney Lake, at a 10,000-foot elevation in the Cloud Peak Wilderness Area, is the site of the four-mile base camp.

The three-day "Custom Trip" is a plan-your-own adventure with an emphasis on hiking, fishing, climbing, or photography, as you wish. This trip is suitable for families with children over 8.

The "Drop Camp Trip" is the ultimate plan-your-own trip. You determine where you want to be dropped and how long you will stay. Cloud Peak packs you in and comes back for you at a prearranged time days or weeks later.

FOR CHILDREN: Adventures like this can start with children approaching kindergarten age. At 4, many children take a step up in their ability to walk for extended periods. At 5 years of age, a child who is motivated can walk for a considerable distance and can be an uncomplaining trail companion.

The Coffmans have two small children who often accompany

them on trips, so they are attuned to the needs of children and plan every aspect of their trips accordingly, from walking speed and distances to campsite selection, menus, and activities. If your young child tires, he or she can take a llama ride for a mile or so. Llamas carry loads of up to 80 pounds and can easily accommodate a weary youngster.

RATES AND PERSONAL GEAR: $ On the Scheduled and Custom trips rates include food, tents, llamas, pack equipment, and an experienced guide. There is a 10 percent discount for children under 12 and for all persons in groups of six or more. You can bring your own sleeping bag or rent one for a nominal fee. Fishing equipment is provided on request.

On receipt of your registration and deposit, Cloud Peak Llama Treks will send you trip information and a personal equipment list. It is advisable to bring your own day pack for raingear, a water bottle, and trail snacks.

OF INTEREST NEARBY: Sheridan is the site of the oldest rodeo in the nation—the Wyoming Rodeo, held in mid-July.

FOR MORE INFORMATION: Write Cloud Peak Llama Treks, P.O. Box 541, Story, WY 82842, or phone (307) 683-2732.

WEST COAST

Kayaking on the Navarro River
Mendocino County, California

To many people, kayaking conjures up images of seal-hunting Eskimos dodging icebergs on Arctic waters, or of helmeted daredevils in sleek plastic boats picking their way through boulders and thundering rapids.

Yet there is another way to think of it: as a family adventure that can combine a peaceful journey through some of America's most idyllic scenery, a camp-out beneath towering redwood trees, and a boating experience that is almost pure fun. California Rivers of Windsor, California, about an hour north of San Fransisco, specializes in the third way.

What makes kayaking a practical recreational possibility for children and beginners is the Kiwi Kayak, an innovation in kayak design that was conceived by Ann Dwyer, the founder and owner of California Rivers. Dwyer is recognized as one of the top white-water experts in the United States. Shorter and somewhat wider than conventional kayaks, the Kiwi has exceptional stability, which it combines with the maneuverability of its sportier cousins. That makes it an ideal boat for children as young as 10 or 12 and adult beginners.

California Rivers schedules its two-day redwoods trip on the Navarro River in April (call or write for precise dates). Excursions on other rivers are available throughout the spring and summer. In addition to kayaks, the outfitter also provides a few canoes for each trip. These may appeal to families with smaller children or to people who prefer an experience that is somewhat less demanding, although also highly rewarding.

The weather in spring is delightfully cool. The air is usually brilliant, and the river winds through canyons of the Coast Range foothills that are alive with spring colors and bird life. Twists and turns punctuate this 16-mile stretch of the Navarro, and the paddler can pleasurably alternate between concentrating on the demands of the water and a serene appreciation of the scenery.

THE OUTFITTER: California Rivers' headquarters is located just off U.S. 101, six miles north of Santa Rosa. The heart and soul of the operation is Dwyer, in her 60s, who presides over everything with a gentle, reassuring competence.

Dwyer is both a certified Red Cross canoeing instructor and an American Canoe Association white-water instructor. An authority on California rivers, she has published one book on the subject and has another in the works. On trips like the Navarro excursion, Dwyer will generally supervise matters from the back seat of the Blue Hole supply canoe.

In addition to a variety of kayaking trips, which last from a half day to five days, California Rivers also offers classes in kayaking and advanced river canoeing.

THE ITINERARY: The kayaking group gathers at Windsor at 8:30 A.M. and is promptly given instruction in the Kiwis and tips on river safety. The typical group is about 20, although Dwyer has escorted parties twice that size. The kayaks are loaded on top of cars, and then it's a scenic 50 miles from Windsor to the put-in point on the Navarro River. The route goes northwest, first through wine country, and then across the Coast Range, past orchards blooming with apple blossoms and pastures thick with sheep. You ride in your own vehicle or with other kayakers.

At Henry Woods State Park, about 3 miles from the town of Philo, the caravan stops by a bridge over the Navarro, and the Kiwis and supplies are hauled down to the riverbank. A good, hearty lunch is served, after which final instructions are given in water safety and the proper stowing of gear in the kayak, which holds more equipment than one might imagine. Then the party sets off in single file, the kayakers, as instructed by Dwyer, relaying back pertinent information about the current, obstacles, and so forth.

The scenery is majestic. Redwoods and Douglas firs tower over the canyon sides. Alders, red maples, bay willows, cottonwoods, tanbark, and dogwood are in abundance. In the river swim steelhead trout and salmon, and overhead, against a blue sky, soar ospreys, vultures, and hawks. Here and there delicate springs flow into the main stream.

By 5:30 or so, Dwyer will have selected a sand bar on which to camp for the night (no facilities). Before the last boat is pulled up on shore, she will have a fire going. The Navarro, at this point, is broad and still, so children can take the Kiwis out for some joyriding.

Everyone pitches in to fix dinner and clean up. A canoe is overturned to serve as the banquet table, and the hors d'oeuvres of paté and cheeses are laid out. Dinner follows: teriyaki beef on skewers, pasta with tomato sauce, salad, and French bread. Wine is provided; dessert is delicious chocolate cheesecake cupcakes.

After dinner, some may linger at the camp fire for songs or a cup of coffee, but most turn in early. To lie snugly in a sleeping bag and watch the stars beyond the tall redwoods and hear the Navarro murmuring softly a few feet away may well be one of the most restful experiences of a lifetime.

Before most of the group has awakened, Dwyer already has the camp fire going again. The routine of shared duties has been well established and smoothly produces scrambled eggs, sausages, English muffins (toasted marshmallow style), orange juice, and coffee.

By the time the group reassembles on the river, the morning fog has burned off, revealing a day of bright sunshine. The kayakers are more proficient now and are more adventuresome in the fast stretches.

By lunchtime, good appetites have developed. The lunch break also provides an opportunity to show off newly acquired skills. A particularly tricky run of the river is at hand, and one by one, with Dwyer leading the way to demonstrate technique, the kayakers shoot downstream.

The take-out point at the Dimmick Recreation Area is reached by late afternoon. The boats are cleaned out, trash is placed carefully in bins, and a shuttle operation quickly produces cars for the ride back to Windsor.

FAMILIES AND CHILDREN: Twelve is the ideal age for a child to begin Kiwi kayaking, says Dwyer. But children as young as 10 can be competent in a Kiwi. At that age, however, Dwyer recommends that the child share kayaking time, either with another child or with an adult.

In addition to the two-day Navarro redwoods trip, California Rivers welcomes children on its one-day trips on Cache Creek in the Sacramento Valley and on its five-day trips on the Klamath, Eel, and Trinity rivers. A minimum age of 12 applies on some of these.

Youngsters are expected to join in the activities of their parents and the others in the group. But that doesn't mean that the special needs of children aren't taken into account. On our trip, a 10-year-old celebrated his birthday with a cake provided by the outfitter.

The rivers and their surroundings are an excellent environment for children to experience nature firsthand, and the abundant opportunities for water play make a kayaking-canoeing trip appropriate for any school-age child.

RATES AND PERSONAL GEAR: $$ California Rivers takes care of virtually everything. All you need do is show up with a few items of personal gear, including sleeping bag.

California Rivers provides Kiwi kayaks, canoes, paddles, life jackets, two dry bags, and food and beverages. Small backpacking tents are optional and can come in handy in case of rain. Kayakers should avoid large, bulky items and restrict the weight of their personal gear to 25 pounds. A small but carefully stocked shop at the outfitter's headquarters offers a selection of river paraphernalia ranging from Kiwi kayaks to little stuffer bags to keep items dry.

In April, the temperature can dip into the 30s at night, so some warm clothing is mandatory. Because wool retains warmth even while wet, it is recommended over cotton fabrics. Bring along separate pairs of shoes for wear on and off the river.

Reservations are necessary.

FOR MORE INFORMATION: Write California Rivers, P.O. Box 1140, Windsor, CA 95492, or call (707) 838-7787.

1. At Strathcona Park Lodge on Vancouver Island, even young children can try kayaking in a protected cove. *(Photo: Martha Shirk)* **2.** The Gunflint Lodge in Minnesota supplies families with all the food and equipment needed for Boundary Water and Quetico canoe adventures. *(Photo: Nancy Klepper)* **3.** Organized hikes around the YMCA's Snow Mountain Ranch are just one of the many activities available at this 4,500-acre nature place. *(Photo: YMCA of the Rockies)* **4.** Camp Denali, which holds majestic Mt. McKinley in clear sight, specializes in guided hiking tours around Alaska's vast Denali National Park. *(Photo: Camp Denali)* **5.** Families can learn about ecology and conservation on the National Wildlife Federation's week-long Conservation Summits. *(Photo: Kent Dannen)* **6.** Bird-watching is one of the organized activities to be enjoyed on the National Wildlife Federation Conservation Summits. **7.** The six-day Family Adventure package at Strathcona Park Lodge offers such activities as canoeing, sailing, and nature hikes.

NATURE PLACES

5

6

7

SOUTHEAST

Watoga State Park
Marlinton, West Virginia

Few state parks are special enough to qualify as a good, solid destination for out-of-state families interested in nature-oriented vacations. Watoga State Park in West Virginia is an exception.

Watoga is a jewel because of its location in a wonderfully scenic area of West Virginia. The park sits astride a rugged mountain range, with the Greenbrier River its northwestern boundary. Watoga is located in a county with one of the lowest population densities of any area east of the Mississippi River. Even on weekends you feel that Watoga is almost yours alone.

ACCOMMODATIONS: $ Watoga has 41 cabins. Eight of these are deluxe cabins with two bedrooms, a kitchenette, living room, and bath; they sleep four people without rollaways and six with rollaways. The standard cabins, log cabins dating from the WPA projects of the 1930s, each have one to four bedrooms, a bath, and kitchenette; they sleep two to eight.

Kitchenettes contain a refrigerator, stove, sink, and cooking and eating equipment. Baths have showers but no tubs. All cabins have woodburning fireplaces. High chairs are available, and cribs are provided on request for a modest fee.

Only weekly cabin reservations are accepted from the second Monday in June through Labor Day. Only the deluxe cabins with central heating are open in winter months.

The park's 88 campsites are located in wooded areas along the Greenbrier River or Beaver Creek. Hook-ups are available.

DINING: The Park has a dining room in the administration building that operates from 8 A.M. to 8 P.M. daily from mid-April to mid-October. The menu is basic, so plan to do some of your own cooking for variety. The small shop in the administration building stocks only milk, bread, and a few staples like ketchup, so you should shop in nearby Marlinton on your way into the park.

ACTIVITIES

 One hard-surface outdoor court.

 In the park's Olympic-size swimming pool; separate wading pool.

Rental pedal boats and rowboats for use on Killbuck Lake. Outfitters in Marlinton offer canoe and raft trips on the Greenbrier River in the spring and tubing during the summer. Elk River Touring Center in Slatyfork (304-572-3771) can offer raft trips even farther afield.

Killbuck Lake is stocked with trout in the late winter and spring; temporary fishing licenses available in the park office. The best trout fishing is April to June. Bass can be caught all summer long in the Greenbrier River.

Both Elk River Touring Center and Appalachian Sport in Marlinton (304-799-4050) rent bikes for peddling along park roads and West Virginia's byways.

Watoga has more than 30 miles of well-maintained hiking trails, including stretches of the Allegheny Trail. The 75-mile-long Greenbrier River Trail passes just outside the Park boundary.

At Jadalee Stables, a very well-maintained facility within the park, open from late spring to early fall. Half-hour and one-hour rides at regular intervals during the day; longer rides and overnight camping trips can be arranged.

 The park has a small nature center with exhibits on local flora and fauna.

A recreation building has Ping Pong and pool tables and video games. Outdoor recreation facilities include shuffleboard, volleyball, and basketball.

 Cross-country skiing over groomed trails and sections of closed roadways.

FOR CHILDREN: "The Junior Naturalist Program" meets for several one and a half hour periods each week during the summer at the Nature Center. Children who complete the program receive patches. Other naturalist activities held during a typical week include a hike in the Park's arboretum or a "stream stomp" during which creatures in a West Virginia creek are captured and scrutinized before being returned to the wild.

A Killbuck Lake Fishing Derby for children 14 and under features friendly competition and prizes.

Evening activities that children will enjoy include nature movies, a beaver pond visit, volleyball and softball games, and a campfire with ghost stories at the stables.

NICETIES: Coin-operated washers and driers are available in the campgrounds.

OF INTEREST NEARBY: Cass Scenic Railroad State Park is a 45-minute drive from Watoga. It preserves the remnants of a company town built at the turn of the century as a base for logging operations in the surrounding mountains. A museum and an excellent slide show tell about early life in Cass, but the high point of a visit is a ride on a train pulled by one of the railroad's original Shay locomotives over 11 miles of original track. The trains run from Memorial Day to Labor Day. Special Saturday night programs with dinner and music are held during the summer.

Not far from Cass, near the settlement of Green Bank, is the National Radio Astronomy Observatory. One hour tours are conducted from mid-June through Labor Day.

Cranberry Glades Botanical Area is a few miles northwest of Watoga. The plant and animal life in Cranberry Glades closely resemble the ecology of a northern Canadian bog. In the last ice age, these plant and animal species migrated here. As the climate warmed, the bog ecology survived because of the high altitude. A self-guided trail over a boardwalk takes you to two of the four glades in this mountain valley. A nearby visitors' center has exhibits on Cranberry Glades and other aspects of Monongahela National Forest ecology.

Beartown State Park is a concentration of heavily creviced rocks that form a maze of passages. Local legend has it that colonies of bears used to stroll up and down the rock passages as if they were streets. Today, boardwalks traverse the crevices, and no bears are in evidence.

FOR MORE INFORMATION: Write Watoga State Park, Star Route 1, Box 252, Marlinton, WV 24954 or phone (800) CALL-WVA or (304) 799-4087.

Great Smoky Mountains National Park
Gatlinburg, Tennessee

Great Smoky Mountains National Park is one of the most beloved parks in the national park system. Its location astride the border between Tennessee and North Carolina puts the park within a day's drive of nearly half the population of the United States.

The 517,000-acre park is one of the most biologically diverse areas in the country. This luxuriant region has more tree species than all of Europe, more black bears than any other national park, more than 200 species of birds, and 27 species of salamanders, some of which grow to more than two feet in length. For this reason, the United Nation's Man in Biosphere Program chose the park as a site for the collection of baseline data against which to measure the impact of humankind on the environment.

The Park also has over 75 historic structures, many dating to the period of first settlement in this region. Costumed interpreters at some of these sites re-create the history of the hardy farmers and mountain folk who made a living in the narrow, wooded valleys of the Smokys.

ACCOMMODATIONS: $ Most visitors stay overnight within the park camp in one of the nine campgrounds, which altogether have 920 campsites. Reservations are essential; make them through your local Ticketron outlet or call (804) 456-2267. Several campgrounds are open all year; Cades Cove, Elkmont, and Smokemont are the best. Backcountry camping at 116 designated sites is allowed with a permit.

The only drive-to hotel within the park boundaries is the Wonderland Hotel, with 27 rooms. Wonderland first opened in the early 1900s as a private club. The rocking chairs on the spacious veranda still provide a perfect setting for daydreaming. Call (615) 436-5490.

Remote LeConte Lodge is at the summit of Mt. LeConte and is only accessible by horseback or a half-day hike (five and a half miles and an ascent of 2,560 vertical feet). LeConte has no showers and no indoor plumbing. Rates include breakfast and dinner. Reservations are essential; call (615) 436-4473.

One of our very favorite family vacation places, the Nantahala Outdoor Center, in Bryson, North Carolina, offers a variety of lodgings from cozy log cabins with kitchens to motel-style rooms. Call (704) 488-2175.

DINING: The Wonderland Hotel has a dining room, and the Nantahala Center has three on-site restaurants, all fairly funky: Relia's Garden, a striking wooden birdcage of a structure; River's End, on the banks of the Nantahala River; and Slow Joe's. The towns at the two main entrances to the Park, Gatlinburg and Cherokee, each have an abundance of restaurants and food stores.

For campers, Cades Cove and Deep Creek Campgrounds have stores that stock basic provision. Picnic sites are located throughout the park.

ACTIVITIES

The Nantahala Outdoor Center (704-488-2175) is one of the nation's premier centers for whitewater rafting, canoeing, and kayaking. Three and four-day family canoe courses and children's kayak courses are scheduled in the summer, as well as one-day raft trips and guided hiking and bike trips. Day care is available for young children.

 Seven hundred thirty-five miles of streams challenge trout and bass fishermen; Tennessee or North Carolina license required.

Rental bikes are available from several concessions in the park. Cyclists are welcome on designated trails. The 11-mile loop through Cades Cove is great for family cycling.

 The park's wild interior is crisscrossed by 900 miles of hiking, cycling, and riding trails, among them a 72-mile stretch of the famed Appalachian Trail. Day hikes on the Appalachian Trail are possible from Davenport Gap, Fontana Dam, or Clingman's Dome.

Guided rides from stables near several of the campgrounds. Hayrides from the Cades Cove stables.

Ranger-led activities and campfire programs are scheduled daily during the summer months. Stop at either the Sugarlands Visitors Center near Gatlinburg or the Oconaluftee Visitor Center near Cherokee, North Carolina for a schedule.

The Smoky Mountain Field School, operated by the University of Tennessee, offers one- and two-day courses. Among the topics are wildlife, spiders, mountain wildflowers, geology, nature photography, and conservation issues. Call (615) 974-6688.

Wilderness Southeast, a not-for-profit outdoor education organization, conducts fully outfitted family camping trips several weekends each year in the Smokies. From a base camp, its groups explore the surrounding country on day hikes. The Wilderness Southeast guides impart a storehouse of information on the forest ecosystem, wildflowers, and animal tracks you discover on any walk. Call (912) 897-5108.

FOR CHILDREN: The six-mile-long valley of Cades Cove was a farming community in the 19th century. Today, it is a living history museum. Families can explore the handhewn barns and cabins and watch corn being ground into meal at the water-powered Cable Mill; some members of the interpretive staff are descendants of the original settlers. From Cades Cove, the nature walks to Abrams Falls and the Skinks Cascades along the Little River Road are negotiable with strollers.

Oconaluftee Pioneer Farmstead, adjacent to the Visitors Center on Newfound Gap Road, is a restored 19th-century farmstead. Pioneer craft demonstrations are offered daily from mid-May through October.

The Great Smoky Mountains Natural History Association (615-448-6709) holds programs for families each July. Their three- to four-day long family camps feature hiking, swimming, storytelling, and a special Appalachian music performance; the fee includes six family-style meals, dormitory housing, and all activities. The association also schedules a special summer Elderhostel program for grandparents and grandchildren.

OF INTEREST NEARBY: The Cherokee Indians are an integral part of the history of the Smoky Mountains. Worth a visit in any season is the Cherokee Oconaluftee Village and Qualla Crafts Shop south of the Park in the town of Cherokee, North Carolina. An excellent museum tells the story of the Cherokee, and the gift shop sells high-quality Indian crafts.

FOR MORE INFORMATION: Write the Superintendent, Great Smoky Mountains National Park, Gatlinburg, TN 37738, or call (615) 436-1200.

Gulf State Park
Gulf Shores, Alabama

Gulf Shores, Alabama has all the amenities American families have come to expect from their beach resorts: miniature golf courses, petting zoos, T-shirt shops, a wave pool, video arcades, and fast-food outlets. There's even an enormous gift shop, Souvenir City, that you enter through the mouth of a giant shark.

But near the easternmost end of Gulf Shores is a jewel of a state park that proves you can have your 20th-century creature comforts and celebrate nature too. Gulf State Park occupies a two and a half mile-long stretch of gorgeous, sugar-white beach on the Gulf of Mexico and 6,000 acres of marshlands, forests, and freshwater lakes. This low-budget, family-oriented resort tries its best to integrate an appreciation for nature into the vacation experience. Gulf State Park manages to please naturalists, beachcombers, sports enthusiasts, sun worshippers, and families at play.

ACCOMMODATIONS: $ to $$ The resort hotel, built out of concrete so it will withstand hurricanes, offers accommodations in 144 beachside motel-type units, each with two double beds, cable TV, individual air conditioners and a private balcony or patio (there's no better gulf view in Gulf Shores). The 18 suites have one room with two double beds or a king-size bed and a connecting room with a kitchenette and a double bed or sofa bed. Children under 12 stay free; older children pay an extra $5 daily. Many package plans are offered. No pets are allowed.

In addition, there are 17 attractive modern cabins built on stilts next to 500-acre Lake Shelby. Each has two or three bedrooms plus a sofa sleeper in the living room, a fully equipped kitchen, and a screened-in porch. There are also four rustic one-room cabins north of Lake Shelby.

The park's nicely shaded campground has 468 sites with water, electricity, picnic tables, and grills; many are located on the shore of 100-acre Middle Lake. Some have sewage hook-ups.

There's a three-night minimum stay required on Memorial Day and Labor Day weekends, over New Year's, and during the annual shrimp festival in the fall.

DINING: The Sandcastle Dining Room at the hotel serves breakfast, lunch, and dinner. During the summer, a special theme buffet is offered almost every evening, ranging from Italian cuisine to a beachside Alabama boil to a luau. Drinks are served in the Fountain Lounge and at the pool bar.

There are snack bars at the Pro Shop, pier, and beach pavilion.

The town of Gulf Shores has scores of restaurants specializing in local seafood and Southern cooking, as well as plenty of fast-food outlets.

ACTIVITIES

 Two lighted courts in front of the hotel; four unlighted courts near the Nature Center.

 Eighteen-hole course designed by Earl Stone; pro shop with equipment rental.

 In the large beachside pool, in the Gulf of Mexico, and in Lake Shelby.

The park's naturalists offer guided canoe trips on Little Lake. In addition, canoes and johnboats can be rented. Launching of powerboats is permitted on Lake Shelby and Middle Lake; water-skiing and sailing permitted on Lake Shelby. Rental Hobie cats, wind-surfers and pedalboats on the beach. Excursions can be arranged on the Cyrus E. King, a 65-foot Chesapeake Bay bugeye ketch. Call (205) 968-6775.

From the 825-foot pier (fee charged), in Lake Shelby, or from charter fishing boats. Bait, tackle, licenses, and other supplies available at the Lake Store.

 Rental bikes available for the day or week from Island Recreation (205-948-7334) in town.

 Complimentary equipment for volleyball, basketball, and horseshoes at the Nature Center.

Several marked trails crisscross the park. Hurricane Ridge Trail wanders through live oaks, saw palmettos, and sawgrass. Bear Creek Trail is accessible to the handicapped. Along Bobcat Branch Trail you'll probably see some marsh rabbits. Alligator Marsh Trail follows Bear Creek and promises sightings of many turtles. Middle Lake Trail offers the best chance for seeing alligators.

 The park's Nature Center has a charming collection of exhibits on the island's natural history, and a touch table with bird's nests, antlers, a pelican skull, and the shells of assorted marine creatures. Tanks hold live specimens such as turtles, snakes, fish, and alligators. There are occasional slide presentations by rangers from the U.S. Fish and Wildlife Service and guided beach walks by the nature center's naturalists.

SOCIAL ACTIVITIES: Guided bike hikes, slide presentations, nature films, needlecraft classes, pot luck suppers, card and horseshoe tournaments, weenie roasts, ice-cream socials, church services, and organized "mind games."

FOR CHILDREN: On summer weekends, the staff at the Nature Center schedules numerous activities for children and families, including puppet shows, crafts workshops, bike hikes, nature talks, kite-flying events, storytime, sandcastle building competitions, evening cartoons, night hikes, and stargazing expeditions. Each summer, Smokey the Bear visits the park to teach children about preventing forest fires. There's a playground near the Nature Center.

NICETIES: There's a laundromat for the use of guests.

OF INTEREST NEARBY: Bon Secour National Wildlife Refuge, at the western end of Gulf Shores, protects more than 4,000 acres of undisturbed coastal barrier habitat. It's a nice place for a hike, birdwatching, and beachcombing.

Fort Morgan, on the island's western tip, guarded the entrance to Mobile Bay during the early 19th century. This star-shaped fort is a fascinating place for children to explore and learn about Confederate history.

It's fun for families to take the scenic car ferry from Fort Morgan to Dauphin Island, the site of Fort Gaines, another Civil War fort. From there, it's only a short ride to Bellingrath Gardens, a 905-acre semi-tropical botanical garden and estate in Theodore.

In the other direction, the free Naval Aviation Museum in Pensacola has an interesting display of aircraft and Navy memorabilia.

FOR MORE INFORMATION: Write Gulf State Park, Dept. SFV, P.O. Box 437, Gulf Shores, AL 36542 or call (800) 544-GULF (for hotel information) or (205) 948-PARK (for campground and general park information.)

MIDWEST

Gunflint Lodge
Gunflint Trail, Minnesota

The glacial shield that covered Canada and the northern United States in the Ice Age scoured out thousands and thousands of lakes. Today the area along the border between Minnesota and Canada is a recreational paradise. Boating, fishing, swimming, and hiking are activities common to all the lodges in the area, but few offer programs specifically designed for families. Gunflint Lodge is one that does.

Gunflint Lodge, 150 miles north of Duluth, opened in 1928 and has been a family business for more than 50 years. A remarkable woman, Justine Kerfoot, was one of the pioneer resort operators along the Gunflint Trail in northern Minnesota. She built Gunflint Lodge from a few cabins with no indoor plumbing or electricity into a modern and comfortable resort. Her son Bruce and his wife, Sue, and their two sons carry on.

Gunflint Lake is a wonderful locale for a vacation. The United States-Canada border runs down the middle of the lake in front of the Lodge. The legendary *voyageurs* traveled this lake in canoes to trade knives and axes and beads for furs.

ACCOMMODATIONS: **$** to **$$$** The 25 cabins at Gunflint Lodge range from older cabins that are basic and comfortable to more recently built earth-sheltered units with wall-to-wall carpets, spa-type bathtubs, and saunas. Most cabins have fireplaces and kitchenettes. The number of bedrooms varies from one to four.

The lodge offers a wide assortment of accommodation packages and plans. Most guests opt for one of the American Plan packages that include all meals, or the Modified Housekeeping Package that includes only dinners.

The Deluxe Family Package, which is offered from mid-May to mid-October, includes all meals, accommodations with a fireplace, a boat and motor with unlimited gas, two canoes, and the lodge's Nature Program. Rates for this package are quoted for stays ranging from two to 10 nights. Children's rates are available; children under 3 are charged a nominal daily fee. A 10 percent service charge is added to rates in lieu of tipping.

If you want to do some of your own cooking and can do without a boat and motor every day, then one of the housekeeping packages may be for you. The rates from the housekeeping packages are in the $ and $$ categories.

DINING: The original main lodge building and dining hall burned down in 1953. Within a week of the fire, work began on the present main lodge building, with its picture windows overlooking the lake and two massive stone fireplaces, one in the dining room and one in the lounge. Using ax and saw, Justine Kerfoot fashioned the comfortable dining-room furniture herself.

Breakfast service starts at 7 A.M. for those eager to start fishing and lasts until 10 A.M., when the sleep-ins rouse themselves. It's an open menu at breakfast.

Lunch includes a tasty homemade soup, a choice among three entrées, and a dessert.

Dinners include soup, salad, and two delicious entrées served family style so that you can sample both. A smorgasbord is served on Sunday evenings. Cocktails, beer, and wine may be purchased with dinner.

The kitchen prepares packed lunches for those who want to venture out for a day.

ACTIVITIES

A refreshing experience in the lakes, which usually are ice-covered until April. The lodge's swimming season officially starts on July 1. A swimming raft is anchored in the lake a few yards from the small sand beach in front of the main lodge building. Children can test their balance on the large log tethered to the raft.

Gunflint Lake is more than a mile wide and about nine miles long. Motoring or canoeing through a short connecting channel takes you into adjacent Magnetic Lake. Motorboats, canoes, and kayaks are always available for use. The boats are sturdy, wide-beamed 15-foot aluminum models with 15-horsepower motors. Among the kayaks are peanut shell models for young children. Life jackets are available in the boat house. The lodge also runs a program of raft trips on the nearby Cross River.

The season runs from mid-May through late September for lake trout, walleyed pike, and smallmouth bass. You can engage the services of a Gunflint Lodge fishing guide for a day or half-day. On daylong fishing trips your guide will prepare a shore lunch that includes some of the fish you catch. The lodge also has a fishing pro whose fishing productivity is astounding. The lodge can supply you with Minnesota fishing permits and arrange for Canadian documents as well. Live bait is available for purchase at the boat dock, and the lodge gift shop carries the essentials in tackle. If you forget your fishing rod and reel, the lodge will lend you equipment.

The Gunflint Nature Program runs from early June to early September, with two or more activities scheduled every day. Some activities are geared for children, like crafts, scavenger hunts, and terrarium-making. For families, the lodge naturalist may take the 20-passenger pontoon boat down the lake to see Bridal Falls or the old Dutch Ovens. Or the day's schedule may include bird-watching, night walking, a nature hike, a walk to Magnetic Rock, an evening beaver study trip, or a van ride to the end of the Gunflint Trail in search of bear and moose. The lodge maintains a network of hiking and nature trails that fan out behind the main lodge building. One of these will take you to High Cliffs, with its magnificent view of Gunflint Lake.

Gunflint Lodge is also open in the winter for cross-country skiers. It participates with other lodges along the Gunflint Trail in a Ski Lodge-to-Lodge program.

Gunflint Lodge serves as an outfitter for Boundary Water and Quetico canoe adventures. The lodge supplies all the food and equipment you need, including canoes and life jackets, tents with mosquito netting, sleeping bags, and mats. A personal guide, who knows canoeing and the out-of-doors well, instructs you in the few canoeing fundamentals you need to know, and then takes you beyond civilization to incredibly beautiful small lakes where your party is likely to be the only visitors. You're sure to see lots of waterfowl and maybe a moose or two. The lodge-to-lodge canoe trip offers six days of guided, pampered adventure.

Gunflint Lodge also will outfit your family for much longer canoe trips in the Boundary Waters.

FOR CHILDREN: Children aged 6 through 15 who are staying at the lodge for a week or more will be taken on a half-day guided fishing trip with other children at no extra charge.

The lodge's playground has horseshoes, swings, a sandbox and sandbox toys, and climbing equipment with a tree house. The swimming, boating, nature program, and overnight canoe trip are other activities that children will enjoy.

A large number of ducks consider Gunflint Lodge to be their summer home. The cracked corn they love to eat is stored in the shed at the boat dock. Children also like to inspect the fishing bait in the same shed. The bathtub full of leeches holds a special fascination.

Baby-sitting can be arranged through the front desk.

NICETIES: The coffee pot is on in the lodge dining room from early morning until late at night. Tea and hot chocolate are also available. Ask the dining-room staff for a thermos bottled filled with coffee for your day trip.

Your fish catch is fileted, wrapped, and frozen at no additional charge.

The main lodge lounge has games, books, and newspapers, including child-oriented materials. It also houses a large collection of Indian relics, objects the *voyageurs* lost when their canoes turned over in rapids, and articles from the fur trade.

Most of the cabins with kitchenettes also have coffee makers and popcorn poppers.

OF INTEREST NEARBY: The town of Grand Marais on Lake Superior at the head of the Gunflint Trail is worth a visit. There you can tour a lumber mill, charter a sailing boat for a day on Lake Superior, patronize one of the local bakeries, visit the Coast Guard Station, go bowling, or tour the Cook County Historical Museum.

Bears gather each evening to check out the bill of fare in the local dumpsters.

FOR MORE INFORMATION: Write Gunflint Lodge, 750 Gunflint Trail, 100GT, Grand Marais, MN 55604, or call (800) 328-3325.

SOUTHWEST AND MOUNTAIN STATES

YMCA of the Rockies
Estes Park Center
Estes Park, Colorado
Snow Mountain Ranch
Winter Park, Colorado

Ringed by the rugged, snow-dusted peaks of Rocky Mountain National Park—and older than the Park itself—the Estes Park Center combines a spectacular high-country setting with down-to-earth rates. Nothing fancy about the accommodations here, though the center offers a wide range of cabins and lodge rooms scattered through 1,300 acres. But the amenities include backdoor access to Rocky Mountain National Park, an ever-present, ever-changing mountain vista, and an extensive menu of activities that you can sample from or choose to ignore. We always leave feeling doubly refreshed—first by the surroundings, and second by the knowledge that we enjoyed them at non-profit organization prices.

On the western side of the park—about 80 miles away by car if you go "over the top" on Trail Ridge Road—sits 4,500-acre Snow Mountain Ranch at an elevation of 8,800 feet. This younger and quieter sister of the Estes Park Center is also operated by the YMCA of the Rockies organization. Although well established as a ski center for many years, in the mid-1980s it got a face lift so it would attract more summer visitors. New at Snow Mountain Ranch in 1991: the Vacation Kidney Center of the Rockies, a joint project of the YMCA of the Rockies, the National Kidney Foundation of Colorado, and University Hospital in Denver. It's a pioneering concept that provides dialysis and post-transplant care for adults and children in a vacation setting.

Both facilities are less than a two-hour drive from Denver. They are popular sites for family reunions; in any given week, you'll find four generations gathered to enjoy the great outdoors.

ACCOMMODATIONS: $ Estes Park Center has more than 200 cabins and 11 lodges designed to accommodate 4,400 guests. If your budget is a primary consideration, you can choose relatively spartan accommodations at bargain basement prices. A family of five can easily be accommodated in a dormitory-style room in one of the Eastside Lodges (rooms include two sets of bunk beds, a day bed, and a bath with a shower, but no tub). Each lodge has a comfortable lounge with a huge stone fireplace; after the children have gone to bed at night, many parents gather here for some adult talk and a cup of tea.

If you're really looking for a bargain, request space in a lodge with a central bath, where rates can go as low as a few dollars a day each for a family of six.

At the other extreme, but still inexpensive, the Estes Park Center offers deluxe three-bedroom cabins that sleep seven. Two-bedroom cabins are among the most sought-after accommodations. Each cabin includes a full kitchen, bathroom, and often a fireplace. There are also motel-style lodge rooms with two double beds and a sofa bed, a balcony, and full bath.

Rates at Estes Park Center are discounted in winter; it books up early for the prime months of July and August. Reservations from the general public are accepted beginning in early April. You would be well advised to reserve then if you can't be flexible about the time and type of accommodations. To improve your chances of getting a reservation, you can pay a nominal yearly membership fee, which allows you to make reservations a month earlier than the general public. Family reunions can be booked through the group sales office.

Reservation procedures are similar at Snow Mountain Ranch, but here you're more likely to run into a crowd during the ski season. Some lodge rooms include a double bed, bunk beds, and a full bath. There are four lodges and more than 40 cabins nestled among the tall pines, with views of the Indian Peaks range to the east and Gore range to the west; the capacity is 1,400.

DINING: Bowls of yogurt, trays of fresh fruit, rows of omelettes, bins of sausage and bacon, and an assortment of pastries thrown in for good measure—that's standard fare at the breakfast buffet every summer morning in the Pine Room at Estes Park Center. If you manage to work up an appetite by lunch, you can return to the Pine Room to order from a menu, or visit the snack bar in the administration building. Another option is the small general store, where you can purchase drinks and simple supplies for cabin cooking and lunches on the trail. Sack lunches may also be ordered.

Dinner in the Pine Room is another smorgasbord, usually featuring several entrées and a wide assortment of salads and vegetables. Once a week, guests adjourn to an outdoor shelter, where singing usually accompanies the barbecue.

No alcoholic beverages are served or allowed in public areas. Guests may drink alcoholic beverages in their rooms or cabins.

For variety, try one of the restaurants in Estes Park, only a short ride by car or public trolley from the Estes Park Center.

No breakfast buffet is available at Snow Mountain Ranch, but three meals a day are served in the Aspen Room. The resort also offers a store. Within driving range for dinner are Granby and Grand Lake, where we found an impressive family-style meal at The Mountain Inn.

ACTIVITIES

 Outdoor courts at both facilities; no court fees.

 Heated indoor pools at both facilities.

 White-water raft trips can be arranged on nearby rivers.

Organized hikes at both locations range from a sedate ramble to an all-day assault on Longs Peak that begins before dawn. The less adventurous can see the park's back roads from touring vehicles that look like oversized jeeps. Periodic instruction in astronomy, conservation, geology, wilderness safety, meteorology, orienteering, and Rocky Mountain flora and fauna.

Trail rides from stables at both facilities. At Estes Park Center, horseback rides take you into Rocky Mountain National Park for some spectacular scenery—all the more beautiful from horseback if your feet are sore from hiking. At Snow Mountain Ranch, the rides visit nearby mountains and meadows.

Crafts centers at both facilities; horseshoes, roller-skating, basketball, hayrides, volleyball, softball, family programs.

Evening programs include camp fires, movies, square dancing, roller-skating, classical and folk music, and an eclectic series of talks by guests.

While both facilities are open year-round, Snow Mountain Ranch is the center of winter action. Within a 15-mile drive are the Winter Park and Silver Creek downhill ski areas. Snow Mountain Ranch itself hosts several cross-country ski races. Ice-skating and sleigh rides are also available. The program building houses a ski rental shop.

FOR CHILDREN: In addition to all the regular programs, which are intended to include children, both facilities offer inexpensive day camps for children from age 3 through high school. Activities include the standard day camp favorites, with heavy emphasis on the outdoors. Most participants get a chance to ride the horses as part of the program.

Children between 3 and 5 meet from 8:30 to 11:30 A.M. and again from 12:30 to 3:30 P.M. Monday through Friday; full or part-day rates are available, and child care can be arranged through the lunch hour if necessary. Children from first through eighth grades meet from 8:30 A.M. to 3:30 P.M. Monday through Friday; lunch is included in the fee.

At the Estes Park Center, the Teen Barn is open from 8:30 A.M. to 10 P.M. Monday through Friday for children in senior high school; teenagers plan most of their own activities.

Younger members of your family may become devotees of the Y's miniature golf courses.

NICETIES: Gift shops at both Estes Park Center and Snow Mountain Ranch will allow you to satisfy the urge for souvenirs at a reasonable cost. Another convenience is a Y charge-card, which allows you to pay for all meals and activities when you check out.

For a rainy afternoon, seek solace in the libraries at both Estes Park and Snow Mountain.

At Estes Park Center, the Lula W. Dorsey Museum will show you what the turn-of-the-century tourist was likely to find.

OF INTEREST NEARBY: Rocky Mountain National Park and the ranges that border it dominate both Estes Park Center and Snow Mountain Ranch. Touring the park by foot, horseback, or car, you can see deer, elk, and, if you're lucky, the elusive bighorn sheep. The simplest park trails, such as the paved walkway around Bear Lake, are as easy as a stroll around the block. But the rugged peaks can challenge the most experienced climber.

An unforgettable family outing is a drive up Trail Ridge Road, one of the highest stretches of highway in the world. Trees thin and finally give way to meadows of wildflowers in the Alpine tundra. A crisp breeze cuts even the warmest day. The thin air will leave you puffing.

Colorado's largest natural lake, Grand Lake, sits at the south-western edge of the park, as well as man-made Lake Granby and Shadow Mountain Lake.

If you tire of the natural surroundings, you can find shopping, restaurants, and other tourist attractions in the cities of Estes Park and Winter Park.

FOR MORE INFORMATION: For Estes Park Center, call (303) 586-3341 or write Estes Park Center, 2515 Tunnel Road, Estes Park, CO 80511-2550. For Snow Mountain Ranch: Call (303) 887-2152 or write Snow Mountain Ranch, P.O. Box 169, Winter Park, CO 80482.

The Nature Place
Colorado Outdoor Education Center
Florissant, Colorado

The full variety of Rocky Mountain scenery, ranging from the desert to Alpine tundra, comes into focus through the exciting natural history programs offered at The Nature Place. On 6,000 acres of private land surrounded by National Forest just west of Pike's Peak, The Nature Place offers first-rate accommodations with in-depth study excursions designed to meet the varying needs and interests of the young and old.

Owners Laura and Roger "Sandy" Sanborn have run separate camps for boys and girls on the site for four decades. In the late 1970s, the Sanborns opened The Nature Place as a kind of camp for families. A passage in a booklet that visitors find in their room sets the tone for a vacation experience here: "In the outdoors we can be reminded that humans have evolved to wonder, that understanding is joy, and that the knowledge of the wholeness of the earth's systems is a prerequisite to survival."

Land surrounding The Nature Place includes pine, spruce and fir forests, meadows, streams, ponds, aspen groves, rocky bluffs, and a 120-year-old working cattle ranch.

ACCOMMODATIONS: $$ Each of the 44 modern, carpeted studio apartments has a full bath, fireplace, two extra-long twin beds, two easy chairs, and a vaulted ceiling loft with two studio couch beds. A small refrigerator, sink, toaster oven, and electric kettle round out a kitchen space. Granite on the hearth adds to the rustic feel of the rooms. Eastern-facing windows look out on Pike's Peak. A spacious lodge houses the dining room, meeting and play rooms, and a lounge well stocked with interesting books and magazines.

Also at the lodge are two telescopes for viewing Pike's Peak or an occasional deer that wanders up to the salt lick near the two outdoor tennis courts. The lodge game room houses a Ping-Pong table, pool table, and television with a VCR.

Rates for a six-night stay vary slightly depending on the program;

children under 5 are free, and between 5 and 15 they pay lower-than-adult rates. The rates include accommodations, three meals per day, all recreation, instruction and guiding, transportation to sites on and off the ranch, plus use of all facilities and equipment.

Daily rates are also available, and there are special rates for weekend programs in the fall and winter. In September, The Nature Place offers a special three-day fall foliage tour, with opportunities to ride horses, fish, hike, and observe an abundance of wildlife, including large herds of elk and deer. You may dip candles, bake biscuits, and make apple cider at the Quick Homestead, a restored 1880s potato farm.

DINING: Excellent home-cooked meals are served buffet style at the lodge. Sack lunches are provided for guests going on outings.

The cooks bake their own bread, biscuits, and desserts. If you are fortunate enough to have a birthday while you are there, just let the staff know; you will be presented with a delicious fresh-baked cake to share with other guests.

During the week-long programs, one night will typically include a barbecue, where Sandy will tell stories of the early settlers or the native peoples who preceded them.

Except for the wine and cheese parties, no alcoholic beverages are available at The Nature Place, but you are welcome to bring your own. Ice is available in guest rooms.

ACTIVITIES

 In heated indoor pool; hot tub.

 Local outfitters can help you plan a day of rafting on the Arkansas River.

 In several stocked trout ponds.

 Besides the pool, the sports complex has a sauna, Jacuzzi, and multi-use game room (tennis, basketball, volleyball, and exercise equipment are available). There's also a one-mile fitness course.

Instruction in such creative arts as photography, pottery, lapidary, sketching, darkroom skills, and weaving.

On a clear evening, the staff may set up a telescope for stargazing. Other evenings may include a slide show on beavers, geology, or the history of Cripple Creek.

Walk 20 minutes through the ponderosa pine forest and you will be at the Interbarn—an ecology center with information on birds, plants, mammals, rocks, and fossils of the area, plus such extra attractions as an inflatable planetarium and a seismograph. During the week-long programs in the summer you can go out on daily excursions with expert rock hounds, bird-watchers, and wildflower specialists. One day you will travel down the "shelf road" into Sonoran Desert country and find 500-million-year-old fish scales in some of the oldest sedimentary rock in the Rocky Mountains. The next day you may visit the Florissant Fossil Beds and see the remains of plants and insects preserved for 36 million years in volcanic ash and mud. You may have a chance to dig for your own fossil specimens on private land a short distance away from the National Monument. Another day you will travel across Leavick Valley and ride up to Horseshoe Mountain to browse among the Alpine cushion plants at 11,500 feet.

The young and fearless go "slickersliding" on the snow patches that remain on into July and August. The hikers head for high country and a lake at the base of the glacial cirque, while the sitters enjoy a beautiful view of the valley below or inspect the wildflowers with greater care.

With golden eagles, broadtailed hummingbirds, western tanagers, and olive-sided flycatchers among the over 50 species seen around The Nature Place, bird-watching is a joy. Bring your binoculars and cameras on all of the day trips. Summer flowering plants vary greatly from the Montane Zone, where The Nature Place is located, to the Subalpine Zone on Horseshoe Mountain.

Day trips leave from the lodge at 9 A.M. and return between 3:30 and 5 P.M. Visitors ride in vans with a driver and specialist guide, plus a cooler of meat, cheese, and sodas for lunch.

Cross-country skiing, ice-skating, tubing, sledding, hiking, birding, and opportunities for seeing bighorn sheep. The special winter program weeks also include a day of downhill skiing at Breckenridge. Especially popular with families is The Nature Place's Winter Family Week, which usually begins right after Christmas. Watching the New Year's Eve fireworks over Pike's Peak is an unforgettable experience.

FOR CHILDREN: On some of the week-long programs, the age range is from 3 to 80, and everyone has a good time. Grandparents particularly seem to enjoy bringing grandchildren for a good week of sharing. Talk with The Nature Place staff before you schedule your stay to find out if any special programs are being offered for children.

In the absence of special kids' activities, children join the adults on the van trips. The experience here is aimed at families who like doing and learning things together.

Many of the educational displays at the Interbarn are especially designed for young learners. For example, a giant cell allows children and adults to get inside the life process.

NICETIES: The one-week programs in the summer usually begin with wine and cheese on a Saturday afternoon and wind up after breakfast on a Friday morning.

Bouillon, tea, hot chocolate, and coffee are provided in the kitchenette in your room, and hot drinks are available in the lodge most of the day.

The library in the lodge has a wonderful collection of books on natural history. It is supplemented by additional books plus a number of video tapes at the Interbarn. Videotapes can be played on a VCR in the lodge, and you may borrow the books to take back to your room.

OF INTEREST NEARBY: If you come by car, plan a drive through Eleven Mile Canyon just 30 minutes away.

The trip to Sonoran Desert country will take you near the Royal Gorge, and some visitors may wish to go back for a drive across that well-known landmark.

In Colorado Springs you can visit the Air Force Academy or the magnificent rock formations at the Garden of the Gods.

FOR MORE INFORMATION: Write The Nature Place, Colorado Outdoor Education Center, Florissant, CO 80816, or call (719) 748-3475.

Yellowstone National Park
Yellowstone National Park, Wyoming

If anyone polled Americans about what they consider their most special national park, the answer would probably be Yellowstone. For a family vacation experience, it beats a theme park hands down.

Yellowstone was designated a national park in 1872—the world's first—establishing the then-novel principle that certain natural features are national treasures. Although the most frequent image associated with Yellowstone is that of Old Faithful, Yellowstone actually encompasses several diverse ecosystems.

Besides harboring the most active and extensive thermal area in the world, it is the site of the Grand Canyon of the Yellowstone River, a spectacular rift sliced through yellow rock walls; Yellowstone Lake, North America's largest mountain lake; many towering peaks, of which Abiathar Peak, at 10,928 feet, is the highest; and the Yellowstone River, the longest free-flowing river in the United States. Surrounding these popular tourist stops are more than 1,000 miles of well-marked hiking trails, dozens of side-roads with spectacular views, innumerable fishing access points, and wildlife habitat that provides sustenance to bison, elk, deer, moose, eagles, coyotes, and even bears.

Most visitors to Yellowstone National Park see the park's sites from the comfort of their cars or a scenic overlook. A relative few venture out onto the park's hiking trails. The lucky fewest—one out of 10,000—see the park in the most intimate way, under the auspices of the Yellowstone Institute, an organization devoted to making visitors fall in love with the park through participation in dozens of field seminars every year.

ACCOMMODATIONS: $ to $$$ TW Recreational Services, the park's authorized concessioner, operates nine separate lodging facilities at six locations, ranging from the old, dignified Mammoth Hot Springs and Lake Yellowstone hotels to the quirky, not-to-be-missed Old Faithful Inn to the strictly utilitarian Lake Yellowstone cabins and Lake Lodge. To best appreciate the park and minimize driving, it makes sense to stay a few days at several different places.

The National Park Services operates 11 campgrounds in Yellowstone, with a 14-day limit during the summer. Campsites fill on a first-come, first-served basis, except for Bridge Bay, which accepts reservations up to eight weeks in advance through Ticketron (call 800-452-1111.) Because of the huge numbers of visitors in the summer, campgrounds fill quickly.

TW Recreational Services also operates a 300-slot RV Park at Fishing Bridge; call (307) 344-7311 for reservations.

DINING: Restaurants at each of the hotels and lodges offer varied menus at reasonable prices; in addition, Lake Lodge, Old Faithful Lodge, and Canyon Lodge have cafeterias. Lake Yellowstone Hotel has an elegant dining room with gorgeous views of the lake (make your dinner reservation in advance of your arrival.) The dining room at the Old Faithful Inn has a lot of charm.

For a fun evening, sign up for one of the Old West Cookouts at Roosevelt Lodge, offered nearly every evening during the summer. Participants ride wagons or horses through gorgeous scenery to Yancey's Hole, the cookout site, where they're served cowboy coffee and charcoal-grilled steaks, corn on the cob, potato salad, corn muffins, Roosevelt beans, and dessert.

ACTIVITIES:

Rental rowboats and outboards at the Bridge Bay Marina on Lake Yellowstone, the hub of boating activities in the park. Several scenic cruises depart daily from the marina on an excursion boat. Docking slips available for private boats. No boating on rivers or streams, except between Lewis and Shoshone lakes.

Some of the best trout fishing in the West on the Yellowstone River and in Yellowstone Lake, where native cutthroats abound. Guided fishing boats available for charter. License required; no charge.

More than 1,100 miles of hiking trails crisscross Yellowstone. Park rangers will be happy to help you plan hikes ranging from a few hours to a few days (backcountry permits are required for overnight expeditions.) Self-guided nature trails suitable for the inexperienced can be found at Mammoth Hot Springs, Grand Canyon of the Yellowstone, the Fountain Paint Pots, Firehole Lake Drive, the Upper Geyser Basin, Norris Geyser Basin, the Mud Volcano, and Calcite Springs Overlook/Tower Fall.

Pick up a copy of "Discover Yellowstone" as soon as you arrive in the park. It lists all of the ranger-led activities that take place in the park during the summer.

The Yellowstone Institute offers several dozen different short courses on geysers, bears, birds, wildflowers, horsepacking, geology, and photography, with the park as its classroom. These are top-quality learning experiences; write the institute at Box 117, Yellowstone National Park, WY 82190 or call (307) 344-7381, ext. 2384 for a schedule.

Guided one- and two-hour rides at Mammoth Hot Springs Corral, Roosevelt Corral, and Canyon Corral between June and September. Thirty-minute stagecoach rides scheduled several times daily on "tally-ho" coaches from Roosevelt Lodge across rolling, sage-covered hills.

Yellowstone is a wondrous experience in the winter. It's the best time to view elk and bison, which come down to the lowlands to graze. And the sight of geysers and fumaroles surrounded by snow is truly other-worldly.

Only two lodgings are open in the winter—Old Faithful Snow Lodge and Cabins, in the heart of geyser country, and Mammoth Hot Springs Hotel, at the park's northern entrance. Winter activities include cross-country skiing (instruction and rentals available), snowmobiling, snowshoeing, snowcoach tours, wine-tasting parties, special theme dinner nights, and hiking.

Special activities including slide shows, ranger talks, and storytellings are scheduled almost every evening at the park amphitheaters.

FOR CHILDREN: Many of the ranger-led activities are aimed at children. And there are seven visitor centers with excellent interpretive exhibits about the park's natural and human history that will help put the scenery in perspective for children.

Each summer, the Yellowstone Institute also offers several programs especially for children or families. Among the recent offerings: "Family Days in Sunlight," "Interpreting Yellowstone with Ranger Ted," "Three Days at the Buffalo Ranch" (for children between 8 and 12), and "Family Days with a Park Ranger Family." Early sign-up is essential.

NICETIES: There are laundromats at Grant Village Campground, Fishing Village RV Park, Canyon Village Campground, and Lake Lodge.

FOR MORE INFORMATION: For information about accommodations and concessioner-run activities, write TW Services, Inc., Yellowstone National Park, WY 82190 or phone (307) 344-7311. For general information about the park and ranger-led activities, call the National Park Service Headquarters at (307) 344-7381.

Pine Butte Guest Ranch
Choteau, Montana

Nestled in the foothills of the rugged east front of the Rocky Mountain Range in Montana is Pine Butte, a unique guest ranch. The ranch is part of an 18,000-acre nature preserve operated by The Nature Conservancy, an international, not-for-profit conservation organization.

The heart of this preservation effort is Pine Butte Swamp Preserve, an area of lush wetlands, rolling prairies, brilliant wildflowers, and abundant animal life. The preserve is one of the most beautiful and biologically diverse places in Montana. The wildlife sheltered here include beaver, mink, moose, elk, mountain goats, and bighorn sheep. And it's one of the few places in the lower 48 states where grizzly bears venture out of the mountains in search of food.

A few miles away lies Egg Mountain, also part of the preserve. Scientists from the Museum of the Rockies at the University of Montana have been working here for several years on one of the most significant dinosaur fossil finds in North America.

ACCOMMODATIONS: $$$$ Pine Butte's rustic but comfortable cabins are set among the aspens, firs, and cottonwoods that line the South Fork of the Teton River. Built of native stone and wood, each spacious cabin is complete with fireplace, full bath and handmade furniture.

Between mid-June and early September the minimum stay is one week, from Sunday to Sunday. Transportation to and from Great Falls International Airport is provided on Sundays during the summer, at no additional charge. Reduced rates are available in May, early June, and mid-to late September, with a two-night minimum stay required.

DINING: All meals are served family-style in the central lodge dining room. The food is delicious, with exceptionally good home-made soups, breads, and pastries. The ranch's own garden supplies fresh vegetables and salads for mid-day and evening meals.

Sack lunches are packed for guests scheduled on daylong hikes or rides. Each week, breakfast and steakfry dinner rides are offered.

No alcohol is served, but guests are welcome to bring their own. Ice and mixers are available during the social hour before dinner.

ACTIVITIES

 In a heated outdoor pool.

Ranch guides will help anglers find the best spots along the Teton River. Beaver ponds and sub-alpine lakes are within easy hiking distance. Montana license required.

Morning and afternoon rides are scheduled each day, and an all-day ride is offered at least once a week. Many rides climb the trails to the surrounding foothills, with spectacular views of mountains and the plains.

Ralph Waldt, The Nature Conservancy's resident naturalist, has developed a trail map and brochure of the preserve and surrounding territory, which makes self-guided hikes easy. Guided hikes focus on the plants, animals and geology of the East Front. A favorite destination is Our Lake, a seven-mile hike with a 1,450-foot gain in elevation. The lake is nestled in a sub-alpine cirque at an elevation of 7,280 feet and is an excellent area in which to view bighorn sheep and mountain goats.

Information on the ecology of the preserve is woven into most of the activities of the ranch. An excursion to the Egg Mountain dinosaur dig is scheduled each week. Excursions to Freezeout Lake State Waterfowl Refuge are made in early summer when migratory birds are still in the area. An ancient seabed fossil-hunting tour, wildflower and birding expeditions, and paleontology tours of nearby tipi rings and a buffalo jump are also on the weekly program. For an extra fee, you can join an all-day excursion to Glacier National Park.

In the spring and fall, week-long natural history tours and workshops are scheduled on such topics as birdwatching, mammal tracking, nature photography, and paleontology.

After-dinner slide shows and talks focus on the natural environment and the Egg Mountain dinosaur dig. Evening programs usually include a square dance or impromptu volleyball game.

The ranch will organize five- to 10-day horseback trips into the beautiful Bob Marshall Wilderness Area upon request.

FOR CHILDREN: Children are integrated into all of the ranch programs. Many horses in the stables are gentle and suitable for children who have little or no riding experience.

The Pine Butte Educational Center holds occasional workshops for children 7 to 18 years of age at the old Bellview School on the preserve. The workshops range from two to four days in length and emphasize hands-on learning. The teachers and naturalists who lead the program cover such topics as the Plains Indians, homesteaders, rare plants and animals, and local dinosaur discoveries. The program also includes group games, skits, nature walks, art projects, and creative writing. There is a moderate additional fee for the workshops.

NICETIES: The ranch's Natural History Center contains a collection of reference books, fossils, animal skulls and other bones, and a small, self-help gift shop with cards, books, T-shirts, and posters. All proceeds go to The Nature Conservancy.

Free laundry facilities are available.

Tea, lemonade, and cookies are served every afternoon in the dining room.

OF INTEREST NEARBY: The eastern entrance to Glacier National Park is 80 miles north of the ranch. See the separate entry on Glacier for more information on the possibilities for family explorations.

FOR MORE INFORMATION: Write Pine Butte Guest Ranch, HC58, Box 34C, Choteau, MT 59422, or phone (406) 466-2158.

Glacier National Park
West Glacier, Montana

The vast majority of visitors see Glacier National Park from their cars as they travel the only paved road through the park, the 50-mile Going To The Sun Highway. It is one of the most spectacular mountain drives anywhere. The roadway literally clings to the mountainside and crosses the Continental Divide at Logan Pass at an elevation of 6,664 feet.

But most of the 1.4 million acres of Glacier Park are inaccessible by car or van, and it is there that a vacationing family will find its most priceless treasures. The park's 10,000-foot mountain peaks hide 50 active glaciers, 200 sparkling clear lakes and fast-flowing streams, and an abundance of wildlife, including mountain lion, deer, bighorn sheep, and Rocky Mountain goats. In its remote wilderness, four threatened species—the bald eagle, gray wolf, peregrine falcon, and grizzly bear—have one of their last strongholds.

Glacier is truly a hiker's park. More than 90 percent of its area is designated wilderness that can only be approached and appreciated by traveling on foot (there are more than 700 miles of trails.) Walks can range from a 30-minute stroll to a two-week expedition. They are the park's truest rewards. Experienced hikers refer to Glacier as the "last, fierce paradise."

ACCOMMODATIONS: $ to $$ Major campgrounds, with hookups, are located near St. Mary, Rising Sun, Apgar, and Two Medicine. Primitive sites can be found at Kintla Lake, near the Canadian border, and just outside the park in Flathead National Forest and Lewis and Clark National Forest. Permits are required for backcountry camping.

Park accommodations include two grand old hotels—Lake McDonald Lodge and the Many Glacier Hotel—and a lodge, Glacier Park Lodge, as well as several motels and cabin complexes. Book early, as all fill up well in advance of the summer season. The hotels are particularly charming. All are operated by Glacier Park Inc., Greyhound Tower, Station 5185, Phoenix, AZ 85077 (phone 406-226-5551 mid-May to mid-September or 602-248-2600 mid-September to mid-May.)

For families who want to head into the backcountry but avoid packing tents, sleeping gear, and food, Glacier offers two wilderness hotels, Granite Park Chalet and Sperry Chalet. These comfortable, rustic mountain retreats are perched near the Continental Divide and are accessible only by trail. Each has private rooms and full meal service, including packed trail lunches for hikers. Either chalet makes a wonderful "base camp" for extended day hikes into the surrounding wilderness; children 8 and over will have no problem with the hikes.

Write Belton Chalets Inc., P.O. Box 188, West Glacier, MT 59936 or phone (406) 888-5511 between April and the end of September.

DINING: Each of the hotels has its own restaurant, and the town of West Glacier has plenty of coffee shops and snackbars as well. The dining room at Many Glacier Hotel is famed for its singing waiters and waitresses, college music majors who actually have to audition for the job of waiting tables. Several times each evening, service comes to a stop and the servers perform. Make dinner reservations in advance unless you like to eat very late.

ACTIVITIES

Rental rowboats and powerboats on Lake MacDonald, the largest lake in the park. Excursion boats take guests across Swiftcurrent Lake, Lake McDonald, Two Medicine Lake, St. Mary Lake, and Josephine Lake.

With a permit (no fee.) The season extends from the third Saturday in May through November 30. The lakes and streams abound with native cutthroat, bull trout, Kokanee, and mackinaw.

Guided trail rides ranging from two hours to all-day are offered by several outfitters in West Glacier. The Glacier Raft Co. (800-332-9995) offers longer trips that combine horseback riding with rafting.

It's easy to take day hikes on your own. If you prefer a guided backpacking expedition, Glacier Wilderness Guides offers guided trips to remote mountain lakes and alpine meadows within the park. The outfitter has a wide selection of itineraries available on trips that range from a day hike to a six-day backpack. Call (406) 888-5333 or (406) 862-4802 from October to May.

The Glacier Raft Co. (800-332-9995) offers one- to five-day raft trips and raft/horseback expeditions in the Flathead wilderness area just to the south of the Park. The three forks of the Flathead River—North, Middle, and South Forks—together make up nearly 10 percent of the total mileage in the National Wild and Scenic River System. Children 5 and over are welcome on raft trips from early summer on, as long as the water is not too high (then the minimum age rises to 8).

FOR CHILDREN: The park's ranger programs are among the best in the national park system, with guided boat rides and hikes, evening campground programs and slide talks in the hotels among the offerings. There are special junior ranger programs each week. Each visitor center has displays about Glacier that will be interesting to children.

Many of the programs offered by the Glacier Institute are open to families with children 10 and older. Summer field seminars run from two to five days; "Explorations" courses are half- and full-day educational experiences. The institute makes the park its classroom as you explore a glacier, raft a river, or hike a wilderness trail. Classes are fun, with the emphasis on being out–of–doors and participating in hands-on nature activities. Your family can learn to track wildlife, identify birds of prey, use a map and compass, sketch the natural environment, and appreciate a bit of Montana history. The institute has limited cabin accommodations for participating families, with a shared kitchen and washrooms with showers. Write Glacier Institute, P.O. Box 1457A, Kalispell, MT 59903, or phone (406) 888-5215 from mid-June to mid-August or (406) 752-5222 at other times.

OF INTEREST NEARBY: The Northern Plains Indian Crafts Association has a trading center with Indian goods just outside Glacier, at St. Mary.

The Museum of the Plains Indian, 12 miles from East Glacier Park at Browning, has exhibits on the customs of the Indians of the Great Plains.

Glacier is the American section of the Waterton-Glacier International Peace Park. Waterton, the Canadian section, is itself worth a visit. A cruise across its lake is a must; you'll understand how insignificant borders are. The Prince of Wales Hotel presides over the landscape here from its perch above the lake. The town of Waterton is charming, with a nice children's museum and many shops that sell imported British goods.

FOR MORE INFORMATION: Write The Superintendent, Glacier National Park, West Glacier, MT 59936, or phone (406) 888-5441. Obtain general information on Montana from Travel Montana at (800) 541-1447.

WEST COAST AND ALASKA

Furnace Creek Inn and Ranch Resort
Death Valley National Monument, California

Death Valley conjures up a host of images and associations: bleak desert landscapes, extremes in temperature and rainfall, prospectors and pioneers perishing from thirst and hunger, a place of foreboding and gloom, maybe even a successful TV show of 20 years ago. If the images run to extremes, so do the reactions of visitors to Death Valley. Few people sit on the fence. They either find Death Valley a fascinating place, a place they return to frequently in thought, if not in person, or they hate it. We found it fascinating.

It is, unarguably, a land of extremes. Summertime temperatures regularly top 120 degrees and only cool off to 90 at night. In June, July, and August, the only tourists are busloads of Europeans who want to go home bragging about having braved the desert heat. Average annual rainfall is less than two inches, much of which evaporates before it hits the ground.

Furnace Creek Inn was built in the 1920s by mining company executives near a creek that flows year-round out of springs. The fields and pastures of the old Greenland Ranch (a provisioning stop for miners) are now the golf course for the inn and ranch, both operated by the Fred Harvey Company.

The Spanish-style Furnace Creek Inn is built against the eastern wall of Death Valley with a commanding view along the valley and across to the Panamint Mountain range on the opposite side. Its three-foot-thick walls of adobe brick were fashioned by Indians employed by the Borax Company. The inn has a garden of semi-tropical vegetation and date palms set among pools and waterfalls.

ACCOMMODATIONS: **$** to **$$$** Furnace Creek Inn, with 69 units, was refurbished and redecorated in the mid-1980s. The larger rooms and tower suites have spa-type bathtubs as well as showers. These accommodations are very comfortable and tastefully done.

The inn operates on the Modified American Plan. There is no charge for a child under 5 staying in a room with parents; a crib or roll-away bed is extra. There's an extra-person charge for children 5 to 12 years and a higher charge for children over 17.

Furnace Creek Ranch, on the valley floor one mile away from the Inn, has 225 motel-style rooms, each with two double beds, in units placed near a swimming pool, golf course, and corral.

The ranch does not include meals in its rates. There is no charge for children under 12; a flat daily rate is charged for children 12 and over. A crib or roll-away is extra.

DINING: The inn's guests eat breakfasts and dinners in the elegant Dining Room with bay window views of the Valley. Alternatively, inn guests may eat dinner in the fancier l'Ottimos. Men dress for dinner in jackets; ties are optional.

À la carte lunches are served in the Dining Room. The inn serves an outstanding champagne brunch every Sunday.

Box lunches can be arranged to take with you on day trips into the Valley. Room service at the inn is available only during the hours when meals are served in the Dining Room.

The ranch has a steak house for evening meals and a coffee shop and cafeteria that are open all day. The golf course has a snack bar as well.

ACTIVITIES

 Four lighted hard-surface tennis courts at the inn, two lighted courts at the ranch. Rental equipment available.

The 18-hole, par 72 course at the inn is 5,750 yards long. The number five fairway has the distinction of being the world's lowest, at 214 feet below sea level. Pro shop, driving range, putting green, electric carts available. The golf season runs from early October through mid-May.

Both the inn and the ranch have swimming pools fed by water from the springs, which is about 100 degrees when it comes out of the ground. The constantly circulating water requires little chemical treatment and keeps the pool at 85 degrees even in December and January. To swim in this delightfully warm pool in winter as the suns sets behind the snow-covered Panamints is a memorable experience. A small sauna and spa are located at the inn's pool.

Rentals in sizes appropriate for every member of the family. There are cycle paths along some roads; a few trails are also suitable for bike rides.

Miles of hiking trails crisscross Death Valley and the surrounding mountains. This is good family hiking territory in the winter. Fred Harvey Company runs sightseeing tours in air-conditioned vans. An introductory Death Valley Tour and tours to Titus Canyon and to Scotty's Castle have been on the schedule in the past.

Rides from the ranch corral two or three times each day. Children must be at least 8 to ride and must be accompanied by a parent if they are under 12. Rides go out across the Valley floor and last about two hours. Hayrides are sometimes scheduled.

Ping-Pong, shuffleboard, volleyball, and badminton facilities are available at both inn and ranch. The inn has a card room off the lobby, and the desk clerk has cards and board games that guests may use. The card room also houses a small library with national newspapers and books you can borrow for the duration of your stay. The inn's front desk has sign-up sheets for guests looking for bridge, tennis, golf, or square-dancing partners. Tours go to performances of the Amargosa Opera in the ghost town of Death Valley Junction during the opera season.

There's entertainment most nights in l'Ottimos at the inn.

FOR CHILDREN: Furnace Creek Inn and Ranch is an attractive winter or spring destination for an outdoor-oriented family vacation. The inn and ranch do not have special children's programs, but there are many activities that family members can undertake here and at the National Park Service facilities in Death Valley National Monument.

A family will enjoy taking a lunch to the sand dunes and frolicking in this huge natural sandbox. Spend some time exploring the old mining equipment in the museum grounds at the ranch. Stop the car along the drives in Twenty Mule Team Canyon or Artists Drive and wander over this desolate landscape. Some scenes from the movie *Star Wars* were shot in Twenty Mule Team Canyon.

Baby-sitters can be arranged through the front desk at the inn.

NICETIES: Large towels are available at the inn swimming pool.

The inn serves an afternoon tea in the lobby.

The inn has a barbershop and beauty salon.

The inn gift shop stocks quality Indian crafts and sundries.

The ranch is a full-fledged village with a U.S. Post Office, service station, and general store. A coin-operated laundry is located on Roadrunner Avenue.

OF INTEREST NEARBY: All the attractions of Death Valley National Monument are easily accessible to guests. The Monument's Visitor Center is a few yards from the ranch. Talk with the rangers there about the daily guided activities and about activities you can undertake on your own. The Visitor Center has a museum and a good collection of books.

Daily National Park Service activities usually include at least one talk on the patio of the Visitor Center, a guided walk, and an evening slide show or movie in the auditorium. Walks take place at sites like the Harmony Borax Works and the sand dunes; there are also sketching and photography strolls.

National Park Service rangers will give you maps and directions for undertaking self-guided auto or walking tours. The rangers delight in telling stories about summertime living in Death Valley. Ask them for the handout on how to tell when it's hot.

FOR MORE INFORMATION: Write Furnace Creek Inn and Ranch Resort, Death Valley, CA 92328, or call (619) 786-2345.

National Wildlife Federation Conservation Summit
Bellingham, Washington

The National Wildlife Federation Conservation Summits set a standard for family nature vacation–education programs that is close to perfection. The locations are wonderful. The programs are great. And there is something for every member of the family (including infant care). What more could you ask?

Three Summits have been scheduled every summer in recent years. Each Summit is located in an area of great natural beauty, within a distinctive North American ecosystem. The Federation strives for geographical and ecological diversity in its choice of locations. Among the recent Summit locations have been the Blue Ridge Mountains in North Carolina; Estes Park in Colorado; Silver Bay in the New York Adirondacks; Bellingham, Washington, in the Pacific Northwest; and the Big Sur region, on California's coast.

These week-long nature retreats offer programs for all age levels —adults, teens, children 5 through 12, and preschoolers, and even child care for infants through 2. The emphasis in all these programs (except for the youngest) is on discovery of nature through outdoor, hands-on, experiential activity. The participants in these programs run the gamut from parents and children, to intergenerational family groupings, to single-parent families, to older couples without children.

Each Summit program is built around the ecology of the area in which the Summit is held and emphasizes a conservation theme. The staff for each Summit is recruited from among environmental educators who have expertise in the flora and fauna of that region. The result is a staff that is skilled in helping Summit participants in their exploration of the local natural environment.

We took part in the Northwest Summit in Bellingham, Washington, and our observations are based on that experience. The basic format of a Summit is the same from one location to another.

ACCOMMODATIONS: $$ to $$$$ The National Wildlife Federation uses the facilities of other organizations to house its Summits —conference centers, lodges, colleges, or resorts. Therefore, accommodations vary from Summit to Summit. At all, access to the out-of-doors, basic human comforts, and good value are common denominators. None of the facilities is luxurious, but all are well suited to a week-long family nature adventure.

The Northwest Summit used the facilities of Western Washington University, where summit participants were housed in dormitories. Some of the dormitories are arranged in suites, with several rooms sharing a bathroom.

Rates for a National Wildlife Federation Summit are divided into program fees and accommodation fees. Program fees are paid to the National Wildlife Federation. Accommodation fees are paid to the host institution and include meals (children's rates are available). Each family must also buy a family membership in the National Wildlife Federation for a nominal fee ($16 in 1992).

DINING: Summits use the dining facilities of the host institution. Food is served either cafeteria-style or family-style.

Every summit participant from the youngest to the oldest receives a brightly colored National Wildlife Federation neckerchief at registration, which serves as the dining room ID card. As the week progresses, participants find ingenious ways to wear their neckerchiefs—as belts, as arm or leg bands, and as headbands.

Box lunches are provided for groups going on daylong field trips.

Often a special dinner is held on one night during the week. A salmon bake was the highlight of the Northwest Summit.

ACTIVITIES: Each age group has its own Summit program. The daily program starts at 8:30 A.M. and ends at 3:15 P.M. Adults design their own program from a catalogue of possible activities that is mailed several months before the Summit begins. You pick and choose from the Summit catalogue and return a request form by mail. Your own personal schedule is prepared and waiting for you at registration.

Adult activities include lectures, workshops, and outdoor experiences. Among the options at the Northwest Summit were explorations of beach, tide pools, woodlands, both long and short nature hikes in the Cascade Mountains of Washington, whale-watch-ing cruises, bird-watching trips in several settings, nature photog-raphy, ecological landscaping, and sharing nature with children.

Late-afternoon and evening programs round out the Summit agenda. Lectures for adults and crafts for all fill the period from 3:30 to 5:30 in the afternoons. Topics included the Northwest coast, whale biology, acid rain, wilderness survival techniques, and the seafood industry.

The entire Summit group gathers for evening programs at 8 P.M. Evening programs included a square dance, a sing-along, Sammy Salmon, and slide programs by nature photographers.

FOR CHILDREN: Children's programs are organized and led by counselors who are teachers, naturalists, or outdoor educators. All have extensive experience in environmental education for young people.

"Your Big Backyard" is a half-day program for 3- and 4-year-olds. Preschoolers develop an appreciation for the natural world through activities that include touch and feel expeditions, short hikes, storytelling, nature crafts, dramatic play, and creative cook-ing. In a week's time, the program's topics range over baby animals and their homes, insects, trees and flowers, mammals, and birds. "Your Big Backyard" ends at noon, when parents pick up their children for lunch. Child care is available from 1 to 5 P.M. for a nominal additional charge if parents want to participate in the after-noon sessions for adults.

Five- to 12-year-olds take part in the all-day "Junior Naturalist" program. The group is broken into four clusters by age: 5 and 6, 7 and 8, 9 and 10, and 11- and 12-year-olds. The emphasis is on nature activities that reflect the diversity of the local ecology. Crafts, games, short discovery hikes, and films are all utilized in the learning ex-perience. But the heart of the "Junior Naturalist" program is field trips. At the Northwest Summit, the "Junior Naturalist" group went on four full-day field trips to nearby state parks and museums—two to beaches and tide pools, one to forests and mountains, and one to a shipyard and fish hatchery. The group studied woodland, beach, tide pool, river, bay, and marsh ecologies. At the end of the day, parents got briefings on crabs, whales, seaweed, rocks, clouds, fishing boats and eagle nests from tired but happy children.

The "Teen Adventure Program" for ages 13 through 17 emphasizes outdoor leadership, group problem solving, and interpersonal skills. Activities may include hiking, swimming, orienteering, a ropes course, and nighttime astronomy sessions. Participants are expected to attend all sessions from 8:30 A.M. to 3 P.M. throughout the week. At the Northwest Summit, teens hiked in the mountains, visited the beach and tide pools, and went on a whale-watching cruise.

Children in the "Junior Naturalist" and "Teen Adventure" programs eat lunch with their groups. After-program care is available for the 5- to 12-year-olds from 3 to 5:30 P.M., allowing parents to participate in all-day programs and afternoon field trips. During the afternoon, children swam, crafted with clay, and learned ballads of the sea.

The baby-sitting service for infants through 2 is available from 8 A.M. to noon and from 1 to 5 P.M. for a nominal fee. Parents provide any supplies—diapers, bottles, snacks—that a child may need.

FOR MORE INFORMATION: Write the National Wildlife Federation, Conservation Summits, 1400 Sixteenth St. N.W., Washington, DC 20036-2266, or call (800) 432-6564.

Strathcona Park Lodge and Outdoor Education Centre
Vancouver Island, British Columbia, Canada

Located deep in the heart of Vancouver Island, this secluded mountain resort is hard to top as a destination for a nature-oriented family vacation. Strathcona Lodge is surrounded by some of the most spectacular recreational land in North America and is just a few miles from the half-million-acre Strathcona Provincial Park, which serves as the venue for many of the lodge's nature activities.

Strathcona Park is largely untouched by humanity, with magnificent snow-capped mountain peaks dominated by the Golden Hinde, the highest point on Vancouver Island at 7,219 feet. The park's valleys are filled with forests of Douglas fir, cedar, and hemlock—trees that were already old in 1778 when Captain James Cook landed at nearby Nootka Sound. Floral displays paint the park from spring through fall, and wildlife abounds. Blue grouse, ruffed grouse, and the rare Vancouver Island white-tailed ptarmigan are found here. Nocturnal wolves, cougar, and black bear are abundant, but not often seen. The park also has unique mammals like the black-tailed deer and Roosevelt Elk that evolved here after Vancouver Island separated from the mainland of North America tens of thousands of years ago.

Staff members at the lodge view themselves as interpreters of the natural world and welcome families as participants in a discovery process, not as spectators. No age limits for participation are set, and single-parent families and large extended families are especially welcome. The programs offer something for everyone who enjoys natural beauty and the excitement of the great outdoors.

ACCOMMODATIONS: $ The cottages, chalets, rooms, and apartments at Strathcona Park Lodge are beautifully situated on the shore of the 30-mile-long Upper Campbell–Buttle Lake chain. All rooms have sweeping views of the lake and mountains and are modestly but comfortably furnished. Extended families should inquire about the Seale House, a large chalet that can accommodate up to 20 people with eight bedrooms, three decks, a loft, and a kitchen.

Daily or weekly rates are available. Units with kitchens require a three-night minimum stay. Reduced rates are available for children under 12. There's a three-night minimum in July and August.

Families can book accommodations alone or an all-inclusive package that provides for meals, unlimited use of equipment, participation in outdoor programs, and instruction in outdoor activities led by the Outdoor Education Centre staff. It is essential to book well in advance, including the equipment and instruction you will need.

DINING: Guests from all over the world converge at mealtimes in The Whale Room. The atmosphere is friendly, casual, and informal.

Delicious home-cooked meals are served buffet style. Vegetarian entrées are available on request.

ACTIVITIES

 In a protected area in the sparkling lake.

The canoes, kayaks, sailboats, and motorboats at the lodge can be rented by the hour or day by families not registered in a program package.

Rainbow and cutthroat trout fishing in the lodge's lakes from mid-April until mid-October; guides available. Steelhead fishing year-round in the nearby Gold and Campbell rivers, summer salmon fishing in the Campbell.

On your first stay at the Lodge you should come as part of one of the "Alpine to Ocean" adventure programs. The wide variety of programs insures that there will be one well suited to almost any family. Program activities include backpacking, swimming, rock climbing, canoeing, kayaking, sailing, and nature instruction. Following are some of the best programs for families.

The six-day "Family Adventure" package, offered several times each summer, is a wonderful opportunity for parents and young children to share outdoor experiences together. Canoeing, sailing, nature hikes, and a ropes course provide the active moments, and nightly campfires provide the quiet times.

The "Strathcona Prime Time" package can be booked for any four consecutive days from late June to early September. In this program you can learn outdoor skills of your choosing and participate in a variety of hikes and other nature activities.

The weeklong "Grandparent-Grandchild" program is immensely popular. This inventive program includes shared activities like canoeing, kayaking, hiking, and nature study as well as activities for grandchildren alone.

Programs continue throughout the winter, which is typically mild on Vancouver Island. A "Folk Music Weekend" in November brings professional and amateur musicians to the Lodge for singing, guitar and fiddle playing, and square and folk dancing. Christmas is a special time for families here, with snowshoeing, cross-country skiing, animal tracking, and even canoeing on the program.

The Hi-Bracer Lounge is a combination bar and library overlooking the lake. It is a quiet, relaxing place to unwind after an active day.

FOR CHILDREN: Children from about age six and up can join with their parents in all program activities, according to their interests and abilities; older children can be enrolled for a charge in the ongoing summer camps offered by the Outdoor Education Centre. Youth Camps are divided by ages—Adventure Camp for 10- to 12-year-olds, Youth Leadership Camp for 13- to 15-year-olds, and Senior Youth Leadership camp for 16- to 18-year-olds. You must book your children in a Youth Camp in advance of your stay.

Baby-sitting can be arranged at the office early on the day it is needed.

NICETIES: Coffee and tea pots are on in the dining room throughout the day. Snacks are offered morning and afternoon.

Camping equipment and some other outdoor gear can be rented at the lodge, or you can bring your own. Inquire about what's available.

OF INTEREST NEARBY: Young children will enjoy a visit to the adventure playground and sand beach at nearby Buttle Lake Campground in Strathcona Park.

The town of Campbell River is renowned for its salmon and trout fishing. Families can book a boat and guide for a day's fishing or fish off the new Discovery Pier. The 600-foot-long pier is open 24 hours a day and has built-in rod holders, bait stands, fish-cleaning tables, and benches. You can rent all the equipment you need for a day of family fishing; be sure to sample the pier's famous ice cream cones while you try to hook a big one.

The Campbell River Museum and Archives is an excellent small museum with artifacts of early settlers and Native Americans. The museum has puppet shows for children in the summer.

Quinsam River Salmon Hatchery is near Campbell River. Take its self-guided tour and explore its nature trails. Picnic facilities are available here.

The Kwakiutl Museum in the Cape Mudge Indian Village on Quadra Island, a 30-minute ferry ride from Campbell River, has a fine collection of Native American artifacts. Potlatch regalia, tribal masks, and costumes recently returned to the Kwakiutl people after 55 years in the National Museum of Man in Ottawa are on display here. Plan a day trip to Quadra Island.

The small community of Gold River, west of Strathcona Park, is in a popular caving area and is the point of embarkation for day cruises to small fishing villages and Indian communities along the west coast of Vancouver Island.

FOR MORE INFORMATION: Write Strathcona Park Lodge, Box 2160, Campbell River, BC, Canada V9W 5C9, or call (604) 286-3122.

Olympic National Park
Port Angeles, Washington

You don't have to go all the way to South America to teach your children about the special significance of rain forests. Olympic National Park protects the continental United States' largest and finest temperate rain forest. Because of its uniqueness, the park has been designated a Biosphere Reserve and World Heritage Site. A vacation here is a wonderful way to introduce children to an environment unlike any they've ever experienced before.

Walking along a moss-carpeted path through a forest of towering 800-year-old Douglas firs as a fine mist moistens your face is an experience you'll never forget. You'll see Sitka spruce and western hemlock trees that reach 300 feet in height and 23 feet in circumference and hundreds of fallen giants that serve as "nurseries" for new seedlings. The carpeting of moss and lichen underfoot and the epiphytes that seem to hang from every branch give the forest a distinct jungle air, and the 145 inches of rain each year ensure that everything stays green.

But Olympic National Park offers more than just rain forest. It actually has three distinctive ecosystems: the rainforest, the scenic ocean strip (the longest stretch of wilderness beach in the continental United States), and the rugged, glacier-clad mountainous core, dominated by Mt. Olympus, with a peak nearly 8,000 feet above sea level. Each of its unique sections is a wonderful place for exploration and learning.

ACCOMMODATIONS: $ to $$$ The park has about 900 campsites in 18 campgrounds; all sites are available on a first–come, first–served basis (groups may make reservations at the Kalaloch, Mora, and Ozette sites). Toilets, fresh water, picnic tables, and grills are provided at all campgrounds, but none have showers, laundries, or utility connections. Backcountry camping is allowed with a permit.

Olympic also has two wonderful hotel/cabin resorts—Lake Crescent Lodge and Kalaloch Lodge, and two motels—Log Cabin Resort, on the northeast end of Lake Crescent, and Sol Duc Hot Springs Resort, in the Soleduck River Valley 40 miles west of Port Angeles. In addition, there's another grand old lodge, Lake Quinault Lodge, just outside the park's southern boundary in the Olympic National Forest.

Lake Crescent Lodge (206-928-3211), open from April 27 through Oct. 27, has 42 motel and cottage units and lodge rooms, some with fireplaces, along the beautiful shore of Lake Crescent at the foot of Storm King Mountain. The main building was built in 1916 and retains the charm of yesteryear, with its lobby furnished with mission oak furniture and dominated by a huge stone fireplace.

Sol Duc Hot Springs Resort (206-327-3583), open from May 15 through Sept. 30, offers campsites and lodgings in 32 cabins, some with kitchens. The main lures here are the three large hot mineral pools and the heated outdoor swiming pool.

Log Cabin Resort (206-928-3325), open May 3 through Sept. 30, has 28 motel units, cabins, chalets, and camping log cabins (you supply our own linens) secluded among old firs and cedars on the sunny side of Lake Crescent.

Kalaloch Lodge (206-962-2271), the only lodging that's open year-round, occupies a spectacular site on a bluff overlooking the Pacific. The stony beach below is littered with pieces of driftwood that look like beached whales. At low tide, hundreds of shorebirds come to feed in the intertidal zone. The lodge offers accommodations in the main building, motel rooms in the detached Sea Crest House, and cozy log cabins with one or two bedrooms (with brass beds), woodburning stoves, and complete kitchens.

Lake Quinault Lodge (206-228-2571) is a charming old-fashioned lodge in a beautiful lakefront setting next to a rainforest. Just outside the park's boundaries, it is well-situated for exploring the park's southern end.

DINING: Lake Crescent, Kalaloch, Lake Quinault, Sol Duc Hot Springs, and the Log Cabin Resort have lovely dining rooms that emphasize regional cooking. Kalaloch has a separate coffee shop as well, and Sol Duc Hot Springs has a poolside deli.

General stores near each of the resorts sell groceries and housekeeping supplies.

ACTIVITIES

Heated outdoor pool at Sol Duc Hot Springs Resort; heated indoor pool at Lake Quinault Lodge. Swimming in the Pacific Ocean at Kalaloch and Ruby beaches, north of Queets, and in Lake Crescent and Lake Quinault.

Rental fishing boats, paddleboats, and canoes at the lake resorts and Fairholm Visitor Service Area.

For salmon, trout, and char. No license required, but a state punchcard must be obtained to fish for steelhead and salmon. Clamming at Kalaloch Lodge; rental shovels available.

The park offers naturalist programs from July to September at several locations around the park; Kalaloch and Hurricane Ridge have the most. Among the offerings: guided beach or coastal walks, meadow explorations, walks through the rain forest, and campfire programs. In addition, the park has many self-guided nature trails. Pick up maps at the Port Angeles Pioneer Memorial Visitor Center, 3002 Mt. Angeles Rd., on the south side of Port Angeles; the center has an interesting slide show, museum displays, and a small nature trail.

The Hoh Visitor Center also has informative displays and is the starting-off point for several self-guided trails. The Hurricane Ridge Visitors Center offers sweeping views of Mt. Olympus and the Strait of Juan de Fuca; there's a slide show every 30 minutes and informative exhibits. Among the things you'll learn is that the park provides shelter for about 5,000 Roosevelt elk and smaller mammals including blacktail deer, cougars, river otters, and jumping mice.

For visitors who want more depth to their experience, the Olympic Park Institute (206-938-3720) offers several dozen seminars and outings each year. Among the topics: the aquatic ecology of the Olympics, ecology of the ancient forest, whale watching hikes, the world of salmon, cedar bark basketry, sharing the joy of nature, and the myths and legends of the Northwest.

FOR CHILDREN: Older children will enjoy the evening programs at the larger campgrounds. Typical topics are "The Coastal Forest from a Slug's Eye" and "Tidepools: Holding on Tight." The daily tidepool walks at Mora and Kalaloch are a big hit with kids of any age. Special children's activities are offered throughout the summer.

Children can qualify as Junior Rangers by completing the activity sections in the park's activities guide, collecting and turning in a bag of litter, going for a nature walk with their families, and attending a ranger program.

The Olympic Park Institute offers some field seminars in which families are welcome. "Peter Puget Voyage" is a five-day voyage of south Puget Sound on replica longboats, with camping at night. "Puget Sound Discovery" is a weekend trip on a longboat replica. Seashore Safari" is a weekend-long exploration of the shore, using games, crafts, dramatics, and creative activities to teach children about life at water's edge. "Making Sense of the Night Sky," offered three times each summer, teaches families about the phenomena and lore of the night sky.

FOR MORE INFORMATION: Write the Superintendent, Olympic National Park, 600 East Park Ave., Port Angeles, WA 98362 or call (206) 452-4501. Request general travel information from Olympic Peninsula Travel Association, P.O. Box 625, Port Angeles, WA 98362.

Camp Denali
Denali National Park, Alaska

For families visiting the 49th state, Denali National Park demands a stop. Not only is it the site of Mt. McKinley, the highest mountain peak in North America, but it is also the wilderness home of over 35 species of mammals, including grizzly bears, moose, caribou, white mountain sheep, and wolves. Bird life and wildflowers abound in the summer months in a wilderness that is both vast and remote. The park is as big as Massachusetts, but only one major road penetrates its heart.

Most Denali National Park visitors stay for one or two nights at one of the major hotels near the Park entrance. But McKinley cannot be seen from the Park entrance, and private vehicle use of the Denali road is limited. Visitors who want more than a short taste of this unique national park will want to stay at Camp Denali, a vacation retreat in the heart of the Denali National Park wilderness.

Camp Denali is Denali National Park's best-kept secret. A wilderness lodge in the center of the park with spectacular views of majestic Mt. McKinley and surrounding peaks, Camp Denali specializes in guided hiking and opportunities to learn about the Park's natural history. The Camp was begun in 1951 as a rustic tent camp. Over the years it has evolved into its present status as a natural history vacation retreat.

Camp Denali staff and vehicles meet guests at the Alaska Railroad depot at the Park entrance for the start of an unforgettable five-hour journey into the center of one of America's great wilderness preserves. The gravel road passes over wooded glacial stream valleys and mountain passes of Alpine tundra. The driver-naturalist gives pointers on how to spot animals in the spruce forest and on the tundra slope. The excitement mounts with each discovery: a cow moose and her newborn calf, half hidden in a dense willow thicket; a group of five bull caribou with this season's antlers partly grown, grazing on a tundra ridge; white mountain sheep—a band of 20 ewes and frolicking lambs—on a precipitous rocky outcropping; a blond grizzly bear digging for roots on a gravel bar. Your own camera and binoculars are put to use continually. The driver stops the bus frequently to set up a 20-power spotting scope on a tripod for more distant sightings. And this is just the beginning!

Those who demand hotel-type accommodation, cocktail bars, and one-night "see-it-and-leave-it" type of stays won't be happy at Camp Denali. But those who seek in-depth vacation experiences away from the hectic tempo of modern life in the company of kindred souls will not be disappointed.

ACCOMMODATIONS: $$$$ Accommodations are comfortable, but basic, without private toilets. Individual log and frame cabins each have a private view of the Alaska Range and Mt. McKinley. Cabins have propane lights, small wood stoves for heat, and charming handmade calico quilts. The main buildings, which include the lodge living room, the dining room, and the central shower and toilet facility, are a short walk from the cabins.

The short season at Camp Denali, early June to early September, necessitates fixed arrival and departure dates and times. All meals, transportation, and activities are included in the Camp's rates. The minimum stay is three nights; children's rates are available. Families receive a 10 percent discount if three or more family members occupy the same cabin.

DINING: Breakfast follows a 7 A.M. wake-up call sounded by a triangle at the corner of the Potlatch Dining Room. The day is started right with Camp Denali's seven-grain hot cereal, sourdough hotcakes with local wild blueberry syrup, sausage quiche, croissants, and rhubarb jam.

With the wide variety of outdoor activities at Denali, lunches are usually taken on the trail. After breakfast each guest constructs his or her own sack lunch from the smorgasbord of homemade baked breads and sweets, sandwich fillings, fresh fruit, home-grown lettuce from the Camp Denali greenhouse, and trail mix.

Dinner is served family style with guests and staff intermingled at tables of 12. Dinner menus include Alaskan halibut, chicken filo, and such energy-replenishing desserts as home-baked pies and cakes and chocolate mousse.

ACTIVITIES

Canoeing at two and a half mile-long Wonder Lake nearby. After a rainy day, nearby Moose Creek may be high enough for a guided raft trip.

The Camp's mountain bikes can be put atop one of the buses. Your family's endurance determines the distance traveled before the staff drops you at the start of your bike trip back to the lodge. The roads are largely empty of traffic, with only the Park's shuttle buses to contend with. You're more likely to see a caribou on the road than a car.

Organized walks. Each day's schedule offers new opportunities to explore nature on hikes of varying difficulty. For instance, one of the naturalist-guides might lead a hike up the 1,500-foot, wildflower-carpeted Alpine ridge line behind the lodge. Mt. McKinley and its snow-clad neighbors dominate the view during the entire hike. A half-day outing toward Wonder Lake by bus and foot is designed for those keen to see mammals and birds. Panning for gold is a favorite with children. Patient staff members instruct in the methods the old-time miners used, and guests invariably find flakes of gold in the cold mountain streams.

After dinner each evening, slide shows, films, and discussions are presented by the camp staff. The topics range from mountaineering on Mt. McKinley, to loons, to the reminiscences of a staff couple about a winter in the Alaskan bush. On the final evening of your stay, Wally Cole, the co-owner, sums it all up with his slide show, "Moods of Denali."

The highlight of your stay will probably be a one and a half hour flight around Mt. McKinley in a light plane. The Coles arrange flights from the nearby Kantishna airstrip with Lowell Thomas, Jr. and other bush pilots. Another world is visible from the windows of these planes—a world of jagged peaks, highways of glacial ice, perhaps a group of climbers like a chain of dots attempting to scale North America's highest mountain.

FOR CHILDREN: Camp Denali does not have specific programs for younger children, and no baby-sitting services are available. But children over 8 with the stamina for moderate hiking, an interest in nature, and the capability to share a wilderness learning experience are welcome here.

NICETIES: The Coles and their staff at Camp Denali treat you and your family as welcome houseguests, not clients. At the end of a one-week stay you'll find that you've become as attached to the people and meaning of this place as you were to the summer camp you attended as a child. The kitchen crew fills cards with recipes, and staff and guests exchange addresses and farewell hugs.

Camp Denali has a storeroom full of things you may have forgotten, like day packs, rainwear, waterproof boots, boot grease, and fishing tackle.

The small library is a retreat for reading and relaxing.

FOR MORE INFORMATION: From late May to early September write Camp Denali/North Face Lodge, P.O. Box 67, Denali National Park, AK 99755, or call (907) 683-2290. From early September to late May write Camp Denali, Box 216, Cornish, NH 03740 or call (603) 675-2248.

Virgin Islands National Park
St. John, U.S. Virgin Islands

St. John is unique among Carribean islands in that more than half its 45-square-mile land mass and most of its shoreline waters are protected by a national park.

Even outside the Virgin Islands National Park, the island's natural resources are without peer in the Caribbean. Some hiking trails follow numerous old Danish plantation roads past the ruins of sugar cane factories, whose cane presses were powered by windmills when the colonial Danes made sugar here in the 18th century. Others lead you to an area where you can see old petroglyphs. The climb to any ridgetop is rewarded with a vista of green islands and blue waters. Along the way you are certain to see many of the island's 100-plus species of birds, and even some feral cats, mongoose, wild donkeys, or goats.

Superb beaches, many of them deserted and pristine, are the major attraction for families. Trunk Bay has one of the world's best beaches and offers an underwater nature trail just off shore for snorkelers.

ACCOMMODATIONS: $ Maho Bay Camps (phone 800-392-9004), our favorite destination on St. John, sits in glorious isolation in the northeast quadrant of the island, surrounded on three sides by national park land. It has been called "a resort with an ethic" because of its owners' determination to show that it is possible to live in comfort and harmony in a fragile environment without spoiling it.

Guests stay in one of 100 tent-cottages set in the lush tropical vegetation of a hillside overlooking Maho Bay. The tent-cottages are built on stilts, surrounded by trees and within sight of only a few other cottages. Each tent-cottage is linked to the central office, store, dining facility, and toilet blocks by raised boardwalks.

The tent-cottage floor plan is simple but functional—a sleeping alcove with twin beds, a small combination kitchen-dining area with a hide-a-bed suitable for two children, and an uncovered balcony. Each tent-cottage has electricity and is outfitted with cooking and eating equipment; cooking is on propane stoves, and food is kept cool in ice chests. Water is stored in a five-gallon plastic container. Toilet blocks have flush toilets and lukewarm showers.

Cinnamon Bay Campground, within the park, offers bare sites for tent campers, sites with tents already erected, and very basic beach cottages. Call (800) 223-7637 for reservations.

The largest hotel on the island is Caneel Bay Plantation, a Rock-resort with unsurpassed accommodations.

DINING: At Maho Bay, the open-air restaurant serves buffet breakfasts and dinners, but no lunches. Dinners feature two main entrees, one of which is almost always vegetarian. The food here is ample, delicious, and healthful. You can eat lunch in your cottage or take a picnic to the beach.

At Cinnamon Bay, a cafeteria offers dining on an outdoor terrace.

The camp stores at Maho Bay and Cinnamon Bay stock cooking essentials—staples, canned and dried foods, dairy products, bread, frozen meats, some fresh vegetables, juice, soda, beer, and wine. Almost all food is imported from the mainland, which is reflected in its price.

The town of Cruz Bay has a wide selection of restaurants specializing in seafood and West Indian cooking. For an elegant meal without the kids, book a table at the Caneel Bay Plantation.

ACTIVITIES

The whole north side of St. John is dominated by a series of beaches with Maho toward the northeast end. At Maho Bay, the safe, sheltered beach is a 10-minute walk from the tent-cabins. The water is clear and calm in most weather, and the bottom slopes gently and is free of coral. Novice snorkelers can easily swim to reefs at either end of the beach. Equipment for sailing, snorkeling, scuba diving, fishing, and wind-surfing is available for rent.

Maho Bay runs sailing and powerboat excursions on request. The Maho staff can arrange a variety of boat trips, scuba diving expeditions, and snorkeling adventures with off-site outfitters.

At Maho Bay, Hamilton Eugene does an excellent job of relating the island's history and folklore and introducing you to its natural beauty. His island tour is scheduled several times a week.

The national park offers tours and lecture programs on the flora, fauna, and history of St. John. Park rangers also lead snorkel trips along the underwater trail in Cinnamon Bay and organize several adventure hikes each week. Other park programs focus on the ecology and history of the island.

At Maho Bay, programs for guests are held several evenings each week, including a "Welcome to Maho and St. John" talk on Mondays and slide and lecture shows on natural history, marine biology, astronomy, and the like on other nights. Some nights there's a reggae band or musical performances by Maho's staff and guests.

FOR CHILDREN: At Maho Bay, there are no special programs for children, and children under 4 are not permitted. But for older children, staying here is a terrific adventure. Birds continually swoop through the branches and land just a few yards away. Hermit crabs and lizards skitter through the leaf litter on the forest floor.

Children will enjoy many of the ranger programs at the national park.

NICETIES: At Maho Bay, departing guests leave leftover food in the "Help Yourself Center," which makes it easy for arriving guests to get a start on provisioning their cottages.

The "Help Yourself Center" also has books and games for borrowing.

OF INTEREST NEARBY: Hawksnest Bay is a good place to introduce children to snorkeling. Zillions of colorful fish dart in and out of the elkhorn coral in water shallow enough to be non-threatening.

The Annaberg Sugar Refinery makes an interesting excursion. Children can learn about how sugar can is processed and watch islanders demonstrate local basket-making, cooking, and gardening techniques.

FOR MORE INFORMATION: Write the Superintendent, Virgin Islands National Park, P.O. Box 7789, St. Thomas, U.S. Virgin Islands 00801.

Index

Note: *Italicized* page numbers indicate illustrations.

Adventure trips, 15–17, 359–417
  midwest, 384–98
  northeast, 360–70
  outfitters, 16–17
  southeast, 371–83
  southwest and mountain states,
    251, 399–413, 453
  west coast, 414–17
Ah, Wilderness! (O'Neill), 75
Air Force Academy, 444
Alabama
  Gulf State Park, 426–30
Alaska
  Camp Denali, *418*, 470–73
  cruise, 349–53
The Alisal Guest Ranch, 215–18
Alpine Meadows ski resort, 279–85
Alpine Slide, 273
Altos de Chavon, 139, 141, 146
Amelia Island Plantation, *22*, 51–55
American Plan, described, 19
Ames Heights, West Virginia, 376
Anasazi Indians, 325–28, 400, 402
Antigua, 344
Apostle Islands Sailing Adventure, 358, 388–91
Appalachian Trail, 229, 425
Aquascope rides, 158
Arapahoe Basin, Colorado, 259

Arapaho National Forest, 175
Archaeological sites
  Crow Canyon Archaeological
    Center, 325–28
  Wolstenholme Towne, 307
Ardastra Gardens, Nassau, 340
Arizona
  Houseboating on Lake Powell,
    399–402
  Pontoon Boat Adventure through
    the Grand Canyon, 402–6
  Tanque Verde Ranch, *164*, 166–70
  Wickenburg Inn Tennis and
    Guest Ranch, 170–74
Arkansas
  Canoeing on the Buffalo National
    River, 379–83
Arkansas River, Colorado, 183, 442
Asheville, North Carolina, 79–82
Aspen area ski resorts, Colorado,
  243–48
Averill's Flathead Lake Lodge &
  Dude Ranch, 190–94

Baggs, Bill, Cape Florida State
  Recreation Area, Florida, 65
Bahamas, cruises, 336–44
Ballard, California, 218
The Balsams, 28–31

Bandelier National Monument,
    New Mexico, 206
Bandera, Texas, 206–10
Barbados, 344
Bayfield, Wisconsin, 389
Beartown State Park, West
    Virginia, 423
Beaver Creek, 264–69
Bellingham, Washington, 459–62
Berthoud Pass, Colorado, 270
Bigfork, Montana, 190–94
Bighorn Mountains, 210–14, *358*
Bighorn National Forest,
    Wyoming, 210–14, *358*,
    410–13
Big Sky, Montana, 194–97
Biking
    Alabama, 428
    Alaska, 472
    California, 121, 457
    Canada, 41
    Colorado, 260
    Florida, 52
    Georgia, 72, 77
    Michigan, 324
    Minnesota, 101
    Oregon, 114
    Puerto Rico, 153
    South Carolina, 85
    Tennessee, 425
    Virginia, 89
    Washington, 468–69
    West Virginia, 421
    Wisconsin, 392–95
Biltmore House, 82
Biosphere Reserve and World
    Heritage Site, 466
Bird-banding program, 167–68
Bird-watching, *418*
    Colorado, 443
    Montana, 450
Biscayne National Park, Florida, 65
Bishop Museum, Oahu, 125, 128,
    357
Bishop's Lodge, 202–6

Bitter End Yacht Club, 155–59
Black Creek Pioneer Village,
    Toronto, Ontario, 43
Black Hills National Forest, South
    Dakota, 213
Blanchard Springs Cavern,
    Arkansas, 382
Blanding, Utah, 402
Boating
    Alabama, 428
    Arizona, 402–6
    British Virgin Islands, 157, 158–
    59
    California, 121, 217
    Canada, 464
    Colorado, 268, 273
    Dominican Republic, 144
    Florida, 57, 60, 63, 67, 69
    Georgia, 72, 77
    Grand Cayman Island, 160
    Hawaii, 124, 131
    Illinois, 97
    Jamaica, 148–49
    Massachusetts, 25
    Minnesota, 101, 395–98, 433
    Missouri, 104
    Montana, 192, 453
    New Hampshire, 30
    New York, 33, 38
    Oregon, 113
    Pennsylvania, 45
    South Carolina, 85
    Vermont, 49
    Washington, 109–10, 468
    West Virginia, 93, 421
    Wyoming, 446
Bolton Landing, New York, 36–40
Bon Secour National Wildlife
    Refuge, Alabama, 429
Boothbay, Maine, 367
Boscobel Beach Resort, *22*, 147–50
Boulder, Utah, 402
Boundary Waters Wilderness
    Canoe Area, 397, *418*
Bozeman, Montana, 197

Bradbury State Park, Vermont, 369
Brandon, Vermont, 367–70
Breckenridge ski resort, *220*, 255–60, 444
British Virgin Islands
    Bitter End Yacht Club, 155–59
Browning, Montana, 454
Bryce National Park, 406
Buffalo, Wyoming, 210–14
Buffalo National River, Arkansas, 379–83
Buttermilk Mountain, Colorado, 243–48

Cabo San Lucas, 347–48
California
    The Alisal Guest Ranch, 215–18
    Dana Point Resort, 119–22
    Furnace Creek Inn and Ranch Resort, 455–58
    Kayaking on the Navarro River, 414–17
    Lake Tahoe area ski resorts, *220*, 279–85
    Rancho Bernardo Inn, 116–19
Callaway Gardens, 69–74
Camden, Maine, 365, 367
Camino Real, 218
Campbell River, Canada, 465–66
Camp Denali, *418*, 470–73
Camping
    Arkansas, 379–83
    Colorado, 406–10
    Connecticut, 289–90
    Georgia, 371–75
    Indiana, 316
    Minnesota, 395–98
    St. John, U. S. Virgin Islands, 473–76
    Tennessee, 424
    Utah, 406–10
    Washington, 467
Canada, 111
    Four Seasons Inn on the Park, Toronto, Ontario, 40–43

Gray Rocks, 222–25
Mont-Tremblant, 222–25
Strathcona Park Lodge and Outdoor Education Centre, *418*, 462–66
Waterton-Glacier International Peace Park, 454
Canoeing
    Alaska, 472
    Arkansas, 379–83
    Maine, 360–63
    Minnesota, 434
    Tennessee, 424–25
Canyon de Chelly National Monument, 402
Cape Cod, Massachusetts, *22*, 24–27, 303
Cape Mudge Indian Village, 466
Captiva Island, Florida, 65–69
Caribbean
    cruises, 332–44
    nature places, 473–76
    resorts, 138–62
Caribbean National Forest (El Yunque), 155
Carnival Cruise Lines, *330*, 344–48
Casa de Campo, 138–42, 146
Cascade Mountains, Oregon, 112–15
Cass Scenic Railroad State Park, West Virginia, 422
Cayman Islands National Museum, Grand Cayman, 162
Central City, Colorado, 181
Centre Island, Toronto, Ontario, 42
Charleston, South Carolina, 86
Cheeca Lodge, 59–62
Cherokee Indians, 82, 426
Chesapeake Bay, 87, 88
Chewonki Wilderness Trips, 360–63
Children
    on adventure trips, 15–17
    on cruises, 12–15
    at guest ranches, 5–7

Children *(cont.)*
  history places and, 11–12
  and nature places, 17–18
  at resorts, 4
  skiing with, 7–10
Children's Museum of
    Indianapolis, 314
Chippewa Indians, 389
Choteau, Montana, 448–51
Cisco, Utah, 407
Clark, Georgie, 402–6
C Lazy U Ranch, *164*, 174–78
The Cloister, 74–79
Clothing
  for guest ranches, 7
  for nature places, 18
  for skiing, 9–10
Cloud Peak Wilderness Area, 410–
    13
Club Med Punta Cana, 142–46
Cody, Wyoming, 213
Coffee, Jamaican Blue Mountain,
    148
College of William and Mary,
    Virginia, 307
Colonial Michilimackinac,
    Michigan, 322–25
Colonial Williamsburg, 304–7
The Colony Beach and Tennis
    Resort, 55–58
Colorado
  Aspen area ski resorts, 243–48
  C Lazy U Ranch, *164*, 174–78
  Crested Butte ski area, *220*, 248–
    51
  Crow Canyon Archaeological
    Center, 325–28
  Estes Park Center, 436–40
  Houseboating on Lake Powell,
    399–402
  The Nature Place, 441–45
  Peaceful Valley Lodge and Ranch
    Resort, 178–82
  Rafting on the Colorado River,
    358, 406–10

Snow Mountain Ranch, *418*,
    436–40
Steamboat ski area, 251–55
Summit County ski resorts, *220*,
    255–60
Telluride ski resort, *220*, 260–64
Tumbling River Ranch, 182–86
Vail/Beaver Creek, 264–69
Vista Verde Guest and Ski
    Touring Ranch, 186–90
Winter Park resort, 176, 269–73,
    436–40
Colorado National Monument, 410
Colorado River, 176, 188
Colorado Springs, Colorado, 444
Connecticut
  Mystic Seaport Museum, 288–91
Conner Prairie, 311–15
S. S. *Constitution* (cruise ship),
    354–57
Copper Mountain ski resort, *220*,
    255–60
Coral Gables, Florida, 65
Coral World, Nassau, 340
Coronado National Memorial
    Forest, 166
Cortez, Colorado, 325–28
Cozumel, 335–36
Cranberry Glades Botanical Area,
    422–23
Crane Lake, Minnesota, 396, 398
Crested Butte ski area, 248–51
Cross-country skiing
  California, 282
  Canada, 41, 224
  Colorado, 176, 181, 188, 246,
    250, 253, 257–58, 262, 266,
    271, 439, 443–44
  Illinois, 98
  Maine, 228
  Minnesota, 433
  New Hampshire, 30, 31
  New York, 34, 38
  Oregon, 114
  Pennsylvania, 45

Cross-country skiing *(cont.)*
  Utah, 275
  Vermont, 232, 236, 240,
    241
  West Virginia, 93, 422
Crow Canyon Archaeological
    Center, 325–28
Cruise Lines International
    Association, 13
Cruises, 12–15, 331–57
  Alaska, 349–53
  Caribbean and the Bahamas,
    332–48
  Hawaii, 354–57
  Mississippi River, 98, 99
  Nantucket and Martha's
    Vineyard, 27
  ports of call, 14
  rates, 19
  tips for, 15
  Virginia, 89
Cumberland Island, Georgia, 79,
    371–75
Cumberland Island Camping
    Adventure, 371–75
Cycling. *See* Biking

Dana Point Resort, 119–22
Darling, J. N. "Ding," National
    Wildlife Refuge, Florida, 69
Dauphin Island, Alabama, 429
Dead River Museum, Maine, 229
Death Valley National Monument,
    California, 455–58
Deer Valley Ski Area, 273–78
de la Renta, Oscar, 139
Denali National Park, Alaska, *418*,
    470–73
Des Moines, Iowa, 308–11
Destination resorts, 3
Disneyland, 122
Dixville Notch, New Hampshire,
    28–31
Dogsledding
  Colorado, 246

Doheny State Beach, California,
    122
Dole Pineapple plant, Hawaii, 125
Dolores, Colorado, 327
Dolores River, 409–10
Dolphins, 126
Dominican Republic
  Casa de Campo, 138–42
  Club Med Punta Cana, 142–46
Donner Memorial State Park, 283
Dorado, Puerto Rico, 151–55
Dungeness Spit, Washington, 111
Dunn's River Falls, Jamaica, 150,
    336
Durango, Colorado, 328
Durango-Silverton narrow guage
    train, 328
Dvorak, Bill, kayak and rafting
    expedition, *358*, 406–10
Dwyer, Ann, 414–17
Dye, Pete, 139–40, 260

Eagle County, Colorado, 264–69
Eagle Ridge Inn and Resort, 96–99
Eagle's Nest Wilderness, Colorado,
    268
Echo Reservoir, Utah, 278
Egg Mountain, Montana, 449, 450
El Dorado, Kansas, 384–88
Elk Mountains, Colorado, 250
Elk River, 188
Emigrant, Montana, 197–202
Estes Park, Colorado, 178, 180,
    182, 436–40
Estes Park Center, 436–40
Eureka Springs, Arkansas, 382
European Plan, described, 19

Fairplay, Colorado, 186
Farming
  Living History Farms, 308–11
  Washburn-Norlands Living
    History Center, 292–96
Fayette County, West Virginia,
    375–79

Feiro, Arthur D., Marine
    Laboratory, Washington, 111
Fernandina Beach, Florida, 54–55
Fishing
    Alabama, 428
    Arizona, 168
    California, 121, 217
    Canada, 464
    Colorado, 176, 180, 184, 188,
        260, 273, 442
    Dominican Republic, 140
    Florida, 53, 57, 60, 64, 67
    Georgia, 72, 77
    Grand Cayman Island, 160
    Hawaii, 135
    Minnesota, 433
    Missouri, 104
    Montana, 192, 196, 200, 449,
        453
    New Hampshire, 30
    New Mexico, 204
    New York, 34, 38
    Oregon, 114
    Pennsylvania, 45
    Puerto Rico, 153
    South Carolina, 85
    Tennessee, 425
    Texas, 208
    Utah, 278
    Vermont, 49
    Virginia, 89
    Washington, 110, 468
    West Virginia, 93; 421
    Wyoming, 212, 446–47
Flathead Lake, Montana, 190–94
Florida
    Amelia Island Plantation, 22, 51–
        55
    Cheeca Lodge, 59–62
    The Colony Beach and Tennis
        Resort, 55–58
    Sonesta Beach Hotel and Tennis
        Club, 62–65
    South Seas Plantation, 22, 65–69
Florissant, Colorado, 441–45

Flying High Circus, Georgia, 70–
    71
Flying L Guest Ranch, 164, 206–10
Folk Trades Summer School, 309
Fort Clinch State Park, Florida, 55
Fort Fincastle, Nassau, 340
Fort Mackinack, 286, 322–25
Fort Morgan, Alabama, 429
Four Seasons Inn on the Park, 40–
    43
Franklin D. Roosevelt Library and
    Museum, New York, 35–36
Frontier Museum, Texas, 210
Frying Pan Lake, Wyoming, 212
Furnace Creek Inn and Ranch
    Resort, 455–58

Galena, Illinois, 96–99
Gallatin National Forest, 198
Garden of the Gods, Colorado, 444
Gatlinburg, Tennessee, 423–26
Georgetown, Colorado, 186
George Town, Grand Cayman
    Island, 159–62, 336
Georgia
    Callaway Gardens, 69–74
    The Cloister, 74–79
    Cumberland Island Camping
        Adventure, 371–75
Glacier Bay National Park, 352
Glacier National Park, 193, 450,
    451–54
Glen Canyon National Recreation
    Area, 399–402
Golf
    Alabama, 428
    Arizona, 167, 172
    California, 117, 120, 216, 284,
        456
    Canada, 41
    Colorado, 176, 180, 251, 259,
        260, 264, 268
    Dominican Republic, 139–40
    Florida, 52, 57, 60, 63, 67
    Georgia, 72, 76–77

Golf *(cont.)*
  Grand Cayman Island, 160
  Hawaii, 124, 127, 131, 135
  Illinois, 97
  Jamaica, 148
  Maine, 229
  Massachusetts, 25, 27
  Minnesota, 101
  Missouri, 104
  Montana, 192
  New Hampshire, 29
  New Mexico, 203
  New York, 33, 37–38
  North Carolina, 81
  Oregon, 113
  Pennsylvania, 45
  Puerto Rico, 153
  South Carolina, 85
  Texas, 208
  Utah, 278
  Vermont, 49, 233, 241
  Virginia, 88–89
  Washington, 109
  West Virginia, 91–92
Gothic, Colorado, 251
Granby, Colorado, 174–78
Grand Canyon, Arizona, 172,
  402–6
Grand Canyon of the Yellowstone
  River, 445, 447
Grand Cayman Island, 336
  Hyatt Regency Grand Cayman,
  159–62
Grand Circle area, 328, 402
Grand Junction, Colorado, 408, 410
Grand Lake, Colorado, 178, 440
Grand Marais, Minnesota, 435
Grand View Lodge Golf and Tennis
  Club, 99–103
Grant, Colorado, 182–86
Grant, Ulysses S., 96, 99
Grant, Ulysses S., Home State
  Historic Site, 99
Graves, Robert Muir, 284
Gray Rocks, 222–25

Great Smoky Mountain National
  Park, 82
Great Smoky Mountains National
  Park, 423–26
Greenbrier River, West Virginia,
  420–23
Green Mountains, 236, 238–42,
  367–70
The Grove Park Inn and Country
  Club, 79–82
Guest ranches, 5–7, 164–218
  rates, 19
  southwest and mountain states,
  166–214, 448–51
  tips for, 6–7
  west coast, 215–18
Gulf Shores, Alabama, 426–30
Gulf State Park, 426–30
Gull Lake, Minnesota, 99–103
Gunflint Lodge, *418*, 431–35

Ha Ha Tonka State Park, 106
Haiti, 336
Haleakala National Park, 357
Hales, 129–30
Harmony Borax Works, California,
  458
Harrodsburg, Kentucky, 318–21
Hawaiian Islands
  cruise, 354–57
  Hilton Hawaiian Village, 122–25
  Kahala Hilton, 125–29
  Kona Village, *22*, 129–33
  Mauna Kea Beach Hotel, 133–37
Heavenly Valley ski resort, 279–85
Heber Creeper, steam engine, 277
Helicopter skiing, 262, 275
Henry Woods State Park, 415
Heritage Plantation, Massachusetts,
  27
Highgate Springs, Vermont, *22*,
  47–50
Hiking, 17–18
  Alabama, 428
  Alaska, 472

Hiking *(cont.)*
  Arizona, 167–68, 172
  British Virgin Islands, 157
  Colorado, 176, 180, 188, 268,
    438, 443
  Florida, 53, 68
  Georgia, 72, 77, 371–75
  Hawaii, 135–36
  Illinois, 97
  Maine, 360–63
  Massachusetts, 26
  Minnesota, 433
  Montana, 192, 195–96, 200, 450,
    453
  New Hampshire, 30
  New York, 34
  Oregon, 114
  Pennsylvania, 45
  Tennessee, 425
  Texas, 209
  Utah, 278
  Vermont, 367–70
  Washington, 468
  West Virginia, 93, 421
  Wyoming, 212, 447
Hilton, Conrad, 125
Hilton Hawaiian Village, 122–25
Historic New Harmony, 315–18
History places, 11–12, 27, 287–
    328
  Canada, 43
  midwest, 308–28
  northeast, 288–303
  residence programs, 11–12
  southeast, 304–7
  tips for, 12
Hogoboom, John, wagon train trip,
    385–87
Holland America Line, 349–53
Honolulu, Oahu, Hawaii, 122–29
Horseback riding
  Arizona, 168, 172
  California, 217, 457
  Colorado, 176, 180, 184, 188,
    439

  Dominican Republic, 140, 144
  Florida, 53
  Georgia, 72, 77
  Hawaii, 124, 136
  Illinois, 97
  Missouri, 104
  Montana, 192, 196, 200, 449–50,
    453
  New Mexico, 204
  New York, 34
  Oregon, 114
  Pennsylvania, 45
  Tennessee, 425
  Texas, 209
  Utah, 278
  Vermont, 234, 241–42
  West Virginia, 93, 421
  Wyoming, 212, 447
  See also Guest ranches
Horse-drawn carriages
  Michigan, 324
  New York, 32
Hot-air ballooning, 38
  California, 283
  Colorado, 246, 250, 253, 262,
    263
  Utah, 276, 278
Houseboating
  Arizona, 399–402
  Colorado, 399–402
  Minnesota, 396
Hyatt Dorado Beach, 151–55
The Hyatt Regency Cerromar
    Beach, 151–55
Hyatt Regency Grand Cayman,
    159–62
Hyde Park, New York, 35–
    36

Ice skating
  Colorado, 246, 258, 262
  New Hampshire, 30
  New York, 34, 38
  Oregon, 114
  Pennsylvania, 45

Ice skating *(cont.)*
 Utah, 276
Illinois
 Eagle Ridge Inn and Resort, 96–99
Independence, Kansas, 388
S. S. *Independence* (cruise ship), 330, 354–57
Indiana
 Conner Prairie, 311–15
 Historic New Harmony, 315–18
International Falls, Minnesota, 395–98
International Folk Art Museum, New Mexico, 206
Iowa
 Living History Farms, 308–11
Irvington, Virginia, 87–90
Islamorada, Florida, 59–62

Jamaica, 336
 Boscobel Beach Resort, 22, 147–50
Jamaican Blue Mountain coffee, 148
James River, 307
Jamestown, Virginia, 307
Jeep tours
 Colorado, 259
Jekyll Island, Georgia, 79
Jones, Robert Trent, 92, 153, 229
Jones, Robert Trent Jr., 113, 251, 254, 260
Joshua Forest, Arizona, 174
S. S. *Jubilee* (cruise ship), 344–48
Juneau, Alaska, 352

Kahala Hilton, 125–29
Kalalua Trail, 357
Kansas
 Wagon Train Trip Through the Flint Hills, 358, 384–88
Ka'upulehu-Kona, The Big Island, Hawaii, 129–33

Kayaking
 California, 414–17
 Colorado, 406–10
 New Mexico, 204
 Utah, 406–10
Kennebec River, Maine, 229
Kentucky
 Shaker Village at Pleasant Hill, 286, 318–21
Kentucky River, 321
Kerfoot, Justine, 431, 432
Ketchikan, Alaska, 352
Kettle Falls, Minnesota, 397
Key Biscayne, Florida, 62–65
Keystone ski resort, 255–60
Kiawah Island Inn and Villas, 83–86
Kilbride, Bert, tours of Virgin Island reefs, 157
Killington Ski Area, 220, 230–34
Kingsfield, Maine, 226–30
Kirkwood ski resort, 279–85
Knotts Berry Farm, 122
Kohala Coast, The Big Island, Hawaii, 133–37
Kokee State Park, 357
Kona Village, 22, 129–33
Kwakiutl Museum, Canada, 466

Labadee, Haiti, 336
Laguna Beach, California, 122
La Jolla, California, 119
Lake Champlain, 47–50
Lake George, New York, 36–40
Lake Gloriette, New Hampshire, 28–31
Lake Granby, Colorado, 440
Lake Huron, 322–25
Lake Mead, 403
Lake Michigan, 322–25
Lake of the Ozarks, 103–7
Lake Powell, 399–402
Lake Shelby, Alabama, 427–30
Lake Superior, 388–91, 435

Lake Tahoe area ski resorts, 279–85

Lantern Bay Park, California, 122

Lapakahi State Historical Park, 137

La Pointe, Wisconsin, 389

Lee Metcalf Wilderness Area, 194–97

Lesueur American Indian Museum, Indiana, 317

Leyritz Plantation, Martinique, 344

Lilly, Eli, 312

Little Bighorn, Wyoming, 214

Livermore, Maine, 292–96

Living History Farms, 308–11

Loma, Colorado, 407

Lone Mountain Ranch, *164*, 194–97

Longboat Key, Florida, 55–58

Longs Peak, Colorado, 438

Long Trail, Vermont, 367–70

Lyons, Colorado, 178–82

Mackinac State Historic Parks, 322–25

Mackinaw City, Michigan, 322–25

Madeline Island, Wisconsin, 388–91

Madison, Wisconsin, 392–95

Maine
  Chewonki Wilderness Trips, 360–63
  Sugarloaf USA Resort, 226–30
  Washburn-Norlands Living History Center, *286*, 292–96
  Windjammer Cruise, 363–67

Mammoth Hot Springs, Wyoming, 447

Manchester, Vermont, 241

Man in Biosphere Program, 423

Mansion Museum, West Virginia, 94

Marble Canyon, 406

Marie Selby Botanical Gardens, Florida, 58

Marine Historical Association, Connecticut, 289

Marlinton, West Virginia, 420–23

Maroon Bells Wilderness Area, 247

Maroon Lake, Colorado, 246

Marriott's Tan-Tar-A Resort and Golf Club, 103–7

Martha's Vineyard, Massachusetts, 27

Martinique, 344

Massachusetts
  New Seabury Cape Cod, *22*, 24–27
  Old Sturbridge Village, *286*, 296–99
  Plimouth Plantation, *286*, 300–303

Mauna Kea Beach Hotel, 133–37

Mazatlan, 347

McLaughlin Planetarium, Toronto, Ontario, 43

Meier, Richard, 317

Mendenhall Glacier, 352

Mendocino County, California, 414–17

Mesa Verde National Park, 327

Mexico
  cruises, 335–36, 344–48

Miami, Florida, 65

Michigan
  Mackinac State Historic Parks, 322–25

Middlebury, Vermont, 369

Mill Creek, Michigan, 322

Miller, Dave, tours of Grand Cayman, 161–62

Millicent Rogers Museum, New Mexico, 206

Minnesota
  Boat-Camping in Voyageurs National Park, 395–98
  Grand View Lodge Golf and Tennis Club, 99–103
  Gunflint Lodge, *418*, 431–35

Mission La Purisma Concepcion, California, 218
Mississippi River, 96–99
Missouri
  Marriott's Tan-Tar-A Resort and Golf Club, 103–7
Misty Fjords National Monument, 352
Modified American Plan (MAP), described, 19
Mohonk Mountain House, 31–36
Montana
  Averill's Flathead Lake Lodge & Dude Ranch, 190–94
  Glacier National Park, 450, 451–54
  Lone Mountain Ranch, 164, 194–97
  Mountain Sky Guest Ranch, 164, 197–202
  Pine Butte Guest Ranch, 448–51
Montreal, Quebec, Canada, 50
Mont-Tremblant, 222–25
Monument Valley Navajo Tribal Park, 402
Moore, Henry, 43
Morgan, J. P., 192
Mt. McKinley, Alaska, 418, 470, 471, 472
Mt. Olympus, Washington, 467, 469
Mt. Rushmore National Monument, 213
Mountain-biking
  Colorado, 268, 273
Mountain Sky Guest Ranch, 164, 197–202
Mountain View, Arkansas, 382
Mount Pelee, Martinique, 344
Mount Snow Resort, 220, 234–37
Mount Zirkel Wilderness Area, 186
Museum of the Cherokee Indian, 82
Museum of the Plains Indian, Montana, 454

Museum of the Rockies, Montana, 449
Mystic Seaport Museum, 288–91

Nantucket Island, Massachusetts, 27
Nassau, Bahamas, 337, 338, 340
National Radio Astronomy Observatory, West Virginia, 422
National Wildlife Federation Conservation Summits, 418, 459–62
Nature Conservancy
  Pine Butte Guest Ranch, 448–51
The Nature Place, 441–45
Nature places, 17–18, 419–76
  Arizona, 172
  California, 121
  Caribbean, 473–76
  Florida, 65, 69
  midwest, 431–35
  southeast, 82, 93, 420–30
  southwest and mountain states, 436–40
  tips for, 17–18
  west coast and Alaska, 455–73
Navajo Indians, 328, 406
Navajo National Monument, 402
Naval Aviation Museum, 429
Navarro River, California, 414–17
Newburgh, New York, 35
New England Maple Museum, Vermont, 233
New Gloucester, Maine, 295
New Hampshire
  The Balsams, 28–31
New Harmony, Indiana, 315–18
New Mexico
  Bishop's Lodge, 202–6
New Paltz, New York, 31–36
New River, West Virginia, 358, 375–79
New Seabury Cape Cod, 22, 24–27
Newspaper Rock State Park, 402

New York
  Mohonk Mountain House, 31–36
  The Sagamore, 36–40
Nicklaus, Jack, 160, 259
Nisswa, Minnesota, 99–103
Noblesville, Indiana, 311–15
Nojoqui Falls, California, 218
North Carolina
  The Grove Park Inn and Country Club, 79–82
Northstar-at-Tahoe ski resort, 220, 279–85
Norwegian Cruise Line, 340–44
Norwegian School of Nature Life, 276

Oak Creek Canyon, Arizona, 172, 174
Ocean Spray Cranberry World, 303
Ocho Rios, Jamaica, 147–50, 336
Oglebay Resort, 22, 91–95
Ojibway Indians, 389
Okefenokee National Wildlife Refuge, 375
Old Fort Harrod State Park, Kentucky, 321
Old Rhinebeck Aerodrome, New York, 35
Old San Juan, Puerto Rico, 154
Old Sturbridge Village, 286, 296–99
Old Tucson, Arizona, 170
Olmsted, Frederick Law, 314–15
Olympic Mountains, 108–11
Olympic National Park and National Forest, 111, 466–70
O'Neill, Eugene, 75
Ontario Place, 43
Ontario Science Centre, 42
Oregon
  Sunriver Lodge and Resort, 112–15
Osage Beach, Missouri, 103–7
Outfitters, adventure trip, 16–17

Owen, Robert, 315–16
The Ozarks, Arkansas, 379–83

Packard, Roger, 97
Painted Desert, 406
Paradise Guest Ranch, 210–14
Parasailing, 38
Park City area ski resorts, 273–78
Parrot Jungle and Gardens, Florida, 65
Paul Bunyan amusement park, Minnesota, 102
Peaceful Valley Lodge and Ranch Resort, 178–82
Pearl Harbor, 128, 357
Pecos Wilderness Area, 204
Pemaquid, Maine, 367
Pennekamp, John, Coral Reef State Park, Florida, 61
Pennsylvania
  Skytop Lodge, 43–47
Penobscot Bay, Maine, 363–67
Pike National Forest, Colorado, 182–86
Pike's Peak, 441–45
Pine Mountain, Georgia, 69–74
Piney River Ranch, Colorado, 267, 268
Pirngruber, Wilhelm, 152
Playa del Carmen, 335
Plimouth Plantation, 286, 300–303
Pliny Freeman Farm, 286, 297
Plymouth, Massachusetts, 300–303
Pocono Mountains, Pennsylvania, 43–47
Polynesian Cultural Center, Hawaii, 125, 128, 357
Ponca, Arkansas, 382
Pontoon boating
  Arizona, 402–6
Port Angeles, Washington, 466–70
Port Ludlow, Washington, 108–11
Premier Cruise Lines, 336–40
Prospect Plantation, Jamaica, 150

Puerto Rico
  Hyatt Dorado Beach, 151–55
  The Hyatt Regency Cerromar
    Beach, 151–55
Puerto Vallarta, 347
Puget Sound, 111
Punta Cana, Dominican Republic,
  142–46
Pu'uhonua O Honaunau National
  Historical Park, 137, 357

Rainbow Bridge, 400
Rancho Bernardo Inn, 116–19
Rates, 18–20
The Resort at Port Ludlow, 108–11
Resorts, 3–5, 22–162
  Caribbean, 138–62
  midwest, 96–107
  northeast, 24–50
  rates, 19
  southeast, 51–95
  west coast and Hawaii, 108–37
Rhinebeck, New York, 35
Riding boots, 7
Rincon Mountains, Arizona, 166–
  70
Ringling complex, Sarasota,
  Florida, 58
Rio Chavon, 139, 140, 141, 146
Rio Grande Gorge Bridge, New
  Mexico, 206
Rockefeller, John D., 304
Rockefeller, Laurance S., 133, 151
Rockland, Maine, 365
Rockport, Maine, 367
Rocky Mountain Biological
  Laboratory, 251
Rocky Mountain National Park,
  175, 178, 182, 436–40
Rodriguez, Chi Chi, 153
La Romana, Dominican Republic,
  138–42
Roosevelt, Franklin Delano, 35–36,
  74
Roosevelt National Forest, 180

Rosalia, Kansas, 386
Ross, Donald, 29
Routt National Forest, Colorado,
  186–90, 254
Royal Caribbean Cruise Line, *330*,
  332–36
Royal Gorge, 444
Royal Ontario Museum, 42–43
Ruby Canyon, 407–9
Runaway Beach, Antigua, 344
Rutland, Vermont, 233

Sabbathday Lake Shaker Village,
  295
Sabino Canyon, 169
The Sagamore, 36–40
Saguaro National Monument, 166,
  168, 170
Sailing
  Maine, 360–67
  Wisconsin, 388–91
St. John, U. S. Virgin Islands,
  473–76
St. Mary's, Georgia, 372–75
St. Vrain River, Colorado, 179, 180
Salt Cay, Bahamas, 337, 338
Salt Lake City, Utah, 277–78
Sanborn, Laura and Roger
  "Sandy," 441
San Diego, California, 116–19
Sandwich, Massachusetts, 27
Sangre de Cristo Mountains, 204
San Juan, Puerto Rico, 154–55
San Juan Mountains, 260–64, 328
San Pasqual Mountains, California,
  116–19
Santa Fe, New Mexico, 202–6
Santa Fe National Forest, 204
Santa Fe Trail, 384–88
Santa Ynez Valley, California, 215,
  218
Santo Domingo, Dominican
  Republic, 141–42
Sarasota, Florida, 58
Saratoga Springs, New York, 39

Science Center, Iowa, 311
Scripps Institute of Oceanography, California, 119
Scuba diving
    British Virgin Islands, 157
    Florida, 60, 61, 63, 65
    Grand Cayman Island, 159, 161
    Hawaii, 132
    instruction, 342
    Mexico, 335–36
    Montana, 192
Sea Island, Georgia, 74–79
Sea Life Park at Makapuu Point, 125, 128, 357
Sedona, Arizona, 174
Sewall House Mansion, Maine, 367
Shadow Mountain Lake, Colorado, 440
Shaker Village at Pleasant Hill, 286, 318–21
Shawangunk Mountains, New York, 31–36
Shaw Park, Jamaica, 336
Shelburne Museum, Vermont, 50
Shelf Lake, Colorado, 184
Sheridan, Wyoming, 410–13
Ships, historic
    Connecticut, 290–91
    Kentucky, 321
    Maine, 363–67
    Massachusetts, 300, 302–3
Shooting
    Georgia, 72
    New Mexico, 204
Sibley, John A., Horticultural Center, Georgia, 70
Sitka, Alaska, 352–53
Ski areas, 7–10, 221–85
    equipment and clothing for, 9–10
    Illinois, 98
    northeast, 30, 31, 38, 222–42
    Pennsylvania, 45
    ski schools, 10, 224, 228, 232, 236, 240, 249, 253, 257, 262, 266, 271

southwest and mountain states, 176, 197, 204, 243–78, 439, 443–44
    in the summer, 10, 225, 247–48, 251, 254–55, 259, 263–64, 268–69, 273, 277–78, 284–85
    west coast, 114, 279–85
    West Virginia, 93
Skytop Lodge, 43–47
Sleigh rides, 236
    California, 283
    Colorado, 253, 258, 262, 267, 271
    Utah, 276
Slickersliding, 443
Snorkeling, 18
    British Virgin Islands, 157
    Florida, 61, 63, 65
    Grand Cayman Island, 159, 161
    Hawaii, 131
    instruction, 342
Snowmass, Colorado, 243–48
Snowmobiling
    California, 283
    Colorado, 246, 250, 258, 262, 267, 271
    Vermont, 237
Snow Mountain Ranch, 418, 436–40
Snowshoeing
    Colorado, 181, 267
    New Hampshire, 30
Solvang, California, 215–18
Sonesta Beach Hotel and Tennis Club, 62–65
Song of America (cruise ship), 330, 332–36
Sonoran Desert, 443, 444
South Carolina
    Kiawah Island Inn and Villas, 83–86
South St. Vrain Canyon, Colorado, 178
South Seas Plantation, 22, 65–69
Spaceport USA, 337

Squaw Valley ski resort, 279–85
Stanley Museum, Maine, 229
Star/Ship Oceanic (cruise ship), *330*, 336–40
M. S. *Starward* (cruise ship), *330*, 340–44
State Historical Society Museum, Iowa, 310–11
Steamboat ski area, 251–55
Steamboat Springs, Colorado, 186–90
Stowe, Vermont, 50
Strait of Juan de Fuca, 469
Stratford Hall, Virginia, 90
Strathcona Park Lodge and Outdoor Education Center, *418*, 462–66
Stratton, 238–42
Straubhaar, Robel, 249
Sturbridge, Massachusetts, 296–99
Sugarloaf USA Resort, 226–30
Summit County ski resorts, 255–60
Sunriver Lodge and Resort, 112–15
Swan River National Wildlife Refuge, 190–94
Swimming
  Alabama, 428
  Arizona, 167, 172
  British Virgin Islands, 157
  California, 121, 216, 457
  Canada, 41
  Colorado, 176, 180, 183, 188, 438
  Dominican Republic, 140, 144
  Florida, 52, 57, 60, 63, 67
  Georgia, 72, 77
  Grand Cayman Island, 160
  Hawaii, 124, 127, 131, 135
  Illinois, 97
  Jamaica, 148
  Minnesota, 101, 432–33
  Missouri, 104
  Montana, 200
  New Hampshire, 30
  New York, 33, 38

  North Carolina, 81
  Oregon, 113
  Puerto Rico, 153
  South Carolina, 85
  Texas, 208
  Vermont, 49
  Virginia, 89
  Washington, 109, 468
  West Virginia, 92–93, 421

Tanque Verde Ranch, *164*, 166–70
Taos Pueblo, New Mexico, 206
Telluride ski resort, *220*, 260–64
Tennessee
  Great Smoky Mountains National Park, 423–26
Tennis
  Alabama, 428
  Arizona, 167, 171–72
  California, 117, 120, 216, 456
  Canada, 41
  Colorado, 176, 180, 187, 256, 260, 438
  Dominican Republic, 139, 144
  Florida, 52, 56–57, 60, 63, 67
  Georgia, 71–72, 76
  Grand Cayman Island, 160
  Hawaii, 124, 127, 131, 135
  Illinois, 97
  Jamaica, 148
  Massachusetts, 25
  Minnesota, 101
  Missouri, 104
  Montana, 191, 199
  New Hampshire, 29
  New Mexico, 203
  New York, 33, 37
  North Carolina, 81
  Oregon, 113
  Pennsylvania, 45
  Puerto Rico, 152–53
  South Carolina, 85
  Texas, 208
  Vermont, 49, 232, 233, 241, 242
  Virginia, 88

Tennis *(cont.)*
Washington, 109
West Virginia, 92, 421
Texas
Flying L Guest Ranch, *164*, 206–10
The Tides Inn, 87–90
Tipping
cruise personnel, 15
ranchhands, 7
Tlingit Indians, 352–53
Tonalea, Arizona, 402
Tongass National Forest, 352
Toronto, Ontario, Canada, 40–43
Tourist information services, 14
Trail Ridge Road, Colorado, 436, 440
Trekking
Wyoming, *358*, 410–13
Tubing, 272
Tucson, Arizona, 166–70
Tulum, 335
Tumbling River Ranch, 182–86
Turtle Farm, Grand Cayman, 162
The Tyler Place, *22*, 47–50

Union Station, Indianapolis, 315
Utah
Park City area ski resorts, 273–78
Rafting on the Colorado River, 406–10
Ute Indians, 328

Vail/Beaver Creek, 264–69
Vancouver Island, British Columbia, Canada, 352, *418*, 462–66
Venetian Pool, Florida, 65
Vermont
Hiking Inn to Inn, 367–70
Killington Ski Area, *220*, 230–34
Mount Snow Resort, *220*, 234–37
Stratton, 238–42
The Tyler Place, *22*, 47–50
Virgin Gorda, British Virgin Islands
Bitter End Yacht Club, 155–59
Virginia
Colonial Williamsburg, 304–7
The Tides Inn, 87–90
Virginian, The (Wister), 210
Virgin Islands
Bitter End Yacht Club, 155–59
National Park, 473–76
St. John, 473–76
Vista Verde Guest and Ski Touring Ranch, 186–90
Volcanoes National Park, Hawaii, 357
Voyageurs National Park, 395–98

Wagon Train Trip Through the Flint Hills, Kansas, *358*, 384–88
Waimea Canyon, 357
Wallace, Henry A., Crop Center, 309
Walt Disney World, 337
Washburn-Norlands Living History Center, *286*, 292–96
Washington
National Wildlife Federation Conservation Summit, 459–62
Olympic National Park, 466–70
The Resort at Port Ludlow, 108–11
Washington, George, 35
Water skiing
Jamaica, 148–49
Waterton-Glacier International Peace Park, 454
Watoga State Park, 420–23
M. S. *Westerdam* (cruise ship), 349–53
Western America Ski Sports Museum, 284

Western North Carolina Nature
    Center, 82
West Glacier, Montana, 451–
    54
West Paris, Maine, 295–96
West Virginia
    Oglebay Resort, *22*, 91–95
    Watoga State Park, 420–23
    White-Water Raft Trip on the
        New River, *358*, 375–79
Westwater Canyon, 407–9
Wheeler Opera House, Colorado,
    246
Wheeling, West Virginia, 91–95
Wheelwright Museum, New
    Mexico, 206
White Mountains, New
    Hampshire, 28–31
White River, Arkansas, 379
White River Gorge, Jamaica, 150
White River National Forest, 266,
    268
White River State Park, Indiana,
    315
White-water rafting, 259–60
    Colorado, 176, 180, 183, 188,
        254, 273, 406–10, 438
    Montana, 195, 200, 453
    New Mexico, 204
    Tennessee, 424–25
    Utah, 406–10
    West Virginia, *358*, 375–79
Wickenburg Inn Tennis and Guest
    Ranch, 170–74
Wildhorse Island State Park, 192
Wildlife Reserve, Barbados, 344
Wilket Creek Park, Toronto,
    Ontario, 40–43
Williams, Esther, 323

Williamsburg, Virginia, 304–7
Wilmington, Vermont, 235–36
Wind-surfing
    California, 217
    Colorado, 273
    Jamaica, 148–49
Winter Park, Colorado, 176, 269–
    73, 436–40
Wiscasset, Maine, 360–63
Wisconsin
    Apostle Islands Sailing
        Adventure, *358*, 388–91
    Bicycle Adventure, 392–95
Wister, Owen, 210
Wolstenholme Towne, Virginia,
    307
Wyoming
    Llama Trekking in the Big Horn
        Mountains, *358*, 410–13
    Paradise Guest Ranch, 210–14
    Yellowstone National Park, 445–
        48

Yampa River, 252, 254
Yellowstone National Park, 196,
    197, 200, 202, 213, 445–48
Yellowstone River, 200
Yesteryears Doll and Miniature
    Museum, Massachusetts, 27
Yorktown, Virginia, 307
Yorktown Battlefield, 90, 307

Zion National Park, 406
Zoos
    California, 119
    Canada, 42
    Hawaii, 125, 128
    Indiana, 315
    West Virginia, *22*, 94

ABOUT THE AUTHORS

MARTHA SHIRK has been a news reporter with the St. Louis *Post-Dispatch* since 1975 and has won numerous awards for journalism. A native of Slatington, Pennsylvania, she is a graduate of Swarthmore College and the University of Chicago. She has lived and worked as a journalist in Washington, D.C., Boston, Philadelphia, and Durban, South Africa, and has traveled on four continents. She is married to William Woo, a newspaper editor. They are the parents of three young sons, Tom, Bennett, and Peter, and live in Webster Groves, Missouri.

NANCY KLEPPER is a consultant in multi-cultural education. A native of St. Louis, she has degrees from St. Louis University, the University of Chicago, and the University of Liverpool School of Tropical Medicine. She has taught in preschools, elementary schools, middle schools, high schools, and a medical school. With her husband, Robert Klepper, a university professor, she has lived and worked on five continents. They currently live with their son, Adam, in University City, Missouri.

Since 1987, Ms. Shirk and Ms. Klepper have written "Families on the Go," a monthly column for the St. Louis *Post-Dispatch* about the rewards of family travel.

The authors and their families are shown on the back cover:
Front row, seated (left to right): Bennett Woo, Tom Woo
Middle row, seated (left to right): William Woo, Martha Shirk, Peter Woo
Back row, standing (left to right): Nancy Klepper, Adam Klepper, Bob Klepper